D0722500

San Diego Christian College
Library
Santee, CA

261.85
G8256

The Blessings of Business

How Corporations Shaped Conservative Christianity

DARREN E. GREM

OXFORD
UNIVERSITY PRESS

OXFORD

UNIVERSITY PRESS

Oxford University Press is a department of the University of Oxford. It furthers
the University's objective of excellence in research, scholarship, and education
by publishing worldwide. Oxford is a registered trade mark of Oxford University
Press in the UK and certain other countries.

Published in the United States of America by Oxford University Press
198 Madison Avenue, New York, NY 10016, United States of America.

© Oxford University Press 2016

All rights reserved. No part of this publication may be reproduced, stored in
a retrieval system, or transmitted, in any form or by any means, without the
prior permission in writing of Oxford University Press, or as expressly permitted
by law, by license, or under terms agreed with the appropriate reproduction
rights organization. Inquiries concerning reproduction outside the scope of the
above should be sent to the Rights Department, Oxford University Press, at the
address above.

You must not circulate this work in any other form
and you must impose this same condition on any acquirer.

Library of Congress Cataloging-in-Publication Data
Names: Grem, Darren E., author.
Title: The blessings of business: how corporations shaped conservative Christianity / Darren E. Grem.
Description: New York: Oxford University Press, 2016. | Includes bibliographical references and index.
Identifiers: LCCN 2015044390 (print) | LCCN 2016007190 (ebook) |
ISBN 978-0-19-992797-5 (cloth: alk. paper) | ISBN 978-0-19-992798-2 (updf) |
ISBN 978-0-19-046700-5 (epub)
Subjects: LCSH: United States—Church history—20th century. | Business—Religious aspects—
Christianity. | Conservatism—Religious aspects—Christianity. | Conservatism—United States—History—
20th century. | Evangelicalism—United States—History—20th century.
Classification: LCC BR517.G74 2016 (print) | LCC BR517 (ebook) | DDC 261.8/50973—dc23
LC record available at http://lccn.loc.gov/2015044390

1 3 5 7 9 8 6 4 2
Printed by Sheridan, USA

For W. Ellie and Phyllis C. Grem

CONTENTS

Contents

ACKNOWLEDGMENTS

My immediate family deserves the first round of thanks. W. Ellie and Phyllis C. Grem always said that an education is the one of the few things in life that no one can take from you. They stood by that belief and sacrificed more than they should have to make sure I took their lesson to heart. They have been supportive beyond words from preschool through graduate school, and they have shaped my life in ways I am only beginning to realize. This book is for them. I also appreciate the love and support of my siblings Marty and Joy, both of whom have taught me that not every part of your education happens in a classroom. My children, Will and Lily, have done much the same. They are already an inspiration, convincing me each day that parenthood is a far richer challenge than any academic or professional endeavor I will undertake.

At the University of Georgia, Jim Cobb offered wise counsel through several dead ends and false starts, pushing me to be as ambitious as possible. He called it like he saw it, and I would never want him to do otherwise. I hope all the "hunkering down" was worth it. John Inscoe saw me through my first research seminar and my first published article. He also asked some great questions at various stages of the research and writing process, and I thank him for the advice he offered over many a free lunch. Laura Mason likewise taught me how to think about whose stories are untold in history and inspired me to think harder about the nature of power and the broad ramifications of the seemingly mundane. Bethany Moreton and I met one another just as the project was getting underway, but she offered help and encouragement when most needed. Similarly, Theo Calderara at Oxford University Press saw promise in the project from the start and let it take shape as it did. His editorial guidance took it from dissertation to manuscript to book, and I appreciate his suggestions and patience.

Archivists at libraries and colleges from Delaware to North Carolina to Illinois to Texas made the research go as smoothly as possible, but I reserve special thanks for the folks at LeTourneau University and the Hagley Library and Museum for bringing several items to my attention that I would not have otherwise had the pleasure of finding. Many friends and colleagues also made this project better, or at least made the process more rewarding. Jenna Mason supported the project for many years, and I thank her for sacrificing in small and big ways so it could find its way to completion. I also single out John Hayes, Tore Olsson, Mike Altman, and Luke Harlow for their friendship and scholarly support. I cherish the many conversations we've had over numerous beers and lunches. Lloyd Benson was first my history professor way back at Furman University, but I now count him as a friend and fellow historical adventurer. Many thanks for convincing me to rethink a life in advertising.

Many other co-travelers and colleagues at the University of Georgia took an active interest in the project or just lent an ear, including Rhiannon Evangelista, Ichiro Miyata, Daleah Goodwin, Bruce Stewart, Chris Manganiello, Robby Luckett, Tom Okie, Blake Scott, Barton Myers, Chris Huff, and Derek Bentley. Back-to-back postdoctoral appointments at Yale University and Emory University helped sharpen the project. I thank the Yale Center for Faith and Culture and Fox Center for Humanistic Inquiry for providing the time and office space to write and think, as well as the chance to meet and work with the likes of Angie Heo, Alan Hurst, Elizabeth Bouldin, Miroslav Volf, Ted Malloch, the late Randy Strahan, and Roberto Franzosi. I also thank Cambridge University Press and the University of Pennsylvania Press for permission to reprint excerpts from previously published versions of chapter 2 and chapter 4.

In the Arch Dalrymple III Department of History at the University of Mississippi, colleagues like Jesse Cromwell, John Ondrovcik, Anne Twitty, Deirdre Cooper Owens, Charles Eagles, Jarod Roll, Marc Lerner, Joe Ward, Sue Grayzel, April Holm, Mikaëla Adams, Vivian Ibrahim, Oliver Dinius, Will Hustwit, John Neff, Jeff Watt, and Elizabeth Payne made the transition to Oxford an easy one. At the Center for the Study of Southern Culture, I thank Charles Reagan Wilson, Katie McKee, Jimmy Thomas, Simone Delerme, Jodi Skipper, Barb Combs, Mary Hartwell Howorth, Becca Walton, and Ted Ownby for the hospitality and encouragement. For scholarly companionship and support, I also thank Phil Sinitiere, Clay Howard, Ben Wise, Steven Miller, Ian Lekus, Paul Sutter, Bryan Simon, Pamela Voekel, Matt Sutton, Randall Stephens, Eileen Luhr, Rob Riser, Darren Dochuk, Michelle Nickerson, Molly Worthen, Matt Lassiter, Joe Crespino, Kevin Kruse, Grant Wacker, Ed Blum, the late Sarah Ruth Hammond, Katie Lofton, David King, Tim Gloege, J. T. Thomas, Matt Bowman, Elesha Coffman, Elizabeth and Ken Fones-Wolf, and John Turner. Kelly J. Baker and Paul Harvey welcomed me on the "blog staff" at Religion in American History, and I thank them for allowing me such a forum to make the online acquaintance of fellow historians and lay out my random thoughts on religion, politics, and SEC football.

Last but certainly not least, I wish to thank the Drive-By Truckers, among many other talented and insightful bands, for getting me through countless hours of writing and rewriting. The roads wind as they do, but I'll keep it between the ditches.

ABBREVIATIONS

BOH Baylor Institute for Oral History, Waco, Texas

CTR *Christianity Today* Collection, Billy Graham Center Archives, Wheaton, IL

DPL Religious Periodicals Collection, Dallas Public Library, Dallas, TX

FFR The Fellowship Foundation Collection, Billy Graham Center Archives, Wheaton, IL

FPC Flower Pentecostal Heritage Center, Springfield, MO

HJT Herbert J. Taylor Collection, Billy Graham Center Archives, Wheaton, IL

IVF Intervarsity Christian Fellowship Collection, Billy Graham Center Archives, Wheaton, IL

JHP J. Howard Pew, Personal Papers, Hagley Museum and Library, Wilmington, DE

LET LeTourneau Family Archives, LeTourneau University, Longview, TX

NAV The Navigators Papers, Billy Graham Center Archives, Wheaton, IL

RLP Roy Lundquist Papers, Billy Graham Center Archives, Wheaton, IL

UGA Hargrett Rare Books and Manuscripts Library, University of Georgia, Athens, GA

VWP Vernon W. Patterson Collection, Billy Graham Center Archives, Wheaton, IL

WBT Wycliffe Bible Translators Archives, JAARS, Waxhaw, NC

ZIG Zig Ziglar Papers, Southern Baptist Convention Archives, Nashville, TN

The Blessings of Business

Introduction

On a sunny July morning in 1952, evangelist Billy Graham slipped on a pair of sunglasses and stepped onto a platform along the banks of the Mississippi River. He raised his eyes toward heaven and asked God to bless a 200-foot-long cargo ship.

The ship was bound for Liberia, and R. G. LeTourneau, a multimillionaire and one of the world's leading manufacturers of heavy earthmoving equipment, had invited Graham to Vicksburg, Mississippi, for the occasion. "The Ark of LeTourneau," as locals called it, contained 500 copies of the New Testament, a dozen "technical missionaries," and a half-million dollars' worth of LeTourneau's wares. LeTourneau was flying ahead to Liberia shortly after the ceremony "to be there when the boat rams that beach."

A year earlier, LeTourneau had signed a contract with the Liberian government granting him a lease on half a million acres of land. His "technical missionaries" would clear surrounding jungles, using a portable sawmill hauled by the largest bulldozer in the world and a 22-ton machine that could reportedly "shear off big trees like a scythe cutting grass." LeTourneau would sell the harvested timber and use the newly cleared land to cultivate rice, grapefruit, banana, and palm trees for export. For the first five years, all profits would be poured back into the mission. Graham applauded LeTourneau's decisiveness, encouraging "more business men to follow in the footsteps of R. G. LeTourneau in making Christianity a part of their businesses and everyday lives." LeTourneau told a reporter for *Time* that he was merely "trying to do a missionary job in a businesslike way."[1]

Graham saw the invitation as a chance to repay a debt. Born in North Carolina, Graham had turned to revivalism and preaching after a brief stint as a salesman for the Fuller Brush Company. After attending Wheaton College, a conservative evangelical school outside Chicago, Graham took a pastoral position before signing on with Youth for Christ (YFC), then a fledgling ministry for teenagers and young adults. In 1946, while Graham was working for YFC, LeTourneau gave $7,000 (nearly $90,000 in today's dollars) to help fund an evangelistic tour of Ireland (See Fig. I.1). That was YFC's and Graham's business strategy in a nutshell: join the fortunes of big donors to the meager offerings of small donors to expand the horizons of conservative Christianity.[2]

Such a strategy was common in evangelical circles at mid-century. Executives underwrote numerous evangelical organizations, quite a few of them in Graham's orbit: *Christianity Today* magazine, the National Association of Evangelicals, Young Life, Intervarsity Christian Fellowship, Wycliffe Bible Translators, The Navigators, and Campus Crusade for Christ. But executives also brought conservative Christianity directly into the corporate world, shaping companies that were—as born-again businessman Marion E. Wade of ServiceMaster put it—"dedicated" to the Lord's service. Their approaches varied, but each executive

EVANGELIST'S EARLY BEGINNING RE-CALLED — Evangelist Billy Graham, right, member of the LeTourneau College board of trustees of Longview, visited at length here Thursday with R. G. LeTourneau, college founder, left, recalling the early days of his evangelistic career which LeTourneau helped with large financial gifts at a time when the evangelist was relatively unknown and without funds during a campaign in Ireland. Le-Tourneau's check for $7,000 to Youth for Christ which was then sponsoring the evangelist in that year, 1946, made it possible for Graham to continue that crusade to its completion. (PHOTO by Wayne Fergason).

Figure I.1 Industrialist R. G. LeTourneau (left) with evangelist Billy Graham (right) in 1968. Courtesy of *Longview News-Journal.*

viewed business as a religious arena and endeavor. The world of private enterprise, it seemed, had many blessings to offer their faith—and vice versa.

With the help of people, methods, institutions, and money from corporate America, conservative evangelicals believed that they could advance a religious, social, and political revolution. They could spark mass revival. They could fund schools and promote new ways of thinking. They could mold the next generation of young believers, defining what it meant to live and work as a modern, cosmopolitan, world-changing Christian. They could inspire others to work hard, knowing that their work was favored by God. They could create media empires and become national celebrities. They could become members of the nation's economic and political elite. Blessed by business, conservative evangelicals believed that they could and would have a hand in the history of nations.

This book tells the stories of the businessmen and businesses behind one of the longest-running and most important social and religious movements of the twentieth century.[3] These stories have gone largely untold in most considerations of conservative Christianity's place in modern American history. To be sure, much has been written on the role of evangelical leaders in giving voice to the millions of ordinary believers who served as the grassroots base for conservative candidates throughout the twentieth century.[4] But focusing on prominent leaders or grassroots activists, or just their political aspirations and election season efforts, does not account for what Graham sought from LeTourneau, what LeTourneau offered Graham in return, or what LeTourneau thought about his own identity as a self-proclaimed "Christian businessman." It does not account for the fact that conservative evangelicalism was formed in boardrooms and private businesses, not just in churches or communities or during political campaigns. It does not account for corporate elites from across the denominational and political spectrum or for countless business decisions. And, most important, it does not account for billions upon billions of dollars.

Every successful movement requires money, and big businessmen used their money—as well as their ideas, values, and organizations—to make and remake conservative evangelicalism in profound and enduring ways.[5] Corporate involvement in conservative evangelicalism did not begin, as is usually believed, in the lead-up to the presidential election of 1980.[6] Collaborations between conservative evangelicals, corporate benefactors, and businesses started around the turn of the twentieth century. For the next fifty years, through a Great Depression, Second World War, and early Cold War, evangelicals, Christian businessmen, and nonevangelical business leaders continued to work together. Similarly, in the 1960s and 1970s, business interests and elites persisted in molding conservative evangelicalism in their own image, building on the investments made in previous decades and spreading their brand of evangelical religion into new sectors of private and public life. Politics was one such sector, and an important one at that, but historians have largely overlooked the parallel story of how evangelical Christianity became both a business-friendly religion and a profitable form of corporate capitalism, with notable implications for business culture, religious culture, and politics in modern America.

How did the alliance between conservative evangelicals and big business come about? In the late nineteenth century, with their grip on the social and political direction of the country loosening, evangelicals realized that the corporation was becoming an important American institution and the corporate elite an untapped source of financial and social capital. To be sure, plenty of working-class and heartland evangelicals were disturbed by the new corporate leviathan and the power it seemed to have over their lives.[7] But other evangelicals were heartened, even excited. To work through business for the "revival" and advancement of their gospel was a new way to be a Christian. As LeTourneau put it, "We are going to sell laymen the idea that they are going to work for Jesus Christ seven days of the week or not call themselves Christians."[8] This quip, delivered in 1941 before a captive audience of "Christian laymen," shows how conservative evangelicals had come to see the corporation by World War II. It was a place where *their* visions of proper and legitimate "religion" could and should flourish.

Over the rest of the twentieth century, evangelicals built a private-sector infrastructure of money, businesses, institutions, philanthropies, and patronage that crisscrossed the country from Chicago to Los Angeles to New York to Dallas to Atlanta and beyond. Particular places mattered, but only insofar as they nurtured local enterprises that went regional or national or transnational—or connected evangelicals and business elites to larger social and financial networks. This was not, in other words, a phenomenon restricted to the so-called Bible Belt. Though places in the South, especially after World War II, certainly shaped conservative evangelicalism, corporate centers in the North, such as Chicago, and the Southwest, such as southern California, mattered as well, and often mattered more.[9]

Conservative evangelicals did more than shape, or strive to shape, the nation's religious, cultural, or political marketplace. They were proactive and strategic about leaving their mark on actual market *places*. In their crusades to garner elite support or create and sustain various business enterprises, conservative evangelicals devised interpretations of work and religious visions of public life that proved attractive inside and outside the evangelical fold. Evangelicals were also strewn throughout boardrooms, suburban shopping malls, and commercial strips; present at self-styled "Christian" radio stations, stores, and publishing houses; and working as managers of a wide range of businesses.[10] Evangelicals had expansive corporate headquarters and set up million-dollar monuments to business success. They founded and ran a Christian theme park and resort, and they sold Christian goods and services to fellow evangelicals and other customers. Evangelicals made it, with the help of business ideas and capital—or as businessmen themselves—into Manhattan office buildings and the halls of power in Washington, D.C. Thanks to corporate sponsors, conservative evangelicals became national and international celebrities, routinely preaching defenses of meritocratic work to packed crowds in sports stadiums and working to push a dual program of "free enterprise" and "family values" in companies and Congress.

Through their business pursuits, evangelicals also became intertwined with the nation's federal bureaucracy. Scholars have long ascribed the federal government a central role in twentieth-century American life. But the state has only just begun to make it into the main narrative of modern American religious history. Indeed, one of the most notable and perhaps unexpected shapers of the evangelical business landscape was the very government that businessmen often claimed was standing in their way. Scholars have largely affirmed that narrative. They have cast evangelicals as growing over the course of the century in their opposition to federal activities or policies, becoming along with other conservatives the state's foremost critics and antagonists. This characterization is not altogether wrong. The evangelical-inflected, regulatory "moral establishment"—resulting in federal Prohibition, for instance, or in countless local and state laws regulating individual personal behavior and public "morality"—crumbled in the mid- to late twentieth century, in large part due to court decisions and political opposition to evangelical power in local and federal politics, customs, and law. And evangelicals did not take such changes lightly.[11]

But in several quieter—though no less important—ways, the state continued to endorse evangelical activities (and continues to do so today). As much as evangelicals might rail against it, the federal government was an ally of business-minded and business-backed believers hoping to assert their religious, racial, gendered, and economic authority. This went beyond evangelical-supported state rituals and proclamations, in full bloom at mid-century, linking an "American Way of Life" to the nation's "Judeo-Christian" heritage or status as "One Nation Under God."[12] Sometimes, state officials directly supported evangelical businesses via private–public partnerships. For instance, LeTourneau owed his spiritual and economic "development" plans not only to up-from-the-bootstraps effort but to contracts for a wide variety of public works projects. Likewise, during and after World War II, LeTourneau benefitted from a private–public partnership with the military, to which his company provided thousands of bulldozers, scrapers, and pullers. State support translated abroad during the early Cold War, as foreign governments opened to outside corporatization, including but not limited to LeTourneau's cadre of "technical missionaries."

The marketplace missions of evangelicals also received indirect government support through the tax code. Evangelical philanthropies, many started or underwritten by businessmen, enjoyed freedom from taxation, as did churches, parachurch organizations, and publications, to which believers could make tax-deductible contributions. At other times, legislation or Supreme Court decisions enabled conservative evangelicalism, especially in the private sector. For instance, Title VII of the Civil Rights Act of 1964, a provision that barred religious discrimination in the workplace, allowed room for conservative evangelicals to bring their religious beliefs to bear on workplace cultures, both in large corporations and in thousands of smaller businesses that tied evangelical influence to monthly and quarterly profits. The state, therefore, was yet another contributor to the corporate landscape of conservative evangelicalism.

Business leaders and elites also shaped the faith's ideological makeup, sometimes in surprising ways. Contrary to the fire-and-brimstone preachers and leaders who became, especially in the late 1970s and 1980s, the public image of evangelical politics, evangelical business leaders often displayed a strategic ecumenism and penchant for moderation, emphasizing a rational, plodding pragmatism that, they thought, might broaden their appeal. Moreover, evangelical business elites often appropriated ideas from progressives, positive thinkers, and the counterculture when constructing what it meant to conduct "Christian business." From as early as the 1930s, evangelical businessmen argued for the freedom to run their enterprises as they wished, based in a managerial philosophy of executive purpose, corporate responsibility, or social "service" borrowed, in part, from more progressive Protestant circles and management theorists. In the 1970s, evangelicals like motivational speaker Zig Ziglar blended positive thinking with Christian revivalism, whooping it up for corporate free enterprise. Mary Kay Ash, founder of Mark Kay Cosmetics and one of the few female executives of note, reinterpreted women's liberation as the right of evangelical women to work for the sake of God, family, and nation. In evangelical consumer culture, countercultural styles redefined what it meant to be a conservative Christian consumer and citizen. To be sure, the faith was a conservative one, and big business sometimes underwrote radical forms of right-wing evangelicalism. But conservative evangelical businessmen and enterprises often borrowed from the left while simultaneously opposing it.

The stories that follow afford a final insight. Historian Kim Phillips-Fein recently noted that historians have only just started to avoid the tendency, common in scholarly or popular discourse, of "read[ing] conservatism's successes backward through postwar history." Assessing where conservatives won and lost certainly becomes clearer when considering evangelical cultural and political ventures through the lens of business history.[13] While businesses were important vehicles for evangelical aspirations, activism, and engagement, the blessings of business were often mixed. A number of business-backed evangelistic experiments floundered or failed. LeTourneau's venture in Liberia, for example, was a mess, underfunded and poorly executed. His "technical missionaries" faced innumerable logistical obstacles and unforeseen setbacks. By 1966, despite sinking hundreds of thousands of dollars into it, LeTourneau considered the project a bust. When he died three years later, his foreign ventures were already largely forgotten by history.[14]

LeTourneau's experience was not necessarily common, but it was common enough to provide a counternarrative to the seemingly inevitable "rise" of conservative evangelicalism, whether one dates that rise to the 1930s or to a post-1960s "backlash." Though they aimed for broad public influence, evangelicals' work through private means—individual donors, the private sector, and corporations—often reaffirmed their parochialism. That is not to say that the evangelicals' corporate endeavors ultimately led to their full-scale marginalization in American public life. It clearly did not. Thanks in part to big business, conservative evangelicals secured billions of dollars for their movement and fixed themselves to corporations large and small. They also won a perennial place in American politics and in the American political establishment via, for instance, inside-the-beltway lobbying groups. But as a religion and social movement routinely framed and funded by big business, by the end of the twentieth century conservative evangelicalism was also surprisingly insular, diffuse, and limited. It was insular because many evangelicals experienced their faith in privatized settings, especially in privately owned businesses. It was diffuse because those settings and businesses were scattered across the country. And it was limited because many arenas of American public life remained—despite a century of corporate empowerment—relatively unaffected by conservative evangelical activities.

This book is divided into two parts, each of which deals with a particular type of collaboration between corporate executives, corporate culture, corporate money, corporate methods, and conservative evangelicalism. Part I focuses on the 1920s through the 1960s, revealing how big businessmen aided conservative evangelicals' attempts to remake, sustain, and extend their religious identity, authority, and influence in modern American life. Part II focuses on the 1960s through the 1990s, detailing what evangelicals did through the private sector by developing—or striving to develop—large-scale business enterprises. Each chapter focuses on specific moments and agents of what I call "corporate revival." In other words, each chapter details a particular manifestation of corporate influence at a given point in modern evangelical history.

My purpose with this book is threefold. First, I show how corporations shaped conservative Christianity into its many private and public forms. Thus, the stories that follow should foment critical discussions about the reach and limits of corporate power in the American past and present. Today, corporate elites enjoy a certain measure of anonymity, and there are few historical roadmaps for understanding their exact influence on American culture and politics. This book addresses this problem by uncovering and evaluating the actions of people too often hidden at the top: corporate executives, elites, and the organizations and the religions, cultures, and popular movements they have made or tried to shape. In doing so, however, I do not attribute undue influence to big business or corporate elites; neither do I offer a celebratory saga of corporate beneficence or a conspiratorial tale of well-planned and well-coordinated corporate empowerment. What follows is a history of corporate power that takes variety, contingency, and conflict into account.[15]

Second, I shed light on the business side of modern American religion, religious culture, and religious politics. In a nation where the corporation and the state became critical shapers of the self, community, and racial, social, economic, and political orders, the business of American religion is too often overlooked. In and through corporate America, conservative evangelicals defined and redefined themselves and attempted to stake their claim on American society. If nothing else, then, the stories that follow are fitting rebukes to the common evangelical impulse to cast themselves as marginalized, victimized, oppressed figures in American history. Such an interpretation of the past—or present— might be vital for evangelicals' sense of embattlement, but it does not accord with the historical record. Business, often big business, mediated by the state, played a key role in shaping conservative evangelicalism.[16]

My third purpose is to place the processes of religious construction within the history of American corporate capitalism. The private sector has been a crucial venue and means by which Americans articulate what it means—and does not mean—to be "religious." Indeed, corporate elites, businesses, and their money shaped the meaning of "conservative evangelical" itself. To be a "conservative" type of "evangelical" or—as they more routinely called themselves—a "Christian" came to mean that one embraced the American business elite, engaged in business-making, and worked out one's religious identity through corporate work, buying patterns, and consumerism. This crowded out other definitions of "evangelical" and "Christian" that might have made more room for, say, working-class concerns or challenges to white privilege and patriarchy. That evangelical progressives struggled to become more than moral minorities in modern America was not merely a matter of failures in persuasion or political strategy. It was a matter of money, power, strategy, and appropriation.[17]

It was also a matter of linking conservative evangelicalism to market exchanges. Millions of American consumers, regardless of their particular faith commitments, played a role in the development and consolidation of conservative evangelicalism's place in modern America. They did so, often unknowingly, when they came into contact with evangelical businesses or businesses run or managed by evangelicals. Dollars that went into such businesses from government contracts or ordinary customers often went on to fund tax-exempt or tax-deductible evangelical ventures, institutions, and campaigns. Hence, conservative evangelicalism's development (indeed, its very existence) was deeply influenced by the forces—supply and demand, labor and capital, state policies, and consumer behavior—that shape the markets in which nearly all Americans participate.

The story of these myriad forces began in an era of corporate and social crisis, when another friend and associate of R. G. LeTourneau and Billy Graham, a fundamentalist executive named Herbert J. Taylor, started to explore what "revival" might mean for him, his business, and the nation at large.

PART I

HOW BIG BUSINESSMEN SHAPED CONSERVATIVE EVANGELICALISM

Fundamentalist Fronts

Herbert J. Taylor, Businessmen, and the "Revival"
of Conservative Evangelicalism

A Republican multimillionaire in a nation with double-digit unemployment, Herbert J. Taylor was out of step with the national mood in Franklin D. Roosevelt's America. But Taylor was not dismayed. In fact, he was hopeful. In the midst of the Great Depression, he believed, the nation was ready to experience a great Christian revival.

Taylor was at ease in multiple worlds. He believed fundamentalism was the future of American Protestantism. He was also a member of a progressive church in Chicago and, more important, devoted to the Rotary Club, a businessmen's association founded in Chicago in 1905, that emphasized community, collaboration, and social service. Taylor thought that the Rotary's tolerant, ecumenical principles could be melded to his zeal for promoting the "fundamental" doctrines of the Christian faith. Business strategies—contracts, alliance-building, private donations, budgetary planning, moderation, and even a certain strategic ecumenism—could also foster fundamentalism.

Like a handful of other like-minded businessmen in this period, Taylor began to consider how he might push fundamentalism forward in a time of economic uncertainty, war, class conflict, and growing state power. Taylor's answer was the Christian Workers Foundation (CWF), a philanthropic organization that funneled money to various evangelical ventures. Founded in 1939, the CWF was a bit of a latecomer to work already underway, most notably through the Christian Business Men's Committee, International (CBMCI). Since 1930, the CBMCI had marshaled the resources of and relationships between businessmen—many fundamentalists, others not quite—to increase Christian influence in the public square. They believed that through hard work, private investment, and measurable rewards they could make this vision a reality. This was in tune with the theological commitments and the beliefs about race and gender held by many

Depression-era businessmen, regardless of whether they were fundamentalists like Taylor or not. Like Taylor, the CBMCI assumed white privilege and male leadership were divine sanctions and confirmed by their authority as the heads of large corporations.

Taylor, the CWF, and the CBMCI represented some of the earliest efforts to create a definitive, elite-driven, business-backed form of modern conservative evangelicalism, a movement that had been underway for several decades but was picking up steam in the 1930s. To be sure, there were other conservative Christian voices in the age of Roosevelt. They also held a certain sway among corporate types, even though their names—Gerald L. K. Smith, Vance Muse, George Washington Robnett—are largely forgotten today, in part because Taylor's more moderate approach won the day.

By the end of World War II, the investments of Taylor and those in his circle were drawing dividends. "Revival" seemed imminent. Millions of dollars had flowed into evangelical missions groups that emphasized private religious experience, most notably Youth for Christ (YFC). These organizations were some of the initial (and longest-lasting) experiments in a discernible, corporate-backed, corporate-minded set of fundamentalist fronts and institutions. More important, such investments laid the groundwork for the early career of another fundamentalist who would fruitfully mine corporations and businessmen for missionary purposes. North Carolina–born, handsome, and newly married, he was a former businessman himself, now a talented preacher working with YFC. His given name was William Franklin Graham Jr. His friends, donors, and fans just called him "Billy."

Birth of a Born-Again Businessman

Herbert J. "Herb" Taylor grew up in Pickford in Michigan's Upper Peninsula. It was an isolated hamlet on the edge of the United States, only miles from the Canadian border. Most men in his immediate family were businessmen. His father ran various businesses—timber-cutting, banking, telephones. His uncles were also involved in business, albeit on a smaller scale. "Uncle Fred ran the hardware store; Uncle Ed the grocery; Uncle Andrew the shoe store; Uncle George the dry-goods store," remembered Taylor years later. His family was Methodist, although Taylor was only a nominal Christian until his late teens. After he was "born again" at a revival at the age of seventeen, he attended Northwestern University and then, when the United States entered World War I, he went overseas, first in the Young Men's Christian Association (YMCA) and later in the Naval Reserves. In keeping with the YMCA's historic mission to instill upright behavior in men, especially when it came to drinking, prostitution, and illicit gain, Taylor oversaw a series of "dry" Christian hotels for soldiers. His knack for commerce was apparent. "So unusual has been Taylor's businesslike efficiency," noted one Chicago reporter during the war, "that many of his large staff of assistants outrank him in point of seniority."

Taylor considered a career in the YMCA. Then, George Perkins, a partner at the banking giant J. P. Morgan and fundraiser for the YMCA in France, intervened. "You have a considerable amount of God-given business talent," Taylor remembered Perkins telling him. Hence, Perkins believed, Taylor should join a company "where you can influence the making of policies," taking time off "for your youth activities." "By the time you're forty-five [roughly by 1938]," said Perkins, "you'll be spending more of your long time on young people's projects than on your business." A few months after Perkins advised Taylor, Taylor received a job offer from the Oklahoma-based Sinclair Oil Company. He returned stateside, married, and hit the postwar oil boom in the Plains at just the right time. Taylor left Sinclair after a year, transitioning into the oil insurance and real estate business and becoming more active in the civic and political life of his adoptive home, the tiny town of Paul's Valley. He also joined the local Rotary Club. The Rotary was still in its infancy when Taylor took an interest in it. But its broad program of uniting businessmen, especially moderate or progressive Protestant businessmen, for the sake of humanitarian "service" to a Rotary club's host community or country deeply affected his business philosophy and religious beliefs. As Taylor moved into management and became further embedded in Rotary culture during the late 1920s and 1930s, the organization would convince Taylor that a Christian's life was meant to be a life of "service" for the "common good." He would draw from the Rotary's vision of service, as well as its brand of ecumenical organizing, in crafting a vision of what it meant to be a fundamentalist *and* a businessman in a midst of a Protestant and corporate America in flux.

Keeping a promise to his wife that they not live in Oklahoma for more than five years, Taylor moved his family to Chicago, her hometown, in 1924. Taylor then proved the adage that "it's not what you know but who you know." The next year, he was hired by an old Navy commander, now the president of the Chicago-based Jewel Tea Company. Landing at Jewel Tea was a turning point in his career and the start of Taylor's climb up the corporate ladder. He networked feverishly and worked long hours. By 1930, as the nation was starting to plunge into the depths of a terrifying economic depression, Taylor's professional career was going in the other direction. He was promoted to executive vice president after only five years at the company.[1]

As an executive with a background at the YMCA and the Rotary, it was almost a given that Taylor would join a congregation that reflected his religious sensibilities. After moving to Chicago, he started a lifelong membership at First

Methodist Church of Park Ridge. (Years later, a young Hillary Rodham would attend there.) Taylor loved his church. He served on various planning boards, paid for the installation of stained-glass windows, smoothed the way for the purchase of an expensive pipe-organ, and attended as regularly as he could. It was a historic, upstanding Protestant congregation, founded in 1856. The church was also in keeping with Taylor's class standing and identity as a white, progressive, respectable businessman. In fact, he could have attended any number of what one Park Ridge resident identified as "several 'fundamentalist' churches of relatively recent origins." One such church, the "revivalistic" South Church, featured "a number of activities for youth," certainly a draw for a man who had spent time as a leader in the YMCA and later underwrote a number of fundamentalist youth programs. But Taylor instead chose a church that reflected his social standing and Rotarian sensibilities. His church's demographic arrangements also fit the community of Park Ridge, which was a growing, well-to-do, white suburb west of a changing Chicago.[2]

After the end of the Civil War, Chicago became the nation's foremost economic center west of New York City. Large-scale corporations abounded there, within reach of national and increasingly international markets. It was a destination for successive waves of European immigrants in the late nineteenth century and, later, thousands of blacks fleeing the oppressive conditions of the Jim Crow South. It was a major center for the nation's union movement and a city strafed by class conflict and violence. It was also, increasingly, a segregated city.

The community surrounding First Methodist Church was lily white. According to the 1930 census, only 14 of Park Ridge's 10,417 residents were black. Thirty years later, the number was 5 out of 32,659. Restrictive housing practices and high home prices kept minorities out. In 1910, residents organized Park Ridge as an independent city to avoid annexation into greater Chicago, helping to keep non-whites out and tax dollars in. Still, the community, or at least its leaders, considered Park Ridge a progressive and tolerant place. The official history of the community, written by local liberal Protestant pastor Orvis F. Jordan, cast Park Ridge "[on] the racial issue" as "on the right side always." "Forty years ago," Jordan noted with a measure of pride, "a negro family lived here and the children were accepted without comment by both church and public school." More recently, he believed, the community's handful of Asian residents had received the same treatment. Such comments, in fact, conveyed the racial comfort Park Ridge afforded. It was easy to believe in racial tolerance and camaraderie if minority residents were almost nowhere to be seen.

Park Ridge's racial demographics notwithstanding, overt racism was not preached in local churches—certainly not at Taylor's First Methodist Church, which prided itself on its progressive theology and ecumenism. Tolerance of other religious groups was a high ideal and a common pursuit. Like other congregations in Park Ridge, First Methodist had a history of "cordial relations" with the nearby Episcopal, Baptist, Presbyterian, Lutheran, and Community churches. It was a member of the Church Federation of Greater Chicago, a reformist, interdenominational Protestant organization that was a local version of the Federal Council of Churches. When politically inclined, the Federation "maintain[ed] chaplains in public institutions" and sometimes "[spoke] out on some legislation that affect[ed] public morals." Once more, however, this social vision fit into Park Ridge's progressive Methodism. The church was, as one observer put it, "a community-serving church, in the proper use of the term," aligning it with other progressive churches in the area, particularly those invested in humanitarianism, "public relief," and public education.[3]

Taylor's church was part of a movement within white Protestantism to bring progressive ethics to corporate capitalism. By forcing corporations to submit to Christian values, reformers felt, they could save capitalism from radical Protestant or communist revolt. The push to tame the corporation through popular reform and state law had been around almost as long as corporations themselves. As far back as the *Dartmouth College v. Woodward* case of 1819, the courts had deemed corporations as private property and, therefore, independent of state ownership but not outside the Constitution's legal authority, protection, or provision. Court decisions from the 1880s onward formalized corporations as legal "persons," able to own property, write and agree to contracts, transfer holdings and assets long past the death of any one corporate founder or executive, and receive certain protective "personhood" rights under the Fourteenth Amendment. Though the courts did not deem them "secular" persons per se, corporations were considered different than independent religious bodies. Unlike churches or other institutions deemed "religious," corporations were subject to taxation, legal restriction, and state promotion through public money. However, their very secularity—particularly their pursuit of profit, seemingly at any cost—did not sit well with many religious Americans. Thus, especially after the Civil War, their growing numbers and rising social and political power caused the nation's religious communities to call for some check on corporate power, either from corporate executives themselves, the state, or some combination thereof.

Vigorous reform sentiments proliferated in the American heartland, and low-church evangelicals gave them religious backing. Sometimes, those sentiments were channeled into fights for government regulation. At other times, they overlapped with or countered the emergence of welfare capitalism, or corporate provisions to quell labor, from the five-dollar day of Henry Ford to paternalistic company towns. Corporate liberalism, or the union of labor's interests with state and corporate interests, was another alternative, popular in the aftermath of the labor wars of the 1910s but not fully realized until the New Deal era. Other managerial innovations, from advertising campaigns to philanthropy to public relations, attempted to improve corporate reputations, address labor's demands, curtail radical sentiment, and—as one historian put it—give the "corporate person" a "soul."[4]

Progressive approaches to the corporation received their most ringing religious endorsement in the same year that Taylor joined Jewel Tea. In his 1925 bestseller *The Man Nobody Knows*, advertising executive and liberal Protestant Bruce Barton cast Jesus as a brawny, efficient, pioneering entrepreneur and "the founder of modern business." Though critics have often viewed Barton's book as a fawning endorsement of big business or of "the glorified Rotarianism" of churches like Taylor's, the book at least provided a popular meditation on executiveship and work in a nation defined by corporate capitalism. Barton's Jesus represented that "all work is worship; all useful service prayer. And whoever works wholeheartedly at any worthy calling is a co-worker with the Almighty." Barton collapsed the "corporation" into "the church," with Jesus serving as a divine corporate executive and moral exemplar. No callous teacher of corporate strong-arming, Barton's Jesus was more than an executive. He was "The Leader" and "The Master" who taught that all must reject the bottom-line "temptation of material success." True leaders and masters of business sought out greatness by becoming the "servant to all," a progressive vision of the ideal corporate executive.[5]

Taylor's Rotary movement similarly attempted to bring reform into the sphere of the corporation through a mantra of executives' social service. At the same time, the Rotary linked religion in the workplace to broader political and social concerns about labor protest, social disorder, and workplace ennui. Taylor routinely went to meetings that, as a West Virginia Rotarian put it in 1925, encouraged "American business men in all lines of commerce and industry to develop high standards of conduct or Codes and Ethics, and eventually get together upon one platform of high ethical principles and conduct of service." Rotarians "had within their grasp to make us missionaries for all time, of a newer and purer conception of man's relation to his fellow man both socially and in business." Such a position was also conveyed through Rotary's official creed: "He who profits most serves best." Through Rotary, Taylor also learned that a businessman's social service was best evidenced through philanthropy, poor relief, and global campaigns against infectious disease, thereby reflecting what lay Christians like Richard Ely had since the 1890s called the "social law of service," the necessity of self-sacrifice "emancipated from the bonds of gloomy asceticism." Though lampooned by writer Sinclair Lewis as "Babbitts" intending to fill their own spiritual void through self-serving rituals of social service, businessmen's clubs like the Rotary—and the Elks or Kiwanis Clubs—mattered as places where many white executives and managers like Taylor built and experienced a profit-minded and progressive, rational, results-oriented, practical Christianity.[6]

Taylor loved the Rotary. He believed wholeheartedly in its mission to fuse Christianity to executive-class identity and daily work. Taylor was also a Rotary man because, in a way, the organization's take on the businessman's role in modern society was—oddly enough—not too far removed from the fundamentalist Christianity that Taylor also affirmed. Hardly "gloomy ascetics" either, fundamentalists, too, thought businessmen and corporate elites could and should play a role in shaping society and godly order through the construction of a more Christian nation grounded in a more Christian capitalism.

Fundamentalism and American Corporate Culture

At least since the "businessmen's revivals" of the late 1850s, businessmen from across the theological and denominational spectrum had worked to shape American society into their idea of a "Christian nation." Evangelical dominance over American intellectual culture, politics, and society had been faltering for at least a generation by the time that Taylor had his "born again" experience in 1910. Long-held interpretations of Christian doctrine and experience, at least for conservative Protestants like Taylor, were under fire. Evolution and natural selection explained the origins and development of species better than the Book of Genesis. Critical studies of the Bible questioned its divine origins. Historical study upended long-held beliefs about the birth, life, and death of Christ, as well as about His divinity. Psychology seemed to explain human motivations better than appeals to inherent or redeemable sinfulness, while various political philosophies—from social Darwinism to Marxism to progressivism—gave Americans a sense of purposeful control over their futures. Evangelicalism's dominance also seemed in doubt in terms of raw numbers, as millions of Catholic and Jewish immigrants flooded into American cities, such as Taylor's Chicago, while the emergence of the academic study of religion undercut the historical claims of American Protestant exceptionalism. Even the exact appearance of Christ was an issue of fervent debate, although white Protestants tended to stay firm on that issue. Jesus was white, no matter what anyone might suggest to the contrary.[7]

One of the first executives to plot a way forward for conservative white evangelicals was a predecessor and contemporary of Taylor's and a fellow Chicagoan: Henry P. Crowell, founder of the Quaker Oats Company. As Richard Ellsworth Day, a biographer and friend, put it, Crowell thought himself a "business-priest . . . a man who acted on the idea that a man's business is not chiefly his way of making a living, but his altar where he serves the King." Crowell was also a financial backer of institutions that taught conservative views on matters of theology, economy, church, and state. In Crowell's Chicago, the city's foremost such institution was the Moody Bible Institute (MBI).[8]

MBI emerged out of the education wing of D. L. Moody's Chicago Evangelization Society (CES). Moody, since the 1870s, had become one of the nation's most popular revivalists, enjoying the backing of corporate executives in thriving economic centers that were nevertheless marked by class conflict: Philadelphia, New York, and, of course, Chicago. In the midst of labor unrest in the 1880s, culminating in the violent Haymarket protests of 1886, Moody planned CES to provide professional training for strategic, class-conscious missions work in the city. "Either these people are to be evangelized," Moody told a gathering of prominent Chicago businessmen, "or the leaven of communism and infidelity will assume such enormous proportions that it will break out in a reign of terror such as this country has never known." Similarly, CES aimed to create a new kind of worker, a missionary "professional" who came to the city's stockyards and packinghouses and served as intermediaries between working-class communities, social workers, and ministers.

Reuben Archer Torrey, a minister and banker's son, attempted to create such "gap-men." Like Moody (and later Taylor), Torrey straddled several spheres of religious thought and politics. According to historian Timothy Gloege, Torrey "brought to MBI a complex mix of experiential religion, an ongoing concern with current urban social conditions, and a growing acceptance of the natural-ness of modern capitalism." Accepting corporate capitalism as a godly social "good" did not necessarily mean that Torrey or others at CES endorsed rapa-cious or cold-hearted accumulation by Christian laymen or the titans of corpo-rate business. The church, like CES, could and should be community-serving, a humanitarian aid to the poor and working classes as well as a grassroots source for continued reform advocacy. Businessmen could and should do likewise with their resources and know-how.[9]

Torrey brought his pragmatic know-how to MBI after he signed on as super-intendent. During his tenure, he recruited potential donors, who could give to religious organizations like MBI without much state oversight, since the modern system of tax exemptions and deductions was not yet in place. (This would begin to change after the Sixteenth Amendment established the income tax in 1913.) Torrey was continuing an established trend as Moody already had many bank-rollers among the corporate elite, including John Farwell, Nathaniel Bouton, Turlington W. Harvey, Robert Scott, Elbridge W. Keith, and Cyrus McCormick. Contributions after Haymarket to Moody's planning for CES pushed upward to $250,000 ($7 million in today's dollars), with the McCormick family contributing $100,000. Farwell and McCormick also joined CES's board of trustees. By 1889, the year CES morphed into MBI, businessmen remained in the project's orbit and continued to shape its activities and internal politics for the next decade. By 1900, however, just a year after Moody's death, the organization had lost some of its early business support and seemed financially in trouble.

Enter Henry P. Crowell. Crowell joined MBI's board in 1901 and helped turn the institute around, reorganizing its educational and evangelistic boards according to corporate hierarchies and working feverishly to keep its books in order and its financial future secure. Crowell asserted his authority at MBI, policing religious opinions and driving it further toward what he deemed "purer" forms of Christian belief and practice and away from anything that smacked of "radical" belief—whether theological modernism or Pentecostalism. Torrey—himself a spiritual dabbler captured by the possibility of faith healing and power of Pentecostal beliefs—attempted to negotiate space for differences of theological opinion at MBI, but he ultimately failed and left the school in 1908. Crowell remained at the head of MBI's board and further "corporatized" the school's curriculum and personnel over the next two decades. By 1925, MBI had a publishing wing that produced thousands of books, pamphlets, and flyers each year, all informed by modern methods of consumer marketing, standardization, and distribution. Thanks in no small part to Crowell, MBI was transformed into a multifaceted center for the promotion of a new kind of socially engaged conservative evangelicalism, one that would rely on big businessmen's influence to perpetually define and "revive" itself. In the 1910s and 1920s, thousands of like-minded Protestants joined Crowell in affirming what they saw by then as a truly "pure" and standardized form of "traditional" or "old-time religion." By the 1930s, they had become a movement with a name: fundamentalism.[10]

Pastors, theologians, and ordinary Protestants all shaped the course of early fundamentalism. But big businessmen also played a crucial role. Consider, for instance, the foundational text of the movement. Published between 1910 and 1915 and edited in part by Torrey, *The Fundamentals* would not have existed without—as the first volume's title page stated—the "Compliments of Two Christian Laymen." The "laymen" were executives at Union Oil, Lyman and Milton Stewart. The former was the real underwriter of the venture, and he was in favor of aligning the "fundamentals" of the Protestant faith with "premillennial dispensationalism," a doctrine then only a few decades old. Although end times prophecy had been around in America since before the Civil War, it took off in a different direction with the teachings of John Nelson Darby in the 1870s. Darby and his followers emphasized Christ's imminent return before ("pre-") a new era or "dispensation" began: Christ's thousand-year ("millennial") reign. Darby's teachings filtered into *The Fundamentals*, which defined a "fundamentalist" largely as a premillenialist who was for evangelism, the preservation of the Sabbath, biblical literalism, and notions of Jesus as "God-Man." A fundamentalist was also a new category of Protestant fervently against "the Decadence of Darwinism," "spiritualism" (communing with the dead), "Eddyism" (Christian Science), Mormonism, and "Rome, The Antagonist of the Nation" (Catholicism). A fundamentalist was also wary of "postmillennialism," or the view that the return of Christ would occur only after a thousand-year reign of the Kingdom of God had been established on earth, a position more warmly received by Protestant progressives who championed reform efforts (a "social gospel") on behalf of the poor and disadvantaged.

Though such cut-and-dried statements seemed to define fundamentalism in an unequivocal fashion, room still remained for debate and interpretation, oddly enough on matters of political economy. For instance, Charles R. Erdman, who wrote a submission on "The Church and Socialism," acknowledged that "capital is often cruel" and that socialist critiques of Christians who uncritically accepted wealth were to be expected, especially if or when corporate barons made their money from the "watering of stocks and from wrecking railroads, and from grinding the faces of the poor." Erdman held no such sympathy toward self-described "Christian Socialists." He deemed them a "gross injustice," since "the Church" should not "invade the field of political economy, nor is it allied with any political or social order or propaganda," especially not one that "minimizes or denies such Christian truths as the incarnation, the virgin birth, the atonement, the resurrection, justification by faith, the work of the Holy Spirit, [and] the second coming of Christ." Sounding like a Rotarian, however, Erdman was hopeful that a renewed Christian conscience would convince capitalists to check certain abuses since "the very principles of industry, fidelity and honesty, taught by Christianity," Erdman concluded, "enable men to increase their power and wealth." Accumulation was good and godly, and "should be true under any form of social organization." Abusive accumulation, however, was questionable, and socialist complaints, if not coming from avowed Christians, were perhaps understandable, even if "unjustly plac[ing] all capitalists under suspicion of dishonesty and selfishness."[11]

Of course, The Fundamentals were not intended as an extended commentary on corporate capitalism per se, but they were crucial for defining a new religion—fundamentalism—in the midst of the social, political, and demographic upheavals that corporate capitalism wrought. Like MBI, the publication was also important because it was an early example of conservative evangelicals recognizing and welcoming big businessmen into their fold to provide both monetary support and organizational direction. Lyman Stewart not only underwrote The Fundamentals; he offered the project a certain level of administrative oversight, often in consultation with Torrey, and added his two cents about content and distribution. Stewart selected the executive board, and he corresponded with them about the purpose and promise of *The Fundamentals*. For instance, Stewart explained that the rejection of one entry was a result of the lack of "chaste and moderate language which causes even the opponent to stop and read." Noting the tendency of the first volumes to focus on high-minded theological issues, Stewart also likely oversaw the transition of later volumes to a vernacular style. "Thus far the articles have been more easily adapted to men of the highest culture," Stewart wrote his brother halfway through the publishing process, adding that "a series of articles adapted to the more ordinary preacher and teacher should follow."[12]

As with Crowell at MBI, Stewart's involvement set another tone for conservative evangelicalism in the twentieth century. Early on, it had a mundane, strategic—at times, even plodding—character, especially when considering who could and should fund the movement and how much power its underwriters should have. Who could and did fund fundamentalism would become even more important as the somewhat nuanced and sympathetic, if hardly tolerant, views that made it into the pages of *The Fundamentals* regarding the economy, socialism, and the state became more suspect to certain fundamentalists in the 1920s and 1930s. In the decades to come, businessmen would also continue to serve as visible hands in defining and shaping the politics of fundamentalists regarding matters of God, Mammon, and Caesar.

Rampant nationalism and anti-immigrant nativism during World War I convinced conservative theologians and bodies that German theological ideas were infiltrating American Protestant seminaries. "Modernist" theology and progressive Christianity seemed merely ploys to undermine the American military effort. Liberal theologians and bodies were no less wary of German "infiltration," but they tended to argue for greater, across-the-board unity among Protestants. After the war's end, a new round of reforms, such as the final push for women's suffrage, angered fundamentalists while the federal prohibition and policing of alcohol—endorsed by a mix of progressive and conservative allies—heartened them. Plans for church and missionary unity among Protestants in an effort to make the world "safer" for democracy and Protestantism merely sparked more division, especially among more creedal and Calvinistic evangelicals like the Presbyterians. Princeton Seminary's Charles Erdman, who had written about "The Church and Socialism" in *The Fundamentals*, came out in favor of unity. A colleague of Erdman's and fellow Princeton faculty member J. Gresham Machen stood opposed. Fights between Presbyterians torpedoed the idea and demonstrated that controversies over ecumenism, the historical Jesus, science, biblical exegesis, public morality, politics, and many other issues were not going anywhere. By 1925, a theological and social civil war was underway, with Protestants settling into distinct "modernist" and "fundamentalist" camps.

Leaders on each side fought frequently, and controversy was especially hot among Presbyterians, who had a reputation for bookishness and a penchant for theological dogfighting.

Taylor was still a young salesman and Billy Graham not yet a teenager in the 1920s, but both would come to know several conservative Presbyterians quite well. (Graham's father-in-law, L. Nelson Bell, was a Presbyterian missionary in China from 1916 to 1941.) "Modernists"—claimed "fundamentalist" Presbyterians and their kin in other denominations—rejected the doctrines of Jesus as divine, of Scripture as inspired or infallible, of the Bible as a historically accurate book regarding creation, of evolution as either erroneous or heretical or both, and of ecumenism as a Trojan horse for theological liberalism. Regarding the end times, fundamentalist Presbyterians were not in full agreement, but they certainly were suspicious of the growing sense that humanity and human institutions might be redeemed by a social gospel or progressive reform. Modernist theologians and progressive Protestants fired back. "Shall the Fundamentalists Win?" asked liberal Presbyterian pastor and theologian Harry Emerson Fosdick in 1922. He answered with a definitive "no." "Fundamentalists," claimed Fosdick and his counterparts, unnecessarily divided the church with take-it-or-leave-it propositions. Conversely, fundamentalists thought Christian pastors, educators, students, and congregants should take a stand and choose—as fundamentalist theologian J. Gresham Machen unabashedly put it in a 1923 book—between Christianity *and* liberalism.[13]

Such denominational and theological controversies could become front-page news, as demonstrated by a single event in the small town of Dayton, Tennessee. The "Scopes Monkey Trial" in the summer of 1925 both summarized and further split Protestant opinion over religious instruction in public schools and, more broadly, elementary questions of human origins, biblical interpretation, white supremacy, and national destiny. After local biology teacher John Scopes, at the behest of Dayton's civic leaders, violated a state law against teaching evolution, a "trial of the century" ensued. William Jennings Bryan, the antitrust populist and former presidential candidate, gave voice to conservative worries about evolution and humans' "apish" or "monkey" ancestors (or, as millions of white Americans interpreted Darwin, "African" ancestors). The proceedings in Dayton also brought national attention to Protestant fractures and, thanks to journalists like H. L. Mencken, cemented the idea of fundamentalism as primarily a "backward" religion of antimodernists living in a Bible Belt that roughly encompassed the rural South, the Ozarks, and the Midwest. The showbiz quality of the Scopes Trial, as well as of other fundamentalist pastors and radio preachers, would inform Sinclair Lewis's *Elmer Gantry*, published in 1927. Gantry was based in part on Billy Sunday, a fundamentalist revivalist popular during the late 1910s who garnered a certain appeal among big businessmen (including John

D. Rockefeller). Gantry popularized the image of the uncouth, unscrupulous, and uneducated evangelical, the fictional equivalent of Mencken's fundamentalists, whom the latter called the "*Homo boobiens* . . . for the precise reason [they are] uneducable." If progressive Protestants had *The Man Nobody Knows* to live up to, then fundamentalists had Elmer Gantry and Mencken's stereotyping to live down. Given the unscrupulous activities of many revival trail evangelists, the rise and fall of the white Protestant and small businessman–led, nativist Ku Klux Klan movement in the 1920s, and the rumors of financial malfeasance and corporate acquiescence that routinely followed Billy Sunday, art was not quite out of step with reality. The business of conservative evangelicalism always had the potential for abuse.[14]

Intra-Protestant relations deteriorated even further after Scopes. Grumbling with one another for years, Presbyterians divided after a series of vitriolic General Assemblies. At Presbyterian Princeton Seminary, faculty fought over fundamental doctrines from roughly 1926 to 1929. Increasingly dissatisfied with Princeton's liberal turn (and looked over for a promotion), Machen founded Westminster Theological Seminary in 1929 with a gaggle of his most talented students, including the separatist Carl McIntire and the more inclusivist Harold Ockenga, the latter of whom would soon be a seminal figure in a "new evangelical" movement. Taylor—and many other businessmen—would underwrite that movement, which they saw as a new and improved brand of an already business-friendly faith.[15]

Of Christian Conservatives and a New Deal

After the booming, post–World War I economy's shaky foundations finally crumbled in late 1929, the nation began a hasty economic slide that seemed to have no bottom, once again raising suspicions among conservative evangelicals that the end of days was near. Progressives thought capitalism's contradictions, like the contradictions of fundamentalist theology itself or of literalist interpretations of the Bible, were finally and unequivocally manifest. This would lead, they believed, to more reform and active political support for labor, a "New Deal" of recovery, relief, and redistributive programs, or (even more radically for the time) the rights of racial minorities. Many denominations, from urban centers to the poorest parts of rural America, not only struggled to make ends meet in the 1930s but also struggled to keep institutional division and religious demagogues at bay. In keeping with a long and growing divide, the Presbyterian General Assembly and missionary boards finally fell apart over conservative resistance to liberal "accommodations" in the early 1930s, eventually resulting in an active purge of fundamentalists like Machen, who in 1936 founded the

Orthodox Presbyterian Church. Adding more fuel to fundamentalist fires, pastors like Carl McIntire thought the Orthodox Presbyterian Church was not sufficiently fundamentalist on points of alcohol consumption and premillennialism. McIntire subsequently founded the Bible Presbyterian Church in 1937 and, in the postwar era, would decry most semblances of moderation or ecumenism among postwar evangelical leaders, such as Billy Graham.[16]

By 1935 nearly every major evangelical denomination was splintering, with members staying or leaving (or being forced out) according to what was taught or practiced regarding the "fundamentals" of the faith. Religious splintering also continued to confirm the racial divisions in Protestant life. Some evangelical theologies were avowedly racist, while others exhibited quieter forms of theological and social racism. Added to this divisiveness was an acute push by both fundamentalists and modernists to leave behind most historical affiliations with Pentecostal practices such as "spiritual baptism," faith-healing, and glossolalia ("speaking in tongues"). Whereas early fundamentalists and moderate Protestants might dabble in or outright endorse Pentecostal or perfectionist ("holiness") teachings, by the 1920s such perspectives had been policed out of formal seminary training, church appointments, and theological publications. Ironically, all this occurred in a nation in which Aimee Semple McPherson, a Pentecostal, albeit not often a terribly public or consistent one, was the most popular evangelist of the 1920s and early 1930s. A national and international celebrity, McPherson preached a conservative message of cultural renewal as a "bride of Christ" from her megachurch in Los Angeles. In the same city, however, fundamentalists like Fighting Bob Shuler lambasted McPherson as a "charlatan," both for her Pentecostalism and for her embrace of jazz culture and interracial services. Shuler was a staunch racist and nativist, infamous for personal attacks. In 1931, the Federal Radio Commission, precursor to the Federal Communications Commission, revoked his station's charter for being a public nuisance, aiming for state regulation of fundamentalists that future activists— most notably, the postwar National Religious Broadcasters—would challenge. McPherson's popularity aside, Pentecostals were increasingly settling into their own distinctive denominations and institutions while internally fracturing over race. Until the postwar era, they also did not have a significant monied infrastructure of big businessmen supporting them. But Pentecostals would not be left out of the corporate world of conservative evangelicalism for long.[17]

By the mid-1930s, divisions between fundamentalists and their opponents calcified. As a result, many fundamentalists left their respective Protestant bodies or denominations (or were forced out, as in Machen's case). Still, they were no less interested in social issues or politics than they had been during World War I or during the prohibitionist 1920s. The search for separation and privatization never quite precluded public engagement. Given that they wanted to protect the private worlds of theological "purity" and social difference they made for themselves, fundamentalists worried about the bureaucratic power of Roosevelt's New Deal program, often viewing it within the context of the war rumblings in Europe. There, the totalitarian regimes of Germany and the Soviet Union seemed the ultimate end-game of secular or "modernist" empowerment. The reformist aspects of the New Deal state seemed similarly foreboding, and fundamentalists theorized about the best response while reading the end times into current events. At the 1932 Democratic National Convention, Roosevelt received 666 votes, a satanic number according to premillennial theology. He spoke in biblical metaphors during his First Inaugural, and, after only a few weeks in office, he oversaw the fulfillment of another campaign promise: ending the federal prohibition of alcohol. Since most fundamentalists were teetotalers and, given that Roosevelt's New Deal seemed to give off signs of either communism or socialism, fundamentalists like J. Frank Norris—and counterparts like Mark Matthews, John Rice, and, to an extent, L. Nelson Bell—came to believe that Roosevelt was tipping toward anti-Christian autocracy. Others, including but not limited to Harold Ockenga, Wilber Smith, and William Bell Riley, theorized that, along with the rise of Mussolini and Hitler, Roosevelt might be the Anti-Christ or was possibly setting the stage for the Anti-Christ through legislation like the National Recovery Act, the formal recognition of the Soviet Union, the expansion of public works projects and welfare provisions, the passage of the prolabor measures, and the proliferation of Social Security.[18]

The Great Depression and rise of the New Deal provided the socioeconomic context for big businessmen to consider backing like-minded and similarly alarmed conservative Christian groups. In the desperate days of the Great Depression, Protestant conservatives, including radical ones, seemed to be, for some businessmen, the best possible collaborators in building a social movement opposed to the New Deal. For instance, Gerald L. K. Smith won attention from some members of the American corporate elite. Though he had fundamentalist friends, Smith was not quite a fundamentalist in theological persuasion and took a collaborationist approach toward those who shared his political sensibilities. Initially schooled and supported by radio personality Francis Townsend and Louisiana governor Huey Long and loyal to a populist view of makers versus takers, Smith advocated for the demolition of the New Deal state before some formulation of socialism, communism, or Nazism took over. His anti-Semitism also endeared him to Henry Ford, who reportedly supported Smith's mission "100 per cent." Yet Ford stopped short of offering monetary aid. Dismayed, Smith later recalled that the wealthy were "never as helpful as people think," but he still trumpeted the automaker's entrepreneurial independence and productive capabilities.[19]

Another conservative Christian radical, Vance Muse, held similar views about the intersection of work, race, and religion. He more successfully garnered business support. Based in Texas, his Christian American Association (CAA) received early support from anti–New Deal oil men like Maco Stewart and John Henry Kirby as well as northern industrialists, including the du Pont family. A segregationist shocked by Roosevelt's inclusion of blacks on the White House staff, Muse became nationally famous in 1936 for distributing photographs of black ROTC officers escorting Eleanor Roosevelt during a public event, implying an intimate relationship between them. Muse also held similar views about Jews and Catholics, whom he believed were behind the New Deal. "That crazy man in the White House will Sovietize America," he once wrote, "with the federal hand-outs of the Bum Deal—sorry, New Deal. Or is it the Jew Deal?" Muse himself held no clear denominational affiliation and no church membership, but the CAA nevertheless worked in and through the culture of plain-folk fundamentalism, albeit with an open-door policy toward potential supporters. The CAA's mission statement joined religious and political rhetoric, declaring its intent "to publish and distribute Christian American literature of a nonpartisan and nonsectarian nature for the promotion of Americanism, religion, and righteousness and to conduct a program of education and organization to combat Communism, Fascism, Nazism, Socialism, atheism and other alien 'isms' designed to destroy faith in God and Jesus Christ, the church, the home, and the American system of one's own conscience." With the help of big business, the CAA attained at least one of its political goals. It held the distinction of being one of the first organizations in the country to champion what it termed the "God-Given-Right-to-Work Amendment" as a political slogan, successfully using racist appeals to fight against the strengthening of labor laws at both the state and federal levels. (Muse thought unions would encourage biracial collaboration and white men and women would have to join "organizations with black African apes whom they will have to call 'brother' or lose their jobs.") Muse died before he could develop the popular, grassroots support for a federal right-to-work amendment, but the impact of the CAA was already apparent at the state level, even in the early 1940s. Versions of the CAA's various anti-union proposals were on the books in eight states during World War II, including Kansas, Idaho, South Dakota, Arkansas, Colorado, Mississippi, Florida, and Muse's native Texas.[20]

Given the New Deal's perceived or actual threat to their economic authority, business elites also underwrote more moderate ventures that were grounded in a sense of fundamentalist immediacy but open to alliance-building and less interested in overtly racist or anti-Semitic appeals. George Washington Robnett's National Laymen's Council of the Church League of America was the paradigmatic example. It was also one of the first evangelical organizations to pair the money of business executives with the method of alliance-building in order to both spark mass conversions and limit the New Deal. Founded in 1937 with the support of an aging Henry P. Crowell, the Church League of America (CLA), as it was later renamed, served as the personal outlet for Robnett's religious politics. An advertising executive in Chicago, Robnett had several friends with connections to corporate power. Frank J. Loesch, a corporate lawyer and former head of the Chicago Crime Commission, joined with Crowell to support the CLA's mission, aiming to promote the idea that Christianity "elevates and dignifies human personality in contrast to the so-called 'Collectivist' or Marxian doctrines." To that end, the CLA published a monthly newspaper—*News and Views*—that tried to convince Protestant ministers of the threat of godless socialism via the New Deal state.

By 1940, the CLA claimed 100,000 members and was hitting up additional donors, including Herbert J. Taylor, and positing its efforts—if properly funded—would reach between 60 million and 80 million Americans (roughly half to two-thirds of the US population) through an expansive network of ministers. This expectation was certainly overstated, but Robnett's social network still had impressive range. Although core CLA-affiliated clergy were fundamentalist ministers, the group also claimed to include conservative rabbis, Episcopalians, Methodists, Lutherans, and Congregationalists. What united these men was opposition to the New Deal. "The league's appeal," noted the *Chicago Daily Tribune* in 1940, "outlines a history of New Deal action on which the predicted crisis is based. It cites changes which it said have shocked the American system, including what it described as one-sided legislation, the burdening of business, decreasing financial support for church, charitable and educational institutions, and the third term for President Roosevelt." The CLA averred that the New Deal's labor acts, such as the Wagner Act of 1935, not only promoted collective bargaining but "tied the hands of every employer (large or small) so that any criminal—any Communist—or any racketeer—could go into any plant and start organizing the employes [*sic*] into a dues paying corral regardless of the merits of the case." Moreover, the CLA chastised all forms of socialism ("Christian socialism" was an oxymoron) and linked freer enterprise to faithful defenses of "the basic liberties of our people and our institutions." "As private enterprise is being taxed more and more by the excessive, ever growing demands for big government," proclaimed one CLA broadsheet, "and as the growth of bureaucratic obstructions and red tape tend to strangle human initiative and stifle opportunity for more employment—it is inevitable that there will be less and less from the profits of business to go for the up-keep of educational institutions—churches and the wide network of human agencies they maintain." Welfare should be provided by churches alone; that was both compassionate and truly conservative. Americans needed to wake up and see "that the anti-business crusade was a stab in the back for all institutions" because "Free

Religion—Free Enterprise [were] Inseparable—One Cannot Exist Without the Other." But the CLA's complaint was not merely about the interconnectedness of fundamental freedoms. If the state got in the way of evangelical effort—of evangelicals' ability to save souls *and* do business freely—then it would reshape the spiritual, economic, and political affiliations of Americans before evangelicals could. Religious freedom was, therefore, synonymous with free enterprise and the freedom to work at will.[21]

Like many anti-New Deal evangelical ventures, the CLA's influence was limited. It had little political effect outside reconvincing the clergy it counted on its mailing lists and rolls. (Never large, it remained a small organization in the 1940s and faded into obscurity in the 1950s, as funding dried up and as Herbert J. Taylor and Billy Graham's brand of business-friendly fundamentalism took off.) Still, the CLA was—like the CAA and other Depression-era organizations on the business end of anti–New Deal evangelical conservatism. The CLA had the backing of specific businessmen who shared its political or religious views, and it often touted the sinfulness of socialism and the power of a faith in free enterprise. Such advocacy was, however, an uphill battle, lacking a political and institutional infrastructure. Even if they were able to get a business leader to cut a check or promise regular support or tacit approval for their revolt against the New Deal, Protestant conservatives—fundamentalists included—had only their own institutions and upstart organizations, which were often disconnected from one another in terms of funding, communication, and personnel. Fundamentalists came to believe that, as in years past, they needed to develop strategies for organizing businessmen and their resources and linking corporate strategies and ideas to their religious and social ambitions. Herbert Taylor and other like-minded Christian businessmen would soon find a way forward. One such way involved writing new corporate creeds. Taylor called his the "Four-Way Test."

Of Fundamentalism and a Four-Way Test

Fundamentalists in New Deal America had plenty of grievances but not much else, at least in terms of corporate insiders or political powerbrokers. The majority of Protestants in the American business and political "establishment"— meaning the heads of large-scale blue chip companies and the holders of high political office—in the 1930s were not quite on the evangelical spectrum. They were mostly churchly Protestants with progressive political and theological leanings. According to one survey, in 1930 53.5 percent of elites (political, cultural, and business) were Episcopalian, Presbyterian, or Unitarian. Catholics and Jews made up a tiny minority of establishment figures (roughly 6 percent together), a figure that changed drastically over the course of the next sixty years (to 23 percent and 12 percent, respectively). Baptists, Methodists, Disciples of Christ, Lutherans, and Reformed Christians provided another 29 percent of elites in 1930, a number that dropped off to 20 percent during the postwar era. Though it is difficult to tell from the survey, it is likely that such Protestants were not generally of the evangelical persuasion and, unlike past exceptions like Lyman and Milton Stewart, were hardly fans of the fundamentalist movement. Moreover, although executives ranged widely in their political opinions, the Great Depression indisputably brought progressive Protestantism and liberal Protestant leaders into closer quarters with governmental movers and shakers. For instance, the Federal Council of Churches—which included any number of big-business supporters and congregational members—supported the New Deal welfare state, labor organizing rights, controls on credit, and farm relief through price controls. The Roosevelt administration basically returned the favor, commending forms of liberal Protestantism as the religious equivalent of state reformism.[22]

As a business executive with fundamentalist leanings, Taylor undoubtedly felt caught in the middle of the Great Depression's political and religious reshufflings. Regarding party politics, he gave minor donations in the 1940s and postwar era to the Republican Party in Chicago, not a small gesture in a city that leaned heavily Democratic. Regarding private enterprise, Taylor did not endorse full-fledged activism for reform and certainly did not favor state involvement in the "private" affairs of labor or management. He was also not in favor of labor organizing or collective bargaining; Christian goodwill between management and labor should be enough to solve most "labor questions," he believed. Still, he was a moderate Republican and not as consistently opposed to the New Deal as some other fundamentalists or his counterparts in big business (such as Pierre du Pont with his American Liberty League, or the anti–New Deal National Association of Manufacturers with its libertarian "American Way of Life" propaganda).[23] When asked to do his wartime duty against "totalitarianism" in 1942 and serve on a price adjustment board for the War Department, Taylor obliged.[24]

Taylor's vision of a good and godly society nevertheless was related to his firm conviction that the solution to most of society's ills—and the heart of the Christian life—lay in the historical interpretations of the Bible and the verity of miracles, the conversion of individual souls, and selective philanthropy. Taylor might attend a white, Republican-leaning, moderate establishment church like First Methodist of Park Ridge, but he repeatedly and consistently held to fundamentalist assertions regarding the nature of Jesus, the Bible, the Virgin Birth, and the need for "social change" primarily through individualistic, soul-by-soul change. Small but revealing acts set him apart from many if not most progressive Protestants, even those he likely sat with in the pews each Sunday. For instance, in 1940 he decided not to fund certain Methodist churches around Chicago because—he claimed—"a real gospel message" did not issue from their liberal pulpits. A few months later, James A. James, the president of Northwestern University—through which Taylor put himself before going off to Europe for World War I—asked him to join the school's board of trustees. A bastion of social gospel teaching, Northwestern promptly received Taylor's rejection of the offer. Garrett Biblical Institute, a small evangelical seminary across town, also inquired as to whether Taylor might consider a small donation, for the sake of scholarship funds. Taylor was forthcoming only after learning that recipients were fundamentalists. Even later, after World War II, it was evident that Taylor retained his disdain for projects that seemed to emphasize social change without soul change. In 1949, he wrote to protest his Methodist church's denominational publishing house, calling it suspect for having little "evangelistic emphasis" in its literature for church schools. (As a lifelong Sunday School teacher, Taylor likely worried about what he deemed heterodox messages being taught to passive youths.)[25]

Taylor's faith also related to his business career and identity as a relatively successful and wealthy corporate executive who had done well for himself during the Great Depression. In 1932, he accepted an offer to become president of Club Aluminum, just as the nation's economy was bottoming out. Unemployment pushed upward into the double digits, reaching one-fourth of the population in 1933. Chicago was rocked by strikes and violence. The New Deal was in its nascent stages. Though Roosevelt and his "brains trust" were rushing to do anything to stem the economic crisis, many Americans were still uncertain about how far the economy could slide.

Like Roosevelt, Taylor exuded confidence in the midst of crisis, especially about his decision to take the helm at Club Aluminum. God, since Taylor's conversion as a teenager, had promised to be on his side. And, Taylor believed, God was transcendent and involved in human affairs, no matter what a modernist or materialist might say. "I was convinced" to take the post (and a significant cut in salary), Taylor later claimed, "because the Holy Spirit told me so." Yet even divine revelation could not hide cold, hard facts. Club Aluminum, a cookware company dependent on door-to-door selling, was not well-suited to a time when millions of Americans did not know where their next meal would come from or—if they ate home-cooked meals—were not inclined to buy specialty cookware. Accountants estimated it was $400,000 ($5.6 million, inflation adjusted) in debt and about to close its doors when the Holy Spirit supposedly moved Taylor to take it over. Aware of its limitations, Taylor contracted out to retail stores and enhanced the company's name-brand appeal by prompting storekeepers to offer food discounts for customers who tried out Club Aluminum cookware.

Taylor's plan worked. By 1940, Club Aluminum was not only turning a profit but garnering a reputation for quality cookware. It had its own radio program,

"Club Time," with millions of Americans tuning in each week. (George Beverly Shea, who would join with Billy Graham and sing for him into the next century, had his big break singing for Club Time from 1944 to 1952.) Taylor's successful turnaround of Club Aluminum established him as a recognizable and influential member of the Chicago business community. From 1939 to 1940, he served as the president of the Rotary Club of Chicago.[26]

Taylor's turnaround of Club Aluminum also reassured him of the applicability of religion in the workplace and in the nation at large. If his faith, duly believed, resulted in his company's success, then Taylor reasoned that God would bless any other endeavor, whether in private enterprise or not, if it followed a few guidelines. Delayed gratification was a myth. Like conversion to the evangelical gospel, the benefits of "conversion" to Taylor's workplace faith brought immediate rewards. It all came down to whether one followed Taylor's self-made creed, what he called "the Four-Way Test."

Taylor thought all executives should ask themselves four questions about any business decision: "(1) Is it the TRUTH? (2) Is it FAIR to all concerned? (3) Will it build GOODWILL and better friendships? (4) Will it be BENEFICIAL to all concerned?" Previous drafts asked "Will it be profitable . . . to all concerned?" as well, but Taylor edited out such references to the bottom line, preferring a test that was applicable to nonprofit endeavors as well. For Taylor, the Four-Way Test was a social ethic as much as a means of applying faith to corporate life. Implicit in the test was the idea that social well-being depended on businessmen asking themselves such questions. Also implicit was the notion that businessmen would be guided by it. If they answered each question affirmatively, then they would proceed with a business plan that would automatically benefit "all concerned," including people directly or indirectly affiliated with their company. If they answered "no" to any question, then businessmen *alone* were the best judges regarding the next step. The Four-Way Test, though certainly an in-office social ethic, was nevertheless an implicit argument for executive authority and freer enterprise, and an argument that businessmen should be free—before their God or sense of personal judgment—to make decisions for corporations and society at large.

Taylor's Four-Way Test brought him cross-over appeal with nonevangelical groups in Chicago, especially with those he would have considered liberal or "modernistic" Protestants. The Rotarian creed also aligned with Taylor's test and undoubtedly informed it. In part, the creed was the product of liberal Protestant approaches to managing corporate power, wedded to Taylor's concerns about state involvement in business. The test linked businessmen's authority to social service and welfare. Rotarians, like their creed, could give the corporation a soul of service and, in turn, ensure that corporate profitability rested on public approval, goodwill, and heartfelt appreciation. In this way, the creed was a precursor to the mid-century managerial philosophy of "servant leadership," which would become a mantra in evangelical, service-oriented firms like ServiceMaster, Wal-Mart, and Chick-fil-A. Setting aside authoritarianism in the office was the key to business efficiency, as was ameliorating "petty" grievances between managers, between management and labor, and between labor and customer. At the end of the day, the customer was, for Rotarians, the godly and moral leader to be served by Christian servants.

As historian Sarah Hammond observed, "By imposing only a behavioral 'yardstick,' not a theological one, Club Aluminum [and the Four-Way Test] exemplified Christianity on Taylor's terms without being officially Christian." Eschewing exclusivist fundamentalism in favor of inclusive Rotarianism, Taylor ran the test past four managers—a Roman Catholic, a Christian Scientist, a Jew, and a Presbyterian—who agreed that the test offended no one's religious beliefs. In this way, Taylor represented one of the earliest efforts by fundamentalists to cross long-standing religious and socioracial boundaries, working with Jews and Catholics to present a social and probusiness theology that, ostensibly, each group would affirm. Nevertheless, the test contained tinges of Taylor's brand of conservative evangelicalism, especially in the immediacy of its promised returns and effect on personal character and labor relations. "The source of character in industry is religious faith," Taylor wrote William McDermott, a Chicago newspaper reporter who had worked on fundamentalist Charles Fuller's revival team. "We have simply incorporated our religious ideals into a simple working code of four points." Taylor thought it killed two birds with one stone: it was a workplace motivator and mollifier. When followed, the Four-Way Test built long-term "goodwill" among everyone in a corporation, acting like a "boomerang [that] will return to you tomorrow with a profit." Unions would have no purchase at a Four-Way company. "Most strikes and lockouts can be traced directly to selfishness, insincerity, unfair dealings, or fear and lack of friendship among the men concerned," Taylor told McDermott for an interview in a 1942 issue of *The Rotarian*. "There are many ways to discover the flaw in a given case, but I think one can usually put his finger on it by applying the Four-Way Test." Indeed, at a Four-Way Test company, it was not that the state's provisions and protections regarding labor were unwelcome. It was that they were redundant.[27]

The Four-Way Test also rested on a contractual view of the world that had its origins in evangelical theology and especially appealed to fundamentalists like Taylor. Contracts, even if they had no religious connotation, were vital for corporate creation. Without them—signed between persons with state approval and in accordance with the law—corporations technically did not exist. Most Protestants, and especially evangelicals, who had a high regard for contractual theologies because of the lack of an ecclesiastical intermediary between them and God, could find much to like in the contracts of corporate culture.

In general, most conservative evangelicals privileged (in their language and material culture) the idea that their "debts" had been *actually* "paid" by Jesus's death on a cross, their eternal fate "sealed" through his resurrection and assurance of his future return. Fundamentalists like Taylor doubled down on this soteriology, deeming it a historical fact; such a contract had *actually* been signed when Jesus died and miraculously rose again. Unwavering faith in the Gospels' accounts of salvation was the key to fundamentalist identity, but so too was all-encompassing devotion to the divine contract, with the steep price of eternal damnation for reneging.

Contractual metaphors for newfound faith had abounded in nineteenth-century evangelicalism, most likening conversion to "signing" on the bottom line in a business deal. Into the twentieth century, such a contractual theology would be found again and again among evangelical businessmen, primarily as an analogy for making sense of their religious experience or worldly position and as a model for social order and goodwill. Any long-suffering patience for heaven was not there. The fundamentals of the faith had no room for otherworldly thumb-twiddling; evangelical activism could thus be a suitable ethic for corporate capitalism. If one could take heart in the rock-solid convictions of fundamentalism as proof that one's work on Earth was affirmed in heaven, then one could work in sectors private and public with confidence and verve. God would keep up His end of the deal. His servants should do the same until the "end times" were self-evident. Therefore, one should work hard and expect blessings *now* because the contract was already signed. The Four-Way Test, its provisions, and its expectations reflected the appeal of this contractual sensibility and served as an early example of an evangelical big businessman's take on what work could and should mean to all Americans in a corporate age.

The Four-Way Test was a hit. Rotarians across the country found it appealing, sending Taylor regular requests to speak about his test at local clubs, schools, and churches. Disseminated by the Rotary, it became a creed for home and office. Rotarians and other civic clubs put it on their letterhead, embossed it on knick-knacks, and set it in picture frames on their desks and office walls. It was popular among evangelical organizations, institutions, and churches. In an ironic twist, the president of William Jennings Bryan University, named for the most prominent anti-evolutionist, anticorporate evangelical of the Gilded Age, sought Taylor's test out for "easy reference" in school operations. Taylor's test and tenure as Rotary president also brought him significant notoriety outside evangelical circles, especially after World War II. In 1955, Taylor earned the seal of approval from the journalistic guardians of middle-brow, respectable, progressive white America. He was the first fundamentalist big businessman to appear on the cover of *Newsweek*.[28]

That *Newsweek* printed nothing about Taylor's fundamentalist leanings demonstrated his aptitude at making certain facets of liberal, establishment, progressive Protestantism work for him and for his brand of engaged, pragmatic fundamentalism. More important, he was hardly alone in taking such an approach to public engagement. Other fundamentalists—such as Billy Graham—would do the same after World War II. Like Taylor, Graham also came out of a circle of fundamentalist businessmen attuned to social engagement and strategic, somewhat ecumenical appeals. Such businessmen had also started to organize themselves slowly over the course of the 1930s into a movement that both overlapped and diverged with Taylor's own efforts, creating new links between fundamentalism, Christian executiveship, and Rotarian respectability. To be sure, outwardly racist or reactionary evangelicals also continued to pursue the blessings of business. But they did not have the longevity or social importance of endeavors like Taylor's, or of the crusades backed by members of the Christian Business Men's Committee, International.

Organizing the Christian Businessman

A brochure, most likely published shortly after the Japanese attack on Pearl Harbor, conveyed how "14 Prominent Businessmen Look at Life." Americans lived "in a strange, unpredictable world." Moreover, "leaders in the political, business, and educational world confess they do not know where they are going." With the Great Depression or the end times also in mind, the brochure mused, "What are diamonds today may be dust tomorrow." What was the believing (white) Christian to do? In whom should he (never she) have confidence and faith?

A cadre of corporate executives held the keys to spiritual, economic, and political vitality—and real-world results. "Leaders in the business world . . . in the vicissitudes of business life," the brochure noted, "have been guided and sustained by an inner force which can be neither measured nor taken away." This "inner force" was no vague spirituality. It was a brand of socially engaged, respectable, business-oriented fundamentalism. Americans should take heart, as the businessmen featured in the pamphlet variously put it, in "the Lordship of Christ," "harmony with the will of God," "the gospel in operation in business life," "the Bible and the Saviour," "Jesus Christ [who] saved me from my sin and myself," "redemption from sin," and "the receiving of a new life through Jesus Christ my Saviour and Lord." This gospel vivified "not an isolated group" but businessmen who "represent a large company of people who in this day of anxiety and uncertainty find comfort in a common faith." This common faith—when put into practice—was concerned with worldly affairs and alliance-building between like-minded businessmen, such as the fourteen men detailed in the pamphlet:

- W. H. Adamson, President of Adamsons, Ltd., Vice-President, Edmonton Stock Yards, Vice-President, Union Stock Yards of Saskatoon, Ltd., and Director of Sterling Trusts Corporation
- Elmer E. Black, Manager of Store Service for Marshall Field and Company
- Philip A. Benson, President of the Dime Savings Bank of Brooklyn and President of the American Bankers Association
- J. C. Black, the President of the Black Manufacturing Company, Treasurer of the Seattle Hardware Company and Director of Pacific National Bank of Seattle
- Arnold Grunigen Jr., Investment Banker for Weeden and Company
- Allan C. Emery, Treasurer of the Emery-Conant Company
- Charles E. Gremmels, President of Providential Realty and Investing Company and Vice-President of Master Rule Manufacturing Company
- Charles L. Huston, Vice-President of Lukens Steel Company and Member of the British and American Iron and Steel Institutes
- A. J. Nesbitt, President of Nesbitt, Thomson and Company, and several Canadian power companies
- Erling C. Olsen, Vice-President of Fitch Investors Services on Wall Street
- Thomas "Apple King" Smith, President of Thomas S. Smith and Sons, Inc.
- J. F. Strombeck, President of the Strombeck-Becker Manufacturing Company
- Henry P. Crowell, Board Chairman of the Quaker Oats Company and the Perfection Stove Company
- R. G. LeTourneau, President of one of the largest engineering and earthmoving firms in the world.[29]

All were members of the Christian Business Men's Committee (CBMC). Founded by A. H. Leaman, a Mennonite with evangelical leanings and faculty member at Moody Bible Institute, the CBMC began as a club for businessmen who wanted to continue meeting with one another after an evangelical revival organized by Leaman in Chicago in 1930, a year of economic panic. The next few years in Chicago were little better, at least from management's perspective. Strikes and violence between organized labor, police, and city officials were common. New Dealers swept into office. In such a tense atmosphere, Leaman's group grew through word-of-mouth and informal invitations. After weekly prayer and testimony meetings attracted small groups and then hundreds of businessmen, the club brought together similar businessmen's groups in the city. From 1930 to 1936, the various groups organized as "committees," which then came together under the banner of the CBMC. Committees met at noon—a time conducive to business professionals taking an hour off for lunch in the city—and received the support of Moody Bible Institute's radio and publishing services.[30]

By 1936, a CBMC-organized revival in Chicago drew 11,000 people. The next year, the infamous "Memorial Day Massacre" of unarmed labor demonstrators in Chicago resuscitated fears of class war. Although such events were not covered in CBMC records, linking evangelical identity and social authority to respectable manhood—especially *white* manhood—and the stilling power of the business elite was a key component of the CBMC. As Arnold Grunigen Jr. put it, men too often "sat demurely in a church pew Sunday morning, if the weather is bad, so they can't play golf." Ministers were also inefficient and bumbling managers, unlike men in "the business world," who would not allow "excess program machinery and ineffectual whirring of wheels." Businessmen could do a better job of giving Americans living through Depression the order, encouragement, and spiritual grounding they seemed to need and want.[31]

As the CBMC increased its membership rolls, it also established chapters outside Chicago, creating one of the first national networks of conservative, evangelical executives and managers in the twentieth century. In Los Angeles, Dr. Paul W. Rood, president of the Bible Institute of Los Angeles (BIOLA), joined with Grunigen to form a West Coast branch of the CBMC in 1937 and 1938. Not coincidentally, BIOLA was another evangelical institution with big-business connections. Three decades before, in 1908, Lyman Stewart—the same oil tycoon who would soon fund *The Fundamentals*—joined with Presbyterian pastors Thomas C. Horton and Augustus B. Prichard to found the school. From the start, BIOLA was intended to be a West Coast version of Moody Bible Institute.[32] The BIOLA model of training students as self-starting, independent, fundamentalist preachers and promoters fit well with the CBMC's model of attracting businessmen to be a type of evangelistic franchisee, first training in small committees and then founding additional committees for maximum social effect, primarily by duplicating the initial training they had received. Every new committee, however, fell under the organizational umbrella of the CBMC, which provided funding, materials, and administrative direction. The various branches of the CBMC added international committees in 1938. After that, it became known as the CBMC International or CBMCI (although both members and outsiders referred to it as either the CBMC or CBMCI).[33]

As a lay organization, the CBMCI deemed itself theologically fundamentalist. In keeping with the fundamentalist privileging of premillenialism, it counted only premillenialists as voting members. But, in keeping with its Rotary Club auspices and an awareness of how controversial premillenialism had become in Protestant circles by the 1930s, the CBMCI did not exclude from fellowship those holding other views about the Second Coming. Still, premillenialism strongly informed the CBMCI's sense of urgency. For leaders and members, the organization was first and foremost a missionary organization, bringing together like-minded businessmen for the evangelization of anyone—regardless of whether they were in business—who came in contact with the CBMCI. The group proved popular. In the late 1930s and early 1940s, the CBMCI became an organizational magnet for businessmen across the conservative end of the evangelical spectrum. From only five committees in 1938, CBMCI membership exploded during the 1940s. By 1947, 162 CBMCI committees were in operation. Roughly a decade later, the CBMCI had 450 committees and 500 up and running by 1960. Its presence was felt in many major American cities, dozens of states, and countries as far-ranging as Scotland to New Zealand. Businessmen from Detroit, Los Angeles, Philadelphia, New York, and Chicago could be counted among its ranks, as well as any number of executives and managers in California, Arizona, Texas, Tennessee, West Virginia, North Carolina, and Florida.[34]

Eschewing the hairsplitting and vociferous controversies that were dividing Protestant churches, seminaries, and denominations in the 1930s, the CMBCI consciously avoided controversy over what one member called the theological or denominational "dust, dirt, and noise" that inevitably resulted from coordinated missions work. But keeping "all spiritual efforts . . . inside church organizations" and under pastoral care was more "dust and noise." "The business men," the CBMCI assured any actual or imagined critics, "are more than ready to cooperate with pastors and Christian forces where the salvation of souls and enrichment of Christian lives is the objective." Moreover, "people will take notice when business men, who have nothing to gain personally through their efforts . . . spend themselves willingly . . . in all sorts of unusual undertakings in order that others might find the Saviour."[35]

As an organization, then, the CBMCI was an advertisement for a new and improved, strategic, moderate (but no less activist), business-backed fundamentalism. It was also an advertisement for the businessman as a religious activist and leader, as a kind of corporate Moses for uncertain economic times. In the postwar era, the CBMCI would turn into a social network for a brand of fundamentalism organized under a new banner, what Machen's student Harold Ockenga called "the new evangelicalism." Ockenga may have coined the term, but he did not invent the method. A "new" evangelicalism had been in operation for a decade by the time Ockenga went public with his call in the 1940s. A new evangelicalism was working itself out in the social engagements of alliance-minded, socially engaged, premillenialist businessmen leading their own revival through the CBMCI. This new form of fundamentalism—lauding corporate work, proclaiming the power of soul-by-soul change, championing active involvement in modern life, vying for social and political influence—built on the investments and involvement of businessmen, forging a new, modern, business-backed, conservative evangelical movement. In large part, what made it a "movement" that "moved" was the involvement of men like Taylor and the "14 Businessmen" who looked at life and saw much in need of change. They were a necessary component, granting shape and sustenance—financial and otherwise—to the movement as it progressed through the postwar era.

The CBMCI had other purposes aside from spreading its gospel of salvation. During the Great Depression, the CBMCI also brought like-minded businessmen together, linking prewar fundamentalist institutions and business activists. But the CBMCI was not merely a social club. It doubled as a public relations firm, legitimizing the idea that corporations were modern institutions that fundamentalists could and should run. Moreover, the CBMCI promoted the conflation of "fundamentalist" with "Christian" in its very name, implicitly arguing that fundamentalism was the truest and best form of Christianity (See Fig. 1.1). To be a "Christian" businessman was to be a fundamentalist businessman. The CBMCI also represented evangelicals as neither reactionary Bible-Belters nor charlatan Gantrys. They were responsible, open to alliance-building, tolerant of other views, and focused on changing society for the "better." A "Christian businessman" was like a disciple of Barton's Jesus, albeit with a fundamentalist soul.

He was also a white man. Though not explicit, white male authority was assumed, mirroring racial and gender arrangements in prewar and postwar corporate America. Women were not CBMCI members. They accompanied their husbands to host cities, but protocols and rituals—such as not having women on local committee boards or scheduling separate programs by women, for women during CBMCI meetings—prescribed gender norms.[36] CBMCI conferences were all-white affairs as well. Not a single photograph, correspondence, or public record from the CBMCI's early organizing or publications feature a person of color. Fundamentalist unity and organizing thus had limits for the business class, in accordance with evangelical precedence and anxiety regarding work, sex, race, and racial proximity. Though concerns about World War II and the Cold War appeared on programs, other political events—the early civil rights movement, for instance—never did, at least not in any obvious way. This was telling. The CBMCI created a space for the evangelical business class to maintain a sense of respectable white distance. Thus it was more than a committee. Much like the Rotary Club, Kiwanis Club, or a private country club, the CBMCI was a cloister in which white evangelicals could affirm their social, racial, and civic authority. One's identity as a "businessman" and right-thinking and acting "Christian" granted access to this private space for discussing matters of religion, society, and business's relationship to both. With no one of a different race or gender at the table, conversations about work, the state, society, or God could occur in a place where one's racial and gendered authority was a given, where white male privilege was assumed and hardly in need of articulation or defense.

Given its national and international presence, the CBMCI also said much about its members' sense of global authority. The world had a social and racial order, with white Christian businessmen at the top, gifted through their own labors and God's blessings to oversee world affairs in the same top-down fashion they believed conducive to running the very corporations and churches that branded them as "Christian businessmen" in the first place.

The CBMCI also affirmed the idea that an evangelical executive could be fundamentalist in personal religious belief *and* operationally pragmatic. Like Taylor's efforts, the CBMCI made the fundamentalist movement a probusiness movement, lauding the authority of the Bible alongside the authority of businessmen as necessary cocrusaders for conservative evangelicalism. In this way, the CBMCI aligned fundamentalism's future with the business executive, a symbol of authority who assuaged risk, assured the managed salvation of souls before the world's end, and settled worries about life in a corporate economy that had fallen apart. The common metaphors used by CBMCI leaders, stationery, and publications drove such points home. In addition to statements that a born-again businessman was unafraid of pragmatic solutions and hard work,

Figure 1.1 The CBMCI organized local revivals from the 1930s onward. Each promoted "Christian" businessmen as religious activists and authorities. Courtesy of the Billy Graham Center Archives.

CBMCI materials featured pictures of hands shaking one another, signifying unity, security, surety, and discretion. The handshake also signified the contractual theology and vision of work promoted by CBMCI members. Signing up for the CBMCI was like signing on the dotted line for any trustworthy business venture or organization—or for salvation itself. With God as the other party in the deal, "success"—defined as the growth of the CBMCI and the social influence of its revival—was a given. Thus the CBMCI cast fundamentalism—joined to business and corporate executives—as a sure bet. Risk, temporal or eternal, was no more, or at least it was easily managed in a world where "diamonds turned to dust." And it was best managed by the foremost symbol of just and godly order—not Roosevelt, not the New Dealer, not necessarily the liberal or progressive or establishment Protestant but the soul-saved "Christian" businessman, the fundamentalist business executive. Corporate power, in the pragmatic fundamentalist's hands, was more powerful than any principality or policy imaginable.

Investing in "Revival"

A friend and associate of many in the CBMCI, Herbert J. Taylor shared their vision of a world ordered around white, virtuous, practical, contractual, conservative evangelicalism. Though a fundamentalist like many in the CBMCI, Taylor stood by the flattening power of business; that is, businessmen had more in common than they generally realized, and religious controversies were secondary to their common goal as business founders, owners, and managers. But what was that common goal? In short, it was the same as it had been for Taylor when he became a Christian in 1910, and as it had been across the years of division and debate. For a fundamentalist, the common goal was the perpetual revival of the individual soul for the sake of turning America into a Christian nation oriented around an "old time religion" that was, in actuality, a brand new faith.

As historian Joel Carpenter has shown, revivalism in the 1930s and early 1940s was never apolitical or confined to an uncomplicated and easily demarcated "spiritual realm" set apart from public life or politics. Revivalism was cultural politics. "Another Great Awakening in America," notes Carpenter, "would not only vindicate [fundamentalists'] stand for Christian spirituality but do much to reinstate America's lost evangelical character." Moreover, a new revival seemed to promise "its adherents tremendous power for social transformation if they would simply stick to the task of evangelization."[37] But revivalism did more than focus evangelical energies for the sake of reaffirming a lost social or political authority. Fueled by the generosity of big businessmen, revivalism also aligned ordinary believers with the *present* social aspirations of born-again businessmen. Indeed, for all its talk of returning to an imagined past or similarly imagined "fundamentals" of the faith, revival was not about the past but the future. It was about crafting a new faith, a new means of religious belief and experience directed on businessmen's terms.[38]

Revival seemed like a solid investment to Taylor. Club Aluminum's turn-around had been like the revival of the self and soul. The company's future changed due to a mix of prayerful decision-making and uncompromising belief in God's promises. Taylor believed that God spoke audibly to him, telling him how to lead Club Aluminum back from near-bankruptcy and moving him to craft and promote the Four-Way Test. If God gave Taylor the acumen to change the fortunes of struggling corporations, then it stood to reason that he could do the same for fundamentalism itself. Club Aluminum's revival, thought Taylor, was merely a prelude to a greater awakening, one with many possible fronts. And a variety of evangelical clients were more than willing to show what they could do with Taylor's time and money.

In 1939, with war rumbling in Europe, Taylor set up the Christian Workers Foundation (CWF) as a nonprofit, tax-exempt philanthropy intended to make and support "Christian workers," or individuals and groups promoting funda-mentalism in various arenas of American life. Recent changes in the tax code, which took effect in 1936, allowed corporations to deduct charitable donations from reported income. Personal income had enjoyed a similar provision since 1917, especially if it went to religious and charitable organizations (known years later and now as 501(c)(3) organizations). As per a 1934 restriction placed on religious organizations, however, philanthropies like the CWF could not have any "substantial part of the[ir] activities" engage in "propaganda, or otherwise attempting to influence legislation."[39] Taylor took advantage of the provisions provided by federal law while navigating the restrictions. Dozens of evangelical businessmen did the same, endorsing religious activities that—because of their emphasis on "soul change" and "revival" instead of reform or radical reconsidera-tions of corporate power—displayed political overtones and social implications without violating the law.

The CWF became a nonprofit recipient of charitable income, most of it from Taylor. It was also a multifaceted organization. On paper, the CWF claimed a kind of separatist fundamentalism, distancing itself from matters of political or economic import. "The Christian Workers Foundation is purely a foundation operating as a public service," wrote Robert Walker, the CWF's assistant secre-tary. "It has no political, religious or racial axe to grind."[40] But read in the context of Taylor's sense of corporate work and social engagement, the CWF's larger proj-ect had a political, religious, and racial axe to grind. Once fundamentalist faith worked its way into the heart of a new believer, Taylor thought, it immediately changed one's political outlook, reaffirming godly, hard-working individualism and serving as a bulwark against political philosophies proffered by "collectivist"

institutions or antimanagement advocates, such as labor unions or social gospelers. The CWF not only advanced fundamentalism in terms of soul-by-soul
growth but also baptized it as the most "Christian" of faiths, thereby legitimizing
conservative evangelical influence in matters of national import. And the CWF
spread money to organizations that, in the 1930s and 1940s, confirmed assumptions that the gospel was of and by whites, if not always just for them.

The CWF spanned historic divisions in born-again America while also
privileging Taylor's brand of fundamentalism. Through the CWF, Taylor
used Club Aluminum stock to finance the expansion of Intervarsity Christian
Fellowship—a British evangelical organization geared toward college-age
youth—onto American college campuses in the 1930s and early 1940s. More
progressive organizations like the YMCA, Pioneer Girls, and the Christian
Service Brigade also received CWF money. So too did Charles Fuller's "Old
Fashioned Revival Hour," which ran religious programming on 650 stations by
1951. In the late 1940s, Taylor's involvement at Fuller Seminary was likewise
a part of its development as a new center for socially engaged, fundamentalist
evangelicalism. When Harold Ockenga and radio evangelist Charles Fuller were
brainstorming about founding a seminary, they both agreed that Taylor could
be a "fleece," or, in administrative parlance, a source of financial support and a
clear sign that God was on the side of the school's establishment. Taylor obliged,
beginning a trusteeship in 1947 that continued for three decades. Taylor's interests also spread into mass media. Evangelical publishers, such as the fundamentalist Moody Press, received small amounts of support while the CWF owned
stock in the Good News Publishing Company, a publisher of evangelical tracts.
No less committed to evangelism, Taylor sponsored the American Institute of
Holy Land Studies and Child Evangelism, an evangelical organization started
at BIOLA in the mid-1930s. Along with other big businessmen, Taylor and the
CWF also underwrote Young Life, an organization started by Jim Rayburn in
1941 and committed to pulling high school–age youths into the fundamentalist
fold through entertainment, age-appropriate marketing, and recreation-based
youth camps.[41]

Taylor's approach to the CWF was similar to the hands-on managerial philosophy of the Four-Way Test. Expenditures related to the CWF were reviewable
by Taylor and had to accord with his sense of moral and financial cost-benefit
analysis—and the accounting of his assistants. For instance, the relationship
with the Good News Publishing Company came with clear-cut contractual obligations. "As agreed during our conversation the last time you were in Chicago,"
Taylor wrote to the company's president, "starting from the date the new company is organized new records are to be kept of all sales and those should be
accounted for as part of the operating statement to the new company." Such
terms were usually revisable, but they were nevertheless set by someone who

ran even his nonprofit endeavors according to his famed corporate creed and his general assumptions about a businessman's superior logic, expectations, experience, and authority.[42]

Like many predecessors and contemporaries, Taylor thought that business involvement in revivalism needed to focus on younger Americans. Reflecting on the CWF's contributions to youth evangelism, Taylor wrote that "with God's help . . . we intended to help pioneer and finance the nondenominational organizations we felt would do the best job of reaching these young people with the Lord's word." Fully two decades before adolescents and young adults would become the focus of conservative activists (through groups like Young Americans for Freedom), evangelical businessmen identified "young people" as in need of discipline and direction.[43]

Historical context helps to explain why the evangelical fascination with youth was strong in Taylor's day. In a way, it was not new. Religious reformers in the nineteenth century—from the Sunday School movement to the YMCA movement that Taylor joined during World War I—had zeroed in on children and teenagers as targets for evangelism. Evangelicals engaged in similar efforts, from youth-centric revivals to seminaries, although the Great Depression amplified evangelical efforts and redirected them. The economy's collapse harmed evangelical churches' ability to serve congregations and families, thereby sparking calls for "parachurch" activities—or organizations that served alongside churches—to retain membership. Economic crisis also seemed to affect the behavior of youths, many of them unemployed and suspected of criminal activity. Since the late nineteenth century and especially since the 1920s, consumer culture, with its presumably "immoral" effects on youthful consumers, raised evangelical ire and, in the midst of the Great Depression and then World War II, fired passions for youth evangelism. So too did the end of prohibition in 1933, which rejuvenated evangelical fears that the state would do nothing to restrict the appetites of all Americans, but youth especially, for alcohol.

For evangelical businessmen, one of the most promising counterweights to such developments was another Chicago-based outfit: Youth for Christ (YFC). YFC's push for adolescent souls showed the possibility of a socially engaged, business-backed fundamentalism. Taylor served on its board and did financial work for it. Early on, he even set aside space in the basement of his Park Ridge house for YFC meetings. Members of the CBMCI contributed time to YFC as well as money. In turn, YFC promoted businessmen as spiritual partners in evangelical revival, primarily because, like other parachurch ministries, they needed the private investors and welcomed big donors. A massive 1944 "Victory Rally" at Chicago Stadium, organized by Baptist minister Torrey Johnson, featured a number of personalities from born-again America, including musicians and singers, army officers, athletes, and YFC directors and organizers. Businessmen, such as Taylor and Robert F. Nelson, the vice-president of the Arma Corporation of Brooklyn, joined the festivities, as did Philip A. Benson, a past president of the American Bankers' Association "widely known for his testimony as a Christian business man." In all, more than sixty different business personalities were featured on YFC committees in Chicago. Women also joined the ranks of those listed from "the business world," although no women were billed as speakers. Still, YFC advertisements included women, marching arm-in-arm with clean-cut, committed Christian men on a mission of national redemption. Smiling, well-groomed women were frequently featured in YFC advertisements and magazines, at times with pictures of Capitol Hill or the intertwined flags of nation and Christ in the background or printed on inserts. The implication was clear. Good and godly women, well-dressed and in union with Christian men, secured the nation's moral future. Christian domestic bliss and nationalism lined up with YFC's version of revival. Saving souls meant saving teenagers from "juvenile delinquency" and preserving women and men's chastity, all the while prepping them for middle-class, suit-and-tie work and a common defense of God and country. YFC's whiteness was also unmistakable at meetings and in organizational literature. It was a movement by white leaders for white youth. Individual and national salvation remained, largely, the business of white America.[44]

As YFC led its revival across the country, it depended on the financial and social infrastructure that businessmen's organizations like the CBMCI provided. Local CBMCI chapters proved, as Johnson wrote to Taylor in 1946, "wonderfully gracious" as YFC held meetings in Seattle. "The contacts we made will prove of immense value in reaching youth for Christ the world around," Johnson continued. "We are grateful to God for the tremendous help and support given by the Christian Business Men's Committee throughout the country." In Minnesota, the local CBMCI "provided not only the necessary finances, but an active and prayerful interest in the meetings" as well as testimonies. Johnson could make and maintain such contacts because he ran YFC with an eye toward marketing, an emphasis on spiritual returns, and an aversion to risk. In 1945, YFC hired Charles R. White, its first business manager, "to carry out the administrative work as efficiently and as expeditiously as possible." White set up an organizational chart, organized correspondence and ledgers regarding donations, standardized forms, and set up working schedules. "I always have an eye for business," White proclaimed, taking pride in his work and the smallest details, such as "a beautifully designed booklet" for YFC rally directors to keep a record of "your contributors." He also ran a tight budget, systematized mailings, redesigned the YFC emblem, and scouted cities in advance of YFC rallies. By 1946, under White's supervision, YFC was a national organization. Meetings not only occurred in a number of northern cities but in Idaho, Washington, California, Arizona, and Oklahoma. White's mantra was predictability, and he sought to ensure that businessmen who encountered the organization walked away impressed. *The Christian Century* certainly was. Even if it questioned whether YFC was "a genuine revival of religion" or "a racket exploiting another form of juvenile hysteria," the flagship publication of progressive Protestantism sensed that YFC was a step ahead of its liberal rivals, at least in terms of public religion and, perhaps, the next generation's religious loyalties.[45]

After World War II, the evangelistic campaigns that business executives and managers organized and the money they raised and spent for revival would continue to challenge any image or presentation of "Christian" that did not affirm conservative theological or social sentiments. Though progressive Protestants certainly remained at the helm in many American business institutions, in the halls of government, and in respectable elite society, they had nothing on par with YFC or any of the other organizations that were within Taylor's orbit. The postwar revival, however, would proceed with a boundary on the right. Outright racists or radicals might play intermittent roles, but they would not lead it; moderate, pragmatic, alliance-building businessmen like Taylor, the CBMCI, and their patrons would. Soul-by-soul "revival" would remain a main goal, primarily because that seemed to widen the tent of fundamentalism and bring many into it. But individual conversion was only one of many goals, which included the normalization of whiteness, the preservation of male authority, and the proliferation of attendant views about the sinfulness of unions or socialism and the sanctity of work, "free enterprise," or the "Christian home." Out of the theological, social, and economic chaos of the modern era and Great Depression, a more orderly stage was being set, with businessmen underpinning it. All that was needed was someone to stand in the pulpit and thunder away.

Business executives like Taylor found their foremost champion and crusader among their own ranks, with a businessman-turned-revivalist scraping by for YFC. Born in 1918 and "born again" in 1934 at a Mordecai Ham revival in Charlotte, North Carolina, William F. Graham Jr.'s first job after high school was as a door-to-door salesman for the Fuller Brush Company. The next year, Graham attended the fundamentalist Bob Jones College in Tennessee for one semester before taking a job as an associate pastor of the Gospel Tabernacle in Tampa, Florida. In 1941, Graham left for a pastor's job at Wheaton Tabernacle in the western suburbs of Chicago. There, Graham embedded himself in the civic and business world of a nearly all-white community of middle- and high-income churchgoers and evangelicals at nearby Wheaton College, which he started attending soon after landing in Chicago from Florida.

At Wheaton, Graham acquired a certain predilection for premillenialism and worked on his chops as a preacher. In 1943 and 1944, Graham's already busy life got busier. He married Ruth Bell, the daughter of Dr. L. Nelson Bell, a physician and fundamentalist Presbyterian missionary to China. Graham earned a degree in anthropology at Wheaton and directed a popular evangelistic radio program for Torrey Johnson of YFC. He also briefly served as a pastor at a suburban Chicago church and directed the West Suburban Men's Fellowship, which one YFC publication described as "a most unique dinner meeting of business men from all over the western suburbs of Chicago." That same year, Graham became involved with YFC after failing to land a wartime commission as an Army chaplain due to a medical condition. Already building a reputation as a talented preacher known simply as *the* Billy Graham, he was the main speaker at Johnson's 1944 Chicago rally. A hit, he spoke at additional rallies in Minneapolis, Atlanta, Miami, and other cities. "Because of his ability as a 'set-up man,'" noted one YFC article on Graham in 1945, "he has helped in starting Youth for Christ [chapters] in Orlando, Florida; Charlotte, North Carolina; Des Moines; Iowa; Norfolk, Virginia; and Jackson, Mississippi."[46]

Being a "set-up man" meant working with other set-up men, specifically those involved in the local business community in each city. Graham, in this capacity, tapped into the expanding national network of businessmen and business interests behind mid-century conservative evangelicalism. In fact, his own organizations—YFC at first, the Billy Graham Evangelistic Association later—were a microcosm of the developing monied infrastructure behind mid-century evangelical activism, building an ever-widening network of donors to support his efforts. But Graham also utilized this network with great skill and to greater social effect than any other evangelical leader at mid-century, or any other evangelical leader before or since. Backed by big businessmen in cities across the country and armed with managerial skills and strategies derived from modern corporate culture, Graham played a key role in shaping modern conservative Christianity, fashioning himself the spokesperson for all evangelicals or even (in his boldest moments) all "true" Christians worldwide, especially white Christians concerned about the many domestic and foreign issues in play in postwar America. Graham married fundamentalism to corporate business while presenting his gospel as any business executive would—as a sure-fire, consumable good that not only proved one's spiritual status but also one's status as a cosmopolitan American citizen in an age of Cold Wars and hot wars against communism. In turn, businessmen rushed to support Graham. From the late 1940s onward, Graham would use his considerable talents in recruiting and working with business executives and professionals to become the most sought-after and influential evangelist—and evangelical businessman—of the twentieth century.

2

Corporate Convictions

Billy Graham, Big Business, and the New Evangelicalism

Billy Graham's father-in-law, L. Nelson Bell, was "deeply disturbed." The previous night he had been "wide awake before three . . . and unable to go back to sleep." Earlier in the day, he had chatted over the phone with J. Howard Pew, a Pennsylvania oil executive. Though Bell did not write down what they had discussed, Pew was not pleased with Bell's decision-making as an editor at *Christianity Today*, an evangelical periodical that Bell had founded in 1956 with a number of like-minded Protestants, including his son-in-law. For almost a decade, Bell had corresponded with Pew about matters they both found pressing: theological debates at various seminaries, the course of Graham's career, and the funds that Pew provided to *Christianity Today*. Although it is unclear how Bell had displeased Pew, Bell felt compelled to assure Pew that no contribution had gone to waste. The magazine, Bell claimed, had already had "a *tremendous* impact for the conservative cause" and "Protestantism." Bell reiterated his agreement with Pew that "the mission of the Church is spiritual rather than economic, social, or political," although he broke with Pew on a matter of prioritization. In Bell's view, articles should focus on issues related to reteaching the fundamentals of the faith, which would influence a reader's social and political outlook. But articles should avoid specific denominational or ecclesiastical issues. Pew disagreed. While believing "the Church must not become involved in secular, controversial issues," Pew thought *Christianity Today* should prioritize articles that were willing to fire salvos at Protestant ministers, especially those who "are diligently striving to put themselves in a position where they can exercise control over the lives and activities of their members."

Undoubtedly concerned about the cost of a strained relationship with Pew, Bell decided to be as diplomatic as possible. On a small scrap of paper, Bell wrote to Pew, "This letter is to be read with the above in mind." On it, Bell had sketched two stick figures, one as himself, and the other as Pew. The Pew figure, seated with his head turned slightly up, hands on his lap, and posture stiff, overshadowed the

Bell figure, who bowed prostrate, arms outstretched on the floor (see Fig.2.1). As a former missionary in prerevolutionary China, Bell had certainly learned how to kowtow in accordance with Chinese custom. Bell was not only asking for forgiveness. He was demonstrating respect bordering on reverence.[1]

Pew and Bell reconciled, as they had done in the past when differences of opinion arose. Aside from Bell's need to reconcile for both personal and financial reasons, common purpose also usually trumped tactical disagreement. Denominationally, Bell and Pew were conservative members in a divided Presbyterian Church, Bell of the more southern Presbyterian Church in the

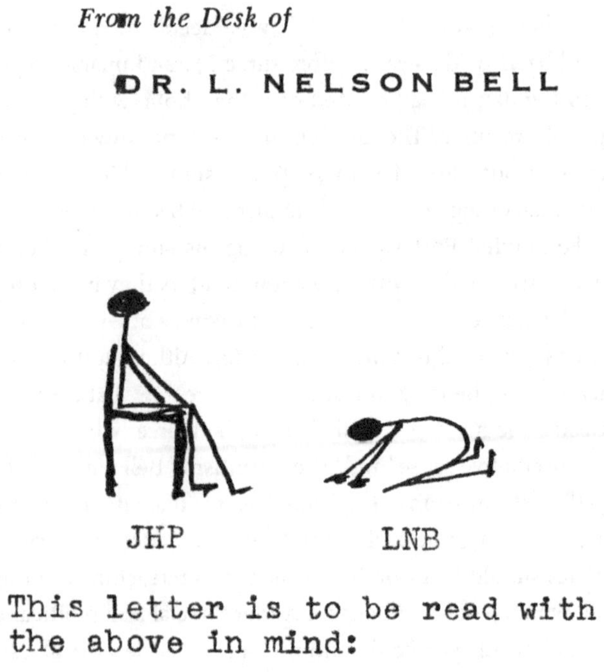

From the Desk of

DR. L. NELSON BELL

JHP   LNB

This letter is to be read with the above in mind:

Figure 2.1 At *Christianity Today*, the relationship between corporate executives like J. Howard Pew (left) and conservative evangelicals like L. Nelson Bell (right) was complex, at times requiring the latter to have a soft touch when writing about financial matters or editorial grievances. Courtesy of Hagley Museum and Library.

United States and Pew of the more northern United Presbyterian Church in the United States of America. Like their mutual friend Billy Graham, a southern Baptist, Bell and Pew held conservative theological views about the Trinity, the authority of Scripture, the divinity of Jesus, and the prioritizing of individual conversion. Both derided the theological ecumenism of the National Council of Churches (NCC), which had emerged from the Federal Council of Churches in 1950. As during the Depression, Bell and Pew were suspicious of the NCC's stance on "social issues," an umbrella term that encapsulated support for civil rights activism, the union movement, the regulatory welfare state, and peaceful coexistence with the Soviet Union. Like Pew, Bell was not a fan of the New Deal either, criticizing it at its inception as a socialistic experiment and hoping in 1940 that Roosevelt would "get the licking he deserves" from his Republican Party challenger, Wendell Willkie. Theology and politics endeared Bell and Pew to each other. Moreover, since *Christianity Today* was committed to presenting a new form of socially engaged, conservative Christianity, it seemed like a good investment to Pew. Thus Pew gave money and advice to Bell and his staff right up until his death in 1971.[2]

The testy but cooperative relationship between Pew and Bell is telling. After World War II, fundamentalists routinely worked alongside interested big businessmen, finding common ground over political and social issues to fund evangelistic missions work and link the "revival" of fundamentalism to a broader Cold War fight for economic freedoms against domestic "collectivism" and foreign communism. Of course, fundamentalists were hardly alone in creating what historian Jonathan P. Herzog has termed a "spiritual-industrial complex." Prompted by business elites and elected officials, millions of Americans in the 1950s and 1960s imagined "religion," and an often vague "Judeo-Christian" brand of "religion," as both spiritual sword for combating the spread of "godless" communism and shield against "collectivist" political ideas. Indeed, fundamentalists were not the religious pariahs or outsiders they often believed themselves to be. The views held by Bell, Pew, and Graham regarding religious faith—as a foundation for anti-communism, or perspectives on race, or a pseudo-consensus around "One Nation Under God" slogans and ideas—were common after World War II. Still, fundamentalists aligned with sympathetic businessmen not merely as a concession to or complement for a general or ecumenical brand of Christian nationalism. Alignment was a strategic endeavor to open up more fundamentalist fronts. The goal was to spread their *specific* convictions regarding the nation's future in a Cold War world.

Businessmen backed the religious projects of fundamentalists for various reasons. In *Christianity Today*'s case, the denominational bond between Bell and Pew, as well as their shared interests in legitimizing conservative theological and social ideas, led to their partnership. Bell's interests diverged from Pew's in that

Bell was a part of a larger fundamentalist project, a reframing of the respectable and socially engaged prewar fundamentalism for maximum social impact in an era of rising state power, Cold War concerns, and the nuclear bomb. Billy Graham was at the heart of this larger project, as were a number of other fundamentalists (and quite a few nonfundamentalists) gathered under the banner of a "new evangelicalism." Big-business interests were crucial to the proliferation of institutions—from schools to youth groups to publications like *Christianity Today* —that began to claim that the new evangelicalism was the only legitimate form of Christianity for the postwar era. Tying the movement together were views about the relationship between faith and social change, a network of institutions, interested businessmen like Pew, Herbert Taylor, and R. G. LeTourneau—and millions and millions of dollars in tax-exempt donations.

Promoting a New Evangelicalism

In the late 1930s, a number of fundamentalist leaders gathered around Harold J. Ockenga, pastor of Boston's Park Street Church, and J. Elwin Wright, a former real estate agent and director of a New England association of fundamentalists. Formed in 1942, their National Association of Evangelicals for United Action (shortened to National Association of Evangelicals [NAE] the following year) hoped to represent "a great unvoiced multitude of Christian people." Premillenialism was generally accepted or endorsed by the NAE's earliest members, while certain non-negotiables included a strict view of biblical revelation, divine authorship, and an emphasis on missions. The NAE was also a lobbying group, mounting opposition to the Federal Council's theological stances, social vision, and political support for the New Deal. Helped by prominent radio preachers like Charles E. Fuller and Walter Maier, both of whom had been in a protracted fight with liberal Protestants and the Federal Communications Commission over radio licensing, the NAE claimed to solicit supporters "regardless of race or nationality," even though it only recruited whites and at first only allowed men to become full-fledged members. Though avowedly apolitical, the NAE used conservative theology to build political influence while eschewing radicalism. The point was to unify fundamentalists while rebranding their efforts as respectable and modern, not reactionary or antimodern. Ockenga termed the NAE's project the "new evangelicalism."[3]

In the 1940s and 1950s, Ockenga was one of a number of figures who started calling on fundamentalists to create a more relevant faith for the postwar era, what he called a "progressive fundamentalism with an ethical message." Fundamentalists were on the defensive against the forces of secularization, and they needed to take action if they wanted to remain relevant. As he preached in 1957, Ockenga was

convinced that "fundamentalism is an honorable word" and "right as far as doctrine is concerned." "If it were confined to that," Ockenga declared, "I would like to
be called a fundamentalist." But regarding "its social approach and social philosophy," fundamentalism was "wrong." In 1947, he had expressed similar views, writing, "In an hour of crying social problems in the realms of war, race, class, liquor,
imperialism, crime, delinquency, etc., fundamentalism stands isolated and aloof,
while all other religious groups are rolling up their sleeves to tackle the threat to
their very existence." A new evangelicalism would tackle such problems head on.[4]

Ockenga was certain his approach was relevant and needed. "The new evangelicalism declares that it is going to face . . . societal questions," which included
not only secularization but the political favor toward New Deal and theological
liberalism, the rise of global communism, "the racial tensions . . . highlighted
by the problem of integration," and much more. New evangelicals offered an
alternative to the social gospel, which "by itself will lead to the welfare state,
to creeping socialism, and ultimately to Communism." But they also offered an
alternative to "the personal gospel," which "leaves out the social consciousness
and may lead individuals to look for pie in the sky and forget all about their relationship to their fellow men." In the end, Ockenga believed, "the new evangelicalism . . . will present Biblical Christianity in such a way that it is going to bear
a powerful influence upon our society."[5]

New evangelicals were also distinguished by *method*. They had an "up-to-
date strategy" based "upon the principle of infiltration." In denominations, in
media outlets, among younger Americans, and in the political structure, new
evangelicals needed "a plan of action" like "Communists in their battles in Korea,
Indochina, and Tibet" and "the liberals, or modernists, [have] been using for
years." Funding was key. Businessmen, therefore, were crucial partners. "We
must take an inventory of our investment of money," Ockenga concluded in
1960. "We should ask, is this institution or movement contributing to the ends
which I seek?" Leadership was no less crucial, and leaders could and should be
drawn from the business world. "Is it folly for businessmen and foundations to
support institutions, movements, and individuals which subvert that for which
the businessmen and foundations stand[?]" "Every evangelical," businessmen
included, "should find his place in the implementation of the modern evangelical resurgence in Christianity."[6]

In reality, Ockenga's "new evangelicalism" was not new to businessmen.
Ockenga might have coined and popularized the term, but businessmen were
pioneers in *acting* like new evangelicals, viewing American society as in need of
"infiltration" and redemption through their God-given authority and resources.
Theologians and revivalists aiming to advance a new evangelicalism in American
life had a willing and ready constituency in Herbert Taylor, R. G. LeTourneau,
and other businessmen who were "worldly" and "respectable" before evangelical

thinkers like Ockenga trumpeted fundamentalist "worldliness" and "respect-ability." Little wonder, then, that leaders among the new evangelical movement looked regularly to conservative, evangelical businessmen and vice-versa.

In time, other worldly and respectable men of business, fundamentalist or not, would also come behind the new evangelicalism. As businessmen had helped fundamentalists differentiate themselves from other Protestants a gen-eration before, they would play a key role in helping new evangelicals differenti-ate themselves. They would do so by donating money to the new evangelical project. In turn, evangelicals, not inclined to bite the hands that fed them, took stances on race, gender, business, state, and society not far removed from those of their benefactors.

Taking up the banner of a new and improved fundamentalism, the NAE set its sights set on quiet infiltration of every level of American society, including the corporate and political establishment. As Ockenga, the NAE's first president, told those assembled at its first meeting, "It is up to us to make sure that the Christian church will return to a new leadership, producing new statesmen for our gov-ernment circles, influencing education, and rebuilding the foundations of soci-ety." With that in mind, the NAE affirmed what its leaders thought were social and economic values that all white evangelicals could or should share. The NAE endorsed "competitive free enterprise and private ownership" and opposed "all forms of communism, regardless of the name it masquerades under" (meaning the New Deal). The NAE published free enterprise tracts, including "Scriptural Proof for the Free Enterprise System," which provided chapter and verse "proof texts" showing that capitalism was a divinely inspired economic arrangement. Jabbing both liberal theologians and the New Deal, the NAE claimed that "good things come out of a man's heart only when cleansed (regenerated) by the sav-ing faith in Christ and not out of a good council, a good planning board, nor a good tax." The NAE endorsed balanced budgets and opposed national health insurance, civil rights laws, and federal aid to education. On the other hand, the NAE saw a positive role for the state in terms of restricting liquor advertising, promoting heteronormative sexuality, and preserving white men's authority and privilege. The NAE also endorsed control over public school textbooks and regulation of television. At the same time, its subsidiary, the National Religious Broadcasters Association, sought to free up airtime for evangelists who had been deemed public nuisances and blocked from wider broadcast by the Federal Communications Commission.[7]

The NAE garnered a willing and wide-ranging constituency of business back-ers. For instance, Herbert J. Taylor served as treasurer for a brief period, and the NAE's administrative boards and subcommittees were loaded with big business-men. Most were friends or associates of Taylor, Billy Graham, or J. Elwin Wright. On the NAE's administrative side, John Bolten, a plastics manufacturer from

Massachusetts, worked alongside timber magnate C. Davis Weyerhaeuser and J. Willison Smith Jr., a Wharton School of Business graduate and lawyer who had served as the vice-president of Bible Magazine, Inc. A special oversight committee for the NAE's administrative decisions, the Business and Professional Men's Committee, consisted of business leaders and managers from Taylor's Chicago circle as well as businessmen who served on the boards of Young Life and Intervarsity Christian Fellowship. Arnold Grunigen of the Christian Business Men's Committee, International (CBMCI) also joined. Florida real estate executive Kenneth Keyes, worked on the Finance Committee, a role that included fundraising. Businessmen at the NAE also coordinated pointed outreach campaigns. Under the direction of A. H. Armerding, an industrial engineer with an anti-union bent, the NAE trained chaplains to work in military-related industries during the war and a wide variety of industries and corporations after it. The NAE also retained a liaison with the National Association of Manufacturers. Still, there were limits to the types of businessmen who partnered with the NAE. R. G. LeTourneau and other leaders in the CBMCI did not join the NAE, partly because they were busy and partly to retain institutional territory, with the CBMCI focusing on organizing businessmen for evangelism and the NAE on advocacy. Regional divisions also remained strong. Many pastors and leaders in the Southern Baptist Convention did not sign on with the NAE, fearing a loss of self-sufficiency to a national and mostly northern body.[8]

If many in the Southern Baptist Convention stayed outside the NAE's orbit, there was one southern-born Baptist who certainly did not. After successful crusades in Grand Rapids, Michigan, and Charlotte, North Carolina (the latter organized by Vernon Patterson, a Presbyterian and segregationist local businessman and later board member at the NAE and director of the CBMCI), Billy Graham turned his gaze westward to the land of Lyman Stewart. Los Angeles seemed a logical next step for Graham's burgeoning career. During the Great Depression, the city was filling up with southern- and Midwest-born migrants, many subscribing to a "plain-folk" Protestantism and up-from-the-bootstraps entrepreneurialism. A small group of Los Angeles businessmen, led by Clifford Smith, the president of Hollywood Togs, Inc., a California-based sportswear manufacturing company, laid the groundwork for Graham's first crusade in the City of Angels. Smith and his associates had collaborated with local fundamentalist pastors for years, sponsoring annual tent revivals through a "Christ for Greater Los Angeles" committee. Smith pushed for a massive revival to be held in 1949 and attempted to garner support from the city's 1,000 Protestant congregations. Fewer than 200 Protestant churches lent Smith their support, but a number of "country preachers" from Oklahoma, Texas, and Arkansas drummed up support for Graham. For instance, Fighting Bob Shuler used his popular radio show to broadcast news about the revival on KGER, a Long Beach station owned by John Brown, an Arkansas businessman and founder of an evangelical college in the Ozarks. A local Youth for Christ (YFC) group provided organizational support and made arrangements for Graham's visit to Los Angeles. From late September to late November, Smith's committee of business leaders worked along with local church leaders, YFC officials, Christian celebrities, Graham's revival team, and other local evangelistic organizations to provide facilities, publicity, and financial support for the event. By revival's end, attendance had reached an estimated 350,000.[9]

A biographer later calculated that only 2,703 had made "decisions for Christ" and 1,475 already-converted attendees had made "reconstitutions" of their faith, hardly a bonanza of soul-winning and a fact that dogged Graham's crusades throughout his career. Far fewer people converted at his events than Graham or his business backers were usually willing to admit. Indeed, figuring out the exact number of conversions at any Graham crusade often depended, as Grant Wacker has recently concluded, "on who was doing the counting." Multiple sources suggested that a conversion at a Graham crusade did stick for some years afterwards, and the rededications to the faith certainly testified to Graham's power as a preacher.[10] Moreover, the publicity brought by Graham's crusades was indisputable. They put Graham on the religious map, brought huge amounts of media attention to the new evangelical movement, and gave the impression that Graham's "crusades" were the hot new Christian "norm." Also, as public events in an era when large-scale gatherings were restricted to politics or sports, a crusade gave an economic bump to local economies. Historians have long recognized that Graham's crusades were good for public relations, offering local Chambers of Commerce a way to cast their cities as cosmopolitan and Christian at once. But the effect of a Graham crusade was also more concrete. With hundreds and thousands of people in attendance, often for weeks at a time, they were good for the mayor's office, local businesses' bottom lines, and the tax base.

Though Smith and other businessmen were crucial to the initial shape of the Los Angeles revival, it was the involvement of the nation's most powerful and reclusive newspaper tycoon, William Randolph Hearst, that helped to make Graham's efforts in the City of Angels a turning point in twentieth-century religious history. Hearst's role entered the realm of legend, when he supposedly decided—abruptly and unexpectedly—to support the Los Angeles revival, instructing his editors to "Puff Graham." In reality, Hearst's support for Graham's career had a backstory. Hearst was not a religious man, but he had shown interest in YFC for years, most likely because of its work among juveniles, its patriotic sensibilities, and its seeming antagonism to a New Deal state that Hearst had come to deplore. That YFC rallies had already attracted nearly a million people also complemented Hearst's most important goal: to sell newspapers. In 1946, Hearst instructed editors at his newspapers to "Puff YFC" or, alternatively, "Puff Graham." (The directive is different according to different historical accounts.) Regardless of his exact wording, Hearst's papers published full-page stories on the organization's rallies in the nation's largest cities. Later, when Graham set his sights on Los Angeles, Hearst provided support through banner headlines in his *Los Angeles Examiner* and *Herald*, as well as in twelve other newspapers. Publicity also came through YFC leader Roy McKeown and R. A. Carrington, the *Examiner's* publisher, who had gained permission from Hearst to cover and publicize the revival's events. Within a few days, the Associated Press, the United Press, and the International News Service followed with stories of their own. Shortly thereafter, national news magazines *Time*, *Newsweek*, and *Life* published features on Graham's revivals. Oddly, Graham did not meet Hearst in person. Well after the conclusion of the Los Angeles revival, Graham was unsure why Hearst had become his most famous booster to that point. "I suppose I could have met him," he told an interviewer in 1987, "but I never thought he would see a person like me at that time." Nevertheless, Hearst's "puffing" of Graham catapulted the revivalist onto the national stage and provided a huge amount of free publicity for the new evangelicalism.[11]

Hearst's support for Graham was neither uncommon nor inexplicable. Graham enjoyed a reciprocal relationship with Hearst and other business leaders, one that seemed to advance the interests of all parties. As William McLoughlin, an early biographer of Graham, noted in 1960: "Billy Graham is equally committed to the belief that Christianity and capitalism, like conversion and success, are inseparably linked and that one cannot exist without the other. When Graham speaks of 'the American way of life' he has in mind the same combination of political and economic freedom that the National Association of Manufacturers, the United States Chamber of Commerce, and the *Wall Street Journal* do when they use the phrase." Hence, like-minded businessmen flocked to Graham's side, sometimes with particular fervor. For instance, Herbert J. Taylor offered in 1962 to hold a revival in Chicago. Graham, who had been recently criticized by both liberals and separatist fundamentalist pastors in the city, demurred, calling himself a "prophet without honor." Taylor worked feverishly to convince Graham otherwise, recruiting 300 "laymen" to pester their pastors to invite Graham. Impressed by a breakfast meeting with 700 local ministers organized by Taylor, Graham obliged, later nicknaming the crusade at McCormick Place and concluding rally at Soldier Field (which drew a record attendance of 116,000) "Herb Taylor's Crusade."[12]

Taylor was fully committed to Graham's success as a preacher. But Graham's gospel appealed to big businessmen for more specific reasons. Though a self-professed Democrat—a political affiliation he would maintain throughout his career—Graham was not quite a liberal or New Dealer. From the late 1940s to the early 1960s, Graham tended to criticize labor unions and strikers, arguing that both undercut productivity and upset the nation's social order. For Graham, workers should be thankful for the opportunity to live in "the land of free enterprise, business, and industry." Unions, by contrast, were "seeking to take advantage of industry and exploit them, just as they were once exploited." Instead of joining a union, "Be a faithful and efficient worker, even if it is screwing a nut on one bolt after another. . . . Let [others] see how a Christian should live." Graham was also on the side of freeing corporate America from regulation. Graham regularly cast free enterprise as an almost magical, inexplicable system of wealth creation. Hence, he argued against "government restrictions," which destroyed "the God-given 'freedom of opportunity'" that the business-built "American way of life" afforded in the 1950s. At times, Graham conflated unionism, socialism, atheism, and communism. More often, Graham championed entrepreneurialism and wealth accumulation, undergirded by both stridently literal and wildly figurative interpretations of the very Bible that he raised from the pulpit as the rock-solid word of God. As he noted in an essay he wrote in 1954 for the US Chamber of Commerce's publication, *Nation's Business*, "We have the suggestion from the Scripture itself that faith and business, properly blended, can be a happy, wholesome and even profitable mixture." Challenging what he perceived as common business practice at mid-century, Graham argued that, "Too long have many helped the idea that religion should be detached from life, something aloof and apart. . . . Thousands of businessmen have discovered the satisfaction of having God as a working partner. It puts integrity into their organizations, sincerity into their sales, and spiritual and monetary profits into their hearts and pockets." He listed the Gideons as "a worthy organization of Christian businessmen" in the evangelistic arena alongside "J. C. Penney, Stanley Kresge, R. G. LeTourneau, and scores of others equally great [men in American business and industry]" who "corroborated the fact that religion and business can be mixed for the spiritual and material profit of all concerned." Graham's views were, not surprisingly, shared by many of his friends and supporters in big business. J. Howard Pew kept his staff busy each day typing letters to friends, associates, and pastors saying the same. Herbert J. Taylor had made such views central to his business philosophy. R. G. LeTourneau, W. Maxey Jarman, and other businessmen in evangelical circles could not imagine the word "businessman" without the qualifier "Christian" in front of it. Neither were Graham's views coincidental. "More than anything else," McLoughlin believed, "his close association with some of the conservative Christian businessmen who supported his campaigns . . . crystallized his views on politics and economics."[13]

Many of Graham's opinions would change in the 1960s. Faced with events he could not easily ignore—rising poverty rates, urban riots, intractable forms of urban and rural poverty—Graham warmed to notions of evangelical social action and state relief. Graham also reconsidered his views on civil rights, foreign policy, and youth delinquency. But regarding the businessman's God-blessed authority, Graham budged little. And, regarding corporate capitalism's excesses and the corrupting power of cronyism in politics, Graham thought, "for the best blueprint of government or business ethics, go to your New Testament." As he wrote for *Nation's Business* in 1969, "Call it what you will, a divine policy paper, a memo from the Big Boss, a heaven-sent management manual, every citizen can use it."[14]

Billy Graham as Big Businessman

Graham's business-friendly faith became full-fledged corporate spectacle in 1964, when the World's Fair returned to New York City. The fair had been there before, in 1939, as Americans were still reeling from the Great Depression and anxious about war in Europe. Various corporations, from IBM to Ford, had exhibited their products for visitors to view then and, twenty-five years later, it was little different. Still, the vastly different economic circumstances in 1964 granted the fair a different aura. Corporate triumphalism abounded. RCA, General Electric, IBM, DuPont, Bell Systems, Eastman Kodak—all had exhibits for patrons to peruse, each touting a particular corporation's contributions to their daily lives and the nation's status as a global economic superpower. The fair also applauded the nation's religious pluralism. The Church of Jesus Christ of Latter-Day Saints (the Mormons) had an exhibit. The American Israel Corporation featured a replica of Solomon's Temple and highlighted Jews' roles in business life and public life. Progressive, nonevangelical Protestants sponsored a "Protestant Center," while an even more pluralistic "Hall of Free Enterprise," set up by the libertarian American Economic Foundation and funded by Pew, pulled from various ancient and modern religions to present free enterprise as a God-blessed system of production and consumption "for the greatest good."[15]

Graham and other evangelicals were among the fair's offerings. Each evangelical pavilion presented the faith as congruous with certain aspects of Cold War culture and American corporate culture, namely scientific discovery, perpetual "progress," and technology. Wycliffe Bible Translators promoted their educational work among the "2,000 tribes" that remained unable to read the Bible. Moody Bible Institute sponsored Sermons from Science, which told about the "links" between traditional faith and testable science (while avoiding any open endorsement of evolution). Graham's pavilion exuded scientific-religious coziness as well. The pavilion accommodated several hundred people and showed a daily film, *Man in the 5th Dimension*, which featured Graham trumpeting the wonders of science in the space age—right alongside the fundamentals of his faith and an altar call—in a style that accorded to the technocratic, optimistic,

business-like presentations at the fair's corporate exhibits. The pavilion advertised Graham as a global religious celebrity and spokesperson for a new evangelicalism, all while bringing his brand of personally affective, modern, worldly,
conservative Christianity to the World's Fair. Thousands visited the pavilion and
saw his film.[16]

The fair was a sign of Graham's arrival at the corporate table, not only as the
religious equivalent of IBM or Bell Systems but as the man who best used business's methods toward religious ends. Graham's pavilion also demonstrated
his place in American popular culture by 1964. His career was, arguably, at its
height, enabled by over a decade of preaching, planning, and working with
big businessmen in a strategic, open-minded, Rotarian fashion. Like Herbert
J. Taylor, Graham developed alliances with evangelical and nonevangelical business leaders. At the same time, Graham tied his religious, political, and economic sentiments together and used fervent language to give his message and
ministry a sense of prophetic immediacy. For instance, in front of a joint meeting
of Rotarians and Kiwanis Club members in 1951, Graham ticked off a laundry
list of national and international threats. All were connected to his reading of
history. "Out of a prayer meeting came the Constitution of the United States,"
Graham told his audience, "Our country was founded by men who believed in
God. Our roots are deep in the Bible and the history of Christianity." Something
went awry "at the turn of the [twentieth] century," Graham believed, likely nod-
ding toward the fundamentalist-modernist controversies of the 1910s–1930s.
"America said we can get along without God and entered into an age of materialism and self-expression. . . . Home, the basic unity, the barometer of society,
began to crumble and crack at the seams. Crime became rampant. It became
good business to lie and cheat." Now, at mid-century, America was "faced with
an enemy more gigantic than dreamed of, a fanatical religion that has declared
war against everything we stand for." Graham finished off with a flourish. "Since
Yalta," he proclaimed, "we have been outmaneuvered by the great unseen enemy
that the Bible speaks of." This enemy was communism. Thus, "If ever there a
holy war was fought," he said, "This is it." The only proper response was for individuals to become "born again." Additionally, "We have got to come back to the
moral principles upon which this country was founded—or we are done for." To
the businessmen gathered around him, Graham urged, "Strike your match until
we have a mighty flame in this country."[17]

He said much the same thing at his crusades. Attuned to the public and political concerns of a nation living in the shadow of the Soviet bomb and in the
midst of McCarthy-era suspicions, Graham injected his views about communism into public services. "Scarcely one of his Sunday afternoon sermons over
a nine-year period has failed to touch on communism[,]" noted McLoughlin in
1960, "and in his regular revival sermons he constantly refers to it to illustrate

his doctrinal points."[18] In a charged crusade atmosphere, Graham's treatment of the subject could be alarmist. To be sure, on that measure, Graham was not necessarily out of step with the political environment of the 1950s, where politicians in both parties often vied to proclaim new communist threats in need of containment or elimination. But Graham's warnings came more from his willingness to—as he put it—"preach Hellfire, when I have to. When the house is on fire, you don't try to use sweet reason to move people out. You scare the daylights out of them—anything to get them moving." Fear-mongering fit with Graham's own fears about world affairs and global politics. Under the tent in Los Angeles in 1949, Graham cast communism as a false faith. "Communism," Graham boomed, "is not only an economic interpretation of life—Communism is a religion that is inspired, directed, and motivated by the Devil himself who has declared war against Almighty God." Throughout the 1950s, Graham called Americans in general, and the American business community in particular, to promote "true" and "authentic" religion—and not a vague Judeo-Christianity—as a powerful weapon against secularization at home and communism abroad. In a 1954 interview with the right-wing magazine *The American Mercury*, Graham said the postwar era would be defined by "a battle to the death" between communism and Christ, with the nation in need of defense by a citizenry devoted to "old-fashioned Americanism, . . . conservative and Evangelical Christianity, . . . prayer, . . . genuine spiritual revival, . . . [and] personal Christian experience." Ordinary Americans, through dramatic and immediate conversion, would become extraordinary Christian citizens and secure the nation's future.[19]

Graham's preaching against communism had implications for the homefront as well. To speak of a "Christian America" was to use a loaded concept, one where the word "Christian" implied and privileged white authority. Speaking against "communism" overlapped with the racial fears of many whites, especially in a nation where "communism" was a handy rhetorical weapon for attacking any form of black activism. Graham did not openly espouse segregationism or anti-Semitism as Vance Muse, Gerald L. K. Smith, and others did. But, until he personally removed the ropes separating black and white visitors at a crusade in Chattanooga, Tennessee, in 1953, Graham respected state laws and Jim Crow customs by preaching in front of segregated audiences. Even after the breakthrough in Chattanooga, as Steven P. Miller noted, Graham was generally unwilling "to discuss the race issue beyond the levels of individual decency and Christian neighborliness." To be sure, Graham was more of a racial progressive than other conservative evangelicals and many of his backers in business, whether a moderate like Herbert J. Taylor or a segregationist—at least in the 1950s—like Vernon Patterson or his father-in-law, L. Nelson Bell. Still, the businessmen who supported Graham's local crusades in the 1950s were nearly all white and lived comfortable, racially secluded lives. Most lived and worked in worlds of white privilege. Even if they held a gradualist view of desegregation or agreed that desegregation might be good for business, they were, like the businessmen behind YFC or the Billy Graham Evangelistic Association (BGEA), passive toward racism and segregation because their station made it easy to be so.[20]

Graham was more consistent on matters of sex and gender. Long after desegregating his revivals, Graham continued to deride deviations from a conservative code of sexual behavior. He thought America's younger generation was overly "obsessed with sex." Fueled by popular music and magazines and disposable income, "You young people who spend your time occupied with sex," he told a packed audience in Madison Square Garden in 1957. "[You] will say a few years later you wished you had taken a different road." Premarital or extramarital sex was bad enough, but female sexuality and autonomy seemed particularly dangerous. In the 1950s, Graham affirmed sexual hierarchies and domestic expectations for women. For instance, preaching at one revival in 1953 on "Women's Responsibility in the Home," Graham admonished "the mothers, wives and sweethearts never to forget God's law that the husband is the head of the home." "And be attractive," he suggested, "Every man wants a pretty wife.... I don't blame some men for not wanting to come home to unkempt and untidy wives." Seeing men as the "boss" in the home, as in the workplace, Graham viewed his spiritual revolution against secularism and communism as requiring the domestication of white women and masculine security of white men. Long before anyone had heard the term "culture wars," Graham and other businessmen posited arguments about the essential or "biblical" rightness of male authority.[21]

It was not enough that Graham's message appealed to American business leaders; he cultivated this appeal by taking on the auspices of a Christian businessman on par with a Herbert Taylor, R. G. LeTourneau, or any number of other businessmen who might have joined the CBMCI or supported his early career. According to *Commentary* writer Herbert Weiner in 1957, Graham reveled in "a peculiarly American brand of evangelism." It was conservative, to be sure. It had hints of premillenialist or strident fundamentalism. But aside from when it tacitly endorsed racial hierarchies or chastised sexual "deviants," it seemed to "[seek] the friendship of all political parties, supports all churches, bids for the good will of intellectuals and refuses to have anything to do with bigotry." A British member of one crusade team described Graham as "evangelism become respectable." Graham cultivated this aura of respectability through his style of dress, grooming, and personal, professional, and political fixations. Graham's boardroom garb left behind the cultural trappings of sawdust trail revivalists and challenged the bumpkin stereotype. As a writer for *Time* noted shortly after the Los Angeles revival, "Graham and his enthusiasm looked disturbingly like something out of Hollywood. His sharply-cut, double-breasted suits and high-decibel ties . . . were a smooth contrast to the rumpled homespun approach of the old school." "Billy Graham is God's top salesman," wrote another reporter in the early 1950s, "He looks like a salesman. Tall—six feet two inches. Handsome. Burning eyes. The sure gesture. The right phrase. The firm handclasp. Wherever Billy goes the celestial balance sheet shows a substantial profit." Graham supplemented his appearance with careful branding, both of himself and of his faith. "Billy Graham" was not just a person. "Billy Graham" was a brand, a persona, an experience, and a product line of books and merchandise all rolled into one. Graham also updated ways of speaking about the Christian faith, repeating slogans during various crusades. Consider "inviting Jesus into your heart," he might preach. Or, try a "personal relationship" with Jesus that was, like one's personal relationship to family or corporate brands: close, life-long, and satisfying. Critics often cast Graham as a crass huckster, but he was undeterred. "I am selling the greatest product in the world," he famously told *Time* magazine in 1954, "why shouldn't it be promoted as well as soap?"[22]

Graham was not the first to add business acumen and corporate cool to the world of evangelical revivalism. D. L. Moody, Billy Sunday, and Aimee Semple McPherson had done so before him. But Graham's efforts were not mere imitation. He was a part of a broader movement, funded and fomented by businessmen, to redefine fundamentalism and advance a new type of evangelicalism. As a result, Graham worked hard to align himself with the racial, sexual, economic, and political concerns of the businessmen and corporate professionals who attended his revivals, served on his ministerial boards, and provided the financial network that supported his crusades. Looking, sounding, and working like a businessman made a fundamentalist like Graham into the business world's Christian.

Given his celebrity status, it was almost expected that Graham would attract the interest of politicians. The symbiotic relationship between evangelicalism, business, and state—never quite as antagonistic as evangelical anti-New Dealers made it out to be in the 1930s—continued into the postwar era. Graham was a respectable religious businessman and a popular figure in an American political context where "One Nation Under God" became a popular mantra, corporate executives underwrote public religious rituals and displays, and presidents like Dwight D. Eisenhower made public pronouncements nearly requiring Americans to pledge allegiance to any god (but preferably a "Judeo-Christian" deity). Eisenhower and other presidents had a great deal to gain from having an evangelical like Graham within their inner circle—or at least on their calendar. Obviously, Graham also gained additional legitimacy for his religious project by having access (however passing or ceremonial) to the halls of power in Washington, D.C. Graham's courting of politicians and presidents was controversial in certain quarters, certainly among white conservatives in the Southern

Baptist Convention and other southern denominations embroiled in a civil rights fight. The doctrine of the "spirituality of the church"—the idea that churches should focus on winning souls, not on social or political issues—was a fitting theological counterpart to the doctrine of "states' rights." Keeping church far from state was a key to racial defense and upholding the shaky theological foundation of segregationism. Such a posture was an exercise in futility and fantasy. Not only had church and state never quite parted ways in America, in the postwar period they were inseparable. After 1953, as a result of the business-backed lobbying of Seattle businessmen-turned-pastor Abraham Vereide, the National Prayer Breakfast became an annual tradition. In 1954, a near-unanimous vote in Congress and quick flash of the pen by Eisenhower added "Under God" to the Pledge of Allegiance. Cold War chaplains in the military had an evangelical edge, speaking about Christian nationalism and "godless" communism in the same breath. Religious missions operated under the auspices of foreign policies like the Marshall Plan and Point Four Program, showing the warmth of officials in the Cold War state toward religion. The "American Way of Life" included a "tri-faith" ideal of Protestant, Catholic, and Jewish collaboration (even if such "goodwill" terms did not necessarily play out in communities nationwide.) In this context, Graham had a place at the White House's table, no matter the protestations about a deleterious blending of church and state from the right or the left.

Graham's skill and identity as a Christian businessman, however, also helped him secure that place at the table. If the president and members of Congress regularly met with the heads of the nation's blue chip companies, then it stood to reason that they would hold court with the nation's foremost Christian businessman. Graham developed friendships with presidents from Truman onward and with many other political insiders as well. They welcomed him as a symbol of the Cold War collaboration between God, country, and commerce. For presidents, Graham was not only another preacher in favor of the spiritual-industrial complex. He was the nation's spiritual chief executive.

The Business of the BGEA

Billy Graham was more than a business-friendly preacher or friend to businessmen and presidents alike. He was an effective fundraiser and businessman himself, albeit of the nonprofit variety. In 1950, Graham faced a problem created (unintentionally) by donors zealous to support his ministry. Accounts vary, but one version tells of thousands of dollars in donations stuffed in a shoebox and given to Graham during a crusade in Portland, Oregon. Not sure what to do, Graham consulted with George Wilson, a friend and revival associate, and they set up the BGEA as a clearinghouse for future donations.

And the donations rolled in. By the time of Graham's 1957 New York City crusade, his largest and costliest to date, the BGEA required the oversight of auditors like Price Waterhouse and Company to keep track of receipts and expenditures. Auditors also added to the Graham brand. Graham was the anti–Elmer Gantry: transparent and trustworthy, especially when it came to managing money given in good faith to what one journalist called "God's Super Sales Man."[23]

By 1960, the BGEA was one of the most well-organized and efficiently run nonprofit corporations in the country. Millions of tax-deductible or tax-exempt dollars went through BGEA's offices. The vast majority of donations were a few dollars given in good faith by Graham's fans and followers. Donations from Graham's benefactors were less common, although in 1956 J. Howard Pew offered a one-time grant of $25,000. Like previous evangelical organizations and revivalists since at least D. L. Moody, the BGEA standardized and specialized the evangelical pitch, all for the sake of mitigating risk. As one of countless procedural handbooks published for BGEA workers and counselors put it, the goal was to "Secure Clean-Cut Decisions." For as much as Graham and his associates spoke of the spirit moving inexplicably through their revivals, every moment at a Graham revival was theorized, planned, tested, organized, assigned, and managed. Workers in the aisles were to "seek those your own sex and age." To communicate with the counselors who would receive potential converts, workers had a six-point hand signaling system to denote the age and sex of the attendee and the needed counselor. Every gesture mattered, from the use and placement of their hands to the decision to kneel with praying attendees to when they raised their head after a prayer. "Watch offensive items: talking too close to face, breath, B.O., etc." suggested one set of instructions. "Be courteous. Do not argue.... Invite the one with whom you are dealing to read the Scripture for himself," suggested another protocol, "Do not be in a hurry. Have prayer with the person before he leaves."

Counselors who spoke with potential converts or with the spiritually moved received the most extensive point-by-point instructions. Aside from other general instructions about courtesy, pacing, and appearance, the all-important decision card was a priority for counselors. "Fill out [the] decision card carefully, getting as complete information as possible," instructed one crusade's handbook along with directions about legible handwriting and taking the new convert on to the next stage in the decision-making process before cycling back to an assigned seat, ready to receive the next person and the next and the next. Graham's organization updated the rules and protocols every so often, but the goals remained the same. Micromanage the event to reduce the chances that someone who might have been converted would walk out the door unconverted. "One soul," noted a set of instructions, "[is] worth infinite price." A conversion was "Life's greatest decision." Hence, workers were to "Follow instructions, for *one* [under-trained counselor] can muff the whole deal." But the goal was also more pedestrian: secure the data. A patron's decision was a data point, a statistic entered into an extensive, typewritten database for record-keeping and analysis by the BGEA for the next revival in another city, or for "follow-up" with local churches and religious organizations. A conversion event was a successfully orchestrated sale, ready to be crunched as a number into a chart, graph, and year-end review, stored in a binder or in a drawer at the BGEA, ready evidence that God's super salesman—and the organization named after him—was good at the job.[24]

As a complex, multilevel, and annually expanding organization with many moving parts, the BGEA, Graham believed, needed the oversight of natural managers. As such, business executives regularly sat on the BGEA's board along with prominent evangelical leaders and preachers. Of Graham's friends in business, Roger Hull, the executive vice president of Mutual Life Insurance in New York City, was an especially important grab. Like Herbert Taylor, Hull attended a progressive church but stayed like Pew on the conservative end of his Presbyterian denomination. Still, his profession encouraged an open-minded approach to doing business and, as such, Hull favored an ecumenical approach to running Graham's largest and most public crusade to date. Serving as the chairman of the BGEA's first New York crusade in 1957, Hull used his clout as a Wall Streeter and his civic influence to introduce Graham to the city. The executive committee looked like "a high commission of the national respectability," according to Marshall Frady. Along with Hull sat many nonevangelicals, including *Time*'s Henry Luce, Ogden Reid of *The New York Times*, Chase Manhattan's George Champion, William Randolph Hearst Jr., and "positive thinking" guru Norman Vincent Peale.[25]

Working with people outside the evangelical fold drew fire from fundamentalists such as Carl McIntire who were suspicious of collaboration with nonfundamentalists and (even worse) Catholics. McIntire stopped supporting Graham after the 1957 crusade. The rift between them had been growing for some time, and it symbolized how far the new evangelicalism had moved past the fundamentalist battles of the 1930s. McIntire kept up what he saw as the "good fight" into the 1960s, scrapping with the Federal Communications Commission over radio programming restrictions even after the government loosened regulations on preachers like him, who regularly attacked any public figure he thought was not sufficiently anti-communist, anti–National Council of Churches, or anti-liberal. The irony was that, for as much as McIntire slammed Graham for working with backers outside the faith, McIntire agreed with businessmen with only tangential or passing theological affinity for his brand of fundamentalist born-again Christianity. Nominal Southern Baptist and Texas oil kingpin H. L. Hunt liked McIntire and other more radical, right-wing fundamentalist advocates in the 1950s and 1960s. Their perspectives, though edged to the pale of conservative evangelicalism in the early Cold War, would remain an important facet of American religion and politics. In the 1970s, the Hunt family and other businessmen would develop relationships with a few heirs apparent to McIntire, including evangelists James Robison and a Virginia-based pastor by the name of Jerry Falwell. At that time, what had been at the radical periphery would move closer to the social mainstream of evangelical America and the political center of American life, once more via the blessings of big business but—oddly enough—with a penchant for collaboration with like-minded nonevangelicals that McIntire might have found disconcerting.

In the 1950s and early 1960s, however, Graham was at the center of conservative evangelicalism's engagement with the American public. Like Herbert J. Taylor before him, Graham was unrepentant about taking fundamentalism into such a public venue via more open-minded strategies, and he had the backing of major evangelical voices like Ockenga and, of course, his father-in-law, L. Nelson Bell. Besides, strategic ecumenism was also a fundraising opportunity. Working alongside many BGEA standard-bearers, including Jerry Beavan and Willis Haymaker, Hull and the crusade's executive board used their experience in business to oversee a massive operating budget for the crusade, which pushed past $900,000 ($7.2 million inflation adjusted). Total contributions topped $2 million. Pew gave $100,000. The board streamlined operations through standard operating procedure manuals, flow charts, and departments organized by function. Shocking racists and segregationists nationwide (but especially in Graham's native South), Dr. Martin Luther King Jr. gave the opening convocation after an over-the-phone invitation from Graham and wired invitation from Leighton Ford, an associate evangelist. On the stage at Madison Square Garden, King advocated "a warless world and for a brotherhood that transcends race or color." His presence further cemented the evangelist's friendship with the civil rights leader, even though Graham saw individual conversion, not necessarily disruptive nonviolent activism, as the best means to achieve racial progress.[26]

The crusade was a huge hit. Initially intended to run for six weeks, Roger Hull extended it for an additional ten weeks. *The Wall Street Journal* was certainly impressed. At the start of the crusade, it published a front-page article on Graham and his efforts in the city. The article offered a rare glance into the internal workings of Graham's business. The BGEA itself, noted the *Journal*, was basically "a mail handling operation" at its headquarters in Minneapolis, leaving most of the planning for crusades to local committees. Still, it was highly organized and thorough, with "seven girls work[ing] furiously opening mail by machine" and separating mail "into donor and non-donor" for the purpose of "counting, checking and receipts." Though housed in "an unimposing building," the BGEA's office was well-decorated and an enjoyable place to work, according to the article, especially for the men. A "trim, dimpled blonde receptionist, Miss June Lazarz," it reported, "would be a decorative asset in the most sophisticated Madison Avenue office." The *Journal* also detailed the exact relationship between the BGEA and local committees: "Local crusades and B.G.E.A., Inc., are organized so as to allay charges leveled against some earlier evangelists that they were piling up personal fortunes on the revival circuit." Publicized audits of each crusade, along with leaving "fiscal control" to local committees, prevented accusations about fraudulent income derived from local crusades, which came from "nightly offerings . . . and contributions (tax deductible) from businesses, organizations, and individuals." In addition to renting Madison Square Garden and paying for advertising, donors supported a vast operation: "Its organizational setup, with eight major operating departments, might cover a major corporation." Responding to anyone who might criticize the BGEA for "bringing business and advertising techniques to religion," Billy Graham told the *Wall Street Journal* that, "The Bible says all things should be done decently and in order. . . . It is a bad reflection on our Christianity to have anything but top efficiency in our work." George Wilson, a Graham associate and "one-time business manager" of Northwestern College in Minneapolis, added, "We try to use the most modern business techniques and still leave room for the Lord to operate."[27]

Such professionalization also meant arranging for businessmen to serve on local crusade boards. Administrative boards most often consisted of local evangelical businessmen or members of upscale businessmen's clubs such as the Chamber of Commerce, Rotary Club, or Lions Clubs. Boards typically included businessmen from various backgrounds, from southern Baptists like "God's Groceryman" Howard E. Butt Jr. to—especially after Graham reached out to them in 1957—Protestants from established, progressive churches and Roman Catholics. The BGEA was aware of this fact and hired Roy Lundquist, himself a former market analyst for Sears and Roebuck, to create in-depth charts and graphs intended to show a local crusade's power in changing religious attitudes or addressing social problems. For Lundquist, correlation was causation. His charts clearly "showed" downward trends in statistics gathered from the Federal Bureau of Investigation's crime indices in nearly every city he studied. After one crusade in Columbus, Ohio, in 1964, statistics remained "favorable for one year after crusade." In the late 1950s and 1960s—when "crime" was a synonym for "black crime" in the midst of unfolding urban crises and rioting—the BGEA promoted a spiritual solution that seemed to quell businessmen's fears and address the promotional aspirations of local Chambers of Commerce. For example, during Graham's 1969 crusade at Madison Square Garden, the "pillars of the business establishment" worked to bring Graham to save the city of New York not from sociostructural problems but a simple excess of "spiritual poverty." Led by Roger Hull once more, a coalition of New York business and ecclesiastical leaders served on the recruitment board, including George Champion (still of Chase Manhattan), Elmer W. Engstrom (president of RCA), and W. Maxey Jarman (head of Genesco). In New York City and elsewhere, the local crusade board worked much like a typical corporation, specializing labor, maximizing efficiency, organizing money flows, and ensuring a steady supply of religious contributors and customers.[28]

Graham's self-made, feature-length evangelical films also illustrated his tendency to hold up the white entrepreneur or big businessman as the quintessential agent of revival—and the object of it. After making Graham's acquaintance, right-wing arms manufacturer Russell Maguire offered Graham a blank check. Graham rejected the offer, reportedly telling Maguire that he could not accept it on the grounds that his "ministry [would] take a nosedive" if his contributors knew "there's a rich man underwriting my work." In other words, a big public donation might discourage other donors, who might assume Graham's efforts were financially secure and sound without their small, dollar-or-two gifts. Still, Graham agreed to a limited donation of $75,000 from Maguire, which he put toward funding World Wide Pictures, a film production company, and likely toward one business-friendly film in particular, *Oiltown, U.S.A.*[29]

Oiltown, U.S.A. was, according to Peter W. Williams, "an undisguised celebration of Texas-style capitalism." In the film, a ruthless oil millionaire from Houston named Les Channing converts to evangelical Christianity and decides to rededicate himself to God's work. "It's Great!" proclaimed one advertisement in 1953 for *Oiltown, U.S.A.*, because it dramatized how the main characters "maintain their testimony for Christ amid the busy world of Oil Town where men acknowledge only the power of money and oil." Other advertisements promoted it as "the story of the free-enterprise system of America, the story of the development and use of God-given natural resources by men who have built a great new empire." Sid Richardson, a wildcat Texas oil baron some speculated was the inspiration for *Oiltown, U.S.A.*'s lead character, also likely contributed money for the film. Critics panned *Oiltown, U.S.A.* Local churches, however, used it, along with other World Wide Pictures films, as tools for evangelism. "Amateurish as they were," noted Graham biographer William Martin, "those first films proved so popular with church audiences that Graham used them to launch a reasonably successful series of films." Businessmen also shaped other media ventures. For instance, the televised version of Graham's *Hour of Decision* depended on a $50,000 gift from two wealthy, anonymous "enthusiasts in Texas."[30]

Most of Graham's early experiments with mass media—other than his weekly radio programs and columns in newspapers nationwide—had limited appeal outside evangelical circles. Still, as with other parts of his evangelistic enterprise, each venture put Graham in close proximity to powerful and well-connected individuals, allowing him access to the halls of corporate and political power in ways he might not have otherwise enjoyed. Plus, each venture illustrated another common aspect of Graham's ministerial model in the 1950s and early 1960s. Graham did not generally refuse support when he could get it, whether from evangelical or nonevangelical businessmen. The strategy had helped make Graham into a national and international star, securing his place as the public face not only of conservative evangelicalism but of Cold War, anti-communist Christianity. But a problem remained, at least according to Graham and those in his circle. Their new evangelicalism aimed for the heart, but it would not hurt if it also aimed at the head. To that end, big businessmen once more offered a helping hand.

J. Howard Pew and the Business of *Christianity Today*

Perhaps no other evangelical venture depended on big business largesse as much as *Christianity Today*. In 1953, Billy Graham began to envision a "strong, hard-hitting intellectual magazine" to challenge the liberal theological and social message of *The Christian Century*, then the most popular Christian magazine in print and one of the only Protestant magazines quoted by mainstream writers and journalists. Harold Ockenga shared Graham's view that an evangelical weekly or monthly magazine would do much good in further defining, clarifying, and promoting the new evangelicalism. But from his experience at Fuller Seminary, which accepted the help of "fleeces" like Herbert J. Taylor and C. Davis Weyerhaeuser, Ockenga also knew that such a start-up venture required capital. By mid-1954, he proposed calling "together a group of leading businessmen" to hear a pitch about fundamentalist social and political engagement. "I should like to present the following to such a group of men," Ockenga wrote to Russell Maguire. "First, present in some detail the spiritual nature of the international threat and national infiltration of corrupting ideas in this critical hour. . . . Second, I would present a practical plan for recapturing the spiritual leadership of the churches by the training of ministers on a post-college level to understand the connection of sound theology with sound economics, and sound politics and sound diplomacy." Maguire had recently acquired H. L. Mencken's old periodical, *The American Mercury*, so he must have seemed like a good person to ask about publishing. (Later, in the mid-1950s, Maguire broke the periodical off from its serious intellectual past, taking it in anti-Semitic and racist directions. Graham and others distanced themselves from Maguire in the 1960s.) For Ockenga, "The basis of this is ideological." "Sound" Christian thinking set one's sights on social and political change through the saving of individual souls. Thus Ockenga planned to "present a definite challenge to those businessmen to undergird a grass-roots movement of sound evangelism as symbolized in Billy Graham."[31]

L. Nelson Bell shared Ockenga's view. Not only were seminarians and pastors "like a bird with a broken wing" when they joined or led churches that focused on "organizational matters, programs, and *social reform* rather than *soul redemption*." They also "have been taught *unbelief under the guise of scholarship*" and "read the CHRISTIAN CENTURY and other liberal magazines and continue to feel they are right in their position." Logistically, there were "two distinct, and yet completely related problems," Bell wrote in early 1955, shortly after quitting his medical practice to "devote all of my time to the promotion and fulfillment of [*Christianity Today's*] objective." "One," he wrote, "is the securing of a group of men who are true Christians, who also have genuine Christian love in their hearts, and who also have the scholarship and ability and vision needed for the text." In other words, Graham's venture needed thinkers and pastors like Ockenga and Bell to write for it: conservative not only in theology but in their social and economic views. "The other is the financial support which such a venture will necessitate," Bell believed. "Those who undertake this must be men of great Christian vision who sense the world-wide significance of this venture and its potential effect on world Christianity for generations to come." Bell also guessed that it would take approximately "a quarter of a million dollars per year for several years" for a publication like *Christianity Today* to get off the ground. Hence, Graham, Ockenga, and Bell sought out like-minded businessmen, some of whom had connections to Fuller Seminary. Others had supported the BGEA or Graham's early crusades. But it was J. Howard Pew who would soon emerge as the single most important and influential contributor to *Christianity Today's* initial direction (See Fig. 2.2).[32]

A backer of nonevangelical initiatives like *Christian Economics*, Spiritual Mobilization, and the Christian Freedom Foundation, Pew had a history of supporting organizations led by conservative pastors or anti–New Deal activists who shared his blending of Christian faith with free enterprise advocacy. Pew's antipathy toward the New Deal grew out of the regulatory framework it established during World War II, which limited large-scale oil producers through production ceilings, the rationing of commercial gas, and price controls. Pew was also reluctant to support racial integration or court-enforced desegregation, and he was a racial paternalist in business. His hatred for progressive Protestant churches and the NCC was a recent development and stemmed largely from their support for the New Deal and labor. After 1950, Pew oversaw a National Lay Committee within the newly formed NCC. Pew was troubled by his Presbyterian denomination's membership in the NCC, believing the latter would corrupt the former's theology and politics, both of which pitched to the left among most NCC leaders and member churches. But even as National Lay Committee chairman, Pew was increasingly marginalized inside the NCC. The committee was little more than an outlet for Pew's view that politics—by which he meant progressive or liberal politics—and religion should remain separate, thereby ensuring the "spirituality" of the church. With the committee disbanded and losing any hope of turning the NCC rightward in 1955, Pew found common ground with fundamentalists who shared his views of soul, state, and society.[33]

Believing that social and economic activism started with pastors and laypeople, Pew and his fundamentalist friends also shared methodology. As Pew wrote to Ockenga during the planning stages for *Christianity Today*, "I determined that the best and probably only way to get libertarian thinking into the church was from the inside." Unfortunately, "a handful of collectivist-minded individuals" in the churches (meaning those affiliated with the NCC) had rebuffed him. Assuming that the NCC's liberal social views did not match those of people in the pews, Pew wrote, "Somehow, someway, a means must be found to make the corporate church truly representative of its constituency." Pew saw right-minded publishing as a viable way to win pastors, congregations, and many unchurched Americans to his economic and political gospel. Referring to *Christianity Today*, "such a publication is most important," Pew wrote to Bell in early 1955, cautioning, "To be successful it must be managed wisely and well." "Its purpose," he continued, "should be to strengthen the minds and hearts of those who are true believers, and at the same time make converts among that vast number who are trying to straddle the great issues." Also paramount was "that the editor of such a publication would always keep in mind that liberty and Christianity are interdependent." "Liberty"—a code word for anti-liberalism in theology and politics— was necessary for faithful Christian living and for turning America away from the allures of state "collectivism." Pew wrote Bell later that, "You cannot take life and divide it into separate compartments—one for your Christianity, another for your economics, another for your social relations, etc." Given Pew's holistic approach, Graham assured Pew that no editor at *Christianity Today* would "allow anything to appear in the magazine [on theology] that will conflict with our views on economics and socialism."[34]

Graham and other board members shared Pew's views and welcomed his help. "Instead of being liberal," Graham wrote, referring to other religious periodicals, "*Christianity Today* will be conservative, evangelical, and anti-Communist." "I sincerely believe," Graham continued, *Christianity Today* "is the greatest possible investment an American businessman can make in the Kingdom of God at this moment." Pew agreed, pledging $150,000 ($1.2 million, inflation adjusted) and assuring Graham and other members of the founding committee that he was "prepared to underwrite the costs for the first year—so that in any event there will be no problem as to the organization expenses." Pew did this because, as he wrote confidentially to Jasper Crane, a friend and fellow executive, he was "keenly interested" in *Christianity Today* and was proud to be a "heavy contributor." Believing that it "should be the most successful church paper ever published," Pew also decided to use his leverage and reputation to write to "as many sound lay people [meaning fellow businessmen and executives] as I can get the names of, who can contribute $100 or more." "No doubt this will cause sparks to fly in certain directions and I am sticking my neck out somewhat," Pew confided in Bell, "but I doubt it will be successful if we pussyfoot."[35]

Concern about "flying sparks" also informed Pew's low profile with regard to *Christianity Today*. Pew was a private man and rarely granted interviews with the press. In ecclesiastical matters, Pew regarded himself a good

Figure 2.2 J. Howard Pew, conservative executive and major donor to *Christianity Today*.
Courtesy of Hagley Museum and Library and Sunoco.

Presbyterian: theologically "sound," committed to good order, and deliberate in decision-making. It is not a stretch to assume that Pew universalized his status as an elder (or presbyter) in his church and denomination, seeing himself as elected by God to steward over society much like he stewarded over his business and church affairs. Moreover, Pew, like most of the "laymen" behind Graham's endeavors, thought denominational or social change could best be accomplished through quiet, behind-the-scenes work. Pew's clandestine approach also fit with evangelical hesitance to have their movement branded as a corporate byproduct, lest other donors consider the venture as hardly in need of continued or continual support. Hence, Pew planned to funnel money—and any donations written out to him from sympathetic lay people—through Ockenga's church fund and the BGEA, which would then make a direct donation to *Christianity Today*. However the money came in, its founders were wary of extended support. Wealthy donors like Pew were seen as necessary but temporary underwriters until the publication had a broader financial base via advertisers and subscribers.[36]

Grand expectations, ideology, and mutual interest certainly drew businessmen to *Christianity Today* but so did rational self-interest. Like any other donor, businessmen could write off donations to the nonprofit periodical—or the BGEA, or any evangelical organization—as tax deductions. Of course, like many religious organizations then and now, *Christianity Today* walked a fine line between legally acceptable religious practice and outright political advocacy. Still, editors were wary of legal infractions. They did not tell readers to vote for any specific candidates, and they couched editorials and articles in "objective" journalistic language and contextual balance. The pursuit of "balance" also fit with *Christianity Today's* mission to intellectualize the evangelical faith and thereby brand it as a respectable mode of belief and practice. Its dual status as a religious charity did the same; the new evangelicalism was presumably like the gospel itself, free of charge and socially beneficial. Initially, approximately four out of five copies were distributed at no cost to pastors and their congregations.[37]

Christianity Today's board of trustees was a who's who of major players in the new evangelical movement. Graham, Bell, and Ockenga sat on the board alongside "business men of considerable means" like Pew, Texas's Howard E. Butt Jr., and Tennessee's W. Maxey Jarman (head of shoe manufacturer Genesco). Together, the board appointed Bell as executive editor with Carl F. H. Henry, a prominent evangelical theologian, professor, and co-founder of Fuller Theological Seminary, serving as another editor. Henry was an obvious choice, having authored *The Uneasy Conscience of Modern Fundamentalism*, a clarion call for conservative evangelicals to assert themselves in American society through personal example and elucidation of the Christian faith's applicability to modern life. J. Marcellus Kik, a Calvinist theologian who shared Bell and Pew's

ecclesiastical sensibilities, was *Christianity Today*'s first associate editor. Unlike
more ostentatious religious leaders, from Billy Sunday in the 1910s and 1920s to
Jim Bakker in the 1970s and 1980s, Bell drew only "a nominal salary." No matter
what readers might think, they could not claim that anyone involved with the
publication was getting rich off naïve donors.[38]

Christianity Today's first issue appeared on October 15, 1956. Calling it
Christianity Today was a clear statement about the publication's self-image and
purpose. The magazine would present the new evangelicalism as the only form
of legitimate Christianity in contemporary America, the only one that mattered. Other forms were suspect. *Christianity Today*'s title also conveyed that it
would cover current events throughout Christian America and take account of
evangelicalism's place in a broader religious context, all while routinely positing
evangelicalism as the only true form of both historic and modern Christianity.
(Theologian Karl Barth's dismissal of the magazine in 1962 as "Christianity
Yesterday" to the face of Carl Henry was a point of pride for Henry and his fellow new evangelicals.) To be sure, the editors assumed too much about the status of the new evangelicalism. It was only one form of Protestantism, much less
Christianity, among many, of course. Moreover, they presented their brand of
"Christianity today" as a predominantly white and male-led religious affiliation
and movement, thereby undercutting its universalist claims.[39] Still, *Christianity
Today* quickly met its goal of becoming the most prominent religious publication
of its day, dominating the Protestant periodical market. Under the editorial lead
of Henry, Bell, and Kik, it blew past *The Christian Century*'s circulation within a
year. By 1957, *Christianity Today* reported an estimated circulation of 120,000 to
130,000, a number that continued to grow to more than 170,000—roughly four
times *The Christian Century*'s—by the time of Henry's departure in 1968.

Aesthetically, *Christianity Today* did not match the look and feel of popular
magazines in the 1950s and 1960s, such as *Time*, *Life*, or *Look*. Presumably to cut
down on costs, editors printed it in black and white, with minimal color text and
few photographs. Articles and editorials were generally printed on paper one
step above newspaper stock but well below the quality of newsstand glossies.
Advertisements were almost always religious in nature, promoting the newest
Bible edition from a mass-market or niche press, a series of devotionals, a private Christian university, a fundamentalist missionary organization, or a revival
series by Graham or other second- and third-tier revivalists. Advertisements
and articles within *Christianity Today*'s covers gave the impression—especially
to its subscribers—that it was *the* only resource for "legitimate" Christianity.
In other words, to be a Christian "today" was to be a "new evangelical" reading
Christianity Today.[40]

Despite its initial popularity, the magazine struggled to make ends meet.
Subscriptions were adequate and donors were generous, but advertisers were

harder to attract and giving away free copies was costly. "In discussing our financial needs I have been disappointed that we have not been able to get more
advertising for the magazine," wrote Butt to Bell in 1957, identifying a problem that hounded the editors well into the 1960s. Though welcomed "editori-
ally," *Christianity Today's* reception "by advertisers has been disappointing"
because to ad buyers it was still a niche magazine.[41] In its first year, the budget
ballooned to over half a million dollars. Expenses overran income by approximately $246,000. Contributions from laymen like Pew and other supportive
donors kept *Christianity Today* from being "forced to fold its tents and silently
steal away."[42] By 1960, it had made budgetary progress. Approximately 90 percent of the magazine's budget was covered by donations and advertising, but
each year it still required hundreds of thousands of dollars—as much as $12,000
per month from various donors in 1960, and then about $27,000 per month
from Pew *alone* in 1962—to stay out of the red.[43] When donations did not quite
fill the gap, additional loans from banks helped with operating expenses, all of
which Pew and other members of *Christianity Today's* finance committee—such
as businessmen Maxey Jarman and Walter F. Bennett—reviewed and usually
kicked up to the board for approval.[44]

In the midst of these challenges, *Christianity Today* presented a relatively
consistent, conservative spin on matters of church, state, and society. It was
more than a magazine reporting on current events or providing commentary.
Occasionally, it was a journal of evangelical economics and politics, one that
in 1960 had approximately five times the circulation of William F. Buckley Jr.'s
National Review. In various issues from 1957 to 1965, *Christianity Today* lauded
free-market economics and pushed for the culling of the "inherently anti-
Christian" welfare state, printed articles by the Christian Freedom Foundation,
and commended Austrian economists like Friedrich von Hayek and monetarist
economists like Milton Friedman. The magazine also insisted on "voluntarism
and [the limitation of] government to a police function" and criticized the "pay-
offs, threats, black-mail, violence and disruptions" of labor unions. As late as
1974, an editor warned that "the welfare state saps individual initiative, increases
the size and cost of sustaining bureaucracy [and] . . . at last assures some form of
totalitarian control that spells the death of democracy."[45]

Christianity Today offered alternative approaches to liberal visions of political economy. For instance, in one editorial, Bell appropriated the famed "Four
Freedoms" of Franklin D. Roosevelt to convey a truly "Christian" vision for the
church's role in poor relief. "*Freedom from want* is not necessarily a good thing,"
concluded Bell. "It is not within the province of the Church or the State to provide to all of its citizens material benefits for life. The scriptural principle is two-
fold [since] those who refuse to work have no right to expect food; but when
a Christian sees a brother in need of help, it is his duty to assist that brother to

the best of his ability." *Christianity Today* also invited book reviews, not only for books on theology or biblical exegesis but also those on "social issues" and state policy. In 1959, the magazine published critical reviews of "Ten Books on Ethics and Economics" promoted by the NCC. Bell's reviewers were "in general agreement that the underlying bias of the series favors the 'New Deal society' against a limited government, free enterprise, private property philosophy." Though "this thesis is resisted in some of the volumes," the books nevertheless smacked of "collectivism" and "left wing social philosophies."[46]

Christianity Today tied economics to foreign policy as well. As with other conservative journals, economic and social "collectivism" at home seemed related to communism abroad. At the invitation of Bell, guest writers, such as J. Edgar Hoover and the Christian Anti-Communism Crusade's Fred Schwarz, weighed in on the Cold War, both arguing that a truly "biblical" Christian faith was spiritual ammunition against domestic or foreign "incursions" by communists. Bell could be as Manichean as Schwarz about the Cold War. Communism was a "ghastly evil" with which there was "no ground for mutual trust or honest discussion." Also troubling was the "communist" or "liberal" dream of "peace" through the diplomatic dropping of "man-erected barriers between nations." Such "forces" were the "very spirit of anti-Christ." For Bell, evangelicals needed to expand their definition of sin beyond gambling and alcohol consumption to "fiscal policies . . . which would long ago . . . have landed prodigal individuals in bankruptcy courts or jails." Bell believed "the American voter" was the biggest sinner of all, having "no one but himself to blame for falling for a program of deficit spending which pushes upward the national debt, accelerates inflation and hastens the day of national insolvency."[47]

Christianity Today was no less vocal about state involvement in the bedroom. Presaging the public complaints of Jerry Falwell and Pat Robertson by a decade (and later evangelical businessmen like S. Truett Cathy and Zig Ziglar), it held as early as 1958 that public "morality" and heteronormativity in America was out of fashion. "Sophistication in matters of sex has arrived at the place where homosexuality has been an underlying theme in two successful plays on Broadway," Bell complained, while "the beauty and rightness of a God-given aspect of life has been perverted to the place where lust and license are paraded as the right way of living, and adultery and fornication as normal and desirable." "This sex obsession has taken such a hold on America," sounding like his son-in-law on the crusade trail, "that nothing less than an aroused Christian conscience, activated at every level of society, beginning with the individual Christian, can check and bring under control the fire of lust which has been the undoing of nations in the past and can prove to be cancer to our own moral foundations." Other issues of *Christianity Today* lambasted public indifference to pornography and "adult films"—meaning edgier Hollywood films—that were little more than parades of "racism, rape, violence, homosexuality, murder, alcoholism, and narcotic addiction, and an open exposure of the psychotic personality and of the futility and nothingness of life." Such "unrelieved preoccupations with naked evil, violence, and sexuality in its normal and abnormal forms" countered the Bible's "admonition to think on things that are true, virtuous, lovely, and of good report." *Christianity Today* did not advocate wholesale censorship. But it did endorse demand-side, organized evangelical protest against pornography, television shows, and movies that were having a deleterious effect on "the moral fiber and spirit of a nation."[48]

For as much as *Christianity Today* commented on hot-button economic and political issues, the magazine stayed on the right side of the IRS. It continued a strict policy of not telling readers to vote for specific candidates, thereby protecting its nonprofit status. But it did cover presidential elections, beginning in 1960. Editors fielded and printed articles that relayed evangelicals' general suspicion of John F. Kennedy's Catholicism. They also worried about Kennedy and the "Catholic question." Bell was strongly opposed to Kennedy's nomination and possible presidency, although Henry took a more tolerant posture. *Christianity Today* did not tell its readership to reject Kennedy, but it did print article after article implying that a vote for Kennedy was a vote against conservative evangelicalism and "freedom of religion." It was more sympathetic three years later after Kennedy's assassination. Ockenga lauded the president as "a man of conviction" who "stood for the separation of church and state," "symbolized a new era in the religious relationships of American citizens" and rightfully "stood for the rights of the Negro as a first class citizen." On other points of political interest, such as the civil rights bill kicking around Congress in Kennedy's honor, the magazine took a theological approach. Bell's "solution" to discrimination and racial violence was a program of church "spirituality," Christian goodwill, soul-by-soul conversion, individual moral judgment, and the pursuit of law and order. This was *Christianity Today*'s stock position in the late 1950s and early 1960s: individual conversion was the solution to so-called "race tensions." "The Church can do what civil law itself is powerless to do," noted one editorial in 1959. By challenging "wrong ideas of God and man as the taproots of race hatred and lovelessness the Church can lay bare humanity's need of redemption from its predicament of sin."[49]

Opinion about civil rights changed little in *Christianity Today*'s pages in the next five years. In 1964, as the Civil Rights Act moved toward passage, the magazine conceded that "the need for legislation exists." Eschewing full endorsement of the bill, however, it argued that "evangelical spectatorism must give way to evangelical action that supports, as conscience leads, such legislation as assures all citizens the freedoms guaranteed under the Constitution." Once again, *Christianity Today* left matters of race and discrimination up to the individual's conscience. As Pew would have put it, "liberty" was the highest Christian virtue, and that included freedom to resist the law through legal means and letters to Congressional representatives. Freedom, however, did not extend very far for protestors on either side of the issue. "Restraint in demonstrations and respect for law" was paramount because "extremism and threats of violence will only impede the processes of legislation."[50]

In 1964, for the first time in the publication's history, Pew himself decided to add his two cents for *Christianity Today*'s readers. The day after Lyndon B. Johnson signed the Civil Rights Act, Pew published his first and only article with *Christianity Today*. It concerned "the mission of the church." As he had done for years in correspondence with editors, Pew sounded off against the "true" Christian's involvement in anything other than strictly "spiritual" affairs. Citing the continuing wrangling between conservatives and liberals in his denomination, Pew argued that privileging social and political questions "prove divisive and weaken the spiritual witness of the church." According to Pew, first-century Christians, Protestant Reformers, early evangelicals, and Presbyterians throughout American history held similar views. "It is obvious from history," Pew concluded, "that in proportion to her engrossment with economic, social, and political matters, the spiritual and moral influence of the Church waned." Likewise, "the social gospel has proved to be ineffective in lifting up the moral standards of our nation" while "the moral corruption and spiritual poverty of our day certainly stem in great measure from the neglect of the Church to carry out her spiritual mission."[51]

Pew's article did not mention the Civil Rights Act, but it came out at a time when liberal domestic policy seemed ascendant. And his views had a clear effect on *Christianity Today*'s public identity. Two weeks later, Ockenga and Henry, most likely with Bell's blessing, took Pew's mantra regarding the "mission of the church" as the magazine's main "objective." In a frontispiece identical in title to Pew's article, *Christianity Today* reaffirmed evangelical theological standards and, once again, held up the "spirituality" of the church, or the focus on conversion and the privatization of one's religious politics, as an ideal. Jesus and the Apostles' ministries were "primarily directed to the spiritual needs of mankind." Readers were "assured that only as the hearts of men are changed can [social, economic, and political] evils be eliminated." "However competent or informed the corporate Church may be or become in social, economic, or political affairs," the editors and board asserted, "these matters are beyond her proper, God-given jurisdiction." At that moment, and for that moment, the synergy between Pew's brand of religious politics and those of the new evangelicals at *Christianity Today* was complete. To be a "new evangelical" was to be a Christian ideally committed to a conservative, big businessman's social and political faith.[52]

Such synergy, as in the past, however, was tenuous, especially after Pew died in 1971. Though Pew's death was not a turning point for the magazine, it might have well have been since Pew's friends at *Christianity Today* either died soon after him or gave way to changing evangelical perspectives regarding religion and political economy. In 1973, after years of failing health, L. Nelson Bell died in Montreat, North Carolina. Carl Henry left the magazine in 1968, in part pushed out by personal quarrels with editors and members of the board, simmering conflicts with Pew over whether capitalism was subject to biblical critique (Henry came to think so), and Henry's uneasy conscience about Vietnam and evangelical disregard for social justice. Henry handed the editorial reins over to Harold Lindsell, a fundamentalist Henry thought relied too much on "theological atom bombing," or strong-arming all parties to conform to his views. Under Lindsell, conservative views continued to direct *Christianity Today's* editorial decision-making. But it was also a different era. Into the late 1970s, *Christianity Today* was both a journal cataloguing the widening array of evangelical sensibilities *and* a place for conservatives to air their grievances about an emerging "evangelical left" that was attempting to redirect evangelical opinions regarding the late Cold War, poverty, sexuality, and a slew of other social and economic issues.

By 1980, *Christianity Today's* circulation had hit a historic high of 200,000. This made it the nation's most popular conservative journal with a circulation roughly double that of *National Review*. It also had, for the first time, a solid financial foundation. The magazine paid off lingering debt on its headquarters, and editors began considering spin-offs, including a magazine for college students (*Campus Life*), for amateur church historians (*Christian History & Biography*), and for lay and academic readers (*Books & Culture*). To be sure, *Christianity Today's* editors and its most loyal constituency—and most common customers—remained conservative pastors, a direct and indirect legacy of its long history of bringing together the mutual interests of publicly engaged religious and business conservatives. But its readership also began to include nonpastors and nonacademics, especially as it transformed from a magazine intent on changing the course of evangelical America to a magazine reporting on events and controversies in evangelical America. After Lindsell stepped down in 1978, subsequent editors kept up this trend. By 1991, *Christianity Today* was, in the estimate of scholars, quoting William Martin, "the most widely read serious religious journal in the nation." Its circulation dwarfed competitors, including its oldest rival, *The Christian Century* and other liberal counterparts, such as *Sojourners*. Like other parts of Graham's corporate revival, *Christianity Today* had made its mark on the nation's religious landscape, empowered by private donations and largesse.[53]

The dual privatization of the faith—privatized financially, privatized as a religious experience—that Graham and his friends in business advanced also unfolded by other means in the immediate postwar era. Indeed, one of Graham's friends and earliest backers, Texas industrialist R. G. LeTourneau, was at the forefront of another kind of mission to the Cold War world, one that treated corporate work, quarterly growth, and evangelical conversions as one and the same. LeTourneau's Cold War crusade had an additional underwriter, namely the very state that other conservative evangelicals cast as the embodiment of secularization and enabler of public godlessness. But in the flat earth of LeTourneau's corporate world, state, enterprise, and religion hummed alongside one another, creating a Cold War venture where economic development and spiritual development seemed attainable and necessary, not only to spread his conservative faith but to open up new fronts against the infiltrations of communists, real or imagined. For LeTourneau, like Taylor and Graham and Pew and Bell, the world seemed flush with promise.

3

Corporate Crusades

Markets, Missions, and R. G. LeTourneau's Cold War

R. G. LeTourneau revered science and technology. An engineer by trade and the idea man behind countless innovative bulldozer and scraper designs, he founded R. G. LeTourneau, Inc. in 1929. His career and fortune depended on applied science and engineering, self-sufficiency, respectability, and innovation. His faith did too.

LeTourneau was a fundamentalist whose views aligned with those of the new evangelicals. He practiced strategic planning, technological innovation, give-and-take ecumenism, and a kind of pragmatic evangelism—much like his friend and contemporary, Herbert J. Taylor. To best promote the faith, LeTourneau incorporated it into his business and used the profits from sales of his high-tech products to underwrite missionary endeavors. LeTourneau's approach was shared by several other elites in mid-century born-again America, including three other important friends and associates of Billy Graham's: the industrialist W. Maxey Jarman, the grocery store magnate Howard E. Butt Jr., and the service sector innovator Marion E. Wade. Each pursued his own form of corporate revival in the early Cold War, linking monetary gain and market share to missionary zeal.

LeTourneau's fortune and faith would not have existed without the direct sponsorship of the federal state. When just getting started, LeTourneau's company received contract after contract from the government for public works projects. During World War II, it supplied hundreds of earthmovers for the war effort. The ensuing Cold War and the growth of the military-industrial complex added to LeTourneau's wealth. Made rich by government contracts, he redirected his millions toward evangelical missions in South America and Africa. Favorable arrangements from governments in Peru and Liberia afforded LeTourneau the opportunity to set up work camps that doubled as missionary colonies. LeTourneau's missions work was colonial to the core. He intended to spread fundamentalism abroad, to be sure. But he also sought to link corporate interests in North America to resources and workers in South America and Africa. His missions were, in both conception and execution, early evangelical exercises in subsidized "free market" globalization. LeTourneau's contractual approach toward the American state set the stage for his contractual approach toward foreign governments. By the time he died in 1969, LeTourneau's corporate crusade had produced demonstrable results for corporations that followed his bulldozers abroad, especially in Peru. But as missionary endeavors, they failed miserably.

A number of mid-century evangelicals joined LeTourneau's mission to the "third world," an imagined and actual mass of countries and peoples not under communist control or (ostensibly) Soviet influence. Once more, big businessmen proved to be important shapers of conservative evangelicalism's worldwide aspirations. Corporate interests and money backed the likes of Dawson Trotman of The Navigators, Cameron Townsend of Wycliffe Bible Translators, and, of course, the Christian Business Men's Committee, International (CBMCI), for which LeTourneau served as president in 1953 and 1954. Most had connections to Billy Graham's network of businessmen, though other businessmen worked to bring different Protestant sensibilities into the American cultural mainstream. Indeed, during the same postwar years, a California dairy executive named Demos Shakarian strove to unite "spirit-filled" practitioners and Pentecostal businessmen under the banner of another businessman's front, the Full Gospel Business Men's Fellowship, International.

Most mid-century, business-backed endeavors did not end up like LeTourneau's missionary program. LeTourneau's work colonies in Peru and Liberia ran aground just as Graham, Trotman, Townsend, the CBMCI, and Shakarian were measuring yearly growth, soul by soul. Though LeTourneau's effort failed, the support granted by the Cold War state to his religious ventures abroad matched the private underwriting of evangelicalism in other corners of America, whether in independent evangelical colleges or in new, business-backed movements that—to use Harold Ockenga's phrase—seemed effective in "infiltrating" mid-century American society.

"Mr. R. G."

Everyone who was anyone in postwar conservative evangelicalism knew Robert Gilmour LeTourneau.

Either by car or by private aircraft, LeTourneau travelled hundreds of thousands of miles every year and spoke regularly in conservative evangelical churches and communities. LeTourneau also gave money and time to the Billy Graham Evangelistic Association (BGEA), The Gideons, and the CBMCI while retaining associations that crossed denominational and regional boundaries. LeTourneau served as a trustee for John Brown University, opened in Arkansas as a vocational school in 1919 and overseen by John Brown, a fundamentalist businessman and radio evangelist who nevertheless welcomed the new evangelicalism. LeTourneau worked as a member of the board of reference for Wheaton College and was friends with George Benson of Harding College, another evangelical school in Arkansas. He was also a friend of the fundamentalist Bob Jones and his family.[1]

LeTourneau's day job enhanced his willingness to collaborate and network. His particular area of expertise, engineering, taught him to try anything and everything to advance his earthly and heavenly goals. LeTourneau embraced the scientific method, valued measurable results, and took a no-nonsense approach to problem-solving. His religious upbringing, however, left an impression and, though an engineer and applied scientist at heart, he never jettisoned the fundamentals of his evangelical faith. In fact, he imagined the secular spheres of science and technology not as threats to his religion but as the most profound means for articulating it.

Born in Vermont in 1888, LeTourneau moved to Oregon as a young teenager and then to California in 1909. He had grown up in a family of devout members of the Plymouth Brethren, a low-church evangelical group that included John Nelson Darby, one of the towering figures in nineteenth-century prophecy belief and theology. The Brethren modeled themselves on the early Christian church and emphasized lay leadership. The latter principle seemed to have stuck with LeTourneau, who became a vigorous champion of lay influence in the evangelical church. Prophecy and premillenialism were somewhat second-tier concerns for LeTourneau. He expected a Second Coming, but he thought less about it and more about what to do with his time beforehand. What he spent most of his time doing was working. A talented workshop tinkerer, LeTourneau started designing earthmoving equipment for the blossoming construction sector. In the late 1910s and 1920s, he perfected his designs and gained patents for a wide variety of haulers and scrapers. His scraper, in particular, was an important innovation, making it possible to level land on a previously impossible scale and helping to usher in the age of modern, industrial earthmoving.[2]

LeTourneau's collaborative tendencies also grew out of necessity. Seeking to win business, he needed to shake hands and sway officials in state governments and, later, in the federal government. Even more so than for his contemporaries in the private sector, contracts defined LeTourneau's world. In 1920, he began work as an independent earthmoving contractor. The next year, he engineered his first designs and opened a small manufacturing facility in Stockton, California. In 1929, he incorporated his company and started selling his haulers and scrapers to local contractors with state and federal contracts. By 1940, the Great Depression had turned into a boon for LeTourneau, much as it had for his friend and compatriot, Herbert Taylor. LeTourneau, however, was on the public's dime. His earthmovers supported a variety of public works projects, especially in the southwest. His machines worked on the Boulder Highway, the Hoover Dam in Nevada, the Marysville Levees, the Orange County Dam, and the Newhall Cut-Off north of Los Angeles. World War II was another windfall. LeTourneau routinely bid for and won wartime contracts, providing earthmoving machinery to the US Department of War. Needing to facilitate the creation of a mobile army via the construction of bases, landing strips, and makeshift roads, the military contracted with LeTourneau for hundreds of bulldozers, scrapers, rooters, and cranes. Troops and engineers in both the Pacific and European theatres used LeTourneau's machines, making them a vital component of wartime operations. Such projects necessitated the expansion of his manufacturing operations eastward and southward, and by 1946 he had plants in Peoria, Illinois; Vicksburg, Mississippi; Toccoa Falls, Georgia; and Longview, Texas. The plant at Peoria was unionized briefly before LeTourneau stopped the effort. The rest were in states with a long history of anti-unionism or, by the late 1950s, were right-to-work states, enabled by Vance Muse's efforts, the Taft-Hartley Act of 1947, and the failures of national unions to make headway in the South.

At each plant, an older model of evangelical paternalism and welfare capitalism prevailed. LeTourneau's factories were miniature company towns, complete with regular chapel services and industrial chaplains, the latter representing what LeTourneau called "Christianity with its sleeves rolled up." LeTourneau paid evangelists to preach at company gatherings. Speakers from evangelical colleges and the Gideons also made appearances. Religious meetings—especially chapel meetings—were so regular that, in 1946, the company's in-house magazine reported that "Few congregations get to hear more preachers than LeTourneau folk." For LeTourneau, a corporation could—and should—have an evangelical soul.[3]

Workplace faith, in LeTourneau's case, depended on a combination of state subsidy and private contracts with various companies. Although the exact number of federal contracts filled by LeTourneau is difficult to determine, according to one estimate, nearly a third of the money the Army Corps of Engineers spent on earthmovers during the war went toward the purchase of more than 75,000 LeTourneau machines. Overall, LeTourneau's company produced 70 percent of the heavy earthmoving equipment used in World War II. In 1943 and 1944, it reaped sales of $36 million ($514 million, inflation adjusted) and $42 million ($566 million), respectively, and netted approximately $2 million ($27 million) in yearly profit. Although V-J Day brought the termination of nearly $21 million worth of contracts, LeTourneau's place in the postwar military-industrial complex was secure.[4] Contracts with the military numbered in the dozens each year during the 1950s and 1960s, including (but not limited to) machinery for US Army and Air Force bases in California, Texas, Florida, Kansas, Georgia, and Oklahoma. Transport carriers for British missile delivery systems and bomb parts for the United States were another part of the company's output. Along with the federal government, LeTourneau's company also depended on dozens of contracts with construction, manufacturing, and oil and gas companies.[5]

In 1948, LeTourneau—already a multimillionaire and approaching sixty years of age—left most of his company's day-to-day operations to his sons, although he continued to provide input and make decisions about acquisitions, new engineering experiments, federal or state contracts, and big deals with private buyers. LeTourneau—known by friends as "Bob" or "Mr. R. G."—also pursued other interests while in "retirement." For the next two decades, he focused fervently on evangelism, donating at first 63 percent of his company's stock (later increased to 90 percent) and nearly 90 percent of his personal earnings toward a personal mission to spread his religious, political, and economic views across the Cold War world.[6] As a beneficiary of the Cold War state, LeTourneau spent the rest of his life defending and advancing its economic and diplomatic program. For LeTourneau, military defense was a constitutionally mandated government duty. Supporting military buildup was patriotic and rightly profitable, especially if the goal was communism's defeat. Thus LeTourneau saw no contradiction in trumpeting "free enterprise" while wheeling and dealing for federal contracts. The federal government was suspect, however, if it usurped the rightful place of businessmen to dictate the terms of workers' welfare or a businessman's free choice regarding property or profits. Like J. Howard Pew, LeTourneau grew suspicious of the New Deal's intellectual underpinnings and thought American students needed "Christian" thinking on matters of state and society. "Our colleges," he wrote in 1956 about the institutions that "Foundations and Christian Industrialists" should support, "should stick to the Faith of our Fathers and the free enterprise system, and not take the path of least resistance into Modernism, Atheism, and Communism." For LeTourneau, Americans had lost faith in free enterprise and needed to believe in it once more.[7]

To that end, LeTourneau also set up his own university, LeTourneau Technical Institute, in Longview, Texas, teaching engineering, science, and math to white male students and foreign students—until the 1960s, when the school desegregated and became coed. From the start, LeTourneau Tech taught not only science and technology but a pragmatic approach toward life and mindful entrepreneurialism. In that sense, it was like John Brown University, which since 1925 had expanded its curriculum in the arts and sciences under Brown's philosophy that "education and manual labor can and should go hand in hand." (John Brown spoke at the opening of LeTourneau Tech.) LeTourneau also promised to "not neglect the most important phase of education; the lack of which renders the life that is otherwise successful a dismal failure." Hence, students took "regular classes for study of the Word of God" and received "every encouragement though chapel services and other means to accept the Lord Jesus Christ as Savior and learn from Him."[8]

As with LeTourneau's company, public subsidy was crucial to LeTourneau Tech. At the end of World War II, Longview newspaper publisher and booster Carl Estes attracted LeTourneau's attention with a nearby army base and hospital that the government was willing to sell to a private buyer. Arrangements for the property's sale were made with the Public Buildings Administration and Federal Works Agency, and LeTourneau was sold the land for a dollar when he revealed his plans to turn the hospital into an industrial training school. Longview's Chamber of Commerce also oversaw the purchase of additional land by LeTourneau, creating a local collections fund to underwrite a lower price for the property. By the winter of 1946, a manufacturing plant was up and running in Longview and enrollment was open for the first classes at LeTourneau Tech, which would later become LeTourneau College and then LeTourneau University. LeTourneau proclaimed it his crowning achievement, brought to fruition not merely by him, the state, or his friends but by divine intervention. Other postwar evangelical businessmen shared LeTourneau's perspective on the necessity and fact of divine involvement in corporate endeavors.[9]

The Postwar Evangelical Elite

LeTourneau was a member of a postwar evangelical elite that included members of the CBMCI, some of Graham's backers, and large- and small-scale businessmen strewn throughout the country. Of those on par with LeTourneau's level of wealth, connections, commitments, and influence, a few stood out: Marion E. Wade, W. Maxey Jarman, and Howard E. Butt Jr.

Marion E. Wade was a conservative evangelical with connections to Moody Bible Institute and the BGEA. Right before the stock market crashed in 1929, Wade started a small mothproofing company in Chicago, a nexus of corporate-backed fundamentalism. Nominally a Baptist, he attended Chicago's Moody Church and, the next year, heard a sermon that led him to accept the basic tenets of fundamentalism. Yet in Wade's retelling of his transformation, personal conversion was not enough to make him into a Christian businessman. He struggled for the next few years, through the Depression and World War II, only to experience another conversion in 1944 when an accident involving cleaning chemicals nearly took his eyesight. Temporary blindness brought spiritual insight. "I found myself wondering what the Lord would do with a company that was entirely His, a company in which every employee, from top to bottom, did his job for the glory of God," wrote Wade, "I pledged . . . there and then I was committing myself to Him entirely—myself, my homes, my business—day and night. I would turn everything over to Him." Wade hired Ken Hansen, a preacher he had heard at a local church, to join his firm. Hansen had the zeal, curiosity, and "real feel for finances" that Wade deemed vital for his company. Wade also met Bob Wenger, a Catholic and "representative of one of the country's biggest rug manufacturers." He "liked the man," setting aside whatever theological qualms he may have had when Wenger agreed that he had "no trouble mixing religion and business" and "had absolutely the same convictions that [Wade] had" about the applicability of faith at work. Like Taylor and Graham, Wade was willing to look past clear historical and theological differences for the sake of integrating business and faith. Together, they formed Wade, Wenger, Hansen, and Associates, later renamed ServiceMaster because of their company's commitment to providing "service to the master," meaning Jesus.[10]

In Chicago, Wade was most likely a member of the CBMCI or at least in its orbit. Having worked at Club Aluminum in the 1920s before it turned around under Herbert Taylor, Wade admired Taylor's management of the company. Wade was a fan of Taylor's Four-Way Test and later developed a version of it for his company. Recruitment also made ServiceMaster a religious venture. Wade placed ads in Wheaton College's paper, encouraging recent graduates to "get in touch with Marion Wade" if they felt "God is calling you in business." (Wade later served on the board at Wheaton, as did Ken Hansen and other ServiceMaster executives.) Scouting at Wheaton resulted in several long-term hires for the company, but it also added to its tight corporate culture, grounded in Wade's particular spin on workplace religion.[11]

Wade's approach was both a complement to and a departure from mid-century managerial theory and practice. In an era before religious discrimination in the workplace was a legal or political concern, business theorists routinely debated whether religion was good for corporate activities and managerial culture, and, if it was, how it best served as a foundation for "business ethics." Conservative evangelicalism, most theorists and practitioners assumed, was not the main source of business ethics; rather, some form of progressive Protestantism was. For instance, the Rotary clubs that Herbert Taylor attended, which provided both community and a place for intellectual reflection on "business ethics," were stocked with moderate and liberal Protestants. Other businessmen's clubs, such as the Kiwanis and Lions Clubs, also provided space for reflection on the varieties of "ethical" business, and most businessmen's clubs had closer ties to liberal Protestant institutions and organizations than evangelical ones. The literature on business ethics also evidenced little to no direct evangelical influence. To be sure, Taylor had his Four-Way Test, but the foremost postwar publication on business ethics, Howard Bowen's *Social Responsibilities of the Businessman* (1953), was based on research sponsored in the late 1940s by the Federal Council of Churches. Business journals exploring business ethics also assumed that liberal Protestantism—or, less specifically, a "Judeo-Christian" perspective—was the place to look for guidance on "proper" governmental regulations, "stewardship" of resources and labor, good management–labor relations, and fair executive pay.[12]

Ethical concerns also shaped the work of Peter Drucker, the most influential management thinker of the postwar era. Protestantism had little to do with Drucker's reflections; Drucker drew inspiration from continental philosophies regarding the "value" of the individual and the verity of "moral universals." Still, Christian philosophers like Søren Kierkegaard influenced Drucker, who also read Friedrich Julius Stahl before writing books such as *The Future of Industrial Man* (1942) and *Concept of the Corporation* (1946). Each book conveyed Drucker's conviction that corporations should always be governed by powerful yet responsible men. A corporate soul was created and sustained by the practical, wise, and responsible executive, the businessman-turned-pastor who recognized that the corporation itself was *the* preeminent form of community in modern life.[13]

By contrast, evangelical managers from Taylor to LeTourneau to Wade thought the best approaches toward work and the best managerial philosophies were authored and promoted by evangelicals in evangelical workplaces. These businessmen used their companies as vehicles for bringing their particular brand of Christian faith into "the world," a buzzword for the private sector. Taking the calling of the "Christian" businessman to be a holistic endeavor, evangelical business executives saw the work done by managers and employees as synonymous with evangelical assertiveness in other places and spaces, whether in urban crusades or on a far-flung "missions field." In so doing, evangelical businessmen made the for-profit corporation a sphere of evangelical articulation, influence, and authority.

They also developed their own theories of executive management, namely that the executive was—as the Four-Way Test implied—directly responsible to God. Not surprisingly, God often pushed these executives to emphasize the individualist, contractual ethic of conservative evangelicalism. To be a "Christian" executive in the evangelical mode meant an executive could and should have significant leeway to shape his company's internal culture and operations. Individual conscience and the interpretation of the Bible as a "heaven-sent" business manual were paramount. God-blessed free exercise of executive authority, in other words, was synonymous with free enterprise and "true" social service to employees and the nation alike. What was good for evangelical business elites was good for reviving Christian America through lively corporate enterprise.

In the 1950s and early 1960s, evangelical executives, employers, and managers could wield remarkable power over the practice of religion in the workplace. But the legal clearance to do so came under increasing scrutiny. The right of employers to discriminate based on religion had, since the early 1940s, been in question, even as labor laws like the Taft-Hartley Act and "progressive" managerial theorizing gave management greater power. Complaints about job discrimination from A. Philip Randolph, black unions, and the National Association for the Advancement of Colored People led Franklin Roosevelt to create the Fair Employment Practices Committee (FEPC), which prohibited employers holding federal contracts from discriminating based on "race, creed, color, or national origin." Though the FEPC certainly opened thousands of jobs to racial minorities, especially in defense-related industries, non-contracted businesses did not fall under FEPC guidelines. Moreover, "creed" was not quite "religion" and was not as judiciously policed as racial discrimination. After the war, efforts to make the FEPC a permanent fixture in federal law faltered in the face of organized resistance from southern segregationists and business-friendly Republicans, many of whom believed businessmen had a constitutional right to discretion (read: discrimination) in hiring, firing, promotion, and demotion.

Given the lack of federal oversight, it was left to state legislatures to take up the issue. Not without opposition, New York, New Jersey, Massachusetts, Connecticut, Oregon, Rhode Island, New Mexico, and Washington had passed fairer employment laws by 1955. Five years later, additional states—including Illinois in 1961—had imitated the FEPC's guidelines or extended them to cover various forms of discrimination in housing, public facilities, and schools. The famed March on Washington for Jobs and Freedom in 1963 put such concerns, especially about race and workplace discrimination, front and center in the American political landscape. A year later, the federal government backed the fuller protection and freer exercise of religion in the workplace through Title VII of the Civil Rights Act of 1964. But until then, the uneven nature of the nation's regulatory framework allowed evangelical executives—or anyone else—to encourage or laud a specific faith at work.[14]

In Chicago in the 1950s and early 1960s, the lack of a robust fair employment law and the support of institutions like Wheaton provided Wade almost free rein to make ServiceMaster an evangelical business. ServiceMaster's in-house evangelicalism, however, also accorded with its labor force and market. ServiceMaster was a service company; hence, by Wade's reasoning, it needed Christian servants willing to do the work required of them. "We must become servants, servants first of all of the Lord and then, in His Name, servants unto all," he wrote. "We must serve. We must give service. Serving the Lord, we must give Him the only things He wants of us: our love and obedience."[15]

Wade's "service to the master" ethic was both individualistic and corporate, and it extended to a growing number of franchisees who contracted under the ServiceMaster brand. Hence, Wade's entrepreneurialism and sense of individual ownership in a free, God-blessed economy was passed down to franchisees who, for the most part, retained a degree of managerial autonomy. In the 1960s, one could contract full-time or part-time, and franchises ranged "from the $1,500,000 annual business to the smallest part-timer with $5,000 yearly business." ServiceMaster's managerial class also grew primarily by word-of-mouth: "About 60% of new management employees who came into our hospital housekeeping and laundry management group in 1968 were referrals by employees, shareholders, suppliers, and licensees." More generally, most "of ServiceMaster's new employees and franchisees [were] generated by referrals." ServiceMaster welcomed such "who you know" growth because it accorded— even if indirectly—with its evangelical corporate culture. Evangelicalism ideally grew through the sharing of the "good news," by a witnessing of a friend or colleague to an unchurched person, convincing them through a personal experience that evangelicalism was a movement worth joining. As ServiceMaster built its franchisee network through contracted relationships, the benefits doubled back in terms of company loyalty and profitability through decreased turnover. "Recruitment of friends and acquaintances," concluded a company evaluation, "illustrates our managers' spirit of commitment and enjoyment of their work." By 1969, company growth through franchising resulted in "approximately 750 franchise cleaning operations in force in the United States and foreign countries."[16]

One of Wade's friends, W. Maxey Jarman, was also a leader in evangelical business circles. The head of Genesco, a Nashville-based shoe manufacturer, Jarman was a longtime supporter of Billy Graham and donor to *Christianity Today*. In general, he was on board with the moderate and measured ethos of the new evangelicals, but he retained a certain affinity for ostentation. "Every well-dressed man," Jarman told a reporter from *Time* in 1951, "should have at least 30 pairs of shoes in his closet," preferably Genesco's brand.[17]

Jarman's flamboyance matched his aggressiveness as a businessman. Taking over Genesco from his father in 1938, Jarman sought to please his investors— the company went public in the early 1930s—with a campaign to grow the business by leaps and bounds in the midst of the war. Like LeTourneau, Jarman excelled at negotiating government contracts, underbidding its primary competitors, US Shoe of Massachusetts and Brown Shoe of St. Louis. During the war, Genesco manufactured approximately 5 million pairs of shoes and boots for US troops. In fact, when the Japanese surrendered to General Douglas McArthur on board the *USS Missouri* in 1945, McArthur wore shoes custom-made for him by Jarman's company. Jarman's fierce anti-unionism helped keep his bids low and his costs lower, especially after the end of the war. Jarman deployed various

tactics to stall or suppress unions. Managers at one plant might intimidate workers while others threw parties with free food and awards to distract from a union
vote or dissuade organizing. "If there was talk of a union at one factory," recalled
a Nashville labor attorney, "they would switch all the work to other factories."
At times, Jarman took more drastic measures. He closed one Massachusetts
plant and moved the work south to avoid unionization. In 1964, when Martin
Luther King Jr. attempted to organize workers at Jarman's only all-black plant
(Jarman's plants were segregated by race until the late 1960s), Jarman shut it
down. Another Tennessee plant attempted to organize a few years later. Jarman
shut it down too.[18]

Jarman's anti-unionism fit his sensitivity to price, which informed his free-
market advocacy despite his own history of contractual camaraderie with the
federal state. Like his father, Jarman kept Genesco's business model focused on
providing low-cost, high-quality shoes. Low rates of inflation and the rise in dis-
cretionary income after the war undoubtedly helped his business, as American
consumers bought status and respect through products like Genesco's footwear.
Advertising for Genesco emphasized not their price but their style and versa-
tility for both the grey-flannel businessman and his fashion-conscious wife or
girlfriend. Jarman's take-no-prisoners approach to competition—which he considered the only means by which a businessman could keep prices low, labor at
bay, and quality shoes available to customers—fit his brand of libertarianism.

Jarman's cutthroat attitude made Genesco a major player in the American
apparel market. By 1955, Genesco was the second largest shoe company in the
United States, a status achieved by an aggressive buy-out campaign and supply-
chain integration that, in the same year, resulted in an antitrust lawsuit by federal
regulators. Genesco fought the lawsuit but then signed a settlement, agreeing
to not acquire any additional shoe manufacturers for five years and to stock
competitors' shoes in its stores. Genesco's power and position in Nashville was
satirized in *The Spiked Heel*, a piece of pulp fiction written by Richard Marsten
and published in 1956. Though Marsten denied the book was about Genesco
and Jarman, its dramatic retelling of a corporate takeover by "Titanic Shoes of
Georgia" was unmistakable to anyone with even a passing knowledge of the
company's chief executive and his union-busting, winner-take-all approach to
marketplace mastery.[19]

In keeping with his authoritarian streak, Jarman was even more forthright
than Wade about religion in the executive's office. "Like his father," noted a 1956
report in *The New York Times*, "Mr. Jarman has made prayer the guiding factor
in his business operations and Christian principles his business policy." Jarman
opened "directors' meetings with prayers" and gave "recognition to the Deity
in his annual reports." He also read "his Bible through once a year and when
[at] home [held] daily devotions with his family." Temperamentally mercurial as

well, Jarman's politics was closer to those of J. Howard Pew than Wade or Taylor. He attended a conservative southern Baptist church in Nashville, one in which fundamentalism was a given and big checks in the collection plate were encouraged. Jarman certainly ran in the same business circles as Wade and Taylor, contributing his financial share to the new evangelicals and their enterprise. But even more so than his friend, L. Nelson Bell, Jarman hated the National Council of Churches and its racial, economic, and political ideas. Jarman was not afraid to air his grievances to board members at *Christianity Today* and the BGEA, both of which he funded and supported. Like Pew (whose publication *Faith and Freedom* praised Jarman for his business practices), Jarman thought that *Christianity Today* should be an organ for conservative businessmen, trumpeting free enterprise and heterosexual "norms" as synonymous with the evangelical faith. Jarman's input was, like Pew's, both welcomed and managed by Bell and other editors.[20]

Privately, Jarman could be bellicose about defending what he saw as the fundamentals of his evangelical faith, both on points of theology and their social, economic, or political application. Publicly, Jarman was mum about matters of society and politics during the early 1960s, focusing on growing Genesco from a regional shoe company into the world's largest supplier of middle-class apparel through the acquisition of a men's suit maker, a pajama company, and even a women's lingerie manufacturer. But in 1965 Jarman went public with his views, publishing a work of theology, *A Businessman Looks at the Bible*, which captured his implicit view of the world: that individual effort and reason was all one needed to succeed in the corporate, free-market free-for-all. Jarman filled page after page with encomiums, treating the Bible as a heaven-sent work loaded with insights for businessman and nonbusinessman alike. Although he claimed up front that his book was "not written to say that the Bible . . . helped me to be a success in business," Jarman argued regularly that an honest acceptance of biblical teachings by readers would positively affect their work and a company's bottom line. The Bible was like a black-and-white presentation of "the truth," relieving the believer and reader of fear, worry, and other personal "shortcomings." It was, like Jarman's fundamentalist faith, a sure thing.

To sell his reader on the applicability and power of the Bible, Jarman used the rationale of the secular business world—fact-checking, pragmatism, clear-headed reasoning, and "measurable" results. "Perhaps I went to work [in writing the book] with a prejudiced point of view," Jarman wrote, "but I believe that the techniques used in the business world are particularly well suited to an analysis of the Bible." "In my business," Jarman asserted, "I have learned that when an idea is presented it must be tested in practice, not just discussed in theory." Such methods were "routine in business, and they were the best tools I had at my command;" hence, Jarman "decided to use them to test the Bible."

Unlike higher critics or social gospelers, Jarman came to the conclusion that the Bible was full of divinely given, plain truths that stood the tests of any honest, pragmatic, rational businessman. Similarly, if readers would trust the authority of Jarman's standard of truth—namely the conclusions of Christian business-men like himself—then they would begin to appreciate its benefits at home, on the job, and in their community. "The Bible is the best self-help Book in the world," offering to those who believed its overall message of personal redemp-tion "a new internal joy, a readiness to meet life's burdens, and a willingness to look forward to the future with serenity and assurance." Jarman did not air some of his more polemical views on race and religion in the book, but he did advocate for social order, ethical business, and Christ-like service in the workplace and public sphere. Moreover, Jarman put his money where his mouth was, using his wealth and executive experience to support the BGEA, *Christianity Today*, and other evangelical ventures. Other businessmen, thought Jarman, should do the same.[21]

And they did. Wade's and Jarman's friend, Howard E. Butt Jr. of Texas, was another service-minded evangelical who viewed building an ever-bigger busi-ness as a vehicle for evangelical empowerment. Like Jarman, Butt inherited wealth and status. In 1905, his grandmother founded H. E. Butt Grocery Store Company (HEB) in Kerrville, Texas. After World War I, her son, Howard E. Butt Sr., took over the store. In the 1920s and 1930s, the company expanded through-out Texas while, according to one 1971 retrospective, it also "became active in food manufacturing and for many years operated the only pineapple canning plant in the continental United States." For Butt Sr., HEB was a company dedi-cated to quality service to customers; assurances of food safety and cleanliness; and reciprocal relations between stockers, suppliers, and managers. HEB's suc-cess, he claimed, also came from "hard work and observance of the Golden Rule." Elements of the Rotarian creed—Butt Sr. was a Rotary member—were similarly front and center. "Our greatest asset is public good will," he believed. "This asset of good will is greater than asset[s] in merchandise. In this business the adage is surely true: 'He profits most who serves best.'" By 1953, HEB's corporate man-tra seemed to be working quite well. According to one observer, HEB employed more than 2,000 people as it continued to "serve the public according to [Butt Sr.'s] guiding philosophy."[22]

Butt Jr. became vice president of the company after World War II while his younger brother, Charles Butt, became HEB's president. In the late 1940s and 1950s, their father expanded the family's holdings through additional invest-ments in banking, real estate, oil, and retailing. Around the same time, Butt Jr. matured in his father's Baptist faith. Having given his life to Christ as a teenager during World War II at Corpus Christi Junior College, Butt Jr. then moved to Waco to attend Baylor University, a Southern Baptist school. After serving as a local director of Youth for Christ (YFC), Butt Jr. honed his craft as a speaker and evangelist during a student-led revival at Baylor in 1946 and 1947. Graduating in 1948, he operated HEB's newest store while gaining additional fame as an effective executive and—in the words of profiles—a "Gospel Bootlegger." By 1955, Butt Jr. had made over 1,650 appearances in twenty-two states and seven countries as an evangelical speaker and had spoken at three Southern Baptist Conventions and the Baptist World Youth Congress. Through connections with YFC, Butt Jr. befriended Billy Graham. He regularly donated to evangelical philanthropies and served with Jarman on the board for the BGEA and *Christianity Today*. Butt Jr. also developed a close-knit network of like-minded businessmen and academics during the 1950s, laying the groundwork for additional forays into business evangelism.[23]

Butt Jr. was more like Wade than Jarman, in that he leaned more toward Rotarian service than rapacious mastery. He viewed his status as an evangelical elite as a precondition for leading other managers—regardless of whether they were evangelicals—into recognizing the need for religion and Christ-like service at work. Like members of the CBMCI, Butt Jr. also strove to create unity and common direction among executives, managers, and business owners. His most important contribution in the latter regard was a self-funded, tax-deductible nonprofit businessmen's organization: the Layman's Leadership Institute (LLI).

First organized in 1955, the LLI was initially an extension of Butt Jr.'s first attempt to organize businessmen, Christian Men, Inc. By 1961, the LLI had brought together "participants, invited because of influential positions as prominent Christian laymen . . . from 42 states and overseas." At LLI meetings prominent evangelical elites, like Jarman and Taylor, met rising stars in evangelical media culture, such as conservative radio personality Paul Harvey. The primary goal of LLI, however, was to teach businessmen to take their faith seriously and use their resources to spread evangelicalism in the private sector and, by extension, the public sphere. As Butt Jr. claimed at a Miami meeting of LLI in 1961, "We have developed a spectator Christianity in which few speak and many listen. The New Testament church, started as a lay movement, has deteriorated into a professional pulpitism financed by lay spectators." To counter this tendency—even as he supported it via his financial backing of professional pulpitists like Graham—Butt Jr. formed LLI to encourage businessmen to live their faith beyond Sunday morning.[24]

The purpose of LLI overlapped with Laity Lodge, another of Butt Jr.'s well-funded experiments. Set up in Texas on a 2,000-acre ranch in 1961, Laity Lodge was an update on the backwoods camps long used by evangelicals to renew their faith or introduce the uninitiated to it. Butt Jr. selected Keith Miller, an Oklahoma oil man also interested in businessmen's ministry and counseling, to be Laity Lodge's first director. The camp yet again demonstrated the porous boundaries surrounding mid-century evangelicalism, especially among businessmen. Indeed, by the end of the 1960s, Laity Lodge was not exclusively evangelical. Representatives from liberal Baptist, Methodist, Episcopal, Mennonite, and Presbyterian bodies attended one program in 1969. More progressive voices, such as Los Angeles Presbyterian pastor Dr. Louis Evans, also preached there. However ecumenical it was, Laity Lodge still had a relatively straightforward and singular mission. According to administrative director Bill Cody, a former personnel secretary for the Baptist Foreign Mission Board and ex-coordinator of the LLI, "The primary thrust of Laity Lodge . . . is in the area of personal Christian renewal, along with family and congregational renewal." "We are re-examining the nature and depth of the commitment called for by Christ in the Gospel," Cody continued. "It is our hope that we can determine what this commitment means in terms of being a part of the body of Christ in our local churches and in our vocational lives. But we also are seeking to enlarge our Christian vision to include the moral and social problems of our generation." To that end, thousands made pilgrimages to Laity Lodge in the 1960s and 1970s. The discussions and seminars that occurred there certainly did not focus on free enterprise ideology. But the anti-union position of HEB and the ethic of executive privilege to determine acceptable faith and practice in business, as well as Butt Jr.'s long association with Billy Graham and conservative evangelical ventures, revealed the social ethic and business practices undergirding LLI and Laity Lodge even as both had a certain overlap with progressive managerial ideas and Protestant ecumenism.[25]

Like Wade, Jarman, and Butt Jr., LeTourneau also crisscrossed liberal-conservative-libertarian lines, all for the sake of extending conservative evangelicalism. LeTourneau's tax-exempt philanthropy, the LeTourneau Foundation, was "one of the largest missionary organizations in the country," according to *Newsweek*. LeTourneau's foundation sponsored the LeTourneau Evangelistic Center (LEC), a clearinghouse for missionary activities founded in 1938 that, by 1945, took its budget from the $13 million per year ($171 million, inflation adjusted) LeTourneau sent to his foundation. Operating out of an office in a citadel of corporate capitalism, Rockefeller Center in New York City, the LEC oversaw the distribution of millions of tracts and pamphlets to churches and individuals. In addition, it trained and managed twelve full-time evangelists who worked abroad. The LeTourneau Foundation and LEC were also involved in various other missionary activities, from distributing "Scripture calendars" to American homes to promoting children's Bible Clubs. LeTourneau's philanthropy backed the Intercollegiate Gospel Fellowship "in organizing Christian students attending colleges in the New York metropolitan area and helping them carry on a progressive program of work in presenting Christ to the student bodies of these colleges." Most audaciously, the foundation sought to create a "mighty armada of flying missionaries" that LeTourneau wanted to send to Africa, China, and Mexico.[26]

Building off the work done via the LEC, LeTourneau began considering in 1951 the prospect of privately funding missionaries to South America and Africa, specifically in Liberia and Peru. Of course he was not the first big businessman with religiously charged transnational business aspirations. In the 1890s, Coca-Cola's Candler brothers, both Methodists, funded excursions to Cuba for the sake of expanding their product's market and spreading Methodism in the Caribbean. Between 1928 and 1945, Henry Ford built and maintained Fordlandia, a "jungle city" in the Amazonian river basin that blended moral policing and capitalism. Similarly, LeTourneau's efforts proceeded as a colonialist endeavor, as a venture sending money and men both for economic gain and for the purpose of proving his dictum that one could "do a missionary job in a businesslike way." Other evangelical entrepreneurs, many in LeTourneau's circle of friends, were captured by the same impulse. They also viewed the Cold War third world as in need of saving as soon as possible, soul by soul and dollar by dollar.[27]

Underwriting Navigators and Bible Translators

"I think Daws . . . personally touched more lives than anybody that I have ever known," Billy Graham remarked in 1956. "Daws" was evangelist Dawson Trotman. Born in Arizona and raised in California, Trotman attended the fundamentalist Los Angeles Baptist Theological Seminary and Bible Institute of Los Angeles. In 1933, he started a ministry for sailors stationed in Long Beach called "The Navigators." During World War II, more than 1,000 of Trotman's Navigators led discipleship groups on US ships and at Navy stations worldwide, yet again demonstrating the linkage between the wartime state and wartime evangelicalism. In 1943, Trotman legally incorporated The Navigators and worked during the late 1940s to spread its message onto college campuses through "spiritual multiplication" (training new disciples by having them teach others) and "routinized spirituality" (Bible memorization, prayer, personal evangelism, and conservative living). The goal of The Navigators, according to Rod Sargent, its business manager, was to create "craftsmen for God" not only among servicemen but among all men, whether in the United States or around the world.[28]

Like the BGEA, The Navigators imitated the business world and the respectability, authority, and risk control it seemed to offer. "We feel the Lord's work," Sargent told *The Los Angeles Times* in 1954, "should be conducted on a businesslike basis." He meant it. Like a military or corporate budget, The Navigators' books divided into highly specific sections and subsections. The group also kept detailed statistics regarding conversions and Bible memorization. All this data proved, at least to those who staffed The Navigators, that they were—in their parlance—"producing reproducers." Trotman's methods also appropriated military culture, which privileged routine, discipline, rank, and the glorification of masculinity and racial order. Naval imagery (the official logo was a sail) and military lingo were common ("B rations" were mini-Bible devotions), thereby affixing evangelical purpose to the wartime valorization of military order and the postwar spiritual-industrial complex.[29]

Businessmen's money emboldened The Navigators in the 1950s, especially after Billy Graham brought Trotman into his fold as a consultant for the BGEA's crusades. Like other upstart evangelical organizations, The Navigators developed a network of bankrollers, which included LeTourneau. Money, donations, and staff were shared with other new evangelical organizations, such as YFC, Young Life, the BGEA, and Campus Crusade for Christ. Shared and ear-marked donations large and small helped The Navigators meet their budget goals in the 1940s and early 1950s. The Navigators shrewdly solicited donors. "Before speaking to the contact at all," one campaign document for the funding of The Navigators' new headquarters suggested to fundraisers and cold callers, "have in mind the man's relative financial ability and suggest that we would like to count on him for an amount of this kind." The pitch created a personal relationship between the donor and The Navigators' global activity. "Stress the Navigators program—what God is doing in Formosa, Europe, in the service . . . in your local area, etc. Show how more men are needed—available but need training. . . . Oh, yes—be able to say, 'I myself have invested,' before suggesting it to others." Guidelines also took a strategic approach toward potentially big donors. "Doubtless it will please him to be able to be one of the larger donors. On the other hand, there may be times when it will be psychologically better not to mention a card [detailing possible donations] at all, particularly in the event of a large donor." It concluded: "We would not want to limit him in this case."[30]

Using such methods, Trotman raised more than enough money to fund The Navigators and, in 1951, to buy Glen Eyrie, a 1,140-acre, 33,000-square-foot estate located near Colorado Springs, Colorado. It had previously been owned by George Strake, a Catholic oil mogul and friend of Billy Graham. Although appraised at $1.67 million ($15 million, inflation adjusted), Strake lowered the price from $500,000 to $300,000 (plus $40,000 for furnishings) when he discovered that Graham was interested in buying the property and using it as a headquarters for religious pursuits. When Graham decided to back out of the negotiations, Strake still sold the estate to Trotman at the same cut rate, accepting a down payment raised via an intensive fundraising campaign among businessmen and other supporters. By 1955, Glen Eyrie was the world headquarters for The Navigators and, for the next few decades, a popular spot for evangelical conferences. It was also a fitting symbol of evangelicalism's fuller integration into big-business culture. Conservative evangelicals now had a spacious, millionaire's mansion all their own on a private estate.[31]

Trotman's personal connections to Graham and LeTourneau also brought The Navigators into the orbit of another important missionary organization with corporate connections: the Wycliffe Bible Translators (WBT) and its affiliates, the Summer Institute of Linguistics (SIL) and the Jungle Aviation and Radio Service (JAARS). All were headed by Cameron Townsend, a Californian, Occidental College dropout, and evangelical missionary who had worked in Guatemala with Central American Mission from 1917 to 1932. According to historian William L. Svelmoe, Townsend "was the classic American evangelical entrepreneur" but "no fundamentalist. . . . He had no patience for quibbles over theology, the 'non-essentials,' as he put it. He preferred the company of business-men to that of pastors for just this reason. He admired 'go-getters,' men who built something, more than thinkers and pietists."[32]

Several smart and dedicated "go-getters" oversaw operations at WBT. Former California insurance broker Edward S. Goodner served as the vice-president of both the SIL and WBT boards until his death in 1957. Lawrence Rough, a North Carolina businessman, was WBT's first regional representative in the South and an avid fundraiser. Converted at Billy Graham's second Charlotte cru-sade in 1958, North Carolina retailer Henderson Belk of Belk Stores gave check after check to WBT. Introduced by Charlotte businessman Vernon Patterson to Townsend and WBT, Belk also donated 256 acres south of Charlotte to WBT to set up JAARS's aviation center in 1960. A local construction company, the Dickenson Company, built a landing strip and runway for JAARS, which sub-sequently shifted operations from California to North Carolina, training hun-dreds of Townsend's missionary-aviators for translation work and aerial support, especially in South and Central America. Chicago businessman William G. Nyman also joined WBT in 1941 after serving as a member of Townsend's home church in Los Angeles and as a chairman of the board at the Bible Institute of Los Angeles. Nyman established WBT's home office and worked as secretary-treasurer, using his extensive business experience and connections to keep the books in good order until his death in 1961.[33]

Through WBT/SIL's work in Mexico, Peru, Guatemala, Ecuador, and other Latin American countries, Townsend applied his entrepreneurial skills, diplo-matic charms, and business connections toward a three-part goal of document-ing Latin American languages, translating the Bible into indigenous languages, and converting what he called "Bible-less" peoples in continental interiors. He received direct and indirect support from multiple nodes in the blossom-ing postwar evangelical network. Along with Billy Graham and YFC's Torrey Johnson, Dawson Trotman became involved in JAARS, promoting WBT on

college campuses, keeping up a correspondence with Townsend about missionary work abroad, and serving on WBT's and SIL's boards.[34]

Townsend was also on good terms with his business backers, exchanging personal and congenial letters. Most mentioned or promised support for WBT's
work. Others vowed to vouch for WBT among colleagues in business or civic
organizations. Much like Taylor, LeTourneau, and Graham, Townsend's network
was expansive. Though hardly supportive of conservatism or evangelicalism, the
Rockefeller Foundation took an interest in Townsend's documentation of native
languages and contributed money for research in scientific linguistics. So too did
stalwarts in the philanthropic money machine of postwar evangelicalism, such
as W. Maxey Jarman and members of the Pew family. Billy Graham fan and Wall
Street titan Sam Milbank also corresponded with Townsend and offered his
financial help and business advice, as did executives at the Washington lumber
company Weyerhaeuser and the Celenese Corporation, a North Carolina chemical company. Norman Hollenbeck, an Illinois trucking executive, and Frank
Sherrill, of S&W Cafeterias in Charlotte, rounded out Townsend's contributors
and correspondents, although other small business owners and managers wrote
Townsend over the years offering their advice, money, or statements of evangelical solidarity. Altogether, the infrastructure of willing businessmen—some
evangelical elites, others not—who stood behind WBT shaped it into one of the
most expansive evangelical organizations at mid-century.[35]

Townsend's favorite underwriter was Henry Coleman Crowell, the son
of Henry P. Crowell, who had reshaped Moody Bible Institute into a fundamentalist powerhouse a generation before. As vice president of Moody Bible
Institute, the younger Crowell oversaw the Crowell Trust, his parents' philanthropic foundation. Crowell and his family's trust supplied money to Townsend
and Trotman's endeavors after 1945. In the late 1940s and through the 1950s,
Crowell regularly contributed checks for hundreds or thousands of dollars to
WBT, SIL, or JAARS. After Crowell died, Townsend called him "a column of
strength" who was "understanding always and anxious to give us assistance in
our efforts to reach the Bible-less tribes with the Word of God." Crowell also
regularly wrote under the pen name "The Kilo Kid," a self-deprecating nickname
given to him by JAARS pilots due to his girth. Letters between Townsend and
Crowell could be mundane, focused on the mechanics of transcription machines
and boat-strainers or complaining about the idiocy of engineering designs in the
aviation industry. Or they could be serious and strategic, as when Crowell consulted with Townsend about airplane purchases, money for servicing planes,
or—as Crowell once put it—saving "a flock of dollars" through cost-cutting
measures, such as asking donors for free gas.[36]

Crowell saw his corporate experience as a benefit to WBT, and he encouraged Townsend to think in terms of risk analysis and networking. For instance,

concerning the purchase of one plane model over another in 1948, Crowell admitted that "I don't know that I am at all qualified to answer such a question. I know very little about your needs and the conditions under which it will be used[.]" Still, Crowell favored the less expensive model that Townsend was considering, not merely for keeping the books balanced but because Crowell offered to purchase the plane "through a local dealer . . . for a 20% discount." In the meantime, Crowell encouraged Townsend to "work on [airplane manufacturer] De Havilland Company for a free gift of the [costlier] plane if possible."[37] This no-nonsense approach toward missions was what made businessmen like Crowell valuable to Townsend's organization—that, along with direct donations. Conditions on those donations varied. Most checks came with no strings attached, as gifts based on needs or requests from the WBT office or from Townsend. Yet when the requests and outlays cycled through the Crowell Trust, which became more common after Crowell's death in 1959, donations could be—but usually were not—"contingent upon the Wycliffe organization's raising a matching amount" by a certain date. For the most part, then, WBT maintained a congenial relationship with the Crowell family, one that doubtlessly advanced the organization's reach.[38]

Overall, WBT showed the importance of big businessmen like Crowell to mid-century evangelical missions. Of course Crowell was well aware of this fact; he was cognizant of Graham's fundraising among business elites and the BGEA's organizational vitality. But as the son of one of the first businessmen to fund fundamentalism, Crowell was keeping the family's side-business alive by putting its newest manifestations on a transnational scale. Hence, Crowell and Townsend worked together, using as many means as possible to make missions abroad a viable component of evangelical activism. Their mission was not only religious but geopolitical. In a Cold War world they sought to ensure that the "bibleless" would affirm an "American way of life" grounded in faith in Christ and capitalism rather than a secular cultural and economic politics (socialism? communism? Stalinism? Maoism?) they saw as anathema.

LeTourneau's missionary work could go forth, in part, because WBT had paved the way into South America. But it also went forth because LeTourneau cut out intermediaries and clients, running and funding a missionary startup all by himself. His ventures in Liberia and Peru were, in large part, an attempt to reproduce the labor arrangements abroad that he had used in his various stateside manufacturing plants. But they were more than business ventures; they fused religious and political purpose to business investment and technological experimentation. In a 1951 essay titled "Why Liberia?" LeTourneau identified stopping communism and promoting technical education and capital investment as major goals of missionary activity, inseparable from proselytizing. "Whether we like it or not," he wrote, "they are not going to stay ignorant, and the Communists will educate them if we don't." LeTourneau acknowledged the efforts of the Truman administration to help "backward nations in the form of lend-lease," but LeTourneau saw another way to save nations such as Liberia from communist dominance: "A better job could be done by teaching them to help themselves, which in the long run will be worth much more to them." This approach to the mostly non-white third world—a monolith of countries, neither fully communist nor fully capitalist, imagined as on the Cold War fence by many American businessmen and politicians—was couched in racial and economic superiority, opportunism, respectability, and Christian duty, a mid-century version of the white man's burden that approximated the white-led philosophy of the CBMCI (but not quite the philosophy of the BGEA or WBT, which made room for racial collaboration if not quite full-scale equality). LeTourneau offered his own spin on this old philosophy. "Maybe a happy medium," he thought, "would be an industrialist who has the know-how to teach them and is willing to take a certain amount of risk to create a greater market for his products especially when they are needed as badly as mine are for roads, railroads, utilities, airports, mining, land reclamation, transportation, etc." In Liberia, as well as in Peru, LeTourneau attempted to establish this "happy medium" of investment, racial "uplift," political conversion, and free-market colonialism.[39]

Of Flattened Earth and Freer Trade

LeTourneau expected free markets to flourish where his earthmovers literally flattened the earth. But this flat earth could not and would come about without state sponsorship. As during the Depression and World War II, LeTourneau's mission to the world accorded to state sponsorship and subsidy.

Once again, LeTourneau's long history of wheeling and dealing with state officials served him well. In 1951, after representatives from Liberia heard LeTourneau speak about industrial improvement at a trade conference, they requested a meeting with him to discuss the potential of using an "undeveloped" area in Liberia as a testing ground for his ideas. LeTourneau gained an audience with Liberian president William V. S. Tubman to discuss opening 500,000 acres of interior jungle for "the purpose of development." In this area, which LeTourneau named Tournata, the primary objective was two-fold: "1. Industrial and agricultural development of an underdeveloped area; thereby providing an opportunity to the people for economic advancement. 2. Evangelizing the area and providing a Christian testimony among laymen of the country." In other words, LeTourneau aimed to duplicate in Liberia what he had developed through his association with the CBMCI, at his industrial plants, and at his university in Longview—putting into practice his "basic philosophy" that conservative Christianity and commerce were mutually edifying. As reported by a sympathetic visitor in 1953, "The LeTourneau project is designed to be a business venture.... and from the soil and trees there can be a much better way of life for Liberians." Mirroring LeTourneau's thoughts on the matter, this observer insisted that "By being business-like we can help them to help themselves, thereby developing in them the self-respect, the sense of accomplishment and dependability, the dignity of common toil, and the diligence that many of them now seem to lack.... Cannot a project be at the same time both good business and true Gospel, with prospect of food for the body and also for the soul? The Liberians need both, as do you and I."[40]

LeTourneau certainly viewed his plan as a way to turn Liberians into the right kind of Christian workers and, subsequently, improve their ability to join American economic networks as willing and grateful recipients of corporate grace. But he also viewed his "African expedition" as an alternative to heavy-handed, collaborationist Cold War policy, writing, "I don't know how much progress the United Nations is going to make toward getting us together, but I know there is too vast a difference between our standards of living to have a peaceful world. The difference in earning power of a laborer in America and a native laborer in Africa is too great." LeTourneau considered his project essential to postwar international politics because he could make "underdeveloped," non-white populations more productive via technology. "If a man doesn't want to work and is satisfied to live in squalor," he continued, "that's not too bad, but when a man can work and wants to work we should provide a way whereby he can receive, as the fruit of his labor, the things his labor can make. And by using machinery we can make his labor very productive. That is why these non-industrial nations must be mechanized before our troubled world gets in any worse shape than it is. And because I'm a mechanic and mechanization is my middle name, I'm on my way to Africa to see what can be done about it."[41]

LeTourneau had a standing offer to do the same in Peru. In 1953, LeTourneau met with WBT's Cameron Townsend. Townsend was aware of LeTourneau's interests in Africa and brought up the possibility of a Peruvian "colonization program." The next year, LeTourneau flew to Peru and contracted with the Peruvian government, led by President Manuel Odría, to build roads in the jungles northeast of the capital of Lima. A settlement named Tournavista developed on the banks of the Panchitea River. By the early 1960s, approximately 15 North American families and 125 Peruvian families lived there. Much as in Liberia, the goals for Tournavista made inseparable the economic and religious. As one pamphlet advertised, LeTourneau aimed to meet the following "National Needs": "In both Liberia and Peru, the philosophy is not to make a donation of material or cultural advantages, but rather to give the people an opportunity whereby they, with their own labor, can obtain these things. It is only as they are made to stand on their own, that they will be able to move forward both technically and spiritually. They need our modern machinery and technical knowhow, but this alone cannot solve their problems. It is only as they put their faith in Christ that they will find the answer to all their problems." Given these challenges, the pamphlet encouraged its readers to pray and give money to the LeTourneau Foundation, which would funnel tax-deductible donations toward the projects.[42]

To elicit further support, LeTourneau spoke regularly during his preaching tours about his endeavors in Liberia and Peru, and he collected thousands of dollars in donations from sympathetic churches and missionary associations from around the country. Students and alumni of LeTourneau's university applied for positions on either his planning teams or on-location missionary teams. He likewise attracted a wide variety of applicants to work in the Liberian and Peruvian missions. Nearly all of the applicants agreed with LeTourneau's business-like way of doing ministry, arguing that they not only had the practical skills necessary for working in the jungles of South America and Africa but also the sense of "Christian mission." Their former and present occupations varied widely: some had just been released from military service; others were college students or had their local minister recommend them to LeTourneau; still others were former farmers looking for a fresh start. News of the Liberian and Peruvian projects made LeTourneau a man worth knowing in the business of Cold War evangelical missions.[43]

LeTourneau intended the Liberian and Peruvian endeavors to be work settlements that opened the areas surrounding them to increased capital investment and production. The goals in Liberia were relatively straightforward: land heavy earthmoving equipment near the western coast settlement of Baffu Bay; set up a base of operations for this equipment, staffed with competent and trained personnel; clear the land in the immediate area and put it to "some experimentally productive use"; teach local populations how to operate and maintain equipment; and, finally, develop schools and churches to "advance Christianity among the natives involved with the project." The goals were much the same in Peru, and at both sites LeTourneau hand-picked a director and instructed him (always a man) to staff the project with willing, well-trained, "Christian" personnel. LeTourneau referred to these personnel as "technical missionaries" who could "handle a Bulldozer as well as a Bible." As LeTourneau saw it, "Machinery in the hands of Christ-loving, twice-born men can help [Peruvians] to listen to the story of Jesus and His love." Relying on such evangelical leaders and laborers, LeTourneau expected a worldwide revolution: "We can't feed the world, but our machinery in the hands of consecrated Christians can open the door to let us in and open the door of the hearts to let the Lord come in, and then the initiative which they lack will come, and that, plus the teaching in the use of machinery will enable them to feed themselves."[44]

LeTourneau's proposed projects not only made him even more popular in evangelical circles. A number of blue chip companies also took notice. In 1959, LeTourneau's son Roy corresponded with Gulf Oil, a Mobil Oil subsidiary, and agreed to build a road from the north banks of the Aguaytia River to their drilling sites, in exchange for which LeTourneau would receive a 3 percent commission from any oil or gas profits that Gulf Oil produced out of the sites. Although R. G. LeTourneau thought this commission "sound[ed] like a mighty small royalty," the contract nevertheless tied his company to the oil business.[45] LeTourneau would continue to contribute to the rise of the global oil economy, both in South America and in other parts of the world. In fact, he had already done so. For instance, in the early 1950s, a war veteran and young executive named George H. W. Bush started a company, Zapata, with the intent of exploring off-shore oil deposits in the Gulf of Mexico. In 1954, he contracted with LeTourneau to build an electric-powered, off-shore drilling platform. The designs that LeTourneau provided were revolutionary from an engineering perspective. LeTourneau's oil rigs helped make Bush one of the richest men in Texas and opened up oil exploration in the Gulf of Mexico and the Persian Gulf. In turn, the design branded LeTourneau as more than an evangelical earthmover. It also marked him as a shrewd businessman interested in advancing the interests of the postwar oil industry.[46]

Oil, however, was not the only commodity worth pursuing. In Liberia, a visitor from *The New Yorker* reported in 1952 that LeTourneau had "been ceded virtual control of ten thousand acres in the Baffu Bay area." There, LeTourneau planned for workers to "engage in lumbering, the mechanized cultivation of rice, and possibly in the raising of livestock, peanuts, and pineapples, along with palm oil, coco, coffee, rubber, bananas, raffia, and other tree crops." Of these products, lumber and rubber interested LeTourneau the most. Along with a newly developed "tree rolling" bulldozer, the tree stinger that LeTourneau developed for road clearance proved useful in the Amazonian and Liberian jungles, encouraging deforestation for the dual purpose of felling profitable hardwoods and clearing land for agriculture. In Liberia, LeTourneau's machines harvested a wide variety of native woods. By the early 1960s, a working saw mill increased production, but it did not fully solve all the problems of industrial lumbering. As one observer noted, "Getting marketable trees out of the high bush to the sawmill site, cut into lumber, and shipped to Monrovia[,] the capital city of Liberia, is a real adventure." Trees were abundant, but trees of marketable value were not. Hence, a number of trees cut by the mill remained at the mission site for use in the construction of employee housing and poultry houses. Raising chickens was an offhand enterprise, as LeTourneau envisioned the reproduction of southern agriculture and agribusiness in the lands cleared by his tree stingers and tree rollers. In Peru, LeTourneau reported that "Extensive experimentation

has been done in agricultural products, [including] poultry, hogs, and cattle."
In general, "the products grown in our southern states do well there," and
LeTourneau imagined that production would not only increase but industrial-
ize in the coming years. Already by 1962, the mechanized means for "butcher-
ing, packaging, and freezing the produce" were established in Tournavista, Peru,
with future plans "call[ing] for entering [in] poultry raising, rubber production,
canning, and eventually manufacturing." Land cleared by LeTourneau and other
developers also ushered in a new industry in Peruvian beef.[47] LeTourneau had a
corresponding interest in Liberia's rubber crops. Since the 1930s, Firestone Tire
and Rubber Company and LeTourneau had been cooperating in the development of heavy-duty, oversized tires for LeTourneau's earthmovers and transports.
By standardizing rubber tree production in Liberia, LeTourneau expected—
like Henry Ford before him in Fordlandia—a fair return on his investment.
One in-house estimate concluded that rubber production might reach as high
as 14,000 metric tons by the project's twentieth year. To facilitate production,
LeTourneau's intended to house his laborers on both small- and large-scale rubber plantations, extracting rubber for sale in the US tire market and, perhaps, for
use on LeTourneau's own machines. Likewise, those he employed in Peru and
Liberia also worked lumbering hardwoods for export to American and European
markets. LeTourneau paid his laborers, although records did not detail their
exact wages in full. (In one report, he noted that he once paid Liberian workers "a little above the going wage," approximately 50 cents per hour, for clearing
a dense jungle by machete. He did this to compare their wages to the cost of
a LeTourneau machine doing the same job, but it can be inferred that he viewed
unskilled work as "worth" approximately this "going wage.") Exploiting cheap
labor, however, was not LeTourneau's long-term goal for either of his missions.
Hence, he paid his "technical missionaries," on average, between $200 and $350
per month ($1,500 to $2,500, inflation adjusted) to train local workers to use his
machines, primarily as a way around paying for what he deemed to be inefficient,
time-consuming work.[48]

Cheap, unskilled labor could not compete with slightly more expensive,
skilled labor, and LeTourneau preferred to develop the latter rather than depend
on the former. Moreover, he preferred to train "unskilled" laborers to become
bulldozer drivers and scraper experts. In other words, LeTourneau's Christian
mission was to "develop" labor. As he put it, "We hear a lot about exploiting labor
and exploiting the backwards countries. . . . It sounds better when we talk about
developing the backwards countries and perhaps we could talk about developing
labor." As he had done in his industrial plants, "development" included the visible hand of management in technical training and spiritual direction. That all of
his managers were white—and the Liberians and Peruvians were not—signaled
LeTourneau's views on race and self-sufficiency. Still, he thought that the costs of

bringing presumably "backwards" populations up to speed in terms of technical prowess and work ethic would be worth it in the end. "All this will cost money," LeTourneau admitted, "but it can be at least partially financed by the raw materials which are being taken out in the meantime." The sooner industrialists tackled the "underdevelopment" problem from this "long range development point of view instead of the short range or exploitation point of view," the better. Through a state-backed Cold War for freer trade, led by evangelicals like LeTourneau, the earth would become flatter. Or, as LeTourneau put it, "the sooner our world will become one world."[49]

To ensure the economic viability of both projects, LeTourneau gained the legal and political support of both the Liberian and Peruvian governments. In a contract with Liberia, LeTourneau's company agreed to make certain concessions in keeping with the government's desire to have LeTourneau "assist in the economic and social development of the country." LeTourneau received the assurance of "the right to import free from all customs duties, tariffs, and all other local and general taxes, all materials, equipment, and supplies for construction and operational purposes." Likewise, via a legislative act that established LeTourneau's company in Liberia, the government agreed to "encourage and assist labour supply and will use its offices to prevent infiltration of radical [likely meaning "communist"] elements that would cause interruption of the corporation's activities or stop production and be dangerous to the peace of the [Liberian] Republic."[50] In Peru, LeTourneau received similarly generous terms. There, he contracted to build 32 miles of the Trans-Andean Highway, which linked the Amazonian slopes with the Pacific Ocean. The highway was undertaken on the heels of the Point Four Program, a foreign aid and economic development policy overseen by the Truman administration. Intended for thirty-five countries, Point Four's goals approximated LeTourneau's: bring third world countries into the economic orbit of the United States, contain communism, foster private investment abroad, and organize world trade.[51] In addition, Point Four did not discourage the expansion of Christianity into its target zones, leading some religious leaders to cast the program as "a twentieth-century missionary vehicle for both democracy and Christianity."[52]

Working with state officials, LeTourneau joined a number of other American and European corporations in taking advantage of the political environment that Point Four created in the early 1950s, what one *New York Times* journalist called in 1955 Peru's "free enterprise and free exchange policy." If LeTourneau opened Peru and Liberia to foreign markets and increased corporatization, he did not do so without complications. Financial and logistical problems dogged the Liberian and Peruvian projects from the start. Both usually ran at a loss, sometimes in the hundreds of thousands of dollars. In addition to organizational inefficiency and wasteful spending, "serious problems developed," surmised LeTourneau's son and on-site manager, "because pastors and congregations [in the Liberian project] could not reconcile the spending of thousands of dollars for machines, equipment, and commercial activities with the Christian message of love." The unwillingness of LeTourneau and his employees to "distribute its 'wealth' freely to all who had a need" led to an inability "to reconcile the concept of 'you must work for what you receive' with the charitable nature of Christianity and what appeared to them, an abundance of wealth." Richard LeTourneau termed this sort of thinking a "limited cultural understanding" and "obviously . . . not the teaching of Christianity," but he admitted that it served as a major obstacle. In the end, the "true concepts of free enterprise and Christianity blending together was understood by very few of the people in the area."[53]

Blaming LeTourneau's "subjects" was an excuse. Government graft, political instability and unpredictability, and broad differences of opinion about the purpose of industry created tensions between LeTourneau and the Liberian government. In Peru, undercapitalization slowed the project, although it also suffered from a lack of in-depth planning for construction and ministerial projects, the rapid regrowth of brush and vegetation in cleared lands, and irresponsible budgeting. Local Catholic activists protested LeTourneau's attempt to create a "Protestant nucleus" in the jungles while the experimental nature of LeTourneau's machinery tended to increase costs and create work stoppages.[54] LeTourneau's interest in Liberia and Peru started to fade. In 1966, he closed the books on the Liberian project and began considering a shuttering of the Peruvian venture.

Three years later, LeTourneau died of a stroke. By then, his ventures in Liberia and Peru were basically moribund. Most of the land and infrastructure that LeTourneau leased or developed had either been turned over to the Liberian or Peruvian governments or was about to be. In Liberia, the extractive side was, according to one memo, "phased out" while the missionary side was folded into the programs of the Christian Nationals Evangelism Commission, a California-based evangelical organization with which LeTourneau had ties. In Peru, the new military government simply declared LeTourneau's contract nullified on the grounds that he had not completed developmental work in the assigned area to its satisfaction. As a result, Peruvian officials moved in 1970 to catalog the land and holdings, successfully pressuring LeTourneau's remaining personnel to abandon the project.[55]

Christian Businessmen Go International

LeTourneau's flat earth vision floundered in Africa and South America, revealing the limits of his free-market mission. But he nevertheless played an important role in the internationalization of another vehicle for corporate evangelicalism, the CBMCI. LeTourneau served as president for the prescribed one-year term (1952–1953). But he never left the CBMCI's administration, staying on as both a board member and one of the group's foremost cheerleaders and consultants.

CBMCI members met the Cold War world with a mix of anxiety and ambition. Citing the Gospel of John's ninth chapter, a CBMCI form letter in 1959 declared, "The night cometh when no man can work." Quoting Indian Prime Minister Jawaharlal Nehru, an architect of Indian independence and, ironically, a secular socialist, the CBMCI claimed, "The world is on the brink of disaster." The most devastating war in human history had laid the groundwork for a new war: an ideological, political, economic, and spiritual struggle against the Soviet Union and its suspected communist allies, whether in China, Eastern Europe, or even the United States. Americans, according to the CBMCI, were in need of spiritual revival.[56]

In some places, the revival had already commenced. Since war's end, CBMCI members had organized dozens of "Crusades for Christ" and regional conferences in cities such as Atlantic City, Washington, D.C., and Minneapolis; growing cities like Charlotte, North Carolina; newly built suburbs like Lakeland, Florida; and secluded spots like the ocean-view Christian retreat at Mount Hermon, California. Members cold-called and sent solicitations to businessmen identified by CBMCI members as people "who might be interested in the establishment of a Christian Business Men's Committee in your area." The CBMCI published brand-name merchandise, including bookmarks, advertisements, and calendars for businessmen to hang in their homes or offices, denoting membership and containing "sixteen devotional messages by CBMCI men." Official CBMCI letterhead linked corporate capitalism with urbane, modern Christian identity, overlaying the organization's logo on a port city, bustling with global commerce, with a New York City–style skyline of skyscrapers in the background. Conservative Christianity was in the midst of the scene. The CBMCI brand of fundamentalism was cast as a part of the hustle and bustle of mid-century corporate America.[57]

By 1960, the CBMCI boasted of "450 Committees of men who know the Lord, banded together throughout the world with the objective of trying to win men to Christ." At annual meetings, the CBMCI focused on the continuing push for revival, though it also addressed the everyday concerns of many Americans: business ethics, family life, employer–employee relations, and— given the Cold War—nuclear war and "world problems." The CBMCI's political concerns were a sign of its international reach. By 1955, it ran loosely affiliated "international" branches of evangelical businessmen's groups. For one crusade in Honolulu, Hawaii, organized on the island because of its location close to members in the Pacific Rim and Asia, members envisioned as on the front lines against Chinese communists, CBMCI officials hoped to "get CBMCI men and their wives to come from Japan, Korea, Formosa, Hong Kong, the Philippines, India, Ceylon, Australia and New Zealand." By 1963, the CBMCI held additional conferences in Sweden, Switzerland, and Scotland (See Fig. 3.1).[58]

The CBMCI's membership remained primarily fundamentalist and premillenialist, but in keeping with past practice, it kept its door open to a wider variety of evangelicals. Most members were evangelical businessmen—like LeTourneau—in denominations that retained fundamentalist leanings, or they were like Taylor, conservative in theological preference but perhaps members of denominations and churches that tilted more liberal. All were businessmen, whether executives at major companies or middle managers and professionals. One group, however, tended to stay outside CBMCI membership: Pentecostals.

Though "higher life" and holiness groups had been in the mix of early-twentieth-century Protestantism and overlapped with fundamentalists into the 1920s, division set in during the 1930s, inspired in part by Pentecostal self-separation and forced in part by fundamentalist purges. LeTourneau actually symbolized Pentecostal–fundamentalist–new evangelical divergences. LeTourneau had grown up in the premillenialist Plymouth Brethren and moved into the Christian and Missionary Alliance. The latter became more welcoming of Pentecostal members by the 1940s, but LeTourneau remained aloof from the charismatic signs of the Holy Spirit, all while retaining a certain premillennial

Figure 3.1 Members of the Christian Business Men's Committee, International gather for a meeting in 1951. R. G. LeTourneau is seated third from the right on the front row.
Courtesy of Margaret Estes Library, LeTourneau University.

vision of the world's destiny. "Moving men and mountains," as his autobiography put it, was not out of line with a view that expected the end times, especially if engineering and earthmoving garnered profits that could be used to spread the gospel before the trumpets sounded and Christ returned. LeTourneau was also not a hairsplitter about collaboration, thus making him more on the new evangelicals' side. Hence, he remained in the CBMCI's orbit.

Others in his denomination did not, joining with "spirit filled" businessmen to form a new group of Pentecostal businessmen: the Full Gospel Business Men's Fellowship, International (FGBMFI). Demos Shakarian, a California dairy heir and executive, set up the FGBMFI as an extension of his revival organizing, a mission that expanded into mutual support, financial interchange, and religious debate and collaboration. The grandson of Armenian immigrants, Shakarian had been raised in a Pentecostal home in Los Angeles. In 1905, around the same time as the famed Azusa Street revival began in Los Angeles, Isaac Shakarian immigrated to America and saved enough money from a job as a newsboy to start Reliance Dairy Farm in Downey, California. In the interwar period, the company quickly grew into a major regional and national milk supplier, and the Shakarian family became notable members of a middle-class Pentecostal community in the Golden State. By 1943, Shakarian was head of the world's largest dairy, with 3,000 cows. Joining his father in the family business—which after World War II included real estate and a series of drive-in "dairy stores"—Shakarian threw himself into streamlining the business, often with high-tech techniques. By 1960, Reliance relied on a complicated quarantining and transportation strategy to cut down on the chance of contamination and spoilage. Shakarian also adopted what the *Los Angeles Times* reported as "the modern method of artificial insemination," whereby Reliance used a bull that Shakarian had purchased from the Pabst beer–brewing family after a revival in Milwaukee to create a company stock of "400 daughters with 1000 or more others assured in years to come from sperm frozen at 350 deg[rees] below zero." As a Pentecostal, Shakarian did not agree with the Pabst family business. But he apparently showed no trepidation about technologies that were good for business. As for LeTourneau, technology made Shakarian's private-sector work more efficient and effective.[59]

Shakarian's enthusiasm for modern business overlapped with his religious work. Like Taylor or LeTourneau, Shakarian sought spiritual miracles through collaboration and careful organizing, fundraising, and planning. Hoping for a postwar Pentecostal revival to match the crusading of Billy Graham, Shakarian collaborated with local ministers and businessmen on his off-days, helping to organize Pentecostal-style revivals and "spiritual healing meetings" in southern California. In 1951, he worked with 300 ministers to bring the nationally famous Pentecostal revivalist Oral Roberts to Los Angeles for a city-wide revival. After the revival, Roberts urged Shakarian to consider inviting other businessmen to set up a more formal Pentecostal businessmen's group, one that accepted Pentecostals of all stripes. For Roberts, having such a collection of business-men behind him would offer the evangelist a base for future revivals and dona-tions, both in booming postwar California and elsewhere. But for Pentecostal businessmen specifically and postwar Pentecostalism generally, such a group seemed likely to create the social and economic capital necessary for the growth of adherents and social legitimacy. As Shakarian later reflected in a written remembrance of his conversation with Roberts, the group would be Pentecostal without hard-and-fast boundaries: "Healing. Tongues. Deliverance. Whatever the man's experience, he could talk about it, just as it happened." But it would also be edifying for "Laymen" and "Ordinary people" because there was no place for proscriptive theories of spiritual experience or sectarian theology. "They tell what they've actually experienced of God to other men like themselves," wrote Shakarian, "men who might not believe what a preacher said—even someone like [Oral Roberts]—but who will listen to a plumber or a dentist or a salesman because they're plumbers and dentists and salesmen themselves."[60]

Established shortly after Roberts's revival in 1951, the FGBMFI grew by leaps and bounds in the 1950s and 1960s through a decentralized campaign analogous to how many Pentecostal churches had grown in a previous gen-eration. Independent ministers and businessmen ran local membership drives that generally resulted in the establishment of longer term, local chapters of the FGBMFI. Two years after its incorporation, the FGBMFI had its own publi-cation, Voice. In its first issue, Shakarian detailed the origins of the fellowship, its cross-denominational Pentecostal nature, and its commitment "to muster a force of Business Men across the nation, and around the world, unitedly work-ing for the cause of Lord Jesus Christ[.]" Organizationally, the fellowship's board consisted of midlevel owners or executives at businesses strewn from North Carolina to California. Theologically, the fellowship was inclusive in its Pentecostalism, much like the CBMCI and the CWF had been with its funda-mentalism. Regarding business practice, it was also little different than other businessmen's fellowships, at times exuding a hint of Roberts's prosperity theol-ogy. (Roberts was famous for requesting audiences to plant a "seed faith," which would inevitably result in a substantial financial return. Roberts also lauded busi-nessmen and for-profit businesses as agents of financial and spiritual revival.)[61]

The FGBMFI was decidedly probusiness and in favor of Pentecostalism in the workplace. According to Voice editor and publisher Thomas Nickel, "Religion in Business Brings Sure Success." An inaugural homily by G. H. Montgomery—the associate editor of Healing Waters magazine, a popular Pentecostal publication—denounced sin, sickness, fear, and death. He also denounced poverty, which was not of heaven, "which speaks of bounty and wealth on every hand." Poverty was "of the devil," who used poverty to keep spirit-filled people "from going forward with missionary programs, from building churches, launching revival campaigns, and keeping the men of God in the field where they should be." Gushing vignettes extolled the lives and work of successful Pentecostal businessmen like Hugh Graham, the vice president of the Utah-based Cal-U-Nite mineral fertilizer corporation, and Miner Arganbright and his associates, who ran a construction and real estate business in Los Angeles and had "palatial homes and landscaped estates in the highlands of La Cresenta."[62] The fellowship also held annual conventions, the first in Los Angeles and attended by several thousand Pentecostals, including a who's who list of speakers and independent ministers: Oral Roberts, Jack Coe, Gordon Lindsay, Tommy Hicks, Raymond T. Richey, and O. L. Jaggers. By the next annual convention in Washington, D.C., the fellowship was on the national political map. In 1954, Vice President Richard Nixon visited the proceedings.[63]

Like the CBMCI, the FGBMFI was initially an all-male organization and thereby affirmed the religious authority of men in local churches, businesses, communities, and the nation at large. Breaking from previous trendsetters in Pentecostalism, such as Aimee Semple McPherson, Shakarian's fellowship also cut counter to the movement's historic fluidity concerning racial lines. *Voice*, the organization's magazine, illustrated the change. The businessmen featured in *Voice*'s early vignettes about spirit-filled success were white. If women attended meetings, they also participated in a mostly marginal fashion. While it affirmed hierarchies of race and gender, the FGBMFI sought cross-class solidarity, reaching out to like-minded working-class and middle-class Americans. Still, through dress and demeanor, Pentecostal businessmen presented themselves as comfortable with conspicuous consumption and corporate culture. Chapter meetings occurred in four- and five-star hotels and had a dignified air about them. Invitations were sent to non-Pentecostal missionary groups and even to the desks of nonreligious businessmen. According to one historian, the by-product of FGBMFI's work was two-fold. "At the banquets of the 'Full Gospel Business Men' [non-Pentecostals] were brought together with Pentecostals in a context that fitted their place in society," which was increasingly in the middle and executive class. The goal was not just social legitimacy. Pentecostals wanted "a hearing for the healing evangelists [like Oral Roberts] in the non-Pentecostal churches" and the movement of Pentecostals "beyond the stage of the sect." In 1960, two visitors to a FGBMFI meeting related the class trappings and "mainstream" appearance of the group, commenting on its relatively staid, Rotary-like character. "Watch out for emotionalism, we warned each other—shouting, arm waving, frenzied testimonies," they remembered fifteen years later, "We watched . . . and nothing of the sort occurred." Rather, Shakarian and his businessmen "conducted the meetings with the hushed sensitivity of one who listened for a voice we could not hear. Instead of the chaos we expected, a restrained and orderly joy governed the convention."

Over the next decade, the FGBMFI set up nearly 300 chapters and boasted 100,000 members. It spawned a number of offshoot groups, including Women's Aglow Fellowship, a Pentecostal women's group. By 1972, Shakarian reported that membership had hit 300,000 and the organization's annual budget topped $1 million. Many new Pentecostal ministers owed Shakarian about as much as non-Pentecostal fundamentalists like Billy Graham owed R. G. LeTourneau and other corporate sponsors. Oral Roberts benefitted from Shakarian's support, but so too did Pat and Jan Crouch's Trinity Broadcasting Network, founded in 1973.[64] Two of the cofounders and first stars of the network eventually became important figures in evangelical business history, selling all sorts of new fantasies and consumer experiences to evangelicals and nonevangelicals alike. Their names were Jim and Tammy Faye Bakker.

"A Good Business Investment"

Fundamentalists—especially those allied with the new evangelicalism—also sought new flocks in the 1950s and 1960s. In tandem with the CBMCI and FGBMFI, independent fundamentalist organizations set up in the 1930s and 1940s continued to spark interest from big businessmen intent on spreading their faith in a Cold War world. YFC kept operating as a business-minded evangelical organization, even after Billy Graham's departure. Businessmen remained important donors and participants at rallies. In addition to standbys like the CBMCI and Herbert J. Taylor, the Pew Foundation had taken an interest in YFC and provided a $10,000 grant in 1958 for a financial drive. YFC administrators also were "hopeful for favorable consideration from the Crowell Trust along and one or two other foundations."[65] By YFC's fifteenth annual convention in 1959, the participation of businessmen was ritualized as an "annual laymen's luncheon." Harry R. Smith, the vice president of Bank of America, joined YFC trustee Herbert Taylor as featured speakers, followed by a "huge patriotic rally" featuring John Noble, a "former communist prisoner." The language and logic of Washington, D.C., and Wall Street penetrated YFC. In the late 1940s, YFC created "a Spiritual Marshall Plan" in tandem with the economic aid program just started by the Truman administration to contain communism in Europe. YFC sought to raise the ambitious amount of $50 million per year until 1951, taking advantage of tax breaks for charitable donations to attract what one report termed "parties ... who now spend huge amounts of money without significant co-operation or co-ordination e.g. with revival movements." Creating a nonprofit YFC foundation allowed wealthy donors or corporations a tax break while helping YFC "make use of all publicity-media like, press, radio, and film." Such Wall Street logic informed YFC pitches to other "investors." According to their 1962 "World" Program, YFC was "a good business investment" for evangelicals and executives alike. "You, too, can have a part in one of the most significant programs for teen-agers on a world-wide basis," YFC claimed. It was not overestimating its reach. By the late 1950s, YFC was operating in more than a dozen countries. Pitches for investments highlighted its global work: leadership training schools in Europe, the Middle East, Africa, and India; a subsidy for a "Spanish teen-age magazine"; direct assistance to YFC groups and conferences in Europe and the Americas, as well as "assistance to overseas nationals training in [the] U.S." Individuals could donate, but YFC also made room for "12 corporations to invest $2,500 [$18,700, inflation adjusted] each."[66]

YFC competed against other postwar upstarts, such as Bill Bright's Campus Crusade for Christ (CCFC). Formerly a California candy manufacturer, Bright founded CCFC at the University of California, Los Angeles in 1951 and became famous in evangelical circles for his ability to get business leaders—evangelical or otherwise—to dig deep into their pockets for evangelism. Jon Braun, who joined CCFC in 1960, remembered that "Bright tended to surround himself with guys who were wealthy ... [and] most of them tended to be Republican conservatives." Bright's appeal to conservative businessmen was straightforward. "A careful examination," he once wrote, "of the Communist strategy to capture the college campuses of America reveals that it *is* happening here." University faculty members were especially suspect, as "hundreds of professors are known to be Communists while thousands of their colleagues are known sympathizers." By contributing to CCFC, then, businessmen assured the extension of evangelicalism onto college campuses, thus undercutting communism's appeal among American youth. Bright could be particularly aggressive when seeking donors. Even after almost twenty-five years of fundraising, he did not let up. As David Hubbard, president of Fuller Seminary, told *Newsweek*'s Kenneth Woodward in 1976, "Whenever I go and meet a wealthy person, I find that Bill Bright has been there first."[67]

CCFC fit into a larger network of money and right-wing politics while crossing the lines that the new evangelicals endeavored to set up between themselves and more radical groups. CCFC received support from business leaders who supported fringe groups like the John Birch Society, the Christian Anti-Communist Crusade, and Christian Crusade. Peter Gillquist, a CCFC staffer in the 1960s, remembered that Bright "had a lot of John Birchers supporting [Campus] Crusade [for Christ], a lot of men that were very politically conservative, like the Hunt brothers and others that really saw [Campus] Crusade [for Christ] as the answer to the spreading threat of communism on the campus." Nelson Bunker Hunt and William Herbert Hunt, whose father H. L. Hunt joined with a wide range of radical radio broadcasters and Carl McIntire's tirades against the Federal Communications Commission, was also behind CCFC, although Bright did not depend solely on the family's oil money. As historian John Turner noted, CCFC was a popular organization in the most conservative regions of the country, especially "in Texas—ranchers and oilmen were major contributors— and the Sunbelt, particularly Arizona and Southern California." A few other big businessmen in the new evangelical nexus, such as Herbert J. Taylor and J. Howard Pew, also granted CCFC intermittent support or at least fielded letters from CCFC administrators in the late 1950s and 1960s. Regardless of who was behind CCFC, Bright was a tireless fundraiser. By the 1970s, he had secured tens of millions of dollars in contributions. In addition, CCFC enjoyed the support and administrative lead of entertainment star Roy Rogers, Nelson Bunker Hunt, and Holiday Inn's chairman Wallace E. Johnson, all of whom served on the fundraising committee for "Here's Life," CCFC's most ambitious evangelistic campaign.[68]

The big businessmen's campaign on behalf of younger Americans—from YFC to CCFC to smaller groups like Young Life and Intervarsity Christian Fellowship—ran parallel to private educational activities funded by corporate interests. LeTourneau's college was one foray into private education, but corporate money flew toward many magnetic educational centers on the evangelical landscape. Evangelical colleges, of course, were not new. Both before and after American universities and colleges moved away from religious curricula and embraced what historian George Marsden termed "established nonbelief," conservative evangelicals founded dozens of small colleges devoted to blending pastoral or humanitarian training with formal education in theology, biblical studies, the humanities and sciences, or some combination of each. The exact degree of engagement between college-age evangelical students and the outside world varied. Some, such as Moody Bible Institute in Chicago or the Bible Institute of Los Angeles, focused almost solely on instruction in theology and exegesis. Others, such as Wheaton College, affirmed the new evangelicalism. At Wheaton after World War II, board members routinely consisted of evangelical theologians and businessmen, not a few of whom were executives at ServiceMaster. As an evangelical liberal arts school, Wheaton had a different mission than a Bible institute. It trained students in evangelical theological principles while encouraging graduates to mimic the National Association of Evangelicals and BGEA, engaging with broader American culture, with the hope of changing it as pastors or laypersons (it was a coed evangelical school, although it upheld conservative teachings regarding male and female roles in family or church life).

Other independent schools were like LeTourneau College, eschewing pastoral training altogether and focusing on lay training for the private sector. Others had a political edge. For instance, at George S. Benson's Harding College in rural Arkansas, Wall Streeters were speakers at lecture series on "Christian Americanism," including Sterling Morton, director of the US Chamber of Commerce; Colonel Robert S. Henry, an associate of J. J. Pelly, president of the American Association of Railroads; Montgomery Ward's Raymond H. Fogler; and James L. Kraft, president of Kraft-Phoenix Cheese Corporation. J. Howard Pew showed an interest in Harding's programs, giving money and keeping up a semiregular correspondence with Benson. Undetermined amounts of money also came in from representatives at DuPont, General Motors, Standard Oil, US Steel, Bethlehem Steel, Republic Steel, Armco Steel, International Harvester, and Quaker Oats. By 1964, the Harding's National Education Program had also produced more than fifty high-quality films, most costing millions of dollars garnered from Benson's widespread network of corporate supporters. One film—*Communism on the Map*—became a staple in American schools, service, clubs, industrial plants, and political forums. An observer of the American political scene in 1967 estimated that more than 15 million Americans had seen the film, a testament to Benson's broad reach.[69]

The National Education Program spawned franchises in "Christian Americanism" at numerous other evangelical colleges from Texas to Oregon. Students educated at Harding—and at a smattering of other small denominational and evangelical schools in the Ozarks area—also served as forerunners to the executive class at several important postwar evangelical businesses while college administrators and departments developed formal and informal connections with companies, such as Wal-Mart. Bob Jones University, however, showed perhaps the clearest route to professional or political influence, training a variety of conservative leaders.[70] As a fundamentalist liberal arts school, the new Bob Jones University in Greenville, South Carolina (the college's move from Tennessee was made possible via a sales pitch by the local Chamber of Commerce and a fundraising drive for the campus) served as an incubator for dozens of elected officials, pastors, and missionaries as well as business executives like Ed Atsinger III and Stuart Epperson and evangelical writers and activists like Tim LaHaye.[71]

Up-and-coming conservative politicians also tapped into the institutional base that evangelical colleges provided. While building links between themselves and evangelicals in California, Barry Goldwater and Ronald Reagan spoke at Pepperdine College and other evangelical schools. Pepperdine, in particular, was on the corporate dole. In 1950, big businessmen saved the school from going bankrupt after George Pepperdine, the auto parts executive who founded it, went bankrupt. By 1957, fundraising and networking by school officials had stabilized the school's budget. The chairman of the university's President's Council was J. H. Smith, a Seven-Up executive who, according to an alumni newspaper, had been "in business in California since the 1920s" and was "prominent in

Southland affairs." Henry Salvatori, the founder and head of Western Geophysical Company, the nation's largest geophysical contracting company in the 1950s and early 1960s, maintained a close relationship with the college, making contributions ranging from a few thousand dollars to tens of thousands of dollars in the 1960s. Oilman Frank R. Seaver and his wife Blanche—personal friends of George Pepperdine—were also important contributors to the university. Their most impressive contribution came after Pepperdine's death, helping the school move from Watts to Malibu in the aftermath of the 1965 riots. During the school's geographic relocation, Blanche Seaver reportedly gave millions "toward the construction of Pepperdine University's Malibu campus." The secluded campus, far from the urban core, matched the privatization ethic of the politicians and evangelicals who saw suburbs and edge cities as places to preach and stump for votes and donors. It also accorded with broader trends. Indeed, in the 1950s and 1960s, the domestic landscape of evangelical business was undergoing revolutionary change toward the ever-more private and even-more political.[72]

With so many big businessmen interested in making conservative evangelicalism into a viable social and religious movement, it was unsurprising that conservative evangelicals also worked to bring their perspectives on faith and enterprise into corporate America. Of course, evangelicals had been shaping big-business culture for over a century. (The shop-floor religion of LeTourneau could be traced back to the first time a pastor was invited to preach in the workplace of pre–Civil War America.) But running heavy machinery and manufacturing earthmovers was different from working in the post–World War II American economy, one increasingly defined by new types of work and new kinds of workplaces. As a result, conservative evangelicals followed the new contours of postwar corporate America, as the nation's economy shifted from the north to the southwest, from industrial work to service work, from New Deal liberalism to corporate libertarianism. In the process, evangelicals not only received help from big business. Conservative evangelicalism became big business.

PART II

HOW CONSERVATIVE EVANGELICALISM BECAME BIG BUSINESS

4

Marketplace Missions

Chick-fil-A and the Evangelical Business Sector

Would-be customers walking down a suburban shopping mall concourse on a Sunday in the late 1960s would have noticed something odd about Chick-fil-A. No one was behind the counter. It was closed for the day.

Incorporated by S. Truett Cathy in 1964 in Atlanta, Georgia, Chick-fil-A made cheap, accessible food available in shopping malls, thereby extending the time that customers might spend there. That made Cathy's company attractive to mall owners and laid the groundwork for the now ubiquitous mall food court. Hence, in the 1970s and 1980s, Chick-fil-A became a fixture in malls scattered around the perimeter of metropolitan Atlanta, with more than 100 locations by 1980. Six years later, this number had risen to 315 mall units in thirty-one states. All followed a common creed: they were closed on Sunday.[1]

Since 1946, when he and his brother Ben went into business together, Cathy had run a small diner called the Dwarf Grill. (The name referred to the diner's diminutive space.) After a strenuous opening week, Cathy decided it best to take a break and close the diner each Sunday. This decision also accorded with his religious upbringing. Cathy was a Baptist, and good Baptists did not—or at least, he thought, should not—open for business on Sunday.

Obviously, closing for a day creates problems for any enterprise, slicing potential sales by at least a seventh. This was especially true for Chick-fil-A. As more businesses nationwide opened their doors on Sundays in the 1960s and 1970s, Sundays became high-traffic days at malls. In general, mall owners discouraged closing, as they expected maximum sales per unit of mall space leased. But for Cathy, these problems reaffirmed the value of closing on Sunday. Cathy affirmed the long-standing evangelical theology of the divine contract; he expected immediate and guaranteed rewards for faithful service. And the results seemed to prove him right. Despite the obstacles closing on Sunday posed, Chick-fil-A showed profits year after year. Cathy felt that this was God's work since, by any other estimation, Chick-fil-A should not have enjoyed continued growth. As Cathy later reflected, "God blessed the seventh day and sanctified it, set it aside. It is made for man, not man for it." Such divine decrees, believed Cathy, were granted "not to make life hard but to make it better." By honoring the Sabbath, Cathy "accepted that as a principle and honored God by doing it." In return, "God . . . honored us and the business because of it." Indeed, the Fourth Commandment, like the Bible in general, was "the formula God has given us for success." If he opened seven days a week, Cathy might literally "miss the blessing" that God wished to grant him as an affirmation of his obedience and devotion to the sensible, godly contract of staying closed on Sunday.[2]

For Cathy, Sunday closing was also like Graham's crusades or Marion Wade's corporate embodiment of Christian service or R. G. LeTourneau's Liberian or Peruvian mission. It was a means of corporate revival, of making and experiencing religion via corporate capitalism. Moreover, Sunday closing was a way to inject his business-friendly religion into contemporary conversations— conversations defined by a series of legal, religious, cultural, and social revolutions. Sunday closing, to be sure, was involuntary and a problem for employees who might want or need to work seven days per week. But, in keeping with new laws like Title VII of the Civil Rights Act, employees were not hired, fired, demoted, or promoted based on their feelings about Sunday closing.

By the 1980s, Chick-fil-A was so unique among fast-food restaurants that its Sunday closing policy was the equivalent of a totem for conservative evangelicals, a symbol that represented the proper posture that conservative people of faith could and should hold toward corporate culture or American society in general. This was because the 1960s and 1970s were revolutionary years for evangelical conservatives. As the legal and customary underpinnings of white supremacy and patriarchy fell away, evangelical business owners were no less alarmed or energized than their counterparts in evangelical churches, grassroots organizations, or upstart political lobbies.

Very few evangelical executives went public with their political opinions about specific candidates or elections. But the Christian cultures of their companies reflected conservative assumptions about work, the state, race, and gender. At Chick-fil-A, Sunday closing complemented other practices—hiring standards, community relations, executive proclamations, tax-exempt philanthropic endeavors—that made the business sector an activist space for evangelical executives like Cathy. A "Christian" company was the evangelical business world's version of a picket line or political rally. And, because many companies, such as Chick-fil-A, were privately owned, their activism had many forms.

Location and context mattered to a company's style of engagement. Conservative evangelicals had a long history as a northern, national, and transnational venture. But by the 1960 and 1970s, evangelical activists were flourishing in other locales. They organized in southern denominations, in racial powder kegs in the Deep South, and in southern churches and communities. At the same time, Chick-fil-A and other evangelical businesses birthed in the 1960s and 1970s developed in racially charged and socially fragmenting urban and suburban contexts, especially in what journalist Kevin Phillips termed "the Sunbelt" states in the southern half of the country.

Sunbelt evangelicals could be assertive because they enjoyed both the material and spiritual benefits of a booming regional economy. Sparked by federal spending and waves of corporate and residential migrations, the Sunbelt economy—based largely around agribusiness, oil and gas, high technology, retail, tourism, and defense—flourished in the 1940s and 1950s, as evidenced by the economic ventures of LeTourneau and other southern elites, such as W. Maxey Jarman and Howard E. Butt Jr. Other Sunbelt evangelicals, from hoteliers like Cecil B. Day and William Walton to industrial magnates like Lonnie "Bo" Pilgrim, extended the mission and meaning of the evangelical "faith at work."

The Sunbelt was an important site of evangelical business activity. But so too were other arenas, namely the struggling industrial cores of the "Rust Belt" as well as a handful of sectors like heavy industry and industrial design, especially in older evangelical centers like Herbert Taylor's native Michigan and adoptive Illinois. Moreover, as in the 1960s and 1970s, the federal government shaped the course of the evangelical business sector. State provisions and case law, framed by antidiscriminatory laws like Title VII of the Civil Rights Act, encouraged a "free exercise" approach toward private businesses, tending to eschew regulation of workplace religion when supposedly "non-coercive." For smaller businesses, the law was often nonbinding, granting relatively free range for religious expression or coercion in the workplace. Thus, for as much as Cathy and other evangelical businessmen might thank God for showering their business with blessings, the state shaped the business aspirations of conservative evangelicals, many of whom opened private-sector fronts in a culture war against the very state that enabled their corporate revivals in the first place.

A New Nation for Evangelical Business

Chick-fil-A and its contemporaries came of age in a new national context, particularly in terms of race and race relations. Though resisted by black activists and white sympathizers since the late nineteenth century, segregation remained a fact of American life well into the 1960s. Racial segregation and discrimination was a national phenomenon, supported by law in the South and by local practice—to varying degrees, particularly in housing and employment—nationwide. The federal government also endorsed segregation through the New Deal, which largely deferred to local officials with little to no interest in breaking down racial barriers. World War II, however, brought serious reexamination of segregation through the postwar desegregation of the armed forces and placement of army and navy bases. Activists who had been chipping around the edges of segregation began to make direct legal challenges. In 1954, *Brown v. Board of Education of Topeka* undercut the legal legitimacy of racial segregation in public schools and ended nearly sixty years of judicial endorsement of "separate, but equal." The next year, the Supreme Court reiterated its position, ordering that all racially exclusive segregated schools desegregate "with all deliberate speed." Local activists, black ministers, and civil rights organizations, who had been fighting segregation for decades, pushed the black freedom struggle into a new phase. In nearly every American municipality, the racial, economic, cultural, and political lines dividing the country came into question, often with life-or-death consequences. By 1960, a civil rights revolution was well underway.

White supremacy was more than a legal and political system. As civil rights activists, moderates, segregationists, and millions of other Americans understood, white supremacy was embedded in American capitalism itself. Race was a factor in nearly every aspect of economic life: banking, mortgages, real estate valuation, hiring and firing practices, property distribution, and a slew of other arrangements and exchanges grounded in "privacy rights" and private ownership. Thus, for civil rights activists nationwide, calls for fairer housing, union membership, or equal access to a lunch counter were assertions of both constitutional rights and economic rights. These actions not only divided the business communities in dozens of cities; they also overlapped with a series of public marches, public coverage of violent segregationist resistance in cities from Los Angeles to Detroit to Atlanta to Birmingham, and the concerns of federal officials and diplomats about the Cold War costs of prolonged civil rights protest. In 1963 and 1964, grassroots advocacy met political possibility, as southern Democrat Lyndon B. Johnson pushed the passage of a comprehensive civil rights bill after John F. Kennedy's assassination.

Though it dealt with many forms of discrimination, from segregated schools to voting prohibitions, the Civil Rights Act of 1964's most important provision concerning religion at work was Title VII. Regarding any employer "engaged in an industry affecting commerce who has twenty-five or more employees for each working day in each of twenty or more calendar weeks," Title VII outlawed employment discrimination based on race, color, national origin, or sex. (In 1972 the law expanded to cover state and local governments. Another amendment redefined "employer" to mean anyone employing fifteen persons or more instead of twenty-five.)[3] Title VII also prohibited religious discrimination, a point of particular importance for religiously affiliated businesses. In 1965, Congress established a federal agency, the Equal Employment Opportunity Commission (EEOC), to oversee complaints about workplace discrimination and ensure implementation of Title VII's provisions.[4] As with other discrimination claims, the EEOC began fielding charges of religious discrimination almost immediately. From 1967 to 1972, the number of such claims filed with the EEOC rose from 169 to 1,176; by 1984, it was over 3,000. To be sure, such claims were rarer than other discrimination claims. From 1965 to 1975, claims of religious discrimination amounted to around 2 percent of the total claims received by the EEOC. Still, by 1984, the EEOC had fielded over 40,000 claims of religious discrimination, averaging 2,000 per year or about forty per week.[5]

Title VII created a new legal landscape for evangelical business leaders. The previous generation could freely bring religion into the workplace and discriminate accordingly. LeTourneau could have hired or fired anyone at any of his plants based on religion. Title VII changed all this. Initially a well-intended but fuzzy law when it came to defining "religion" and "religious discrimination," the EEOC, Congress, and various courts clarified Title VII's intent. In 1967, the EEOC amended its guidelines to require employers to "accommodate" religion in the workplace unless such an accommodation caused "undue hardship" on the business or employer.[6]

But what *exactly* constituted "religion" and its "accommodation"? What was "undue hardship"? Title VII and the EEOC initially proffered no clear, universal, applicable, and enforceable definitions. Hence, in 1972, Congress defined what it meant by "religion" in the workplace, amending Title VII to read, "The term 'religion' includes all aspects of religious observance and practice, as well as belief, unless an employer demonstrates that he is unable to reasonably accommodate to an employee's or prospective employee's religious observance or practice without undue hardship on the conduct of the employer's business." As one scholar has noted, after the 1972 amendments, courts also "began to broadly interpret the definition of religion ... [including] everything from major to obscure religions, and even as far as self-proclaimed religions where the harmed party is the sole adherent." In such a new legal environment, all employers—evangelical ones included, of course—were incentivized to ensure corporate cultures ostensibly "open" to anyone's religion. The federal state and courts endorsed private-sector pluralism.[7]

Subsequent cases further clarified what forms of employer "religion" were acceptable in the workplace and how far employers or executives could go in promoting their form of religion. For instance, in 1975 a Fifth Circuit Court in *Young vs. Southwestern Savings & Loan Corporation* offered a firmer interpretation of unacceptable forms of workplace impressment, awarding damages to an atheist employee who left a company to avoid attending mandatory employee meetings that doubled as Christian devotionals. The Court concluded that employers could still hold such meetings in the workplace, under their right to "free exercise" under the First Amendment, but attendance and participation always had to be "voluntary" and decoupled from hiring, firing, promotion, and demotion. Voluntarism—making a personal, independent, and "uncoerced" decision to affirm a given religion—aligned with evangelical sensibilities and, ironically, empowered them to promote their religion in the American workplace as a take-it or leave-it proposition. In 1976, the Supreme Court clarified the legal definition of "voluntary," deciding that employers could present religious views in the workplace, but they could not harass employees or base employment on adherence to an employer's religious beliefs or practices. In 1977, after the Supreme Court's landmark decision in *TWA v. Hardison*, employers also had to "reasonably accommodate" an employee's religious practices, including but not limited to days off for Sabbath observance. At this point, however, employers won back a remarkable measure of religious authority. Accommodation had to occur without "undue hardship" on a company's everyday operations or bottom line. Employers, more often than not, would determine the meaning of both "undue" and "hardship," which could include monetary cost or loss of production. By siding more with "undue hardship" over "reasonable accommodation," the Supreme Court granted employers a slight edge over employees regarding the freedom of religion at work. After *TWA v. Hardison*, the proportion of plaintiffs winning religious accommodation cases against employers fell by half.[8]

For evangelicals specifically, Title VII's case history mattered because the for-profit business had historically been an important sphere of religious and cultural influence. More important, evangelical assumptions about racial and gendered authority rested on having the freedom to exercise their faith in the workplace. The essential "practicality" of a workplace religion or faith's contribution to corporate profits and social improvement had been used for decades to justify the authority of white male evangelicals. After Title VII, evangelicals had to be more selective and strategic about religious expression lest they land in court. Still, the EEOC and Court's stance on privileging the "free exercise" of religion at work—even before the Court assured free exercise in case law—granted a certain leeway. As long as executives, owners, and managers worked under the guise of pluralism and noncompulsion, the court was usually satisfied. In a way, employee voluntarism—that is, the free choice to work in an evangelical company or practice their faith at work—could confirm an executive's evangelicalism as the "best" source of workplace culture. Unlike the state, which seemed unjustly restrictive or coercive, the evangelical business supposedly collected and directed individual wishes, dreams, and grievances as well as satisfied the demands of customers for a more "moral" or "religious" company. "Free enterprise," therefore, and the free exercise of faith were, once again, synonymous, albeit in a new legal and cultural context, one informed not only by local or world-traveling crusades but also by the deployment of evangelical social and political values in the domestic private sector.

The freedom to exercise faith at work was vital for reasons other than propping up the faltering power of white evangelical businessmen. Not only did the legal and economic foundations of white supremacy crack in the 1950s and 1960s, so too did the legal foundations for the nation's "evangelical moral establishment" and the cover granted to evangelical activities in public spheres by Cold War–era affirmations of "Judeo-Christianity" and public rituals affirming the essential "Christian-ness" of the nation and state. In the landmark *Engel v. Vitale* decision of 1962, the US Supreme Court struck down the authority of state officials to compose prayers for use in public schools or encourage students to pray while in school. The following year in *Abington School District v. Schempp*, the Court decided that mandatory Bible reading in public schools was likewise unconstitutional. More fuel was added to the fire over women's rights in the late 1960s, as states reconsidered patriarchal divorce laws and, more important, the illegality of abortion.

Evangelicals were not automatic reactionaries to court decisions or state policies regarding abortion. Although plenty of evangelicals disliked the rulings, not a few southern Baptists, including prominent pastors and denominational leaders like W. A. Criswell, initially were hesitant about fighting them. More often than not, in state-level battles during the late 1960s, conservative Catholics and bishops were the most ardent anti-abortion activists, facing off against advocates of abortion access from California to Connecticut. With *Roe v. Wade* in 1973, the Supreme Court granted federal protection—under the constitutional right to privacy and due process clause of the Fourteenth Amendment—to women seeking an abortion. Anti-abortion Catholics then built closer alliances with conservative evangelicals, cementing a union over "social issues" and "family values." There were precedents for this among evangelicals—like Taylor, Wade, and Graham—who had hit up Catholic donors or counted certain Catholics as friends and kindred spirits in supporting evangelistic work. But by the mid-1970s, conservative Catholics and conservative evangelicals were joining forces on an unprecedented scale, regularly linking abortion to other "social" issues worth fighting for, ranging from heteronormativity to abstinence education.

If court decisions seemed to convey to evangelicals that the federal government was abandoning them, then protests over sex added to their distress. Feminist activists further questioned misogyny and sexism in corporate America and in broader American culture while state-level women's activists fought for the resurrection and ratification of the Equal Rights Amendment, first proposed in the 1920s to cement that "equality of rights under the law shall not be denied or abridged by the United States or by any State on account of sex." The student movement against the war in Vietnam also gained ground on college campuses and expanded to include a wide range of "New Left" activists who saw the war as an imperialist endeavor parading as "democratic" errand. Gay rights activists forced new public debates over human sexuality and whether sexual expression or orientation should receive equal protection under the law. Other grassroots movements, whether focused on environmental degradation, ethnic discrimination, or workplace rights, added to the volatile political culture of the 1960s and early 1970s.

Conservative evangelicals, to varying degrees, protested court decisions and laws as a state-backed assault on *them*, a widespread push by wrongheaded government bureaucrats and their liberal constituents to replace their Christian America (or halt their postwar crusades in spheres private and public) with a post-Christian "secular humanism," a catch-all term deployed in the 1970s by evangelical thinkers like Francis Schaeffer to mean the "destructive" forces of centralization, feminism, scientific rationalism, and moral relativism. Of course, reality was more complicated but, for many conservative evangelicals, perception was reality. The American state and American culture were no longer "under God." Their American way of life was going away. The nation was once again in danger of losing its "God blessed," exceptional status. Another revival was needed—another corporate revival.[9]

Altogether, the so-called culture wars had broad-ranging political effects. Alongside and often overlapping with political activists, business elites carved out places and spaces where conservative evangelicalism could retain a certain measure of social influence via private enterprise, even within the new regulatory environment created by Title VII. Indeed, in the late 1960s and 1970s, many evangelical-owned businesses—big and small—became vehicles through which evangelicals could achieve the social and political changes they deemed most important. Keeping religion active and based upon the "free" choice of workers was necessary because it had been "taken out" of other arenas, such as in public schools or state law. In pushing this, however, conservative evangelicals often created new social, racial, and ethical orders. If one signed on with a work ethic based in purposeful work, then one was deemed God-blessed and keeping God truly "at work" in America, whether in a small business or large corporation. Or in a suburban shopping mall.

Of Shopping Malls and Sunday Closings

In 1960, Truett Cathy's concerns were hardly so broad-ranging. His brother had suddenly died in a plane crash in 1949. Going it alone, Cathy had turned the Dwarf Grill into a popular local diner in the 1950s, but the accidental burning down of a second Dwarf Grill in 1960 discouraged him and did not bode well for his financial stability. Concerned about keeping his diner's doors open, Cathy began reviewing his menu's offerings. Cathy noticed that his chicken entrees often sold well, especially his fried chicken sandwiches. Unfortunately, such items often took a long time to prepare and had higher wholesale costs than cheaper offerings like hamburgers and fries. These problems vexed Cathy until 1961, when he discovered that a food equipment manufacturer had recently developed a relatively cheap pressure fryer, nicknamed the "Henny Penny." Like LeTourneau, Wade, Shakarian, and many evangelicals before him, Cathy had a certain fascination with modern technology. Technology shortened the time from not yet to now. With this fryer, Cathy reduced cooking time for chicken breasts to roughly the same amount of time as the average hamburger. To reduce the cost of raw chicken, Cathy solicited the services of Goode Brothers Poultry Company. Goode Brothers primarily supplied airline companies with boneless, skinless chicken breasts but agreed to sell Cathy any pieces deemed too large for packing in airline trays. Although it is unclear who first contacted whom, Cathy's relationship with Goode Brothers continued for the next few decades. As the chicken processing industry transformed from a peripheral to a central industry on the southern economic landscape, Cathy's fortunes would depend on this relationship in more complex (and disconcerting) ways. In the 1960s, however, his connection to the Sunbelt's burgeoning chicken industry was relatively straightforward. Poultry processors supplied Cathy with cheap chicken breasts, which he battered, seasoned, and fried, topped with a few pickles, stuck in a buttered bun, and sold as a finished product—which he termed the "Chick-fil-A"—to a new customer, the suburban mall shopper.[10]

Enclosed, climate-controlled malls gradually moved to the center of American consumer capitalism in the three decades after World War II. Originally developed as a way to make shopping convenient year-round in northern cities, air-conditioned shopping malls also proliferated in suburban zones in the Sunbelt. Because of civil rights activism, the move to the malls was acute and unmistakable in cities like Atlanta. In the 1950s and early 1960s, civil rights advocates targeted various Jim Crow institutions: schools, churches, public facilities, and, especially, downtown business establishments that promoted or maintained a policy of segregated seating and service. Downtown "sit-ins" between 1960 and 1962 brought violence and the fragmentation of business–civic coalitions in cities and small towns across the South. One byproduct of the successful desegregation of private, downtown businesses was that droves of white residents and business owners moved to the suburbs, with shopping malls often serving as the new nodes of community and commerce. (Residential and commercial "white flight" presaged a subsequent wave of "black flight" after the mid-1970s, as middle-class blacks and businesses moved out of central city communities to stake their own claim in suburbia.) The shift in Atlanta's metropolitan economy was dramatic. In 1960, Atlanta's central business district contained approximately 90 percent of the metropolitan area's office space. By 1980, the outward migration of businesses had cut this percentage by more than half. Between 1963 and 1972, retail sales in the central business district of downtown fell to just 7 percent of the total sales in the Atlanta metro area. By 1973, dozens of business centers and office parks were strung along the perimeter highway, many of them employing thousands of new arrivals in white-flight zones on the edges of Atlanta. As thousands of jobs and hundreds of businesses relocated to the suburbs, employment and the tax base declined precipitously in the central city. Atlanta became blacker and poorer between 1965 and 1980, creating an urban crisis similar to that in other metropolitan centers around the nation.[11]

The rise of the suburbs created new incentives for companies and owners to relocate to inner-ring, outer-ring, or edge cities. Relocating empowered additional rounds of suburbanization, as well as the continued depopulation and destruction of urban economies. Cathy took advantage of these complex racial, spatial, and economic restructurings, exploring the market options that the shopping mall economy and Atlanta's suburbanization made possible. In doing so, he not only followed national trends. He also made Chick-fil-A a national company, since the market conditions of various suburbs around the country were usually different by degree, not by type.

Suburbia, a majority-white place, was also in line with Cathy's racial and religious inclinations. Cathy promoted an ostensibly "color-blind" work ethic, one oriented around the sanctity of work as a godly arbiter of social order and authority. This was a remarkable ethic to promote because Cathy could not have been unaware of his company's racial context. He had come of age in a world of striking racial and economic limitation. Born in 1921 in rural Putnam County, Georgia, Cathy moved to Atlanta during the Great Depression. Near desperation, like many southern families, his family lived in Techwood Homes, an all-white, New Deal housing project that was the first of its kind in the United States. After serving abroad during World War II (before getting sent home early on a medical release), Cathy's first ventures into the diner market occurred in Hapeville, Georgia, an inner-ring working-class suburb of Atlanta that local papers advertised as "98% White." Much like other communities in and around Atlanta, Hapeville maintained a segregated economy. The local Ford plant, nearby airport, and other commercial enterprises adhered to the standards of legal and spatial segregation common in the South of the 1940s and 1950s. Regardless of whether Cathy practiced or promoted racial segregation (no hard evidence exists either way), Jim Crow certainly shaped the commercial world he inhabited.[12]

It is instructive that the hagiography of Chick-fil-A never mentions the company's genesis in the racial environment of Hapeville. According to the books that Cathy wrote, the company's diner days were merely spent in an ostensibly race-less, small southern town. This might be chalked up to strategic forgetfulness or true "colorblindness." But historical amnesia was *vital* to Cathy's myth of personal uplift. To show that his work ethic and contractual theology provided the keys to immediate "success," the bars to entering the elite class had to be low and any help (from white privilege, legalized racism, or the New Deal state) or limitation (such as systemic racism or poverty) had to disappear. Moreover, such a myth also fit with the massive, national flight to suburbs. As he and thousands of other whites moved to the suburbs, they fled their racial history and the downtown or small-town fights over race, moving away from it politically, rhetorically, geographically, and *religiously*.

But by focusing on religion as the proper way to sort the blessed from the rest, Cathy also strategized a path away from a racial past that still bound all too many of his contemporaries. Case in point: in Atlanta, other civic or business leaders, such as Mayor William B. Hartsfield, sought to manage the course of desegregation to the city's benefit. Others followed the hardline stance of segregationist businessmen, such as Cathy's contemporary and fellow Baptist, Lester Maddox, who sold off his own chicken restaurant in 1965 in the face of court-ordered integration. Both were unsuccessful in forging the racial future to their liking. But in the shopping malls around Atlanta, Cathy's religiously infused social and political perspective would take root in an age of white flight and new white "rights" regarding the sanctity of home, church, bedroom, and boardroom.[13]

In 1964, a year before Maddox closed his restaurant and the year Lyndon B. Johnson signed the Civil Rights Act, Cathy started to reconsider his business model. Three years later, in 1967, Cathy brought his chicken sandwich to Atlanta's Greenbriar Mall. Opened in 1965, Greenbriar Mall was an enclosed regional shopping center, one of only a few large malls near Atlanta. Located west of downtown, near an exit on the I-285 perimeter, it was a popular spot for a wide range of Atlantans. A 1973 report on regional shopping centers ranked Greenbriar third out of twelve "shopping areas" in Atlanta, with 18 percent of all Atlanta adults visiting it in an average thirty-day period. Though the surrounding suburbs were nearly all white, one out of four shoppers at Greenbriar Mall was "non-white" and, in terms of purchasing power, Cathy's first mall customers ranged from lower-middle to upper class. Leasing a tiny, 30-by-13-foot space in a vacated hearing aid store, Cathy set up his first Chick-fil-A along the main concourse and complemented it with architectural touches intended to mimic the Dwarf Grill's storefront. His chicken sandwich was the menu's centerpiece, supplemented with waffle-sliced potato fries, slaw, lemon pie, and soft drinks supplied by Atlanta's Coca-Cola company.[14]

Cathy was like thousands of business owners in the 1960s. He moved beyond Hapeville and outside city limits, to a new promised land where churches and businesses—or, in Chick-fil-A's case, a "Christian" business—created and legitimated new forms of community and conservative politics. Suburban life, however, came with its own particular challenges and costs, which Cathy sought to address. By affirming a company like Chick-fil-A and its values of work, faith, and family, suburbanites of any race (ostensibly) could share in Cathy's merito-cratic, postsegregationist dream. In Cathy's hands, as it was in the hands of a new generation of evangelical business leaders, the evangelical movement would not only "move on" from its racial history; it would do so in an environment almost exclusively defined by the common denominators of modern conservative Christianity: privatization, meritocratic uplift, moral authoritarianism, familial "rights," and corporate power.

Cathy's faith-based suburban strategy was also emblematic of other shifts in evangelicalism's business history. Whereas a previous generation of evangeli-cal activists depended on big businessmen to drive their movement forward by funding churches and parachurch organizations, by the late 1970s building an evangelical business was *itself* a way to further the movement. So too was mak-ing sure that a wide variety of evangelical practices were essential to corporate culture, from Sunday closing to Bible reading to public prayers to public activ-ism. In fact, such practices took on special meaning in a nation in which the Supreme Court had judged unconstitutional a wide range of state-backed reli-gious practices. One may not be able to require Bible reading or prayer in the public sphere, but in the private sphere of a privately owned business like Chick-fil-A, Bible readings and prayers remained permissible, as long as they were not required or tied to conditions of employment. If employees "freely" accepted top-down endorsements of a given religion, then it seemed like one more vote for bringing conservative evangelical faith into the workplace and, by proxy, broader society. Through a mixture of executive and employee choice, evangeli-cals could retain a semblance of control over public displays of religion via the private space of the for-profit business. Like-minded consumers could decide to support a "Christian" business with money and word-of-mouth endorsements. Evangelical executives could also take on greater authority through role mod-eling and "public" stances on the social and personal benefits of private-sector religious practice. The state may no longer endorse conservative evangelicalism. The nation may not resemble *their* vision of a Christian America. But Chick-fil-A was a "Christian" company. If enough spaces and places in corporate America could be "born again," then with enough money from organized consumers, perhaps they could use corporate America to reinstate their vision of Christian America.

Differing models of business ownership, however, put limits on religion at work. "It would be very difficult to close on Sunday if the stockholders could see that the profits were feeling it," Cathy told the *Wall Street Journal* in 1989. "It makes it easier as a private company to carry out your philosophy." Cathy was right. Consider the case of Tropicana, also a company taking shape at around the time Chick-fil-A made its move to the shopping malls. A publicly traded, Florida-based, agribusiness run by Anthony Rossi, an Italian immigrant who converted in the early 1940s from Catholicism to evangelicalism, Tropicana should have been, on paper, an evangelical company. But nothing about Tropicana suggested Rossi's evangelical leanings. The lack of evangelicalism in the fields, factories, or refrigerated "Juice Train" that supported his company's production line was related to its status as a large-scale, publicly traded operation. In 1969, Tropicana went public, and public companies had to deal with multiple factors that tended to tamp down on religion in corporate culture: nonreligious stockholders, religiously disinclined board members, legal prohibitions regarding executive free rein, and public disclosure of corporate accounts. Capitalization via public stock offerings also served as a shortcut to competitiveness or market share that many companies—even those headed by evangelicals—prioritized over religious mission. In Tropicana's case, public capitalization resulted in an expansion of operations that, by 1973, netted the company over $120 million in revenue, almost $100 million more than it had earned a mere ten years before. Still, at no point in its history was Tropicana an evangelical or "Christian" company. Only Rossi's private, tax-deductible philanthropic interests revealed his religious aspirations. In the 1970s, having become a billionaire, Rossi supported the Gideons, the Billy Graham Evangelistic Association (BGEA), and the Aurora Foundation, a missionary organization he founded for the purpose of training American missionaries for evangelism in Europe and Asia. Such missionary work continued well after Rossi retired in 1978 and Tropicana was acquired by Beatrice Foods. Its relationship to evangelicalism, tangential at best before that, became even more distant after the sale.[15]

Tropicana's un-evangelical corporate culture contrasted with that of another privately owned, then publicly traded company: Holiday Inn. At Holiday Inn, evangelical practices were primarily dependent on the tenure of one executive working in a relatively constrained environment. Founded in Memphis, Tennessee, in 1952 by Kemmons Wilson, an off-and-on Baptist churchgoer known to drink and gamble, Holiday Inn was the trendsetter in providing hospitality services to a new postwar middle class of mostly suburban vacationers. In short, Holiday Inn attempted to transplant suburban "family-friendly" expectations to the hotel business, previously known for seediness or—as Federal Bureau of Investigation Director J. Edgar Hoover put it—the "hot pillow trade." (Little wonder the Gideons continued their long mission of putting Bibles in hotel rooms nationwide after World War II.) In 1955, conservative Baptist, friend, and funder of Billy Graham William B. Walton joined the fledgling Holiday Inn enterprise, which then had only twenty hotels. Thanks to annual expansions in the federal highway system, however, Holiday Inn had a growing market. And thanks to willing investors and stockholders, it had the capital to expand. By 1960, it had 100 hotels and was opening new ones at the rate of two a week. In 1963, Holiday Inn opened its 500th hotel; in 1969, it had 1,000. By the early 1970s, Holiday Inn was the nation's largest hotel chain, a growing conglomerate with contracts for onsite Gulf Oil fill-up stations and a portfolio of fifty companies under its umbrella, including a bus company, cardboard manufacturer, and meat-packing outfit.[16]

Like Tropicana, Holiday Inn was a publicly traded company. Walton soon learned about the limits this placed on him. As the company became an international conglomerate, Walton attempted to place his stamp on its corporate culture. His evangelical sensibilities framed his managerial approach, but public ownership and the company's franchisees encouraged religious inclusiveness. As a result, for Walton, "the underlying management philosophy, and corresponding employee attitude, at Holiday Inns" was not merely profit and reputation but also "respect for the dignity of every individual and the Christian principle of love for your neighbor." Running Holiday Inn was supposed to be like running the inn that the infant Jesus never had—one that was hospitable and welcoming. Custom-fitted for a publicly traded company, Walton's hospitality mantra—he called it "The Attitude"—boiled down to an inoffensive, universal message suited to contemporary American life: work hard, respect each employee, offer great customer service, and exemplify upstanding corporate integrity and morals. "Who could object to anything so basically humanitarian as that?" Walton believed.[17]

Walton's definition of "Christian" was outwardly and legally nondiscriminatory while, in company culture, "Christian" meant evangelical, at least in terms of who shaped the religious course of Holiday Inn. Indeed, despite his seemingly universal "Attitude," Walton gave full access to the Gideons to distribute Bibles in rooms and lobbies nationwide. Evangelical chaplains or local ministers were on-call for guests and staff, and Wilson started voluntary "prayer breakfast" meetings at the company. Yet, as a second-in-command executive at a publicly traded company in flux, Walton's personal and professional evangelicalism eventually isolated him at Holiday Inn. In the 1970s, much to Walton's chagrin, Holiday Inn's executive board moved the company overseas and branched out into the gambling business, buying Harrah's Casinos in 1980. Alcohol was served in rooms and certain practices, such as voluntary prayer breakfasts, were stripped of their evangelical overtones and turned into the more generalist "fellowship breakfasts." Chaplaincy calls were no longer available, although the Gideons were allowed to continue supplying their wares. Walton increasingly thought that his evangelical values were marginalized and maligned at Holiday Inn. Frustrated, he reluctantly took a leave of absence in 1980 and finally left the company in 1985.[18]

Other evangelical companies and executives also gradually shifted in religious affiliation—after a public stock offering or changes in management.
ServiceMaster went public in 1962 a few years after Marion Wade handed the
company's future over to Kenneth Hansen. Shortly before his death in 1973,
Wade claimed that his company maintained a pluralistic corporate culture,
telling *The Wall Street Journal*, "I've never hired a gentleman because he was a
Christian, and I've never not hired one because he wasn't. . . . but we do insist
that a man be of high moral caliber." After Wade died, Hansen oversaw the transition in leadership to Kenneth T. Wessner, a former ServiceMaster field manager.
ServiceMaster employees later worked for another of the nation's most prominent evangelical executives, C. William Pollard. A Wheaton College graduate,
corporate lawyer, and former vice president at Wheaton, Pollard took over
as chief executive in 1983. Under Pollard, ServiceMaster began gobbling up
brand after brand, "pursuing a growth-oriented approach based on an aggressive acquisition strategy." In the early 1980s, ServiceMaster started to become a
behemoth, buying out brands like TruGreen, Terminix, American Home Shield,
Merry Maids, and AmeriSpec. By 1994, it had annual sales of $4 billion.[19]

During ServiceMaster's expansion, Pollard downplayed the company's evangelical overtones. Instead, Pollard sought to construct within the company what
he called "the soul of the firm." "Servant-leadership," as in decades before at
ServiceMaster, was a common mantra and managerial practice, but Pollard also
held an open-door policy toward religion. "We can't and shouldn't and don't
want to drive people to a particular religious belief," Pollard wrote. Arguing that
"a key to success in developing the soul of your firm is to harness the power of
diversity," Pollard opened the company's culture to as wide a range of faiths as
possible, primarily because the company's stockholders, payroll, and market had
become large and diverse, increasing the chances of disgruntled customers or
discrimination litigation. "At ServiceMaster," Pollard advocated, "we never allow
religion or the lack thereof to become a basis for exclusion or how we treat each
other professionally or personally." Little about ServiceMaster's range of religious offerings, from corporate chaplains to routine devotionals to dedicatory
prayers, signaled the company's evangelical origins, a striking irony given the
Wheaton-educated, conservative, Rotarian evangelical executive at the helm.[20]

Chick-fil-A was different than Tropicana, Holiday Inn, or ServiceMaster. It
was a privately owned company more conducive to private and public forms
of Christian expression. At the company's main headquarters in Atlanta, Cathy
established a voluntary, Monday-morning prayer service. Local ministers from
both evangelical and nonevangelical churches led the group in prayer. By 1985,
Chick-fil-A headquarters was a sprawling, 75-acre campus that mimicked the
evangelical backwoods youth camps of Cathy's upbringing (save for the company's expansive, five-story office building). It also was a private evangelical space,

much like the megachurch campuses just beginning to pop up in other suburban locales or another sprawling Christian enclave, Jim Bakker's Christian theme park, Heritage USA. At Chick-fil-A, a bell tower tolled well-known evangelical hymns each morning at precisely nine o'clock. Employees regularly walked a 1.4-mile long trail lined with Bible verses mounted on wooden stands every tenth of a mile. Regular tours of the complex were available to visitors, who were treated to an onsite museum that featured a life-size replica of Cathy—the ideal Christian businessman—working inside a built-to-scale reproduction of the Dwarf Grill's interior. Other visitors, whether potential clients or potential hires, usually passed by and read five large plaques that adorned the main lobby's walls, each featuring encouraging quotes by Cathy—"It's easier to succeed than to fail," "No goal is too high if you climb with care and confidence"—next to a Bible verse, such as Proverbs 22:1's injunction that "A good name is to be chosen rather than great riches."[21]

Common corporate practices also signaled the company's evangelical leanings. At each new Chick-fil-A unit's opening, Cathy held a dedication ceremony, often inviting managers, employees, and special guests, ranging from local politicians and boosters to pastors and celebrities. In the early 1980s, when Cathy opened a Chick-fil-A unit in a suburban Miami mall, Cathy told those present that "Chick-fil-A operates in a different way from just about any other business." "We try to base our principles," he continued, "on Scripture," as well as on the more general injunctions of the Golden Rule and a universal call for all Americans to steward available resources. (Both were ideas pulled in from managerial theorist Peter Drucker, whom Cathy mentioned as an inspiration, as well as other common schools of business ethics, in part informed by Rotary and other forms of liberal Christian managerialism.) After these words of encouragement, Cathy asked a local pastor to lead everyone in a "prayer of dedication . . . to the honor and glory of the Lord and [to] ask His blessing on us." The pastor declared that "America is on the decline because of the decline of the Christian work ethic" and then thanked God "for the possibility of this being a real demonstration to a skeptical world that a business can operate on Christian principles."[22]

Such ceremonies were not mere spectacle but a necessary part of developing and demonstrating the corporate culture of Chick-fil-A. Other corporate policies, publications, rituals, and initiatives revealed Cathy's commitment to making his suburban company an active participant in the nation's post-1960s debates over matters of work, faith, sex, and family. First and foremost, Cathy presented Chick-fil-A as a devoted, purposeful, corporate family with Cathy as the *pater familias*. To be sure, the "family" motif in corporate management strategies had precursors long before Chick-fil-A; and paternalism was a long-standing method of labor "management." But in Cathy's estimation, both methods worked to instill values imagined by evangelicals and other conservatives as "lost" in more recent decades.[23] Thus Cathy urged all new employees to follow the lead of the unit's operator, who would train them, motivate them, and model for them how to dress, act, talk, and work. Various in-office activities and policies promoted these views. By the early 1980s, company policy encouraged Chick-fil-A's employees to sing songs of devotion to the company and their operators. One song, titled "Movin' On," went:

> We are strong hand in hand.
> We are happy side by side.
> Our hearts are joined together,
> By a sense of family pride.
> Every day is an adventure,
> When you're striving for a goal.
> There's a spirit of excitement,
> When we see the dream unfold.

> **CHORUS:**
> *Chick-fil-A we're movin' on.*
> *Chick-fil-A we're growin' strong.*
> *We're one big happy family,*
> *That's the way at Chick-fil-A.*

> It's so fun to make our living,
> Doing what we love to do.
> When you're working with your friends,
> Every day is fresh and new.
> We're exploring new horizons.
> Reaching, striving every day.
> And the way we work together,
> Is the pride of Chick-fil-A.

Cathy's emphasis on the immediate, on seen things, and on spiritual adventures unfolding anew each day was not hard to miss in such songs. Neither was the extolling of the familial and contractual, as employees joined in song with a company that affirmed togetherness and spiritual bonding. Such values also grounded Chick-fil-A's corporate philanthropy. Any employees who exemplified Chick-fil-A's corporate values regarding work and family were duly rewarded for their "familial" piety with the symbol of postwar upward mobility—the college scholarship. Any employee who maintained a C average in school and had worked part-time for Chick-fil-A for at least two years could be eligible for a $1,000 scholarship to the school of his or her choice, depending on the manager's recommendation. By 1991, Cathy had given away millions of dollars to this scholarship program, benefitting more than 6,500 former employees.[24]

Private Ownership and the Varieties of Corporate Evangelicalism

If Chick-fil-A were a public company, it is doubtful that Cathy would have been able to maintain its religious character. Private ownership created notable commonalities among evangelical businesses but also fostered important differences, often shaped by location, executive discretion, labor markets, and business models.

For instance, in 1970 Cecil B. Day, an Atlanta real estate executive and Baptist, founded Days Inn to be an extension of his evangelical activities. Like Kemmons Wilson of Holiday Inn, Day offered clean, relatively cheap rooms for customers in suburban Atlanta. Later, Days Inn sought out the business of tourists at the ultimate middle-class suburbanite vacation spot in the 1970s, Florida's Disney World. Intentionally placing his hotels along the "Golden Triangle" of interstates connecting several Deep South states to Florida, Day capitalized on the tourist traffic running up and down these highways during the spring and summer months. Unlike Cathy, Day did not have the option of closing on Sunday. In the hotel business, Sunday closings were impractical: one could not kick guests out on Saturday night. Hence Day explored other options. Alcohol was not available at any Days Inn, thereby marking the room as equivalent to the ideal, godly home. Patrons could read and take home the bedside Bibles that Day provided ("Steal This Book!" they advertised). Given the possibility of having guests far from home and family, each hotel offered pastoral services and a "Chaplain on Call" card, prominently displayed in every room. This integration of evangelicalism into his management strategy and corporate culture won Day effusive praise from numerous evangelical and business leaders. Paul Harvey, Kemmons Wilson, Gerald Ford, Richard Nixon, Billy Graham, John Haggai, Bill Bright, Norman Vincent Peale, and Pat Robertson all considered Day a friend and lauded Days Inn. Sitting presidents and former presidents even weighed in on Day's life and work. A businessman himself, Jimmy Carter thought Day "demonstrated by example how a rich family life and professional success can be achieved based on biblical principles." Gerald Ford cast him as "a stalwart believer in and fighter for the highest American principles," while Ronald Reagan thought that Day proved that "the American Dream can be fulfilled without compromising a sense of values."[25]

Day sought to shape American evangelicalism and society in ways particular to his professional life and personal interests. He tithed regularly to his local church, the upscale, all-white Dunwoody Baptist Church in suburban Atlanta.

(It was a church that was socially and politically on par with Herbert Taylor's home church, albeit in a southern setting and stocked with both old and new money.) Day also gave 10 percent of Day Realty's profits toward missions and his nonprofit and tax-free religious organization, the Day Foundation. Founded in 1968 and funded straight from Days Inn's profits in the 1970s and early 1980s, the Day Foundation focused especially on what he deemed to be the most troubling aspect of post-1960s America, namely the decline of conservative, evangelical churches and religiosity in New England. According to Edward White Jr., who began directing the Day Foundation in 1976, "Mr. Day" felt that northern churches had "started getting away from the truth of Scriptures [in the 1960s], preaching the gospel, and sharing the essence of what faith and following Christ is all about." Day's complaint had been common among fundamentalists earlier in the century and southern conservative evangelicals since L. Nelson Bell corresponded with J. Howard Pew about the National Council of Churches' "takeover" of American Protestantism. But Day took a different tack to counteract the trend. The Day Foundation acted as both a conduit for funds to support evangelical church growth and as an intermediary for like-minded evangelical groups and organizations. The Foundation's investments ranged from evangelical campus ministries to worldwide missions groups like the Haggai Institute. In the late 1970s, Day fell ill with bone cancer; he died in 1982. Soon after, the Day family relinquished the name and majority stock holdings in the company. Days Inn was no longer an evangelical company. The Day Foundation, however, continued to receive funding from Day's investment portfolio and donations from a wide variety of business supporters, churches, and nonsectarian associations.[26]

Sunbelt evangelical executives like Cathy and Day had counterparts in the old northern centers of conservative evangelicalism. For example, Herman Miller was another privately owned company with evangelical leanings and auspices. Founded in 1923 in Zeeland, Michigan, only a few miles away from the evangelical publishing center of Grand Rapids, the De Pree family had run the company for more than four decades as a small but well-respected manufacturer of office furniture. The company's transformation from small regional manufacturer to national company came in the late 1960s. In 1968, noted one business historian, Herman Miller "revolutionized the workplace by introducing Action Office II, a modular, open-plan approach to office space configuration." In other words, Herman Miller invented the now-ubiquitous office cubicle. The cubicle was seen, at the time, not as a spiritual or psychological cage but as a labor-empowering arrangement, freeing workers from the confines of fixed seating and desks. Thus the cubicle was a direct product of the company's overall take on in-office management and corporate relations, one strongly informed by the De Pree family's connections to Dutch Reformed evangelicalism. De Pree affirmed covenantal relationships between management and employees as well as a sense of doing "high" design as a form of art and Christian calling. After hearing a lecture at a trade show in 1949 on "Enterprise for Everybody," the company's executives developed a bonus and profit-sharing system tied to each employee's ability to solve problems and improve efficiency, whether in the design of a product or its production. Known as the Scanlon Plan, it received another dose of managerial theory when Max De Pree and his brother Hugh took over the company in 1962.[27]

The main shaper of executive practices in the 1970s, Max De Pree stepped into the top office in 1980. De Pree had attended Wheaton College until World War II called him into service in Europe. He later studied at Hope College, a Dutch Reformed school, before entering the family business. Since at least 1970, De Pree had been a fan of Robert Greenleaf's vision of "servant leadership." An off-and-on Quaker, spiritual wanderer, and business theorist with no connections to the evangelical movement, Greenleaf published in 1970 his pithy essay, "The Servant as Leader." Greenleaf's work promoted a philosophy of corporate management as self-deprecative service to employees and customers that evangelicals like Herbert Taylor, Marion Wade, Howard E. Butt Jr., and De Pree had been using for years.[28]

Greenleaf's philosophy was a good match for service executives who liked to think of themselves as servants leading servants, but its application in evangelical businesses was never uniform. At Chick-fil-A, for instance, Cathy adopted a servant leader philosophy in the late 1980s, writing in tomes like *It's Easier to Succeed Than to Fail* that Christ-like service was the key to developing good customer relations and a smoothly operating franchise. A Sunday School teacher and Rotarian like Herbert J. Taylor, Cathy aligned social service with profit-making, all for the sake of philanthropy toward "the least of these," which included foster children in need of temporary housing. The training of children also fit with his notion of social service, as Cathy funded summer camps based on the idea that "It's better to build boys and girls than mend men and women."[29] At ServiceMaster, Pollard's version of servant leadership similarly matched the premium long placed by the company on service work.

At Herman Miller, a manufacturing and design company, De Pree applied Greenleaf's ideas as a counter to the "greed is good" and "buy out and kick out" culture of management in the early 1980s. In 1983, Herman Miller extended stock options to its employees as an act of "servant leadership." In 1984, De Pree capped his annual cash compensation at twenty times the compensation of his full-time employees. Two years later, De Pree established a "silver parachute" plan in which all full-time and part-time employees were guaranteed generous severance benefits after two years of work, regardless of whether they were fired or pushed out due to a buy-out. "This is the chief difference in being a Christian," noted De Pree, "that you accept the idea of moving capitalism in the direction of making it possible for everyone to be a participant, to be an insider.... If top management takes care of itself first, that's wrong. You are supposed to take care of the bottom half of the ladder." De Pree's blend of evangelical and servant-leader beliefs provided the justification for top-to-bottom corporate care, although he was aware that in a post–Title VII America, other faiths could have a place in corporate affairs. Religious diversity and pluralism was a positive good. Echoing other evangelicals, De Pree cautioned against "secularism" in management even while endorsing the secular notion of religious freedom and tolerance. "The question is not, Am I being successful? It is, Am I being faithful?" he told Laura Nash, a business scholar, "There is a reasonable temptation to adopt a secular standard. It happens without thinking about it. Unless somebody articulates something different, you are going to adopt a secular standard without even thinking about it."[30]

But a religious "standard"—or holding to either a vague or specific religion in the private sector—was by no means guaranteed to become permanent in any company, privately owned or not. For instance, attendance at weekly Bible studies was routine at Reell Precision Manufacturing, Inc., which after 1970 was a major supplier to Xerox based out of Minneapolis–St. Paul, Minnesota (also home to the BGEA). Founded by three former 3M engineers, Reell was intended to be a Christian company, albeit one with a relatively unique form of private "tri-ownership," ostensibly as a play on the doctrine of the Trinity. To encourage unity among executives, "in one of the [regular] Monday morning breakfast meetings in the early '70s, [executive] Dale [Merrick] recognized the spiritual dimension that was growing in our relationship and our working experience together," remembered Robert Wahlstedt and Lee Johnson, the company's cofounders. "He wondered if there could be ways to share that dimension with the other employees." Voluntary, weekly Bible studies "on company time" attracted "almost 100% voluntary attendance." The company issued a statement of purpose that was "strikingly explicit in its affirmation of Creator, Redeemer, and the need for Judeo-Christian values in the work environment." Ironically, Reell's Bible studies soon undercut the very reason they were started: to ensure unity between executives and employees. Wahlstedt recalled how increasingly "one person 'blew off' another's point of view because it was not based on a particular version of the Bible. And practices that not everyone was comfortable with[,] such as praying aloud[,] were suggested. A division developed between the more 'spiritual' and the rest." By 1980, the voluntary Bible meetings were discontinued.[31]

Reell was a manufacturing company, and though religious rituals there faltered, it nevertheless demonstrated that evangelicalism still had a place in the American industrial sector. Indeed, the industry-centric managerial philosophies of the postwar era, ranging from welfare capitalism to hired chaplains, remained a viable part of evangelical approaches toward "labor relations." And, in the 1970s, as industrial manufacturing was rocked by plant closures, union fights, global outsourcing, and corporate migrations, evangelicals sought to relate to—and direct—the last vestiges of industrial order and working-class community via corporate revival.

One dramatic event in particular granted an evangelical executive a brief time in the spotlight and an opportunity to publicize an evangelical strategy for "saving" industrial America. In 1973, workers and executives at Pittron, a steel foundry, claimed that the assumption of a chaplain's role by evangelical Vice President Wayne Alderson assuaged relations between company managers and workers. Located in Glassport, Pennsylvania, about 20 miles south of Pittsburgh, Pittron was a division of Textron, Inc., a Boston-based company that had become a multifaceted industrial conglomerate and the nation's seventy-sixth largest firm by 1970. A union town, Glassport had a reputation for labor disputes stretching back to the 1930s. Though pay and time off had increased for Glassport's unionized workforce, especially under Textron's management, by the early 1970s it was still a tense place to work. According to Samuel Piccolo, the president of the United Steelworkers local, "the weekly grievance sheet looked like a laundry list." In the midst of a business slump in 1971, the union agreed to a temporary freeze "on extended vacations, supplemental unemployment benefits, and other fringe items," but managers claimed that the union had agreed to a permanent relinquishment. The union and Piccolo, a "determined first-term president," disagreed. A subsequent strike lasted almost three months and, according to a Pittsburgh-based paper's estimate, "left the foundry on its last economic leg."

Little had been settled when the Pittron plant came under new management in the form of President George V. Hager and evangelical Vice President Wayne T. Alderson. "Hagar and Alderson," noted one report, "were taking control of a plant where over 80 per cent of the employes [sic] had 10 or more years [of] service and where dissent had been rampant." Their approach to this dispute, however, would focus not only on labor grievances but on matters of the spirit. Bible in hand, Alderson met with labor leaders, coordinated prayer sessions, and set times for workers to air complaints and suggestions. Labor relations were set right. Productivity soared. Employment increased from 420 to 700 workers. Even labor leaders were reportedly astounded. "Prior to the strike, it was not uncommon for six or seven grievances to be filed daily," a local newspaper reported, "[but] Norval Boyd, [the local union's] grievance chairman, said no grievances have been filed by workers in the past 21 months." Workers also attended "Bible meetings and union meetings and act[ed] like gentlemen." According to the local union's vice president, Alderson's approach reportedly "improved family relations" in Glassport due to a relaxing of labor tensions, thereby linking God's spiritual union of work and home. By the end of the year, Alderson was an evangelical celebrity. *Christianity*

Today and other evangelical publications recounted Alderson's efforts. A television documentary "The Miracle of Pittron" aired. "Some 7,000 persons," noted one account, "visited the foundry earlier this year to view the results of the new program." President Gerald Ford, already embroiled in an effort to bring evangelicals into the Republican fold and promoting his feckless "Whip Inflation Now" program, received Alderson's suggestions regarding labor relations, which included an industry-wide "moratorium" hour each day, during which "management at all levels and labor" would "embark on a process of communication that would open new avenues of discussion and understanding."[32]

Alderson's successes were short-lived. Alderson was let go by management in 1974. A year later, the Milwaukee-based company Bucyrus-Erie bought the foundry, renamed it, and then sold it in 1981. It permanently closed in the mid-1980s, and a fire destroyed the remaining facilities. Still, Alderson spent the next few decades preaching his "value of the person" ethic, rebranded in the early 1980s as Theory R management, for "respect." Alderson's myth of Pittron—as ruined, then redeemed industrial garden—remained a component of the evangelical business press well into the 1980s and 1990s. Alderson, who left business management to become an in-demand speaker and writer, promoted the myth of Pittron's "turnaround." So did R. C. Sproul, an evangelical theologian who wrote a biography of Alderson, characterizing his Bible-centered, "value of the person" ethic as the key to creating bonds between labor and management that were "stronger than steel." Evangelical writers, from theologians like John R. W. Stott to popular writers like Tony Campolo to evangelical politicos like Charles Colson to business executives-writers like Jack Eckerd and Zig Ziglar, repeated the myth as fact well into the late twentieth century.[33]

Alderson's myth had clear implications, namely that evangelical business leaders were reliable authorities on labor relations. Moreover, the myth held that labor relations worked best on a person-to-person basis. The problems facing the American working class, therefore, were best handled by properly trained Christian workers and managers with Bibles in hand. It was a perspective with a genealogy that could be traced back to D. L. Moody's "gap men" or Herbert J. Taylor's Four-Way Test and his Rotarian brand of labor relations. And it now had up-to-date counterparts in other evangelical companies, from service-oriented businesses to heavy and light industries. It was certainly the mantra at Interstate Batteries, a manufacturer of automobile batteries in Texas. As at Pittron, the company underwent a conversion of sorts when Norman Miller took over operations in 1978. Miller had been an alcoholic until 1974, when he experienced a dramatic conversion after attending an evangelical Bible study and became a lay preacher. Shortly after coming on board at Interstate, he introduced routine, quasi-voluntary prayer meetings among his executives, made prayer a part of corporate culture, and started a chaplaincy program. Other facets of corporate culture betrayed his Christian leanings. Employees could check out a wide variety of evangelical books, magazines, tapes, and videos from its corporate library. Bibles were presented to new hires, along with the option to watch a film about Jesus while the chaplains gave "prayer cards" to volunteer "prayees" to pray for Interstate's wide range of missionary beneficiaries. For the holidays, the company mailed out Christian gifts to distributors and dealers. Employees routinely received Bibles and newsletters that included Bible quotes, reflections about God and Jesus, or an invitation: "If you have any interest in understanding how you can receive Jesus Christ as your Savior, contact Chaplain Henry Rogers," read one solicitation. Terminations were made "the result of a consensus that's been fully covered in prayer—usually over an extended period of time." Miller wanted the company's "soul" to be "sensitive and kind, not ever desiring to offend anyone but to be appropriately bold and obedient to share His love with others as He would lead." The company's corporate purpose, drawn up in 1990, was to "glorify God as we supply our customers worldwide with top quality, value-priced batteries, related electrical power-source products, and distribution services." A millionaire executive, Miller gave freely to the conservative Dallas Theological Seminary and served on its board. Later, in the 1990s, he was a bankroller for Campus Crusade for Christ's *Jesus* film. Politically inclined, Miller also donated, according to *U.S. News & World Report*, "$8,650 a year to the Free Market Foundation, an organization that helps voters identify socially conservative candidates in Texas who want to end legal abortions, establish prayer in public schools and drastically decrease welfare spending."[34]

The differences among Chick-fil-A, Days Inn, Herman Miller, Reell, Pittron, and Interstate Batteries were the result of public versus private ownership and the matching of executive aspiration and discretion to differences in customers, employees, and locale. Thousands of other small or growing companies in the 1970s and early 1980s also revealed the varieties of business-based evangelicalism and the importance of private ownership to evangelical assertion in the marketplace. Indeed, without private ownership and the legal allowances granted by Title VII, an important complement to the evangelical big-business sector—the evangelical *small* business sector—would not have been as prevalent or varied.

The Evangelical Small Business Sector

Small businesses were granted even more license than bigger businesses under Title VII. Any business with fewer than twenty-five employees (after 1964) and fifteen employees (after 1972) fell outside its regulatory purview. Thus evangelical small businesses were pockets where religious presentations thrived and outright discrimination might continue. But context also mattered. As local businesses serving local markets, small-business owners and employees also had the freedom to create a remarkably varied evangelical small-business sector, albeit one more susceptible to changes in employment pools, consumer demand, and demographics. Regardless of local variations and challenges, however, the evangelical small-business sector was filled with evangelicals no less committed than some of their large-scale counterparts to reinserting evangelicalism into the public sphere as their businesses—owners hoped—grew bigger quarter after quarter, year after year.

As with Chick-fil-A, many evangelical small businesses served suburban markets. Others did not. Hence there was little uniformity among evangelical small-business owners or in-house religious practices, although observers were quick to note a few generalizations. Open prayers, for instance, were common. Companies also often implied that their "evangelicalness" assured honest business relations. For instance, an upholsterer for suburban homes implied its staff was on the up-and-up because they were "all Christian," while the owner of a drain-cleaning company pitched himself as "the sewer man with a conscience." Christian unity through prayer, sale, or service was another common mantra in evangelical small-business culture. A swimming pool company "Serving North Dallas" asked customers to "Pray About Our Service," while Christian Consumer Services advertised "honest dependable Christian help" and had special offers for "Believers at cost." Born-again buying achieved perhaps its greatest synergy, however, at Check-Up's, a company offering Christian-inspired checkbooks and checks. By paying for their purchases with their checks, Check-Up's assured buyers that "each check you write reaches 16 persons," thereby aligning the very act of purchasing with the act of evangelical witness. The specific purposes of certain businesses also added variety to the "Christian" appeals and identities of small enterprises. Connecticut Mutual Life Insurance cited 1 Timothy, using Paul's epistle to advertise "sound financial management" by challenging the manhood and familial commitments of Christian breadwinners. "If a man does not know how to manage his own household," presumably by buying insurance policies, "how will he take care of the church of God?" A greasy-spoon restaurant in suburban Dallas, Texas, advertised "Southern Fried Chicken & Country Fried Dinners," linking prayer and pun by citing Christ's petition in the Lord's Prayer to "Give Us This Day Our Daily Bread."[35]

Like ServiceMaster, numerous evangelical businesses used Christian ideas and symbols (Jesus fish, church spires, crosses doubling as "T's") and religiously suggestive names (SonShip Recordings, Master's Automotive, Earthly Residences, The Master's Press, Covenant Transport). Other companies printed biblical passages on merchandise or in advertising. Such public presentations showed how religious affiliation supposedly related to public reputation. As Robert Stansell, who owned and operated an eponymous trucking company in Florida, noted, "Christians ought to use their business as a platform for their

ministry. . . . We should be Christians seven days a week and not just on Sunday."
For this reason, Bible studies, led by a visiting minister, were a part of Stansell
Trucking's business. Bookshelves at his main office were filled with evangelical
tracts and devotionals. Walls were adorned with posters "quoting Bible verses
and small wooden crosses," and callers put on hold listened to "hymns or sermons piped in from a Christian radio station." "Truckin' for Jesus" was emblazoned in huge letters on the sides of nearly all of the company's long-haulers.[36]

The preference for the ostensibly inclusive term "Christian" was also common among evangelical small-business owners. Of course, evangelicals had long
used the term interchangeably with "born-again" or "fundamentalist" or "new
evangelical" or just "evangelical," proclaiming themselves as the only true form
of Christianity today. And, at Chick-fil-A and many other evangelical-owned or
affiliated companies, the "Christian" tag was no less purposeful, normalizing the
idea that the only normative Christian was an evangelical and the only normative Christian business was an evangelical business.

Another upstart business in the 1970s, evangelical business directories,
placed the "Christian" tag's meaning in high relief and deployed it with particular purpose. The foremost, *The Christian Yellow Pages* (CYP), was based in
Modesto, California, but distributed nationwide. The CYP was founded in 1972
by two evangelical businessmen "to help raise the consciousness, especially
of born-again Christians, in order that they can contribute to lifting the moral
vision and behavior of the business and trade practices of all their neighbors in
their communities." If born-again buyers responded to such a call, together with
business owners they would "build a community life based on . . . fundamental
moral and democratic values and principles." In keeping with the CYP's place in
a presumably postdiscriminatory marketplace, "people from all religions, races,
and ethnic groups" were welcome "to join us in bringing morality into the marketplace."[37] Through the CYP, then, evangelicals could also use their purchasing
power to take a stand against state empowerment, secularization, and "immoral-
ity." Instead of withdrawing purchasing power to advance a political goal, as in an
organized boycott, CYP invited evangelicals or anyone else to direct their purchasing power toward evangelical enterprises. Evangelicals could engage in what
amounted to a "buycott" at CYP-listed small businesses, thereby demonstrating
evangelical activism via their individual and collective purchasing power.

The CYP's editors conveyed other messages to its audience, namely that evangelical businesses were exceptions to the rule of a materialistic and morally vacu-
ous corporate America. "The unspoken assumption," wrote Aubrey H. Haines in
1977 for *The Christian Century*, "is that the Christian consumer should find such
[Christian] merchants to be more honest, reliable and ethical in their business
dealings than other merchants, who may identify themselves as Jewish, as secular humanists, [or] as Christians who reject the 'born-again' tag." Moreover, as

the front matter of an early issue of the CYP in Dallas noted, "As the publishers, our prayer is that CYP will help to instill sound moral and ethical principles in the relationship between consumer and the business community. Application of this concept would, to a large measure, provide an increase in individual liberties and we firmly believe this to be the will of our sovereign God." The CYP further argued that solidarity between Christian consumers and Christian businesses would prove "our free enterprise economy" was "an alternative to government policing agencies." Copycat publications took an even more expansive view of Christian business. According to Bill Bray, an entrepreneur from Wheaton College's business community and organizer for Campus Crusade for Christ, his *Christian Business Directory* was the solution to the nation's "moral slide away from God." "The smaller Christian society becomes and the more pagan America becomes," Bray concluded, "we'll be forced to put these out to cling to each other." Solidarity through business was a way of organizing evangelical business owners, customers, and money in the midst of a society in flux.[38]

Nonevangelical observers deemed such solidarity to be fundamentally exclusive and discriminatory. In fact, in 1977, the Anti-Defamation League sued the CYP for not allowing a Jewish-owned business to advertise within its pages, based on California's antidiscrimination laws (and not Title VII per se). After the lawsuit and an appeal in 1984, the CYP and the *Christian Business Directory* had to accept advertisements from anyone, regardless of religion. Still, the CYP did not actively solicit advertisements from nonevangelical businesses, and the vast majority of advertisements were from self-professed born-again Christians.[39]

Evangelical small-business owners sought other means of exuding a sense of control, community, and direction in a competitive, market economy. Hiring was one. As a small-business owner in Georgia put it in the late 1980s, "I just explain to non-Christian applicants what we stand for and hope it scares them away." Smaller, more homogeneous workforces often gave owners a "pass" for open proselytizing. Citing data gathered from an expansive study of "Christian-based" (likely evangelical-affiliated) firms in the 1980s, a marketing professor at Georgia State University concluded that "the smaller the company, the higher the share of Christians" in its workforce.[40] Smaller businesses also granted managers leverage for religious coercion or exclusion through indirect strategies, customary rituals, public presentations, or outright proselytizing. A 1991 study of more than 100 "Christian-based" firms—many likely run by evangelicals and most of them small businesses—listed a wide array of activities that certainly walked a fine line between "free expression" and proselytizing, including:

> distribution of "Christian" books and gospel literature; inviting customers to meetings where "Christian" testimonies are heard; displaying "Christian" principles in a prominent area, such as the company's

reception area or lobby; enclosing biblical quotations in product con-
tainers, packaging, invoices, stationery, monthly statements, or customer order forms; inviting customers to Church, to worship together;
giving "Christian" gifts to customers, such as "Christian" calendars and
bumper stickers; using "Christian" symbols, . . . [such as] a cross or a
fish in company logo; conducting "friendly Christian" conversations
with customer; "ministering" to clients from the scriptures; distributing company brochures and literature with biblical messages; praying
with customers, inviting customers to pray together on an ad hoc basis;
printing biblical verses on restaurant menus; playing "church music"
on company premises.... [In general,] a majority of the firms (73%)
engaged in active proselytizing to their customers.[41]

Overall, evangelicalism showed up in varied forms among small businesses,
much as it did among larger businesses. But, given the smaller workforce, there
was greater potential for universal acclaim by employees for explicitly religious
displays at work. "I heard much less groaning . . . at Christian-based companies
than at others," reflected Leslie Rue, a management professor, about interviews
she conducted with employees. And, given Title VII's allowances for small businesses, such complaints would—more than likely—never turn into a claim,
especially if an employee shared the company's religious sense of mission or
affiliation.[42]

By the 1980s, evangelical-owned or -affiliated businesses were a notable,
if still niche, part of the nation's private sector. A 1989 estimate by a consortium of evangelical businesses claimed that "committed Christians" owned
300,000 small businesses. According to another anecdotal estimate in 1995,
self-described "born-again" Christians made up "nearly half of all small-business
owners," a number undoubtedly overblown but still repeated in at least one
peer-reviewed study. In reality, nailing down the exact number of evangelical-
owned small businesses required guesswork for any scholar or journalist keeping track of this new phenomenon in postwar evangelicalism. As one study
concluded, "there does not appear to be any single authoritative estimate of the
number of self-proclaimed 'Christian-based' companies." But even if substan-
tially lower than available estimates, the presence of evangelical small businesses
mattered beyond numerical strength. From the mid-1960s onward, evangelical
businesses evidenced a complex interplay between work, religion, the law, business culture, and evangelical identity politics. Evangelical businesses, by casting
themselves as "Christian," also monopolized the meaning of what it meant to be
"in business" for "Christian" reasons while linking consumer purchasing to cultural politics. Moreover, when creating their own workplace religion, evangelical small-business owners exercised wide discretion. Private ownership allowed

such freedom, especially when community context encouraged it, thereby assuring that whatever forms of religious expression or exclusion happened in the evangelical small-business sector would go forth without much state involvement or oversight. Free enterprise and free exercise, at least at a small business, was not merely a rhetorical linkage or electoral season platform. It was a Monday through Saturday potential and actuality.[43]

Community context was similarly important at the dozens of mall units that S. Truett Cathy was opening in the late 1970s and early 1980s. Indeed, in the racial and gendered environs of a suburbanizing South and nation, Chick-fil-A's distinctly Christian corporate culture took shape. What made this culture "Christian," however, were not exclusivist religious proclamations or practices. Rather, at Chick-fil-A, "Christian" approximated what it had meant for years to other conservative evangelical organizations with businessmen behind them, whether the Christian Business Men's Committee, International or *Christianity Today*. It meant a pragmatic, strategically ecumenical, collaborationist, results-oriented faith intended to reshape the social, economic, and political direction of the nation. "Christian" was synonymous with "conservative evangelical" but also worked as shorthand for conservative social views regarding meritocratic work and familial "promotion" and "preservation," practiced by executives and employees who—if acting like "one big happy family"—advanced an evangelical faith grounded in corporate persons, places, and practices.

The "Christian" Business of Chick-fil-A

As Chick-fil-A expanded beyond Atlanta's city limits, two factors underscored Cathy's corporate philosophy. The first was a growth strategy that slowly left the malls behind. After reaching a saturation point around 1978, mall building in America slowed in the early 1980s. Stand-alone shopping strips, accessible only by automobile and often anchored by commercial strips or "big box" stores, became more common, challenging the dominance of public shopping malls and encouraging the fuller privatization of American life. In response, Chick-fil-A considered free-standing restaurants, following the precedents set by McDonald's, Burger King, Kentucky Fried Chicken, and other fast-food establishments. In 1987, Chick-fil-A had 347 mall units and only one free-standing restaurant. By 1993, however, it had opened eighty-three additional mall units and fifty-nine free-standing restaurants. By 1994, Chick-fil-A redirected all plans for future expansion away from malls (See Fig. 4.1).[44]

Second, in a shifting suburban market, Cathy and his company aimed for further mass appeal to a suburban customer base. Regarding this second pursuit, Cathy's evangelical religion was especially important. Evangelical

Figure 4.1 As Chick-fil-A matured as a "Christian" business, it left behind the shopping mall market, expanding with stand-alone restaurants in suburbia and other locales. Photo by author.

churches were popping up or moving to the suburbs in droves by the 1960s and 1970s, along with other religious institutions, especially those of middle-class white Protestants and Catholics. "Megachurches" appeared in the 1980s, mimicking the marketing strategies and organizational arrangements of corporations. (Megachurch pastors like Rick Warren and Bill Hybels might cast their ecclesiastical strategy as new, but it had many precursors, from Aimee Semple McPherson in the 1920s to, more immediately, the church-building of Baptist pastor W. A. Criswell in Dallas during the 1950s and 1960s.)

Nationwide, no matter their religious affiliation, churches served as important arenas for suburban politics. In general, in evangelical churches, the privatization ethos of suburbia fueled cultural politics and positions on the hot topics of the 1960s and 1970s. Place by no means determined one's willingness to back conservative social views. But demographics did matter. Suburban communities were largely heterosexual zones defined by high numbers of married adults. Any communities—from new civic organizations, public schools, or religious institutions—built in such an environment therefore tended to resist or stand askance to challenges to the heterosexual, nuclear family ideal, whether coming from the state, gay rights activists, feminists, or pro-choice advocates.[45]

As a Christian business executive, Cathy never addressed "hot-button" family issues directly. He never mentioned abortion or gay rights in any book he wrote or speech he gave. He did, however, align Chick-fil-A with heterosexual ideals via its corporate culture, administrative arrangements, and philanthropic endeavors. In this way, Cathy attempted to both reflect and meet the heteronormative desires of his suburban customers, as well as the general sensibilities about work and sexuality held by Christian conservatives. Moreover, through his hiring practices, managerial rituals, and corporate mantras, Cathy also linked familial "norms" and "family values" to the corporate identity of Chick-fil-A. Religion was the glue that held it all together; hence, it was vital for Cathy to be able to practice his evangelical religion at work as freely as possible. For this right, ironically, Cathy had cover from the very federal government that he and many other evangelicals deemed in need of redemption. Indeed, by the time Chick-fil-A was becoming a big business in the 1980s, Cathy had relatively free range via Title VII to make his corporation a "Christian" business and, therefore, a private-sector front in yet another public conflict for the social and political direction of the nation.

Cathy, like Taylor, was a relatively quiet activist. Cathy was also a Rotary member and prominent figure in the Southern Baptist Convention after 1980, albeit not a hardline fundamentalist. But Cathy's views on work, sexuality, and race operated in a different social and historical context. Like Taylor and many other evangelical executives before him, Cathy did not take up militant, culture war rhetoric. On race, he was no Lester Maddox. Rather, Cathy imbued his company with the cultural characteristics he thought ideal for the shifting sexual, racial, and political landscape of late-twentieth-century America. As Chick-fil-A grew and its corporate culture developed in the 1970s and early 1980s, the company's public initiatives signaled a new kind of focus on work and youth and, therefore, a new kind of cultural politics.

In 1983, Cathy started the nonprofit, tax-exempt WinShape Foundation at Berry College, a former junior college turned four-year liberal arts institution in the foothills town of Rome, Georgia. Though not officially linked with any evangelical denomination, Berry College "was holy ground" to Cathy "for God had sanctified it for his purpose." "With God's heading," he thought, "we could not fail." Intended to "Shape Individuals to be Winners," the foundation first emerged as an offshoot of Cathy's scholarship program, offering a $10,000 per year scholarship to Berry College for any Chick-fil-A employee who exemplified Cathy's desire to "equip college students to impact the world for Jesus Christ by following Him and living out His unique calling." Cathy expanded the foundation to include a foster home for "good children with potential to be winners but who would not have the chance without our program." As WinShape expanded,

Cathy explicitly cast his foundation as filling a gap in state-run social service programs. "You have other programs for drug addicts, alcoholics, and children with sexual abuse problems," he noted. "But where are the people who will take those who haven't been in trouble, those who want to be winners despite their circumstances?" The government, Cathy believed, did not offer programs for such children and, in fact, often mismanaged those under its care. WinShape, by contrast, was a "ministry" designed to turn children into "winners" in ways the state never could. By modeling a familial ideal, Cathy believed that the foundation could prepare children to stand on their own two feet and make their way in the world, thus proving that the American Dream was still available to anyone who—with God's provision—sought it and worked for it. To encourage a sense of entrepreneurial drive and moral direction, Cathy funded the construction of Camp WinShape at Berry. Much like an off-the-beaten path, evangelical revival camp, Camp WinShape aimed "to guide . . . children in their moral, spiritual, and physical growth." For Cathy, meritocratic work, combined with godly respect for authority and good decision-making, were the keys to turning children into "winners." As such, Camp WinShape staff members strived to teach "Christian stewardship and hard work" through camp programs and curricula.[46]

Chick-fil-A's identity as a Christian company also dovetailed with Cathy's mission to preserve, promote, and protect heteronormative family arrangements in American society. Cathy might avoid a public stance on abortion and gay rights, but he nevertheless linked family solidarity, gender roles, moral virtue, and meritocratic work. Family matters bled over into business and vice versa. "Next to a person's salvation and the choice of Christ as Master," Cathy once averred, "the most important decision is choosing your mate." Like other conservatives, Cathy emphasized distinct roles for men and women. Such roles might be implied in his company, but they were explicitly prescribed for marriages: "Father is chairman of the board, president, and chief executive officer in the world's greatest institution—the home. Mother is executive vice president in charge of public relations, bookkeeping, interior decorating, the commissary, infirmary, hospital, and all those things that make a house a home." By sticking to this arrangement, Cathy believed that couples would achieve marital peace, thus resulting in greater productivity on the job.[47]

As such, Cathy funded marriage seminars and implemented an annual "marriage retreat" for his operators, later expanding their availability to the wider public. Sponsored by his WinShape Foundation and run out of a retreat facility at Berry College, Cathy's programs aimed to assist "couples in maintaining and growing their relationships" while "experiencing the presence of God" via "prayer, worship, group discussions, and couple mentoring." Focus on the Family, a conservative group headed by Dr. James Dobson, was one supplier of marriage materials to WinShape. After the 1990s, the National Institute of

Marriage and the Center for Relational Care, both nonprofit Christian marriage organizations, supplemented its programs. Couples could also pay for general relationship seminars or for more specialized weekend packages. For instance, the "Courageous Hearts" package promoted techniques for "restor[ing] communication and rekindl[ing] affection," the "Prepare to Last" package counseled "those considering engagement for a successful Christian marriage," and the "Romantic Adventure" package offered an "exciting retreat for couples who want to increase their passion and have a blast doing it!"[48]

Chick-fil-A also linked its cultural politics to hiring decisions, its workforce, and public relations. Hiring at Chick-fil-A was like of a rite of passage. When Cathy hired someone, either as an operator or an employee, he was not merely building a labor force or encouraging good relations with customers. He was showing that hard work and heteronormative families—whether private households or corporate "families"—were duly rewarded in corporate America, especially when united under an ethos of faithful devotion to God and company. When looking for potential operators to run his restaurants, then, Cathy sought out a seemingly contradictory person: a fiercely loyal organization man (less often a woman) who doubled as an innovative and driven entrepreneur. On the one hand, Cathy presumed that "our commitment is going to be like a marriage," a sacred vow of principled, mutually beneficial work "with no consideration given to divorce." On the other hand, Cathy encouraged operators to consider themselves innovative, out-of-the-box entrepreneurs. As one advertising campaign put it, operators had the potential to "Be Your Own Boss" at Chick-fil-A, unlike with other fast-food restaurant chains. To attract such operators, Cathy offered a remarkably lenient financial arrangement between them and his company. Since the 1950s, many fast-food owners had made their companies public and grown through franchising, an arrangement that often forced operators to absorb significant start-up costs. Since Chick-fil-A was not a public company, Cathy spread ownership among members of the Cathy family and eschewed the traditional style of franchising.

Chick-fil-A's franchise model approximated Baptist ecclesiology. Southern Baptists tended to endorse congregational autonomy, although financial resources pooled into the Southern Baptist Convention for redistribution to particularly needy Baptist congregations, institutions, colleges, missionary organizations, or humanitarian endeavors. Chick-fil-A operated in a similar, if not quite copycat fashion. "Operators" or franchisees, like Baptist pastors educated at a denominational school or seminary, were independent entrepreneurs, trained and licensed via Chick-fil-A's front office and its training program. (Although, unlike Baptist pastors, they could not be fired by their "congregation" of employees or an equivalent "board of directors.") Chick-fil-A allowed any potential operator to open a location with a modest "buy-in" investment of $5,000, instead of the tens or hundreds of thousands of dollars that a McDonald's or Wendy's operator often had to provide up front. Cathy's company covered, with money pooled from other franchises' profits, the rest of the new location's capitalization and the operator's training. Fifteen percent of gross sales went to Cathy, who then split any future sales 50-50 with the operator. The Cathy family and their executive board, much like the Southern Baptist Convention's president and board of favored pastors or denominational insiders, doled out top-down declarations of corporate theology that, nevertheless, was left up to the local franchisee to implement or ignore (although most did the former). Inspirational revivals, held at Chick-fil-A headquarters or at convention centers nationwide and intended to remind attendees of their corporate loyalties and earthly rewards, approximated the intermittent revival schedule in the Baptist annual calendar (complete with travelling corporate revivalists, such as Zig Ziglar, a personal friend of Cathy's). Franchise operators also enjoyed rewards for high sales numbers, from all-expense-paid vacations, merchandise, and cash bonuses to free Lincoln Continentals for any operator who raised sales by 40 percent or more in a given fiscal year. Like the Baptist faith itself, such incentives made Chick-fil-A a popular choice for those seeking to work quasi-independently and serve an established corporation while retaining the sense that they were masters of their own spiritual and commercial futures.[49]

Cathy's Human Resources department conducted a stringent interview process for operators. Religion was not an explicit part of the interview process, obviously to avoid Title VII violations. But the politics of hair and dress, raised by the counterculture and sexual revolutions of the 1960s, were important to Cathy. He firmly believed "it is rather easy to size up an individual [operator] in the first two minutes." "If the shoes are not shined, the handshake is not firm, the hair is not groomed," then an applicant had no chance of getting in Cathy's good graces. The application process, and the incentives that came along with it, also seemed to ensure the loyalty and productivity Cathy sought among his operators. In 1989, Chick-fil-A averaged a loss of only 5 percent of operators per year, in stark contrast to the 25 to 35 percent turnover rates for operators in the fast-food industry as a whole. Again, such statistics reaffirmed Cathy's notion that he had passed along to his managers a winning mix of corporate family values, loyalty, and leadership.[50]

To make good on Cathy's offerings, operators were expected to hire and train equally loyal and driven employees. Yet again, religion was not the determining factor for employment. Still, employees were mostly teenagers or young adults, and Cathy and his operators tolerated none of the youthful rebellion, sexual license, surliness, or laziness that seemed to conservative Americans to be the most significant legacies of the 1960s. As with operators, the politics of hair and dress mattered. Applicants needed to have a "good general [physical] appearance" and demonstrate, like operators, a "sense of significance" to gain employment at Chick-fil-A. "If a man's got an earring in his ear and he applies to work at one of my restaurants," Cathy told the Associated Press in 2000, "We won't even talk to him. It's not becoming for a man to wear an earring. . . . I can't take that risk." The risk was more than a matter of professional appearance. It was also the risk of condoning such gender formulations as a new standard of behavior.[51] Because of its evangelical and familial overtones, Chick-fil-A became a popular employment option for parents interested in managing their children's exposure to unsettling or non-Christian work environments. Though not always from evangelical families, homeschoolers nevertheless served as an important labor pool for Chick-fil-A's recruiters. "They're smart, ambitious, and very driven," observed Andy Lorenzen, a Chick-fil-A representative. "They have a high level of loyalty to the business, are diligent and have a good work ethic." Alexa Mason, a seventeen-year-old homeschool student in Charlotte, North Carolina, "enjoyed the flexible hours" and "great environment" that Chick-fil-A offered, as did her parents, who, like many homeschoolers, sought out Chick-fil-A because of its Christian affiliations. Of course, homeschoolers did not make up most of Cathy's workforce. One operator claimed that only 10 percent of his employees had been homeschooled.[52] Still, hiring a disproportionate number of homeschoolers lined up with Chick-fil-A's continuing commitment to hire workers of a "different" background than most fast-food companies, which helped brand it as a "different" type of fast-food enterprise. "Like its competitors, Chick-fil-A targets high-school students to work the counter," observed business writer Frederick F. Reichheld, "but it goes after the upper end of the class, typically higher achievers and more dedicated workers who have long-term intentions of attending college." Thus, on average, Chick-fil-A's rank-and-file tended to be whiter, more middle class, more educated, and more loyal than those working in the fast-food industry in general. Whether or not they were Christians like Cathy, they at least in appearance and attitude exuded the cultural conservatism that Cathy deemed most desirable for corporate work.[53]

Obviously, Cathy's college scholarship fund helped attract and keep such workers. But since most did not earn this scholarship, other factors kept the job applications coming. A corporate culture that emphasized the value of middle-class work certainly helped, as did hourly wages a few dollars higher than the industry standard of minimum or near-minimum wage. Its Christian proclamations and affiliations also marked Chick-fil-A as a business where, presumably, young workers would not be overworked or undervalued. Its managerial role models—heterosexual, religious, like Cathy and his "family" of executives— would also offer a different "lifestyle" for teenagers and college-age workers to consider, ostensibly contrary to other role models. In short, Chick-fil-A was a fast-food corporation that middle-class, suburban parents (or any other involved parent) would not mind their children working for. It was a place where a parent's moral outlook—whether oriented around conservative evangelical-ism, household or corporate heteronormativity, the perceived need for teenag-ers to have a productive job, or just the notion that hard work pays off and state support is superfluous—seemed to flourish and be rewarded in ways unusual in the fast-food industry at large.

Supply Chains

As with other evangelical-led companies, Chick-fil-A's market shaped its mission as well as the work undergirding that mission. Higher pay for hourly workers accorded with Chick-fil-A's push to fit into the labor market of middle-class sub-urbia. For evangelical executives in other markets and locales, however, labor's demands were more of an obstacle to be overcome than a need to be addressed. Profit maximization and pay squeezing, downscaling, or the privatization of public resources seemed the goals of several other evangelical-led or -affili-ated companies. For instance, according to supermarket HEB's 1988 guide for workers, "The company will oppose a union at H-E-B by every legal means." Oklahoma-based Hobby Lobby—founded in 1970 by the conservative evangel-ical David Green—also opposed unions and located its stores in smaller towns and atomized suburbs, thereby making organizing difficult. With a middle-aged workforce of working women and mothers, Hobby Lobby's employees also had much to lose from joining a union and generally did not do so. Other evangelical companies were generally non-union organizations, a product of a middle-class or transient workforce (such as Chick-fil-A's) or outright suppression by man-agement (as in the case of Tyson Foods). Given their respective business mod-els and markets, few evangelical companies garnered direct public contracts as LeTourneau once had. But the few that did generally worked to privatize public institutions and resources. For instance, in the 1970s and 1980s, ServiceMaster was a popular resource for states and municipalities frustrated with unionized or public workers. Although evidence is sketchy, ServiceMaster's franchise arrangement certainly made unionization difficult across the company, as in other franchised or locally controlled companies. It did not have an officially published stance against unions in the 1960s and 1970s, but by the late 1980s ServiceMaster was a popular option for localities seeking to cut costs through subcontracting or the privatization of public or unionized workforces.[54]

Along with privatization efforts, the history of one evangelical-led company made it clear how far evangelical businessman could push their in-house and pub-lic authority. Lonnie "Bo" Pilgrim, a Texas Baptist in a right-to-work state, was an evangelical authoritarian intent on building his own personality cult. Pilgrim owned and ran Pilgrim's Pride, a poultry processing company. Federal agriculture subsidies undergirded Pilgrim's business model, as since the 1950s agricultural policy tended to privilege highly scaled, well-capitalized poultry processing companies over smaller scale suppliers. Pilgrim, like another evangelical family, the Tyson family of Arkansas, benefitted from and lobbied for such subsidies, using political connections and regulations to crowd out competitors and establish highly integrated companies. Most of the typical, post–Title VII practices flourished at Pilgrim's Pride in the 1970s and would come to define parts of Tyson Foods's corporate culture in the 1990s, primarily through a chaplaincy program and voluntary prayer breakfast among Tyson operators. Employees at Pilgrim's Pride were not hired or fired based on their religious persuasions, but voluntary Bible studies were available in Pilgrim's plants. Prayers were also common at corporate headquarters, as were other forms of religious expression that related Pilgrim's view of himself and his evangelical mission. In the late 1970s and 1980s, he regularly dressed in the garb of a Mayflower pilgrim when touring the state or appearing in nationally televised advertisements, and the company's primary logo—the cameo of a pilgrim, complete with silver-buckled black hat—emphasized the myth of America's Christian origins. At the company's headquarters in Pittsburg, Texas, Pilgrim also commissioned a giant on-site statue of his own head, donned with the signature pilgrim's hat. Pilgrim also gave money for the construction of a "Prayer Tower, which [sat] on triangle-shaped Witness Park, near downtown Pittsburg." Completed in 1992, the 75-foot-tall stone tower contained "beautiful stained glass, French bells, and Belgian clocks. Inside [was] a small chapel, chairs, a long kneeling bench, and a large, thumb-worn Bible on a lectern. There [were] no locks on the doors. Visitors come day and night to enjoy the quiet elegance and peacefulness of the place."[55]

Bo Pilgrim's public witness did not push him toward ensuring healthy labor relations; rather, it seemed to invigorate his authoritarianism and bullish approach toward state regulators. Once, in 1989, Pilgrim shocked the Texas state legislature when he walked onto the Senate floor and proceeded to hand out $10,000 checks along with his personal business card to legislators just two days before a vote on workers' compensation laws. One Senator called the stunt "outrageous" while a state representative promised to propose a law prohibiting such contributions on Capitol grounds. Two swing voters took Pilgrim up on his offer but the bill floundered and, in fact, reopened discussions of campaign finance reform to prevent Pilgrim and other businesses interests from having too much sway in Texas legislative politics. (A subsequent bill passed, prohibiting lawmakers from taking contributions while in session or physically inside the Capitol building.)[56]

The poor treatment of workers at Pilgrim's plants also overlapped with his increased dependence on immigrant work. Pilgrim admitted to *The Dallas*

Morning News in 1996 that he was more than willing to hire migrant labor. In fact, he spiritualized the issue. "God wants poor people to have jobs," he said. He stuck to this position a decade later. "We're not looking for cheap labor," he told another reporter. "We're looking for available labor. How many people can you get to squat down and catch chickens?" Pilgrim's active recruitment of Latino laborers—many lacking legal status in the United States—garnered an investigation into Pilgrim's Mount Pleasant, Texas, facility under the suspicion that Pilgrim officials were looking the other way when workers presented false documents and engaging in discriminatory hiring practices at other plants, rejecting non-Latino male applicants and Latino female applicants "in favor of Hispanic male applicants." Neither did Pilgrim's evangelical convictions seem to bring a reevaluation of his company's environmental impact. Though he once stated that, "when you sin against the environment, you are sinning against the Lord," Pilgrim seemed less than inclined to repent of his company's sins. Between 1985 and 1999, Pilgrim was cited dozens of times by state and federal officials for violations of air and water laws. Pilgrim paid over $500,000 in fines during the same years.[57]

When investigating such instances of corporate "hypocrisy" and illegality, labor lawyers, investigative journalists, and government regulators rarely noticed that any exposé simply demonstrated how embedded evangelicals were in the structures of the American economy. On this score, Chick-fil-A was no more exceptional than ServiceMaster, HEB, or Pilgrim's Pride. In Chick-fil-A's case, following the supply chain back to its source revealed the full-scale dependence of the company on the low price of chicken and the low-wage economics of poultry processing. Although Chick-fil-A did not receive its chicken from Pilgrim, it did receive it from two other poultry conglomerates. At an undetermined point in either the late 1980s or early 1990s, Chick-fil-A dropped its affiliation with Goode Brothers Poultry Company, a Georgia processor that had supplied it with ready-made chicken fillets since the company's early days. Instead, it began receiving its processed chicken meat from other suppliers, most notably Perdue Farms, the second largest poultry processor in the United States, and Wayne Farms, the nation's sixth largest vertically integrated poultry processor and a subsidiary of food conglomerate ContiGroup.

Like Pilgrim's Pride or Tyson, Perdue Farms and Wayne Farms became industry leaders by specializing in what anthropologist Steve Striffler termed "the industrial chicken." In plants throughout the economically depressed and deunionized rural South, Perdue Farms and Wayne Farms gained full control over all points of production, from hatcheries to transportation to processing to packaging, marketing, and distribution. Both companies also fully rationalized and specialized the chicken processing line, resulting in a new type of finished chicken, one processed into myriad cuts for wholesale to restaurants, grocery store freezers, and fast-food vendors like Chick-fil-A. (In Perdue Farms's case, after it bought a 500,000-square-foot plant in Perry, Georgia, in 2004, it supplied Chick-fil-A with nearly 350,000 birds per week for its restaurants.)[58]

Despite federal and state prohibitions, both Perdue Farms and Wayne Farms also regularly employed undocumented workers from Central and South America.[59] In Surry County, North Carolina, field researchers for the University of New Hampshire's Carsey Institute found that "80–85% of [Wayne Farms's] work force is Hispanic" with "many employees [living] in a trailer park adjacent to the chicken plant." Sidestepping the law was common in other ways. After investigating the death of an undocumented worker at an Alabama Wayne Farms plant, the US Labor Department's Occupational Safety and Health Administration found no less than twenty safety violations, warranting fines of nearly $60,000. Such labor and safety violations, however, were not the company's only problem. During at least one test period between 1998 and 2005, five of Wayne Farms' seven plants failed federal tests for salmonella contamination.[60]

Such violations hardly hurt the company's profits. With a client list that included Chick-fil-A, as well as Zatarain's, Jack in the Box, Costco, Nestlé, and Applebee's Restaurants, Wayne Farms posted approximately $1 billion in sales in 2004, with expectations for a "10% annual growth in sales for the next five years." What worked for the chicken processing industry also apparently worked for Chick-fil-A. In 2008, Chick-fil-A's annual sales pushed close to $3 billion, a 12 percent jump over the previous year. Though facing an economic recession and stiff competition from McDonald's (which produced its own plagiarized version of Cathy's signature sandwich), Chick-fil-A remained one of the fastest-growing fast-food chains in the country. Reflecting on his company's standing over forty years after its founding, Dan Cathy remarked, "I do think that God has blessed our business."[61]

One might read an ethical problem into the supply chains undergirding Chick-fil-A. Behind the counter lay a vast, highly scaled system of exploitation and abuse. Whether or not Chick-fil-A's executives or customers wanted to accept it, this system fueled the company's quarterly growth and evangelical activism. Indeed, Chick-fil-A's funding of philanthropies that supported heteronormative "family values"—a commitment that only came to light in the midst of investigative reports in 2011 and 2012—was another facet of the "blessings" that the Cathy family saw as forthcoming from Chick-fil-A's transformation into an evangelical big business. And, without the cheap chicken sandwich, and the workers who made it, Chick-fil-A could not do big business or "take stands" for its vision of evangelical culture or the heteronormative family. More distressingly, the economy of Chick-fil-A, much like the economy of any evangelical business, big or small, placed customers in an ethically intractable position. To buy at Chick-fil-A, whether merely to satisfy lunchtime hunger or as a form of evangelical "buycotting," was to back the poultry processors behind Chick-fil-A. To retract consumer support was to do the opposite, albeit with the effects of quarterly losses likely felt first by hourly workers behind the counter or on the line at a Wayne Farms or Perdue plant.

Acknowledging that evangelical businesses were not isolated entities but institutions embedded in complex and scaled market arrangements also pointed to another fact about conservative evangelicalism. By building bigger and bigger businesses, evangelicals created situations where the consumer needs and desires of ordinary Americans became the engine behind evangelical influence. Corporate forms of conservative evangelicalism, then, ensured that evangelical activities would be directly subsidized by consumer demand just as the state had subsidized LeTourneau's marketplace missions. This was not necessarily a cynical or craven strategy. For the most part, evangelicals opened businesses for the same reasons that anyone opens a business, the purpose of religious activism notwithstanding. Still, whatever its exact configuration of faith, labor, services, goods, and executive oversight, American consumers underwrote evangelical endeavors and certain facets of their social and political activism.

From the late 1970s through the 1990s, evangelical executives—some political conservatives, others moderates, others somewhere in between—chaired a wide range of large-scale companies, including General Motors, Borg-Warner, The Boston Company, Raytheon, Chemical Waste Management Inc., Burger King, Wendy's, Eckerd's Drugs, Knight-Ridder, Rayco, Buford Television, In-N-Out Burger, The Allen Morris Company, Snyder Oil Corporation, Hall-Mark Electronics, Highland Park Cafeterias, The Medart Companies, Wyndham Hotels, Williamson Cadillac Company, Pizza Hut/PepsiCo, Martin Sprocket and Gear, Westaff Inc., Cavan Real Estate Investments, The Miami Herald, Comps. com, eHarmony.com, FlowData Inc., Hobby Lobby, Kinetic Concepts, SYSCO, Forever 21, and World Wide Technology. To be sure, evangelicals remained a distinct minority of board members or CEOs in corporate America. Neither were they at the helm of most of the nation's small businesses. But, as sociologist D. Michael Lindsay put it, evangelicals had clearly "entered the American elite."[62]

In reality, evangelical business executives had been members of the American elite long before the new experiments in corporate evangelicalism in the late twentieth century. Moreover, conservative evangelicals had long retained sympathizers and backers in the American elite. Still, the particular legal and economic context of the 1970s and 1980s ushered in nuanced, varied, and uneven strategies to retain and expand their religion's presence and power in and through corporate America. With leeway granted by the courts, employers and executives were relatively free to encourage the diffusion of the evangelical movement via the private sector. This was a new direction in the business history of born-again America. Whereas a push for unity of religious purpose might have driven evangelical business leaders into relation with one another in the 1940s and 1950s, in the 1970s they moved toward independence and diffusion.

The preference for privatization, which simultaneously empowered evangelical executives and underpinned their brand of identity politics and familial conservatism, drove evangelical corporate aspirations and activities elsewhere. In another suburban locale, the small edge city of Fort Mill, South Carolina, 18 miles south of the burgeoning metropolis of Charlotte, North Carolina, a promising new vision of evangelical America appeared, a fantasy world delivered by a new evangelical business conglomerate made possible by the same federal government that shaped the Cold War ventures of LeTourneau and marketplace missions of Cathy. Outside Fort Mill were a number of new cultural industries that similarly delivered evangelicals a set of ready-made identities, constructed and capitalized by a new class of evangelical businessmen who found a great deal of profit—social and financial—in making evangelical culture into the next big thing in business.

5

Culture Industries

Heritage USA and the Corporatization of Evangelical Culture

In 1978, televangelists Jim and Tammy Faye Bakker opened Heritage USA in the suburban edge city of Fort Mill, South Carolina, just across the North Carolina border. Funded by bank loans and millions of dollars in contributions to Praise the Lord (PTL), the Bakkers' television ministry, Heritage USA would grow into a sprawling 2,500-acre Christian resort that cost $175 million to build. It featured outdoor amenities, a shopping mall, a water park, and a four-story luxury hotel. (Another high-rise hotel was in the works by 1985, funded in part by a Maryland savings and loan.) It was a huge business, on par with a Fortune 500 corporation. By 1986, Heritage USA was the third-most-visited theme park in America, attracting 6 million visitors per year. Heritage USA was also one of the largest employers in the Charlotte metro area, with a full-time staff of 2,000.

Newsweek's religion editor Kenneth Woodward visited Heritage USA in 1986, proclaiming it a "Disneyland for the Devout." He was not far off with that assessment. The Disney corporate empire was Jim Bakker's immediate inspiration. "Why is it we can almost enshrine a mouse, a Mickey Mouse or a Donald Duck?" Bakker asked. "Why can't we have something where young people will be connected to Jesus Christ?" But Heritage USA wasn't just for children. It was a "Total Living Center," branded to serve the dual purpose of edifying the faithful and evangelizing others. "Jesus said that we were to be fishers of men. And with some of the bait that we have used in the church—I call it dill-pickle religion—I've never seen anyone catch a fish with a dill pickle and sourpuss religion. . . . The thing that I have resented in the past is that somehow there is almost an unseen force that says religion has to be boring and dull and dreary. And I rebel against that. I think true religion is a relationship with Jesus Christ. . . . It should be beautiful, it should be creative."[1]

Bakker's critics were less sympathetic than Woodward. "Interesting that the same God who inspired the cathedral at Chartres, Westminster Abbey and the Sistine Chapel also inspired this," wrote humorist P. J. O'Rourke. "That Big Guy Upstairs can be a real kidder." The park made a similar impression on journalist Hunter James, who cited the "fetid, cloying stench of PTL wholesomeness and good fellowship" as the park's defining characteristic. Heritage USA was religious kitsch at its worst.[2]

Critics were far too dismissive. Bakker's "rebellion"—through creative, privatized consumption—signaled a fuller alignment between conservative Christianity and corporate enterprise. He was at the vanguard of a new generation of evangelical leaders who doubled as business executives. Most were as flexible toward religious boundaries as the most effective evangelicals of the past, seeking out youth markets and warming to the very countercultural motifs of the 1960s and 1970s that they wished to contain or appropriate in other arenas, particularly electoral and legislative politics.

Bakker was also in the growing big business of televangelism, a culture industry that paralleled and—at times—intersected with several other growing evangelical industries: in retail, publishing, and music. The term "industry" is important and appropriate. Though each began as small or niche businesses, by the mid-1970s, they were going corporate. Various executives brought disparate, competitive enterprises under one corporate roof while nonevangelical businesses interests— such as mass-market book publishers and music labels—shaped the distribution to and demand of consumers. Evangelical culture was, by the mid-1980s, a multimillion-dollar business. Ten years later, it was a multibillion-dollar business.

The evangelical culture industries that provided the images, goods, and ideas for sale at Heritage USA also matched the park's ownership and executive model. They were more like large corporations than the individualistic and entrepreneurial proclamations Bakker and others used. In the evangelical television industry, corporatization worked hand-in-glove with a changing federal government. After changes in "fair use" and "paid time" regulations, televangelists quickly used up-to-date marketing and fundraising strategies to transform television stations and programming into vehicles for religious community and political expression. By the 1980s, they dominated the religious media market. In the 1950s and early 1960s, evangelicals backed by big businessmen aimed to align the word "Christian" with "fundamentalist" or "new evangelical." Likewise, the evangelical culture industries worked to ensure that the only "Christian" many Americans saw on television or in stores was bearing the conservative evangelical brand.

In a way, then, the broader move toward large-scale corporations and Wall Street empowerment in the deregulatory environment of the 1970s and 1980s had a precursor and parallel in the corporatization of conservative evangelical culture. To be sure, the goods that stocked the shelves at Heritage USA told a story of evangelical assertiveness and corporatization that had been developing since before the Great Depression. But especially after the 1960s, large-scale, mass-market evangelical industries emerged, including a niche-market Christian music industry and mass-market radio and publishing conglomerates.

Evangelical retail businesses also grew by leaps and bounds in the 1970s, promoting notions that "buying Christian" was analogous to "being Christian," with the meaning of "Christian" precluding most any definition other than "conservative evangelical." New forms of capitalization came via nonevangelical business interests and corporate investors who sought to get a profitable piece of the evangelical culture industries. Indeed, whereas big-business largesse had long been vital to nonprofit startups, such as Moody Bible Institute or *Christianity Today*, media conglomerates, big music labels, and investors now began to shape for-profit evangelical culture industries. Shared religious or political interest sparked investor interest, as did a sheer desire on the part of investors for more market share. For outside investors, evangelical identity politics, a politics defined by "revival" through routine consumption, was great for the bottom line.

There is no doubt that Heritage USA and Christian television, music, and radio were personally edifying for evangelicals and enabled new directions in evangelicals' long-standing religious mission and broader social or political crusades. Each enlivened the faith for millions and exposed it to millions more. In the living room, at home, in the car, or at church, to be "evangelical" or "Christian" in America was to be defined by personal, private, and communal revival via the goods, images, sights, and sounds created by evangelical culture industries. Of course the lived religious experiences of American evangelicals, as well as the opinions of evangelical intellectuals about life in a corporate America, remained diverse and dependent on what one did with a consumer good after buying it or what one felt when a song came on the radio. Yet, by the mid-1980s, the evangelical culture industries flattened the definition of the "Christian" life to roughly match Bakker's definition—the consumption of goods and experiences proffered on the television, over the radio, at the retail store, and, of course, inside the confines of Heritage USA. To be a born-again Christian was to consume perpetually, to be born again and again by buying what corporate executives, sellers, retailers, and producers provided. The links between evangelical consumers and corporate providers was no story of economic hoodwinking or false consciousness. Evangelical consumers knew exactly what they were doing and desiring. Buying evangelical goods seemingly made them good and godly evangelicals. Enriching their personal faith through consumer goods also, by proxy or purchase or profit margins, advanced a religious and cultural movement driven by suppliers who fused ever-bigger business to conservative evangelicalism and vice versa.[3]

Federal Law and the Rise of Televangelism

Heritage USA would have never existed without a number of dramatic shifts in how the federal government regulated religious media. As with most forms of new media, evangelicals jumped at the chance to tap into the television market in the 1940s, primarily because television afforded the chance to reproduce the revival experience. Unlike print or radio, television simulated the face-to-face exchange between preacher and audience, drawing observers and advocates of "televangelism" alike to call it a new form of "electric church." But in the immediate postwar period, evangelicals' place on the television dial was in peril. During World War II, the Federal Council of Churches worked feverishly to keep many evangelical radio broadcasters—such as Fighting Bob Shuler and Charles Fuller—off major radio networks. In 1949, the Federal Communications Commission (FCC) instituted the "fairness doctrine," which required all licensed stations that broadcast nationwide to avoid controversial topics and editorializing for the sake of "public service." On the chance that controversial topics—including religion—were a part of programming, "balance" had to be maintained. Any religious viewpoints expressed on a given program had to be met by opposing religious viewpoints, leading to many network radio broadcasts that featured a Protestant, a Catholic, and a Jew. Regulatory prescriptions, at least according to the networks, seemed good for the bottom line. Religion could be a "splitter" subject, something that potentially repelled listeners. Broadcasters were therefore incentivized to avoid controversy, aim for the middle, and avoid regulatory oversight and fines. Firebrands were assumed to be bad for business.

As television matured in the 1950s, the National Council of Churches upheld and endorsed the fairness doctrine. NBC and CBS supported the move, which followed a policy drafted by Charles F. McFarland, the general secretary of the National Council of Churches' predecessor, the Federal Council of Churches, and a member of the NBC Advisory Committee on Religious Activities. McFarland's policy encouraged nondenominationalism, the use of one speaker through broadcasts, the shouldering of production costs by religious groups, and "avoiding matters of doctrine and controversial subjects." At NBC, ecumenical incentive also governed what did and did not receive airtime. "The National Broadcasting Company," its Advisory Committee had declared in 1928, "will serve only the central national agencies of great religious faiths, as for example, the Roman Catholics, the Protestants, and the Jews." For the most part, it followed this stance into the postwar era, as did ABC and the Mutual Broadcasting Company.[4]

The evangelical fight for airtime was led by a consortium of evangelical preachers and businessmen: the National Religious Broadcasters Association (NRB). The National Association of Evangelicals set up the NRB in 1944 to counter the networks' policies. Herbert J. Taylor and J. Elwin Wright were vital to the NRB's early formation, although dozens of evangelical radio broadcasters were its most fervent members and supporters. Effectively a lobbying group, the NRB pressured the networks to allow more "paid time" slots. In short, a paid time slot was a slot in daily programming that was readily available for sale to anyone with the upfront cash. Paid time slots were usually reserved for local stations that wanted to fill a daily schedule with nonbroadcast programs, both to avoid dead air and to maximize the profitability of every hour. Paid time slots, however, still had to comply with the fairness doctrine. The NRB sought to change this to allow "independent" religious broadcasters—generally conservative evangelicals—a chance to have their voices heard outside minor markets. Long before the privatization push of the 1970s by neoliberal economists and politicians, evangelical activists wanted radio and television programming—then defined as "public goods" for the "public interests"—turned over to the market.[5]

Statistics alone convinced evangelicals that television was the wave of the future. Television was the nation's fastest-growing mass medium, rising from just over 250,000 sets in use in 1948 to 17 million in 1952. By the end of the decade, 90 percent of American homes had at least one television. And the regulatory climate shaped the brand of religion that Americans saw on their screens. Aside from Billy Graham and a few other evangelicals, television was dominated by Catholics and progressive Protestants. For instance, the nation's leading televangelist was Roman Catholic Bishop J. Fulton Sheen, who presented ecumenical, inspirational, and informational lessons on subjects ranging from communism to art, science, war, and family life to an audience of millions each week from 1952 to 1957. Softer-toned and well-financed evangelicals, such as Percy Crawford, Rex Humbard, and Robert Schuller, did make it onscreen during the 1950s, paying for programming on independent stations or negotiating deals with major networks to air their offerings. Pentecostal preacher Oral Roberts did the same. That many of them adopted the more inclusive approach of the "new" evangelicals or moderate, business-minded Rotary Club style of evangelism was crucial. By eschewing sectarianism, each fell ever so slightly within the regulatory boundaries of the "fairness doctrine." Mass appeal also mattered. By the late 1950s, Crawford, Humbard, Schuller, and Roberts had become popular brands in and of themselves. Each had a loyal and predictable audience—one that crossed denominational and social boundaries—that they had cultivated via years spent building a name for themselves as capable, respectable evangelicals and businessmen to boot. Style also mattered. Onscreen, at least, none traded in wild-eyed tirade but rather took their cues from the variety shows on the "big three" networks to sell their message of eternal salvation and earthly satisfaction.[6]

Though prominent evangelicals were already taking advantage of the television revolution, the NRB did not stop stumping for more paid-time programming on the largest networks, namely NBC and CBS. From 1955 to 1960, it repeatedly lobbied the federal government against what NRB members saw as a conspiracy by the FCC, big-name networks, and liberal Protestant groups to use the fairness doctrine to keep evangelicals off the air. In 1960, however, the FCC released a policy statement that revolutionized religious programming in America. In short, the FCC relaxed its regulatory standard, allowing radio and television stations to count paid time as "public service," thereby financially incentivizing radio and television networks to make time slots available to anyone who could pay. Uncoupling "public interest broadcasting" from "free air time" effectively destroyed part of the liberal media establishment, namely its hold on the networks or local stations. As mainline Protestant denominational and church budgets slid in the 1950s and 1960s, they were unable to retain media dominance. Representatives from nonevangelical denominations argued that they deserved the continued backing of the FCC, but the networks had already moved on to other, more profitable options. Ready and willing to fill paid time programming were a number of independent preachers and upstart "televangelists." Each was thrilled to put their gospel on the air, and networks and stations were happy to oblige, especially since evangelicals offered top dollar for time. *Christianity Today* and other evangelical outlets supported the NRB's efforts, occasionally printing articles that called for the fairness doctrine's nullification, applauding "paid slots" for spreading the gospel, or airing evangelical grievances regarding an assumed— and often actual—favoritism showed by FCC regulators toward more liberal programming. Firebrand fundamentalists, such as Carl McIntire, still had difficulty getting or staying on the air. In 1967, McIntire engaged in a lengthy fight with the FCC, which ended badly for him. By 1973, his station's license was not renewed and, deeply in debt and out of step with the media environment of the 1970s, McIntire began a slow fade into further obscurity.[7]

Freed from state prohibition, evangelical televangelism took off in the 1970s. One of the first to garner a notable audience was Trinity Broadcasting Network, which Jim and Tammy Faye Bakker helped to popularize with Pat and Jan Crouch and the help of the Full Gospel Business Men's Fellowship, International's Demos Shakarian in 1973. A member of the NRB known for Pentecostal and prosperity gospel leanings, Trinity was one of many to move to cable in the 1970s. From 1970 to 1978, independent evangelicals who purchased airtime through donations increased in number from thirty-eight to seventy-two. By 1977, religious programming denoted as "paid-time" programs was at 92 percent, a dramatic change from 1959 when only 53 percent of religious programming was purchased. In the estimation of one scholar, the move to paid programming "left evangelicals with virtually no competition, except among themselves." The rise of televangelism led to a spike in NRB members. "It's a phenomenon, no question about it," noted Dr. Ben Armstrong, head of the NRB, in an interview with *New York* magazine in 1980. "Membership in

NRB . . . has increased 900 percent since the sixties." Armstrong was not too far off in his estimation. The NRB grew from 104 members in 1968 to 900 in 1980, with NRB members producing "at least 70 percent of all the religious broadcasts in the United States." Again, stations had strong incentives to field airtime orders, especially from televangelists with cash in hand. In fact, there was an imitation effect as televangelists garnered more space on local and regional programming. In 1971, the Broadcast Institute of North America found that, at least when it came to religious programming, station managers were not influenced by local interests or community responses. Instead, they usually made their decision on which televangelists to privilege according to what their competitors and coun-terparts were deciding to air. As a result, evangelicals sought out non-network television stations and cable-access channels to build or expand their audiences, encouraging a fundraising race to marginalize competitors.[8]

A decade's worth of competition and consolidation left a handful of televan-gelists at the top of the heap. As one expert on religious broadcasting noted in 1984, "These broadcasters, who once could not get enough time, have been so effective in their struggle that they now hold a virtual monopoly over airtime used for religious programming, having forced most other religious programs off the air by their cut-throat purchase of time." Now in charge of the market, a small number of televangelists dictated terms, showing "none of the consideration for other types of programming which they originally sought for themselves." A lack of government oversight encouraged authoritarian tendencies, but so too did the religious logic of televangelists. Casting themselves as having a direct line to God's will and purpose, televangelists rejected "the general principle that oth-ers should regulate their broadcasting activities," much less that the government should impose regulations that were "both inappropriate and unnecessary and, therefore, unwelcome." In short, televangelists used the logic of many an evan-gelical business executive. Accountability to God was enough.[9]

Consolidation centralized money and power. Spurred by slick advertising, clever branding, and perpetual appeals for donations, hundreds of millions of dollars flowed into the coffers of a few prominent televangelistic operations dur-ing the 1970s and 1980s, making them commercial entities on par with many large-scale businesses in terms of cash flow and potential social influence. The Bakkers certainly exhibited such characteristics, but so too did the television ministries of Rex Humbard, Pat and Jan Crouch, Jimmy Swaggart, Billy Graham, Pat Robertson, and James Robison. Though varied in style and message, each needed an ever-expanding network of donors to set quarterly budgets, hire additional technicians, and buy time. Differing—and sometimes overlapping— financial bases revealed both market segmentation and a kind of competi-tive consolidation. By the mid-1980s, evangelical televangelists dominated the market, even after almost a decade of declines in audience after the initial explosion in viewers from 1970 to 1975. Estimates by analysts noted that only eight televangelists, all conservative evangelicals of some stripe, were watched by 85 percent of the "religious television audience." Gallup and Arbitron, however, disagreed about the exact size of that audience, with televangelists lauding Gallup's larger numbers ("one in three adults [60 million] had watched religious television" in the past month) and their critics lauding Arbitron's smaller estimates of "between 7.3 and 9.2 million persons." Regardless of whose numbers were accurate, few other types of "Christian" were to be found on television. Wherever the viewer went on the dial, evangelicalism was the televangelist's brand of conservative Christianity—predominantly white, heterosexual, male-led, and consumerist.[10]

Televangelism's business model was both entrepreneurial and corporate. Perpetual pitches to donors for hitting higher marks in terms of financial support joined with a personality-driven, top-down organization focused on controlling risk. This was, of course, not a new way of organizing evangelical money. In the 1950s, Percy Crawford had pioneered the solicitation of subscribers to support his early ventures in televangelism. Billy Graham, Rex Humbard, Oral Roberts, and many other predecessors had run their television ventures in similar fashion. But the freewheeling approach toward hitting monthly fundraising goals was certainly new and in keeping with the upsurge in evangelical assertiveness in the public and commercial spheres of American life. Televangelism's accounting model also broke from evangelical trends. As nonprofit, tax-free organizations, the Billy Graham Evangelistic Association and *Christianity Today* had been scrupulous about finances, publishing audits and paying modest salaries to directors, board members, and editors. Televangelists, by contrast, often reveled in ostentation and conspicuous consumption. So, asked many observers, were televangelists merely modern-day Elmer Gantrys running—as one book put it—a "ministry of greed"?[11] Newspaper reporters obsessed over this question. And with the amount of money flooding into televangelistic enterprises in the 1970s and 1980s, it was a fair one to ask. Televangelism was a big business operating with few referees. Televangelists also exuded libertarian defensiveness toward any form of governmental or ecclesiastical oversight. By 1976, only 13 percent of religious organizations—which included many televangelist organizations—had provided any audited financial information to the Better Business Bureau. Two years later, three-quarters of televangelists offered no financial information to any public watchdog group.

In response, in 1979 a consortium of evangelicals set up the Evangelical Council for Financial Accountability (ECFA). Moderate evangelical Senator Mark Hatfield led the way, threatening to regulate televangelism and evangelical organizations unless evangelicals got their house in order. "Legislation is not important; disclosure is," reiterated Thomas Getman, Hatfield's chief legislative

assistant, to a group of evangelical leaders in Chicago. "[Hence,] a voluntary disclosure program" was needed that "preclude[d] the necessity of federal intervention into the philanthropic and religious sector." Stanley Mooneyham, head
of World Vision, agreed, noting that "this threat of governmental action was
one of the stimuli" for the creation of the ECFA. Still, creating such a voluntary
council did little to bring televangelistic enterprises to heel. Jerry Falwell, the
Billy Graham Evangelistic Association, World Vision, and Campus Crusade for
Christ joined the ECFA, but no other syndicated television ministry did. Citing
"religious freedom" and First Amendment rights, televangelists continued with
little to no oversight into the 1980s. Jim and Tammy Faye Bakker's PTL ministries did so with particular aplomb, pulling in millions of dollars that kept the
Bakkers' television show on the air but also went toward the newest venture in
evangelical big business, the creation of a private evangelical resort where feeling
and buying "Christian" defined what it meant to be a conservative evangelical in
modern America.[12]

Consuming Evangelical Culture at Heritage USA

Calling Heritage USA the "biggest bargain family vacation in Dixieland," one
travel reporter noted that it was "an exciting moment when guests approach[ed]
the . . . resort in its national park setting." Once past the park's gatehouse, visitors encountered numerous examples of Bakker's extensive borrowing from
the Disney Corporation and Disneyland culture. For instance, Main Street
Heritage USA, a twenty-five-store shopping complex, was an unabashed copy
of Disneyland's pastel-splashed, faux-Victorian Main Street USA. Both seemed
to resurrect an idyllic small-town life, which Bakker saw as a central part of his
1950s upbringing and many other evangelicals believed to be a casualty of sit-
ins, desegregation, urban riots, and other social upheavals in the 1960s. Both
featured a litter-free, crime-free, worry-free downtown of years past, restored to
its imagined former glory. As at Disneyland, the colors of the buildings—yellow, pink, green, purple—invoked freshness and frivolity. Food and souvenir
shops similarly dotted the Bakker's Main Street, inviting guests to sample "your
daily bread" from Der Bakker Bakkery or take home a bottle of perfume from the
Heavenly Scents shop. Each November, Heritage USA even donned Christmas
flair to rival Disneyland's annual holiday celebration, thereby signaling that
Bakker's appropriation of Disney culture was a year-round affair.[13]

Heritage USA took the ethos of suburban privatization and policing on vacation. Security and seclusion were paramount. A thirty-person security force
regularly patrolled the grounds, looking for any signs of alcohol, drugs, or dis-
orderly behavior. Anyone found breaking Heritage USA's long list of rules was

immediately asked to leave. Bakker's handling of other threats, such as disgruntled workers and volunteers, was likewise swift and direct. Since Heritage USA's early days, Bakker held the opinion that "You don't serve God for eight hours a day and then punch out." Accordingly, unpaid overtime and layoffs to "prod or punish those who balked" reportedly became standard operating procedure, although Bakker did hire back about half of the workers he released, at least on one occasion.[14]

Though trading in privatized security and consumption, the park offered more than that. It also indisputably addressed certain psychological and emotional needs. "Underneath the cordial jollity," wrote one reporter, "dwells a free-floating mass of emotion. The pain of past lives and current troubles.... All come spilling out in the ongoing effort to replace the anguish with an all-encompassing faith in Jesus." The emotional baggage that many visitors brought with them to the park varied widely. Some wanted relief from alcoholism, drug addiction, and suicidal thoughts. Others sought miraculous healing for crippling diseases or painful cancers. Still others desired counsel for their marital breakdowns or rebellious children. "We get a lot of widows coming here trying to deal with the change in their situation," reported Bill Ingram, a pastor who served in the Upper Room, the park's round-the-clock counseling center. Such concerns were met with family-centered, conservative solutions. For instance, in 1984 Bakker opened Heritage House, a counseling center for unwed mothers who chose birth instead of abortion. The facility had first-class furnishings that "looked like they came straight from an Ethan Allen showroom." Heritage House also provided cooking and child-care classes, private rooms, and the Tender Loving Care Adoption Agency, which found Christian foster parents for children whose parents had decided against terminating the pregnancy. Another facility, the People That Love Center, was located on the westernmost edge of Heritage USA and provided donated food, clothing, and furniture to underprivileged families. In the southwest corner of Heritage USA, the 30-acre Fort Hope complex offered housing, educational programs, and drug rehab to homeless men and women aged seventeen to forty. In keeping with evangelical perspectives regarding work and personal reform, Fort Hope did not accept all cases, admitting only those who—as one observer noted—were "serious about trying to learn a trade and the living skills necessary to lead productive lives."[15]

Privatized recreation and middle-class hospitality services, both facets of the Sunbelt economy that supported Chick-fil-A, Holiday Inn, and Days Inn, defined Heritage USA's brand of evangelical culture. Once more, as at other youth-oriented evangelical organizations and businesses, first-class recreation seemed to prevent "sinful" activities, especially those that might lead to unintended pregnancy or "deviant" sexuality. With the smaller, yet popular, Carowinds Amusement Park only 5 miles away, Heritage USA was in direct competition for youngsters and teenagers seeking a more "secular" recreational experience. Hence, after three years of construction, Bakker opened in 1986 a $13 million water park on Heritage USA's property. Wrapping around an expansive lake and named Heritage Island, the water park was, according to one observer, "a dissonant mix of ornate Victorian outbuildings, intended to blend with the adjoining Partner Center and the centerpiece volcano of artificial rock that Bakker wanted." The volcano was "supposed to evoke images of old religious movies and serve as a stage for fireworks displays." For Bakker, the water park was his most ambitious attempt at both marketing evangelicalism to nonbelievers and selling a safe space for evangelicals to find spiritual rest, relaxation, and reaffirmation. "Well, if the Bible says we are to be fishers of men, then a water park is just the bait," Bakker noted in an interview with *The New York Times*, "and I don't seen [*sic*] anything wrong in using some pretty fancy bait."[16]

Mythical visions of Christian history and a "Christian America" rounded out Heritage USA's privatized recreational offerings. Another of Bakker's most impressive attractions was the park's 3,000-seat amphitheater. The facility featured a $1 million replica of an ancient Jerusalem street as its main stage, but the amphitheater's fixed design hardly limited its range. Each summer, it played host to "Musical Heritage," a weekly presentation of American history through song, dialogue, and costume—a patriotic, city-on-a-hill vision of the nation's God-blessed past. A weeklong circus and Fourth of July celebration were likewise held at the amphitheater, as were regular performances of various biblical stories and concerts by prominent Christian musicians. The high points of the amphitheater's dramatic season, however, were the Easter Passion Play and the Christmas nativity reenactment. The Passion Play had a cast of 120 actors, "all committed Christians." Bakker contracted freelance actor Gary Morris, a spot-on look-alike of the iconic, long-haired, white Jesus for his services, which included a PG-rated crucifixion. Fitting the celebratory mood of the amphitheater's regular offerings, the Passion Play concluded with Jesus's resurrection and end-time victory over a red-suited, horned Satan, accentuated with strobe lights, lasers, and smoke machines. Beginning in November each year, the amphitheater took on a decidedly more subdued tone, showing a nightly reenactment of Matthew and Luke's nativity stories. A common occurrence in evangelical churches around the country, this nativity drama had the same intention behind it: drawing believers and nonbelievers alike toward an appreciation for the "true" reason for the season.[17]

Bakker also believed that a trip to Heritage USA trumped a Disney vacation because of the goods and consumer experiences offered by the evangelical culture industries. Like an increasing number of shopping centers around the country, Heritage USA's Main Street concourse contained retail stores specifically aimed at evangelical consumers (See Fig. 5.1). At Heritage USA's Christian bookstore,

Bibles in nearly every available size and color lined the shelves. Customers even had the chance to have their Bibles personalized with 24-karat gold lettering. Numerous selections from the Christian publishing industry were also available for purchase. Jim and Tammy Faye Bakker's spiritual guides *You Can Make It!* and *I Gotta Be Me* received special displays, but the Bakkers did not have a monopoly on the store's shelf space. Other inspirational literature included *The Exodus Diet Plan*, the spiritual biographies of Roy Rogers and Dale Evans, and sermons by Billy Graham. Dolls in the toy store were "Praise Dolls" that sang "Jesus Loves Me" and cooed "God is Love . . . Plus five other sayings!" And in the event that one's child threw a tantrum, the store also sold "a spanking paddle

Figure 5.1 The enclosed shopping mall concourse at Heritage USA. Courtesy of the Flower Pentecostal Heritage Center.

emblazoned with the words 'YOU train YOUR CHILD.' " Parents who used physical punishment to train their children to respect authority, thereby seeking to stem the youthful rebellion that evangelicals saw as rending the nation's moral fabric apart, could now do so through a simple act of evangelical retailing.[18]

Evangelical retailing itself, of course, had existed since long before consumers at Heritage USA strolled down Bakker's concourse. For Heritage USA's visitors, the Christian stores along the indoor mall concourse were intended to serve as a trip down memory lane, a nostalgic reference to either the small-town proprietor or the independent Christian bookstore of some vague and timeless past. Memory, of course, simplified and distorted history. The independent evangelical bookstore was a relatively new invention. Moreover, by the time Bakker set up his own retail stores at Heritage USA, the Christian retail business was no longer quite the mom-and-pop operation of the park's presentation. It was, like televangelism and Heritage USA, yet another evangelical big business in the making.

Of Business, Bookstores, and Bibles

Before the 1950s, independent evangelical retailers were generally an extension of Bible publishing houses or Sunday school suppliers. Alternatively, evangelical retailing and bookselling happened through the famed traveling Bible seller of popular lore. The postwar, independent "Christian bookstore" broke from these historical precedents. Bakker's bookstore did have one thing right. Christian bookstores were small businesses, independently capitalized and entrepreneurial to the core. Most were also quite modest in terms of inventory, specializing in goods branded by evangelical celebrities and oriented around lifestyle consumption. But Bakker's bookstore also did not convey, at least not at first glance, one of the more important facets of the evangelical retail business. Most independent retailers and booksellers strove as much for evangelical unity and collaboration as their counterparts in the Christian Business Men's Committee, International. Indeed, the evangelical retailer was the foundation of yet another evangelical trade organization, the Christian Bookseller's Association (CBA).

Founded in 1950 in Chicago by Ken Taylor and Bill Moore, both of Moody Press, and John Fish, manager of Scripture Press Store, the CBA worked like any other trade association, holding yearly conventions and serving as a supportive business community for Christian bookstore owners. Membership grew steadily in the 1950s and 1960s. By 1976, 5,000 booksellers attended the annual meeting, a number that doubled by 1990. Some in the CBA debated the particular ups and downs of running their "business ministries," but the profit motive was never questioned. "It is to their [Christian booksellers'] credit that most of them are motivated by a desire to spread Christian literature more than to make a profit," asserted a speaker at the CBA's first convention, "although that too [making a profit] is absolutely necessary." Howard E. Butt Jr., who was one of many evangelical businessmen to speak at annual meetings of the CBA, congratulated members for their work. For Butt, evangelical retailers were a crucial business front in America's culture wars over work, sex, enterprise, and evangelical identity. "Business in America now gets the Black Hat. . . . If you want glamour look poor in blue jeans; to be a dull clod you buy a business suit," he told the CBA at its 1979 meeting. "Rich men are Robber Barons; success means you're a dirty capitalist pig. . . . Everyday [*sic*] you breathe this atmosphere which cuts you down. I'd like to say a word to build you up." Butt continued, "I wonder if [youngsters], surrounded by so much popular condemnation of all us greedy businessmen and our capitalistic system, ever think how much they owe that old man in the picture," meaning businessmen like himself and the retailers in the audience. The CBA was doing more than selling books. It was taking an activist's stand against any challenge to business authority or any ideas that discounted business freedom as the source of all freedoms. "Personal freedom, political freedom, religious freedom," Butt claimed, "all freedom includes freedom in your economics." Christian booksellers and their businesses were a godly "incarnation" because "The Almighty God has elected to do his business of love, joy, and peace through you. . . . You men and women have been called as surely as any pastor. Your bookstore is your sanctuary. You stand on holy ground. Your name is Mr. God." Through Christian bookstores, thought Butt, CBA members—the majority of whom were men and, therefore, not "Ms. God" or "Mrs. God"— were servant leaders in a unique corner of the new service economy: "[You] stand in a titan's place; you serve the servants of God; you carry fantastic power. You represent Christ in the world of ideas. In you the message gets packaged for a bookstore." For Butt, CBA members and their customers were also prophets. By supplying goods that met demand, evangelicals were made into better Christians, helping their children, neighbors, and friends turn away from the "sins" of the counterculture or mass culture materialism and thereby win the battle of "flesh versus spirit; immediate versus everlasting; instant versus always." Revival was secured through retail.[19]

Butt may not have captured the sentiments of every Christian bookseller in the room, but he did identify a real link between buying and evangelical identity politics, one on which Heritage USA and its bookstore depended for their very existence. During the 1960s and 1970s, evangelical bookstores nationwide expanded their wares, selling not only Bibles and books but a wide array of Christian-themed merchandise that, for the buyer, doubled as private edifier and public pronouncement. Equating "evangelical" with "Christian" and banking on the potential of selling "Christian" as a "lifestyle," Christian bookstores increasingly stocked their shelves with what detractors called "Jesus junk" or "Christian bric-a-brac," which ranged from clothing to posters, souvenirs, jewelry, stationery, gifts, films, games, toys, plaques, artwork, and more. Though nominally inclusive spaces filled with mass-produced goods, most Christian bookstores were located in majority-white suburban neighborhoods and communities. Much like a Chick-fil-A restaurant, no race-based law prevented employment or patronage. But the evangelical retail space was more often than not a culturally white space. Shelves were filled with white faces and white Jesuses and white characters from the Bible. T-shirts and other products rarely featured any Jesus other than a white Jesus, suffering for the sins of the world or wooing the would-be believer to accept God's offer of eternal salvation. Continuing the long history of retaining separate retail establishments in evangelical America, black Christian bookstore owners and bric-a-brac sellers routinely catered exclusively to African American customers.[20]

Nationwide, the "Christian" lifestyle that retailers primarily sold was a white, male-led, middle-class evangelical ideal. It was also a life of purposeful conspicuous consumption. To buy was to "witness," buying goods from retailers for the sake of edifying one's faith, affirming one's Christian identity, or pronouncing one's right to public complaint and redress of grievances. In the 1970s, the proliferation of "Jesus fish" stickers and car magnets met with WWJD ("What Would Jesus Do?) bracelets, T-shirts, and bumper stickers in the 1980s. (Ironically, WWJD was appropriated from a book written by Gilded Age social gospeler Charles Sheldon, who had advocated social activism on behalf of the poor.) In the 1980s and afterward, the alignment of lifestyle consumerism, corporate culture, buycotting, and Christian witness was so indivisible that entire clothing lines featured T-shirts with logos taken from corporate culture. Instead of Coca-Cola's famed cursive logo, noting that the soft drink was "The Real Thing," evangelical T-shirt companies printed the same logo bearing the words "Jesus Christ: He's the Real Thing." Other reinterpretations were knock-offs of logos and slogans for Pepsi, Mountain Dew, Sprite, Hershey's, Reese's, Arm & Hammer, and other companies. Even if tongue in cheek, such appropriations and reinterpretations added a literalist's take on what it meant to grant American corporations an evangelical "soul."

The rise of what scholar Colleen McDannell called "independent Christian bookstores" was dramatic. Between 1965 and 1975, Christian bookstores ticked up in number from 725 to 1,850. Store sales, on average, grew annually at 16 percent between 1975 and 1979, exceeding the national retail growth rate of 9.7 percent over the same years. In 1978, 68 percent of sales in Christian bookstores came from books, Bibles, and Sunday school curricula. Fifteen years later, print materials made up 49 percent of total sales, while sales of Christian music rose from 12 to 15 percent, a less impressive increase and possibly related to the inclusion of Christian music at nonreligious retailers and music shops. Sales of "nonprint merchandise"—shirts, stickers, and other Christian retail items—nearly doubled from 20 percent to 36 percent. The number of outlets and overall sales also increased. Increasingly, Mom and Pop might still run the local bookstore, but large-scale book publishers generally served as their main suppliers. Going or almost gone were the small-scale publisher or denominational press. In their place were Zondervan, Moody, NavPress, Thomas Nelson, Eerdmans, and Intervarsity Press. The Christian book market was concentrated in fewer hands, as nonreligious presses and corporations were acquired by big buyers and distributors like ABC. HarperCollins (owned by Rupert Murdoch) bought a stake in the Christian publishing industry, buying out Zondervan in 1988, which at that point had $106 million in annual sales. Since publishers and producers acquired shelf and floor space for their books and goods at Christian retailers, integration was tight between corporation, local retailer, and consumer.[21]

The links between evangelical retailers and mass-market presses allowed evangelicals to pursue that most cherished of publishing achievements: a *New York Times* bestseller. One of the first was Hal Lindsey's apocalyptic *The Late Great Planet Earth*. First published in 1970 by Zondervan (and ghost-written by Carole C. Carlson), the book was vital to the resuscitation and mainstreaming of one of fundamentalism's earliest fundamentals, namely premillenialism. Although even "new" evangelicals like Billy Graham might speak openly—if intermittently—about end-times prophecy or expectations of an imminent Second Coming, Lindsey unequivocally embraced it, popularizing prophetic readings of current events in the Middle East. He also preached Darbyist ideas like "the rapture" and "the tribulation," and he pontificated about the identity of an "anti-Christ" figure, which filtered throughout American popular culture and even captured the interest of Ronald Reagan. A nonevangelical press, Bantam, picked up the book in 1973 and, through an aggressive marketing campaign, helped to turn it into a worldwide phenomenon. A film version, narrated by the legendary and reclusive Orson Welles, appeared in 1979. Though Lindsey wrote in a follow-up to *The Late Great Planet Earth* that "the 1980s could very well be the last decade of history as we know it," the book continued to sell well into the 1980s and 1990s. By the close of the century, it had sold an estimated 30–40 million copies. Lindsey's books also demonstrated the Christian book publishing industry's overlap with mass-market distributors and markets. Sequels, such as *Satan Is Alive and Well on Planet Earth* and *The 1980s: Countdown to Armageddon*, also came out with Bantam, helping to create a subgenre of apocalyptic literature that Billy Graham explored in the early 1980s with books like *Approaching Hoofbeats: The Four Horsemen of the Apocalypse*, published by the paperback giant Avon.[22]

Lindsey's books also demonstrated a certain faddish element in evangelical publishing, as marquee writers could achieve brief appeal through books that hit on highly specialized demands from Christian or non-Christian consumers. To be sure, Lindsey's progeny—such as the multimillion-selling *Left Behind* series written by Tim LaHaye and Jerry Jenkins—showed the longevity and profitability of corporatizing the end times, as well as the ability of certain evangelical writers to normalize one interpretation of human destiny. But dozens of other subgenres explored and developed by Thomas Nelson, Zondervan, and their competitors suggested the range of Christian publishing by the early 1980s. Whatever one's identity or interpretation of what it meant to be a faithful "Christian," there was a book, video, or devotional series available for purchase. There were Christian sex, child-birthing, and parenting manuals, Christian homeschooling and supplementary educational materials, Christian perspectives on child discipline and teenagers, Christian money management and financial planners, Christian biographies and devotionals, Christian psychoanalysis and treatment guides, Christian handbooks for grief and personal tragedy, Christian approaches to geriatric care and the stages of death—and, of course, books on Christian business management and entrepreneurialism.

Gender and sexuality also shaped evangelical choices at the local bookstore or online retailer. The sexual revolutions of the 1960s, both in terms of the bedroom and the workplace, opened up avenues for evangelicals to debate "new" meanings of masculinity, femininity, sexuality, work, and family life. But the evangelical desire to control sexual decision-making by younger Americans continued and was clearly apparent in books on male–female relations, sexuality, and "family" training or "values." Anxieties about the feminization of work or the feminization of Christian men were also prominent, and it was not surprising to see reassertions of an essentialist Christian "femininity" and "masculinity" appear via consumer-based goods and marketing campaigns, ranging from Marabel Morgan's *The Total Woman* (1974) to Tim and Beverly LaHaye's bestselling sex manual *The Act of Marriage* (1976). But Christian book publishing ran the gamut, stretching far beyond marital relations or sexual matters. Taking the fullest interpretation of the personal as commercial, publishers attempted to cover as much of daily life as possible, primarily because any part of daily life not covered was a potentially untapped market. Evangelical consumption was often a communal act, as many evangelicals bought books for reading in groups with other like-minded individuals or in church group studies. Consumption also helped firm up a sense of evangelical social authority—evangelicals had something to "say" in the public sphere about all matters of political or social import because they had read what a well-marketed "born-again" writer had written on such subjects. Race and class also mattered, as Christian authors regularly assumed middle-class, white norms as the standard for "family" or workplace life. Few Christian authors touched on matters of race, white privilege, or class (one exception was Ron

Sider, whose 1977 book *Rich Christians in an Age of Hunger* did so, albeit indirectly). Whatever fads came and went, whatever or however books drove or responded to demand, the main market was for whites, by whites of a certain class, professional station, and social perspective.

In the evangelical culture industries, brand names were important, granting a select handful of evangelical writers a legitimacy that might supplement or even replace local pastoral authorities. As in D. L. Moody's or Billy Sunday's day, who became a household brand name among the glut of Christian authors was the result of a combination of personality, historical moment, and corporate backing. Fan followings developed accordingly, whether it be for prosperity preachers following in the wake of Oral Roberts, older new evangelicals like Billy Graham, or newer evangelical celebrities like Francis Schaeffer, Tim and Beverly LaHaye, or James Dobson.

Even C. S. Lewis, a high-church Anglican who died in 1963 and held theological, sexual, and eschatological views at odds with those of many evangelicals, became an evangelical sensation. A respected professor of literature, Lewis's religious musings were not well-received in British intellectual circles. His radio program, however, did reach over half a million listeners and his books, particularly *The Screwtape Letters*, sold well in the United Kingdom and United States. He landed on the cover of *Time* in 1947, but he was not an evangelical celebrity in America until after he died, coincidentally on the same day as John F. Kennedy's assassination. After Lewis's passing, evangelicals outside of the academic circles of a Wheaton College or Fuller Seminary increasingly took solace and gained intellectual confidence from Lewis's works, especially *Mere Christianity* and *The Screwtape Letters*, as well as his collection of children's tales, *The Chronicles of Narnia*. Readers who closely read Lewis's work might have been nervous about the sexual relations detailed in his autobiography *Surprised by Joy*, his interpretation of biblical accounts through the lens of mythology in *God in the Dock*, and his conceptualization of heaven and hell in *The Great Divorce*, which had no basis in even the most imaginative biblical exegesis. But whatever his contrarian background or religious views, Lewis added gravitas to evangelical interpretations of the Bible and the identity of Jesus, both because of his commitment to "apologetics"—or building persuasive, rational arguments for orthodoxy—and for his witty, engaging writing style. In evangelical consumer culture, Lewis was like Billy Graham, a commodity as much as a personality, a purchasable icon of intellectualism, wit, and edification. The effect of Lewis's posthumous commercialization and popularization was certainly meaningful for Marion E. Wade, ServiceMaster's founder. After he died in 1973, Wade's family used a portion of the ServiceMaster fortune to collect Lewis's works and the works of other British authors popular in evangelical circles, like orthodox Catholics G. K. Chesterton and J. R. R. Tolkien, for storage and study at Wheaton College.[23]

The Bible was also not immune to corporate influence, identity politics, and lifestyle marketing. Historian Randall Balmer noted as much after visiting the CBA's annual convention in 1988. For Balmer, the various types of Bibles available at the CBA put the twin trends toward specialization and corporatization in high relief. "Bibles are big business," he noted. "In order to sell more and more Bibles, publishers have devised all sorts of angles: new translations, new typefaces, new colors, new bindings." Zondervan was at the forefront of the Bible business, offering new "contemporary" translations in the 1960s and 1970s to provide a readable alternative to the King James Version (KJV), at the time the most common Bible in Christian homes. Zondervan significantly cut into the KJV market while crowding out more "liberal" versions of the Bible with the New International Version (NIV), first published in 1978 as a concerted effort of conservative Bible scholars and the National Association of Evangelicals. The NIV hardly developed in a social and political vacuum. Contrary to other versions, the NIV continued the use of masculine pronouns for God and rejected "gender neutral" language. It cast Genesis's creation accounts as historical instead of figurative and interpreted Paul as demonstrably anti-homosexual, with homosexuality assumed a "choice" against God's fixed, heterosexual ideal. Future versions added commentary that applied biblical stories and teachings to nearly every political or social matter in the 1980s and 1990s, from divorce to abortion to evolution to war. NIV versions for the business professional also appeared, as did other devotional versions for women, teenagers, and pastors. Most evangelical business executives writing faith-based "how to" books after the NIV's publication used it to build their "biblical" arguments for executive authority, servant leadership, or "faith at work." Zondervan's acquisition by Harper & Row in 1988 meant that the NIV was not only the Bible of millions of evangelicals. It was also another asset of Rupert Murdoch's media empire.[24]

At times, interested evangelical businessmen added their two cents to the crafting of new versions of the Bible, aligning their political or theological desires with editorial decision-making. For instance, as "an independent layman" for the Overview Committee of the New King James version of the Bible in 1976, W. Maxey Jarman joined with 100 of "the most outstanding group of conservative evangelicals" and "conservative scholars" to publish with Thomas Nelson an "inerrant, infallible, inspired Word of God," albeit with "archaic words replaced, some word changes where meanings are now different, and new punctuation." The point was to repackage the old KJV for modern audiences, especially for younger evangelicals whom Jarman believed were falling away from the fundamentals of the faith. By the late 1980s, however, Jarman's conservative version was only one of dozens of options for the would-be buyer. "First there was The Word," wrote a reporter for *The Boston Globe*. "Today, there are Words, and Words and Words." By 1999, more than 3,000 different versions of the Bible were on the market. Most were not new translations but "specialty Bibles" for each potential customer segment: men, women, preachers, students, business leaders, and so on. Most were published by a short list of major publishers, including Thomas Nelson, Zondervan, and Tyndale.[25]

Large-scale suppliers and distributors stocked the shelves of Christian bookstores, including the one at Heritage USA and at outlets for new chain bookstores, such as Family Christian and LifeWay. In the 1990s, retail corporations like Wal-Mart and Barnes & Noble also became vital spaces for consumers interested in buying Christian goods. As a result of the general trend toward corporatization in the production and distribution of Christian books, the small-scale, independent Christian bookstore of the immediate postwar era became a thing of the past. "The generation who grew up going to Christian bookstores is dying," reported one California minister. "There are a lot of people in the 'CBA market' now working with Barnes & Noble." A smaller Christian book retailer in Lynchburg, Virginia, agreed and had mixed feelings. Though happy that such "books are calling people back to their roots" and causing Americans to realize "their need for God and family," she admitted that "we can't compete with the big chains on discounts."[26]

Making Corporate Christian Music

Along with books, Jim Bakker's bookstore sold music by Christian pop groups, Christian folk groups, Christian heavy-metal groups, and Christian rap groups. Bakker's broad embrace of artistic expression as creative rebellion largely accorded with the business models of the companies, record labels, and musical acts that supplied the tapes and records to buyers at Heritage USA.

Evangelical spins on the youth "rebellions" met corporate modes and money in the early 1970s. This was an important shift in evangelical culture. Previously, and for much of the immediate postwar period, the emphasis of evangelical organizations had been on setting certain boundaries around youthful license, tamping down or directing youth creativity, and precluding rebellious attitudes or inclinations. In other words, the purpose of an organization like Youth for Christ was to align young lives with adult lives. It was to make social, racial, and gendered copies. The end product was largely assumed to be converted youngsters who affirmed the conservative evangelical ideal and, more specifically, the ideals of their parents, ministers, or the movement's business backers, namely businessmen like Herbert Taylor, R. G. LeTourneau, or J. Howard Pew. At worst, youth organizations sought to make good evangelical Rotarians. At best, they intended to make them into crusaders like Billy Graham.

Beginning in the late 1960s, the suit-and-tie evangelicalism of Campus Crusade for Christ, The Navigators, and Youth for Christ had new competition from one of the most important and influential movements in American evangelical history: the Jesus Movement. Emerging alongside and out of student protest groups and countercultural activities in California, the Jesus Movement valued free expression and experiential spirituality over the relatively staid respectability of other evangelical youth movements. Chuck Smith, a California pastor whose daughter exposed him to the burgeoning Jesus Movement, called himself and his followers "radical Christians." In that vein, as Carol Flake noted, "the Jesus revolutionaries demanded their own culture—their own rituals, rallies and music." In constructing this culture, Smith and others in the Jesus Movement borrowed extensively from the counterculture. Slogans, rituals, and clothing marked followers as youth of a different sort, as rebels for Christ's sake. Through music, participants in the Jesus Movement sought to separate themselves from both their parents' generation and the "do what you feel" message of popular "secular" music. Hence, the first wave of "Jesus music" blended evangelical messages with musical elements borrowed from the folk music revival of the late 1960s and contemporary forms of rock. Of course, this sort of hybrid music was not an original concoction. Various big-name singers and groups—from Elvis Presley to Johnny Cash to Bob Dylan to James Taylor—had dabbled in religious music throughout the 1950s and 1960s. And gospel singers and hymn books stretching back to the nineteenth century had incorporated sounds and styles borrowed from contemporary music. Still, "Jesus music" was a popular alternative for young, mostly white and middle-class evangelicals seeking to reconcile their religious "rebellion" with American popular culture. Thanks to the Jesus Movement in general and its musical endeavors specifically, Time claimed in 1971 that "Jesus is alive and well in the radical spiritual fervor of a growing number of young Americans who have proclaimed an extraordinary religious revolution in his name."[27]

For all its rootsy radicalism, business interests shaped both early and later iterations of Jesus Movement music. Evangelical artists might imagine themselves as "Christian rebels" or countercultural Christian artists working outside the "mainstream" of American culture or even against a suit-and-tie evangelical establishment. But they soon joined with music labels already invested in the profitability of rebellion tropes and countercultural identity. Various self-styled "countercultural" groups from the 1950s through the early 1970s provided corporate marketers with new and profitable forms of "cool." Selling "lifestyles" alongside products—and linking such products to one's lifestyle—became a tactic of corporate advertising to a broad swath of the white middle-class.[28] It was little different in evangelical circles, as business concerns shaped the production and distribution of evangelical pop and rock music, much as it had for gospel music for almost a half-century. In 1968, Larry Norman—often hailed as the Father of Christian Rock—and his band People!, a soft rock group, attempted to break into mainstream pop music with the album *We Need a Whole Lot More of Jesus and a Lot Less Rock and Roll*. Interested in distributing Norman's group but wary of its religiosity, Capitol Records changed the album title to the less didactic *I Love You*, which also shared its name with their Top 40 hit. The cover of the original album was to feature a picture of a long-haired, white Jesus, which Capitol replaced with a simple picture of the band. Troubled, Norman left both his band and Capitol, starting up Solid Rock, his own record label. Yet, Capitol still released *I Love You* and followed it in 1969 with Norman's solo work *Upon This Rock*, widely regarded as the first "Christian rock" album.[29]

Over the course of the next few years, Norman worked in an uneven and unformed market. Christian musicians came from many backgrounds. Some, such as Faith Flight, Love Song, Children of the Day, Country Faith, Selah, Blessed Hope, and Debbie Kerner, worked via Maranantha! Records, a small music label set up by Calvary Chapel, a center of the Jesus Movement in southern California. Others, like Andraé Crouch and the Disciples, joined black gospel to a premillennialist vision of the future, inviting their listeners to convert while there was still time. Barry McGuire, a former drug addict known for his 1965 hit "Eve of Destruction," converted in 1971 and formed an evangelical band, 2nd Chapter of Acts, to tour the nation. Dozens of other guitarists and vocalists also appeared around the country, playing in a variety of venues, from street corners to churches to coffee houses to high schools to bars. The experimental spiritual and commercial context of the late 1960s and early 1970s contributed to the music's appeal. But a new, countercultural Jesus was also a hot commodity. He was on Broadway in musicals like *Godspell, Jesus Christ Superstar,* and *Hair*. He was sung about and talked about as a soul-satisfying lover or admirable rebel by musicians signed to major labels and steeped in black gospel and soul music, such as Aretha Franklin, Al Green, Marvin Gaye, and Earth, Wind & Fire. Bob Dylan and Johnny Cash experienced very dramatic and public "born again" conversions and resuscitated interest in a populist, evangelical-inflected roots music that seemed to come out of and speak for down-and-out America. In such a religious, musical, and commercial context, opportunities for crossover appeal appeared for groups affiliated with the Jesus Movement. Though hardly a huge draw outside evangelical circles, it was no small achievement when Norman and People! opened for the Grateful Dead, Jimi Hendrix, The Doors, and the Byrds.[30]

Evangelical music turned a corner at Explo '72, a youth festival held in the Cotton Bowl in Dallas. A "Christian Woodstock" planned by the Jesus Movement in tandem with businessman Bill Bright's Campus Crusade for Christ, Explo '72 was specifically designed to reach out to what Billy Graham called the "Jesus Generation." (Graham spoke multiple times at the event.)

Norman performed along with other emerging Christian artists and born-again crossover country artists like Johnny Cash and Kris Kristofferson. Explo '72 also served as a precursor and model for other Christian music festivals, including "Jesus '74 in Pennsylvania, Salt '75 in Michigan, Fishnet '75 in Virginia, Jesus '75 Midwest in St. Louis, the Sonshine Festival in Ohio, Lodestone in Vancouver, Road Home Celebration in Colorado, the Jesus Festival of Joy in Wichita, and the Hill Country Faith Festival in Texas."[31]

In addition to spreading a younger generation's brand of evangelical culture and music all over the map, Explo '72 presaged a shift toward a new business model for a dynamic and developing genre. Shortly after Explo '72, a music minister from Waco, Texas, named Billy Ray Hearn turned into the genre's Sam Phillips, its first hands-on producer and business mogul. In 1972, Hearn founded Myrrh, believing that he could tap into the youth market he found at the Cotton Bowl. "He realized that these kids would listen to Christian music if it just existed," remembered his son Bill Hearn. "Young church people realized that there was good music out there that also had lyrics that affirmed their faith, that was consistent with their lifestyle. They said, 'Hey, we didn't realize that we needed this, but we really like this, and we want it.'" Initially, Myrrh was under Word Inc., a Texas-based book publisher and gospel label, and filled with established acts, such as Billy McGuire's 2nd Chapter of Acts, and bold new voices, such as Randy Matthews. According to his son, Hearn "built the first national [evangelical] record company" until he left Word in 1976 to start Sparrow, another foundational evangelical label.[32]

Though the spirit was willing, it took investment from large-market labels to make this upstart form of hybrid religious-folk-rock music a successful industry. As in the publishing industry or with Hollywood studios, distribution was the key to a broader audience. To be sure, some evangelical artists or labels did not want wider appeal. Some wanted to remain distinct from broader American culture and rejected all dealings with mass-market labels as threats to the sanctity and sincerity of their music.[33] If evangelical musicians were at times stand-offish toward big labels, corporate music entities were also slow in investing. In the early 1970s, there was no clear market for it, despite Hearn's assumptions. To be sure, gospel music was a well-defined market and one with backing from labels. But gospel albums sold poorly among younger white listeners and "were generally left at the bottom of the promotion stack when records were pitched to radio." Evangelical music—rebranded and sold as an ostensibly all-encompassing, big-tent "Christian music"—tended to have mostly white musicians blending rock or folk musical stylings with original Christian lyrics, not merely covers of hymnbook songs or gospel standards. Though initially less attractive to major labels than gospel music and interpreted as gospel music marketable to white buyers, a few major labels tested the feasibility of a white-based Christian music market in the late 1970s and early 1980s. The motive, as one executive at CBS put it, was the bottom line: "I'll not pretend that we're here because of some new burst of religious faith. . . . We're here because of the potential to sell records in the gospel market. We want to put gospel records in stores that don't currently carry them. We want to transform gospel from a specialty market to a mass-appeal market."[34]

Trying to tap into the niche evangelical market and broader mass markets, ABC bought Word and then Myrrh. Hearn's Sparrow became a part of MCA's holdings in 1981, while CBS started up its own Christian label, Priority (though CBS later closed it down in 1983 as "a matter of sheer economics"). Elektra briefly distributed Christian music put out by the Light label, while MCA Records distributed the Christian label Songbird from 1979 to 1983. Joint ventures, such as Exit and What? Records, had their artists' work distributed by big-name, mass-market corporate labels Island Records and A&M Records. After 1978, a for-profit magazine, *Contemporary Christian Music,* served as the industry's *Rolling Stone,* thereby signaling the emergence of Christian music as a distinct genre in commercial pop music and, yet again, the terminological linkage of "evangelical" and "conservative" with "Christian." Editors and writers for *Contemporary Christian Music* did the work of most music magazine staff, promoting new artists alongside interviews and industry-specific reviews. But the magazine also further identified Christian music as "contemporary," as presumably more creative, expressive, "rebellious," different, and distant from "traditional" Christian hymns and church music. Operating quasi-independently until the late 1990s, *Contemporary Christian Music* was then bought out by the for-profit Salem Communications, a radio conglomerate owned and operated by two Bob Jones University graduates.[35]

Despite corporate restructuring, buyouts, and hints of popularity, contemporary Christian music had unimpressive sales and only halfhearted backing from mass-market labels and distributors until a Nashville teenager named Amy Grant proved the genre's viability and profitability. Cutting her first album with Myrrh in 1976 at the age of sixteen and selling 50,000 copies of it by the time she was seventeen, Grant became the first profitable "crossover" artist in Christian music history. "By 1983," Grant had become "probably the most popular Christian female vocalist in the country," wrote Paul Baker, an early chronicler of the Christian music industry. Her 1982 album *Age to Age,* released by Myrrh and backed by ABC, was a huge hit. Filled with praise and worship songs, *Age to Age* became the first "gospel" album to gain platinum record status for selling a million units. Her appeal demonstrated that the complex racial or countercultural world that birthed "Jesus music" had flattened into a better defined, standardized, and predictable genre. Christian music was not "gospel" music even though it won awards in that category. Unlike gospel, which had mostly older or middle-aged listeners, Christian music was white pop music marketed toward youth. Moreover, it was marketed less as churchly music and more as a "wholesome" alternative to overtly sexual pop artists like Madonna or Prince. Grant was sexually pure and restrained. She was white and seemingly virginal. Moreover, Grant embodied the conservative feminine ideal in the midst of evangelical activism against feminism or sexual expressiveness in popular culture. Her marriage to Christian songwriter Gary Chapman in 1982 created the first celebrity union in the genre's history. (And, predictably, the couple's subsequent divorce in 1999 sparked a minor controversy in evangelical circles).[36]

By 1985, market experts watching the burgeoning Christian music industry claimed that "a window's open in this country for this kind of music, and it's open because of Amy." As in the past, some saw this "window" as a threat instead of an opportunity, as too much blending of the secular and sacred. As Barry Alfonso of *Billboard* observed, "Amy Grant's popularity opened a Pandora's box of troublesome issues that the Christian music industry has wrestled with to this day." Christian artists were forced to deal with a number of questions: Are we "selling out" for the sake of broader appeal? Will we have to give up certain religious emphases in our music to garner more of a stage? Will the profit motive overtake the pastoral or proselytizing motive? Regarding the social and political questions of the 1970s and 1980s, Christian musicians also wrestled with how overtly political their music should be. These questions concerned Christian musicians and their followers alike, and much ink was spilled in the popular and evangelical press over how "acceptable" Christian music was for evangelical listeners. Still, in terms of business decisions, into the 1980s and early 1990s, many Christian musicians made a no-nonsense deal with large music corporations. To get their music distributed to a wide audience—presumably with the intent of evangelizing or edifying as many people as possible—they worked with these companies and sought out their distributive channels. "The bottom line," argued Billy Ray Hearn, "is we needed the resources in order to grow, in order to fulfill our vision."[37]

Though lyrical content and marketing might convey that Christian artists were "different" from their "secular" counterparts, contractual arrangements and sales expectations were often similar. By the 1990s, most major labels and many smaller, independent labels required artists to cover the cost of recording and road trips or wrote contracts that covered such start-up costs, albeit with clauses that any sales from singles or albums sales, merchandise, or tickets went toward paying down the label's upfront extension of cash. A further squeeze on a musician's take-home pay came from the fact that Christian music remained a popular but niche industry, even after two decades of involvement with big-name labels. "In the business sense, Christian music is economically disadvantaged even in the best of times, something that Christian music fans might not realize," noted John Styll, President and CEO of the Gospel Music Association. "Since most [Christian] radio airplay is on non-commercial stations, which pay a fraction of what commercial stations pay in royalties, our songwriters receive far less income than those in other genres." Ticket sales and merchandise sales—the key to staying afloat for all working musicians, whether a struggling band or a chart-topper—also lagged behind more mainstream acts. At the turn of the century, as the music industry at large faced additional financial problems and economic pressures due to digital piracy and online downloads, Christian musical acts were not immune to the siphoning off of sales. The end result was a labor arrangement between Christian bands and labels that was usually in the latter's favor. To compensate, many Christian bands and artists moonlighted as worship leaders at local churches, played as studio or supporting musicians, or wrote worship songs on a pay-by-use basis. "I think sometimes people get this out of proportion," reflected Paul Baloche, a worship leader with many friends in the industry, in 2008. "They have this image in their minds that people are making millions and millions of dollars, and it's just funny. If they really knew." What about those who did more than make ends meet, who enjoyed a truly "rock star" status? "Gosh," said Baloche. "Maybe there's a small handful."[38]

In addition to major labels and media conglomerates, radio distributors and companies served as gatekeepers, determining who were "acceptable" artists and evangelical celebrities. Once more, the trend was toward corporatization and conservatism. Only select forms of artistic or political expression got on the air. To be sure, Christian radio stations had been around since the dawn of radio itself, and many early innovators in the field—Fighting Bob Shuler and Charles Fuller, among others—were fundamentalists. But after the same 1960 change in federal law that encouraged the rise in televangelism, a new breed of Christian radio stations flourished. Up until 1960, Christian radio stations had primarily devoted most of their programming to preaching, with musical acts and hymns interspersed. After 1960, music and commentary began to crowd out preaching, resulting in programming that mimicked Top 40 music stations. At the same time, federal communications law redefined "non-commercial educational use" as meaning religious programming as well, thereby allowing churches and religious organizations to qualify more readily for air time on established stations. Conservative talk show hosts certainly benefitted and capitalized on this shift, but so too did radio stations that might play the latest hits from the Christian music scene or the newest worship song. Christian radio stations took off, especially in metropolitan markets, rising from 111 stations in 1973 to 1,052 in 1989. Indirectly, a failed attempt in Congress to codify the "fairness doctrine" in 1987, vetoed by Ronald Reagan, spurred another decade of growth (and, concomitantly, the rise of a one-sided, conservative talk radio industry). By 1996,

Christian music and talk programming was on 1,807 stations, and 2,513 by 2002, approximately 19.1 percent of the total radio market.[39]

Through such restructurings, commentators and call-in hosts could more readily get programs on the air. For instance, conservative, politically minded evangelicals like Dr. James Dobson used radio as the primary means to advance their own take on evangelical social engagement. For Dobson, who grew up in Oklahoma and attended medical school in southern California, changing American culture was a project that had to start at home. Dobson presented himself as a combination of pastor, father, entrepreneur, counselor, and activist. He was also a savvy evangelical businessman and a culture warrior, a purveyor of ideas and practices that, if implemented, would forestall the decisions that impressionable children or teenagers might make that would result in sexual frivolity or "deviant" lifestyles. With his bestselling 1970 book, *Dare to Discipline*, Dobson pushed back against parental strategies that seemed too congenial to childhood independence and anti-authoritarianism. The book was a hit, published by Bantam (a subsidiary of Random House) and selling over 2 million copies. As the evangelical Dr. Spock, Dobson moved into radio, setting up a national radio program, *Focus on the Family*, in 1977, and taking full advantage of the growing market in Christian radio and book publishing. Blending practical advice about parenting or marriage maintenance with an increasingly political message that cast homosexuality as a learned condition and abortion as abominable, Dobson became, by 1995, the third most popular radio broadcaster in America. Dobson's books sold millions in Christian book stores around the country, and his mailing list reached 3.5 million names, many of them evangelical women who, according to one historian, "were delighted to discover a Christian psychologist who seemed to understand their problems."[40]

Dobson and other evangelical public figures took advantage of the liberalization of radio laws, as did businessmen like Bob Jones University alumni Edward Atsinger III and Stuart Epperson, who founded Salem Communications Company. By the mid-1980s, Salem Communications was a huge business, the largest evangelical media company in America. Epperson entered the radio business with his brother-in-law Atsinger in 1972, when they bought a Bakersfield, California, station. In 1974, Atsinger put his first full-time Christian music and talk show station on the air. Three years later, he convinced Epperson to join him in developing additional stations, all on a for-profit basis. Nine years later, they formed Salem Communications as a conglomerate of thirteen Christian radio stations in some of the nation's largest radio markets, including New York, Los Angeles, and Boston. Salem added five more cities during the late 1980s and early 1990s. When the Telecommunications Act of 1996 loosened cross-ownership rules, which encouraged consolidation among media companies nationwide, Salem benefited tremendously, adding new markets and new stations. In 1999

Salem Communications went public and used the capital infusion to gobble up additional market share. By 2006, Salem had ninety-eight stations in thirty-eight markets, with "60 stations in 23 of the top 25 markets." Salem was the "third largest operator of stations in the nation's top 25 markets," trailing only radio giants Clear Channel Communications and Infinity, a subsidiary of media behemoth Viacom. Epperson and Atsinger were the William Randolph Hearsts of corporate Christian music and radio.[41]

At the very moment Salem started to thrive, Jim and Tammy Faye Bakker's business model fell apart. Investigative reporters from *The Charlotte Observer*, along with the IRS and FCC, discovered outright fraud in PTL's bookkeeping. In addition to spending donors' money on private purchases, the Bakkers and their associates had sold free overnight rooms at Heritage USA's Grand Hotel and a new high-rise luxury hotel in exchange for $1,000 "life time memberships" in the PTL Club from 1984 to 1987. The addition was still under construction, and the promised rooms did not exist—and would never exist. More troubling, the project's budget was set to only $11 million, but $50 million in solicited funds had come into PTL's coffers. In a nationally publicized trial, Jim Bakker was found guilty of fraud and sentenced to forty-five years in federal prison. (His sentence was later reduced to eight years.) An affair with Jessica Hahn, a church secretary, and rumors of several homosexual trysts added to Jim Bakker's tarnished reputation in the evangelical community. In 1992, Jim and Tammy Faye Bakker divorced.

Heritage USA closed its doors for good in 1988. Jerry Falwell, a Virginia-based fundamentalist pastor and conservative activist who had taken over management of the park after the Bakkers left PTL in disgrace, seemed oddly unable to contain his delight. He had always disliked Jim Bakker, in part for Bakker's Pentecostal leanings, in part out of a personal dislike for the Bakkers' gaudiness and popularity. Rumors that Falwell intended to use the park as another node on his political network mixed with rumors that he had intentionally sought the Bakkers' downfall in a larger scheme to kill off any viable competitors in the burgeoning market of evangelical activism. Regardless of his personal or professional dislike of the Bakkers, Falwell had no clear plan for Heritage USA. Within a few years, he oversaw the property's transfer to the first in a series of investors, each more flighty or incompetent than the last in their attempts to turn the park into a viable tourist attraction or private business endeavor. By 1992, the park largely sat vacant, its buildings in decay, its former glory fading.[42]

It was not without a bit of irony that Heritage USA, a space created to endorse and affirm evangelical fantasies, public assertiveness, and privatized revival now appeared like a monument to the economic, religious, sexual, and national vicissitudes of the 1960s and 1970s. Heritage USA looked like a blighted inner city or boarded-up downtown. It looked like a run-down church, a religious experiment gone awry. It looked like a shuttered commercial strip, a Sunbelt Christian business gone wrong. Indeed, it looked like what supposedly happened when the corporate evangelical vision of godly, familial work was rejected, when sexual desire, instead of moral fortitude, directed a business or, by proxy, America at large.

Heritage USA's fate, however, was not representative of the evangelical culture industries in general. Evangelical conglomerates continued to make millions for executives and investors well into the 1990s. The Christian music industry alone was a big business, undergoing continued corporatization and transformation into the late twentieth century. Gaylord Entertainment Company bought Word in 1998 and then sold it to Warner Music Group in 2001. EMI bought Sparrow in 1992, then set up an entire division for Christian music, headquartered in Nashville, Tennessee. Nashville, of course, had long been a center of country and gospel music and Christian book publishers such as Thomas Nelson (which bought Word Records in 1992). But the move by EMI, as well as subsequent purchases of Christian labels like Reunion Records by BMG in 1995, helped turn Nashville into the official headquarters of the Christian music industry.[43]

Backed by large, mainstream labels, Christian musicians also found their albums on shelves in Christian bookstores, chain record stores, and big-box retailers like Wal-Mart and Best Buy. A few garnered occasional rotation on mainstream rock stations. Most others provided the primary content to regional and mass-market stations devoted to Christian music programming, which exploded in both number and audience during the 1990s. In fact, by 1995, Christian music was "the fastest-growing form of popular music, driving its message home to the tune of $750 million a year." In 1999, Christian music bested the combined sales of jazz, classical, and blues artists, making up 6 percent of overall sales in the US market. Two years later, it comprised 7 percent of the market.[44]

Though billions of dollars and millions of customers now backed them, the evangelical culture industries also continued the long trend toward religious privatization, both in terms of placing the seat of "religious" experience and activity in the private sphere of paid-for and for-profit consumption and linking religious activity and production to private investors and corporations. Still, commercial assertiveness and the market share that evangelicals garnered certainly corresponded with their public assertiveness in other arenas, especially the arena of ideas about what it meant to live and work in a nation of corporations and in the midst of drastically shifting patterns of work and political economy. Throughout the late 1960s and 1970s, evangelicals positioned themselves to have a prominent voice in an era of economic change, corporate empowerment, deregulation, middle-class anxiety, and apparent national "malaise." And, especially for an evangelical businessman like Mississippi-bred Zig Ziglar, the economic context of the 1970s and 1980s served as a catalyst for interpreting economic deprivation and blessing as per his own experiences a generation before in the nation's poorest state. Ziglar's tales of uplift met with those of other evangelical storytellers, granting the long-running, if somewhat intermittent, free market crusades of many conservative Christians an emotional and narrative core. Their stories aimed to inspire all Americans to fight for the conservative side in the emerging culture wars by believing—with heart, mind, dollar, and vote—in the powers of a free-wheeling corporate economy.

6

Free-Market Faith

Zig Ziglar and the Business of Evangelical Culture War

Born near the rural hamlet of Enterprise, Alabama, in 1926, Hillary "Zig" Ziglar grew up poor. Around the time of Ziglar's birth, the Great Depression arrived in rural Alabama, several years before it brought Wall Street and the rest of the country to its knees. The Depression devastated Enterprise and rural Alabama in general, pushing thousands of families off the farm while driving others into deeper poverty—or into sharecropper unions, into antiracist communist organizing, or to cities as far north and west as fortitude or money might take them. The Ziglar family made ends meet in Enterprise until 1932, when Ziglar's father died. Desperate, his mother moved with him and his eleven siblings to find work. They landed in Yazoo City, a tiny town in the Mississippi Delta, a flat, sparsely populated floodplain on the eastern side of the Mississippi River.

When Ziglar was a teenager, Franklin D. Roosevelt called the South the "nation's number one economic problem." It was not hard to believe after a trip to the Mississippi Delta, even if only through the imaginary vehicle of a photograph. The hollow eyes, haggard faces, and hungry children that federal agents photographed in southern towns like Yazoo City—and published nationwide—regionalized the face of American poverty. To live in the rural South, believed many Americans, was to live like Ziglar's family, on the far margins of the economy and on the fringes of normalcy. There was much truth, to be sure, in such photographic visions of Ziglar's South. Indeed, Ziglar's family struggled mightily to get by on one income.

Ziglar's early experiences with poverty and deprivation taught him many lessons. The foremost lesson concerned matters of religion and political economy. Indeed, Ziglar's hardscrabble upbringing served as a resource for his faith not in governmental action or relief but in the free market, in the merits of a meritocracy, and in a theology of personal uplift and empowerment.

Also foundational to his free-market faith was one of the more important influences in evangelical business circles, Norman Vincent Peale. Peale was a liberal Protestant in terms of theology but a conservative and anti-communist on political issues. Peale's philosophy of "positive thinking" shaped Ziglar in powerful ways but also shaped the approach of a number of other evangelical business executives in the 1960s and early 1970s, including one of Ziglar's closest friends and supporters, Mary Kay Ash. One of the first and only female evangelical business leaders, Ash's direct-sales company, Mary Kay Cosmetics, granted Ziglar a boost for his career. She also blended Peale's positive thinking with evangelical feminism, crafting a free-market message for women entering the competitive marketplace for the first time. Like S. Truett Cathy (also born poor) and other conservative, evangelical business leaders, Ash's message of personal uplift was custom-fitted to a South and nation undergoing demonstrable sexual, social, economic, and racial change. Framed by the civil rights movement and women's movement, both of which emphasized economic freedom in addition to personal or cultural freedom, Ash's company joined with Ziglar's to legitimize the corporation as the best arbiter of economic freedom and rights. Through work, blended with positive thinking and evangelical social and sexual conservatism, anyone might enjoy the fruits of the free-market meritocracy. This was a message that overlapped with the institutional and corporate culture of many evangelical businesses and fit the economic philosophies posited by other rags-to-riches evangelical business leaders. It also made Ash, Ziglar, and a new generation of mostly southern evangelical business executives into another iteration of the evangelical elite: wealthy, ready, and willing to remake America according to their vision of personal and professional revival.

Ziglar was no voice in the wilderness. In fact, he was nearly as well known, read, and revered as any other evangelical writer or public figure save Billy Graham. To be sure, Hal Lindsay sold millions more books, but he was controversial and divisive. Writers like C. S. Lewis had many fans, and popular intellectuals like Francis Schaeffer were influential among the same crowd who might read *Christianity Today*. But in general, they went for the head and therefore appealed to a notable, if influential, subset of evangelical leaders and intellectuals. Especially on personal and professional issues, Ziglar was unmatched—truly a national and international celebrity. The reason was his consistent engagement with the two issues that, by the 1970s, were of paramount concern to millions of evangelicals and millions more Americans: work and family. By 1995, he regularly filled arenas, stadiums, and convention centers around the country and made at least as much as $30,000 per appearance. (A decade later, he could command $100,000 for each speech.) "According to Gallup polls," estimated one report in 1995, "37 percent of Americans [knew] his name." Millions attended his seminars over the course of his career, and his most popular books usually sold several million copies. Monetary contributions from mass-market corporations were also never far from the enterprise. Although records are spotty or anecdotal, direct-sales companies like Mary Kay Cosmetics, Shaklee, and Amway and larger companies like Century 21, Holiday Inn, Days Inn, Chick-fil-A, Wal-Mart, Halliburton, AT&T, and Aramco were corporate clients, often paying for their employees to attend Ziglar's seminars.[1]

Ziglar's popularity, like Ash's, came not only from personal charisma or clever marketing. Ziglar used a mythological South, the imagined Mississippi of his upbringing, to universalize his message. Cathy and other evangelical business leaders had one set of narratives and religious culture to frame their companies, attending to middle-class suburbanites leaving behind the racial, municipal, and political contexts of central cities. Familial emphases had one meaning in a sub-urban shopping mall or strip-mall Christian bookstore. They might have a differ-ent meaning elsewhere among people living on the bottom rung or struggling to hang onto a house or business. Ziglar's deployment of a personal story of uplift, of rising up from Mississippi, was thus even more universal than Cathy's. To come out of Mississippi via changes of mind and habit meant, at least for Ziglar and his customers, that anyone could dig their way out of any social, racial, and economic circumstances, no matter how difficult. It was a message intended to appeal to anyone, whether living in an urban ghetto, a Rust Belt city, or a poor rural town like Enterprise, Alabama.

Taken together, by the mid-1980s, evangelical business leaders had mil-lions of Americans covered in the marketplace of ideas. There was a gospel of free-market uplift for anyone and everyone to believe in. For northerners and southerners, service workers and industrial workers, small-town resi-dents and suburban homeowners—the evangelical "free market" faith was for them.

That anyone or everyone—regardless of race, class, or gender—might join Ziglar's revival did not mean that Ziglar thought everyone could or should. Along with Mary Kay Ash, Ziglar wrote early and often about who was not included in his vision of a hardworking and prosperous Christian America. As a disciple of W. A. Criswell, one of the nation's most vocal Baptist conserva-tives and the head of a prominent and wealthy Dallas church, Ziglar endorsed and fell behind a "fundamentalist takeover" of his home denomination, the Southern Baptist Convention (SBC). Ziglar's posture in denominational mat-ters signaled his broader commitment to define and promote conservative norms of race, gender, sex, and the state in America. Ziglar also showed the multiplicity of means available to evangelicals intent on transforming America through corporate capitalism. They could use the written word, the corporate boardroom, or a revival stage like Ziglar's. They could even help to remake the internal politics and political leanings of the largest Protestant denomination in America. Why not think about climbing even higher, perhaps as high as the Oval Office?

Up from Mississippi

By 1939, Ziglar's mother had garnered a semblance of economic security for her twelve children. Charity certainly must have helped, as well as friends and neighbors. But she also scratched out enough social and economic status for the family to feel at home at the town's foremost white congregation, the Yazoo City First Baptist Church. Attending "every Sunday morning and evening for church services and Wednesday evening for prayer meeting," Ziglar learned the evangelical basics: the need for conversion, the rewards of moral rectitude, the unquestionable authority of the Bible, and the salvation afforded by Jesus Christ's death and resurrection. "As we would say over in Mississippi," Ziglar later wrote, "I was 'raised right.'"[2]

A rambunctious teenager, Ziglar joined the Navy for World War II, but the war ended before he completed his training to become a fighter pilot. Returning to civilian life, his wartime service fast-tracked him for enrollment at the University of South Carolina. He married in 1946 and tried to make a few bucks as a salesman, enough to spend on cheap suits and cheaper thrills. At this point in time, he later wrote, "there were few Sundays I was really excited about going to church." Ziglar believed he was merely a "Carnal Christian" and "living a double life since I pretended to be serving God while daily following Satan's dictates." Ziglar might have been spiritually adrift, but he was good at his job. Working for Wearever, a door-to-door kitchenware company, Ziglar had the second-highest sales out of 7,000 salesmen. He soon became the company's highest-paid sales manager.[3]

Professional volatility defined the next two decades of Ziglar's life. In 1955, he left Wearever for the Dale Carnegie Institute in New York City. The author of the Depression-era classic *How to Win Friends and Influence People*, Carnegie had established the Institute to train businessmen in public speaking, communication, leadership, and sales. As a salesman, Ziglar was well versed in the popular self-help literature of the day, including Carnegie's work and Napoleon Hill's *Think and Grow Rich*. But Ziglar held a special affinity for Norman Vincent Peale's bestselling 1952 book, *The Power of Positive Thinking*.

On specific points of theology, Peale might seem like an unlikely source of inspiration for a southern-born, Baptist-raised salesman like Ziglar. A northern Protestant minister associated with the National Council of Churches, Peale also dabbled in theological and religious experimentalism. In the late 1940s, he began pulling together a century of various spiritual currents—transcendentalism, "New Thought," mind cure, Christian Science—to create a coherent approach to individual behavior and personal change he called "positive thinking." Peale worked hard to make his ideas stand out in an already crowded market. Since the 1930s, writers like Carnegie and Hill had been selling hundreds of thousands of books with their suggestions for winning friends, influencing people, thinking positively, and growing rich. With his 1952 bestseller, *The Power of Positive Thinking*, Peale summarized and updated Carnegie and Hill's views and threaded in nonsectarian language about God's endorsement of prosperity and "faith in faith." Peale became a household name. His influence spread far and wide in American popular culture while his politics leaned rightward. From 1932 to 1952, Peale joined anti–New Deal organizations like the Committee for Constitutional Government, Spiritual Mobilization, and the Christian Freedom Foundation, all of which were backed by J. Howard Pew. Pew and Peale also corresponded semiregularly about politics and publishing, and Peale had other friends in big business. He served on Texas oilman H. L. Hunt's *Facts Forum* program, and he worked as the editor-in-chief at the conservative-leaning *Guideposts* magazine. As Robert S. Ellwood points out, Peale's "political world was staunchly conservative Republican" and he personally had "little sense of the realities of life for laborers, minorities, and others outside the realm of religion-inspired businesspeople with whom he connected so well." Still, he maintained membership in more liberal, establishment religious federations like the Protestant Council of New York and the National Council of Churches, even though his economic perspective was certainly not shared by those bodies.[4]

Peale had many friends and admirers in evangelical America, including Billy Graham. But his foremost evangelical disciple was Ziglar. Ziglar was eager to teach Carnegie's sales courses, which mirrored Peale's lessons about positive self-image, optimism, and tenacity as the keys to personal satisfaction and success. Homesickness and big-city living, however, got the best of Ziglar. After only three months with the Carnegie Institute, he moved himself and his growing family back to South Carolina. Unable to hold down a steady job and with debts mounting, Ziglar returned to the kitchenware business in the early 1960s, moving to Texas to sell pots and pans for the Dallas-based Saladmaster Corporation. Ziglar took advantage of the emerging Sunbelt economy in Dallas. A center for defense spending, high-tech enterprise, and in-migration of professional workers, Dallas was a fertile market. By 1964, Ziglar had paid off the last of his debts and began working with American Salesmasters, a company that offered business advice and motivational seminars to would-be entrepreneurs. For the next four years, Ziglar drifted out of sales work and into the field of motivational speaking, selling the power of positive thinking for American Salesmasters and on an as-needed basis for a variety of other companies. Holiday Magic, a multilevel seller of cosmetics, attracted Ziglar as a speaker and sales trainer. Shady business practices and disagreements over business plans led Ziglar in 1968 to leave Holiday Magic for a sales director's job at Automotive Performance in Dallas. Ziglar enjoyed the big bump in salary and perks. But, two years later, the company went belly up, leaving Ziglar once more out of work and in financial straits. Deciding to commit fully to the self-help business and the motivational speaking circuit, Ziglar set up his own company in 1970, incorporating it as We Believe! (In 1977, Ziglar changed the company's name to the Zig Ziglar Corporation.)[5]

Ziglar's company specialized in self-help materials and motivational seminars for corporations and individuals. With few clients on his docket, Ziglar was fortunate that executives at Mary Kay Cosmetics contacted him about conducting a series of motivational seminars for their sellers. Mary Kay Ash, who had founded Mary Kay Cosmetics in 1963, liked what she saw during one of Ziglar's seminars. She hired him to teach Mary Kay representatives—mostly women entering the workforce for the first time—"how to get motivated and how to stay motivated" with various goal-setting procedures and sales techniques. As Ziglar remembered, "During the following two years [from 1970 to 1972], [Mary Kay] was my principal source of income."[6]

Soon, Ziglar's relationship with Mary Kay Cosmetics went beyond professional expediency. On July 4, 1972, Ziglar dramatically rededicated his life to Jesus Christ after a religious epiphany he experienced while floating in his backyard pool. Details about this event varied. In second-hand accounts, he was alone and unexpectedly moved. In most first-hand accounts, Ziglar claimed that an elderly black woman named Sister Jessie had witnessed to him a few days before his conversion.[7] The first-hand version suggested that Ziglar had not worked the racial culture of his upbringing entirely out of his system. In other words, Ziglar traced his spiritual awakening to her fundamental understanding of the spiritual universe, a long-standing white assumption of black spirituality that simultaneously worked to delegitimize black autonomy. Or, Sister Jesse granted Ziglar another source for proclaiming his color blindness. If he and Sister Jesse were friends and she his spiritual mentor, then they were both equals at the foot of the cross and, by extension, the commercial sphere. Regardless, one thing was clear: Ziglar's born-again experience revived his personal and professional life, inspiring him to use his fledgling company as a platform for addressing the social and cultural "problems" facing contemporary America. "I'm a satisfied customer who has shopped in the marketplace of Satan and in the eternal love of Jesus Christ," he later wrote. "I never had it so good—never had so much love, peace, joy, happiness, security and contentment along with better physical, mental and spiritual health." Sounding like Marion Wade at ServiceMaster in the 1950s and 1960s, under the "leadership of the Eternal Director," Ziglar had made "more financial progress in the past twelve years than I did in the preceding forty-five years." Ziglar was now an evangelical entrepreneur defined by a pragmatic, results-oriented faith. He was also determined to become a big businessman with an activist's taste for cultural politics.[8]

Ziglar was in good company. Mary Kay Ash was also a positive-thinking Peale disciple and evangelical who tried to bring her faith to bear on her business. Of the evangelical executives to play a major role in the evangelical movement during the 1970s, Ash stood out because of her gender. In general, evangelical businesses mirrored corporate America. Evangelical corporate hierarchies put men in charge of other men or women. Though more women were entering the workforce, evangelical companies tended to retain the common arrangement of men over women and white over black, whether in older industrial workplaces or at newer, service-oriented companies like ServiceMaster, HEB Stores, and, later, Chick-fil-A, Hobby Lobby, and Wal-Mart. Mary Kay Cosmetics was different. It was a company founded for the sole purpose of bringing women—regardless of race or class—into corporate America and up the corporate ladder. It was a feminist company, at least according to what Ash thought "feminist" should mean.

Ash started Mary Kay, Inc. in 1963 with her son, Richard Rogers. Like Chick-fil-A, it was a suburban company, growing mostly at first in newly built subdivisions outside Houston and Dallas, Texas. A divorcee whose second husband died tragically from a heart attack in the same year she founded her company, Ash had spent almost twenty-five years in the direct-sales business, working first for Stanley Home Products in Houston and then as a national training director for World Gift Company of Dallas. When her bosses passed her over for a promotion, granting it to a male coworker she had trained, Ash resigned and decided to write a "how to" book for professional women seeking to survive the male-dominated business world. The book became a business plan for her new company.[9]

Capitalizing Mary Kay Cosmetics with $5,000 ($36,500, inflation adjusted) of her own savings, Ash designed it as a company run by and for women. In doing so, Ash fit into a longer and broader history of direct-sales companies selling home products as an enabler, rather than oppressor, of women.[10] But Ash was also building her company in the midst of a changing culture. Middle-class women were reentering the workforce. Women were challenging glass ceilings, undercutting traditionalist interpretations of female ability, and pushing employers for equal pay for equal work. As historian Nancy Peiss has noted, Ash's company rode the crest of protest, "although [Ash] criticized feminists for effacing sex differences in the pursuit of equality." Ash deliberately "reached out to displaced homemakers and other women rocked by the social and economic turmoil of the 1960s and 1970s. . . . Lauding female ability, opening job opportunities in her own organization, addressing women's needs as mothers—all the while avowing women's desire to appear feminine—Mary Kay fused feminist economic aims with traditionalist ideals of womanhood." In interviews, Ash regularly argued that feminists needed to "come off it . . . and get with it." "[Women] have to help themselves, too. And looking repulsive won't do it," she told one columnist in 1970 after the Texas governor appointed Ash to a state commission on the status of women.[11]

By retaining as strong a commitment to their Christian faith as they did to cosmetic beauty, thought Ash, women could make their way in business without losing their feminine distinctions and sense of Christian, motherly duty. As Ash put it, her company's core philosophy was "God first, family second, job third," a direct challenge to what she assumed was a feminist assault on God and family *through* female careerism. As one former Mary Kay beauty consultant put it, "Everything [Mary Kay Ash] says, even listening to her inspirational tapes, is all directed to women. It has an undertone of 'we are capable, but we still have our place.'" Ash urged beauty consultants hoping to work at Mary Kay to ask their husband's permission before starting work. Likewise, Ash encouraged women to forego company business if family obligations or emergencies were more pressing, generally with the implication that family matters were first and foremost women's work.[12]

In keeping with Title VII's recent requirements, Ash claimed that she would never "impose my personal religious beliefs on anyone." (The company went public in 1968, which encouraged a certain corporate pluralism early in its business history; it went private again in 1985.) Still, at Mary Kay, evangelical devotion to a personal, all-encompassing faith remained the company's "bottom line," since "on that day when God calls you to accept your relationship with Jesus Christ, nothing else matters." "Each of us will come to that day," Ash concluded, "and we must ask ourselves whether or not our lives have been meaningful." A meaningful life, like a meaningful company, was one devoted not to feminist political or cultural values but to the conservative values of serving God, family, and faith. In Ash's estimation, "miracles happen[ed]" for men and women who kept their priorities straight. To incentivize such "miracles" and prove the immediacy of rewards for hard work, Mary Kay gave pink Cadillacs to top sellers, thereby aligning several gendered tropes with entrepreneurship. Not only did the vehicle reference Elvis culture and southern forms of conspicuous consumption, it also taught that any woman could "make it" in a masculine sphere (the world of competitive, often combative business) and attain a man's trophy (a Cadillac) on their own terms (pink). The pink Cadillac branded Mary Kay representatives as the right kind of entrepreneurial woman: manicured to perfection, modest in appearance, molded by "family" concerns.[13]

Mary Kay's message landed at a time when women's work and the economics of American families were in flux. Given the flat-lining male wage in the 1970s, female work was becoming more valued in the household and workplace. The emerging service economy seemed, to employers, suited to women while sexist hiring practices that set women's wages below men's dragged overall wages down, with cost-cutting benefits accruing to companies making do in the midst of oil shocks and rising inflation. Hence, included in Mary Kay's definition of "family concern" was the first or second income afforded by Mary Kay, earned for the sake of a family's economic well-being. Most important, Mary Kay representatives were role models to other women, selling conservative womanhood to their friends and family and customers—who were sometimes one and the same. A Mary Kay woman was a careerist and feminine but not sexually promiscuous or overly assertive. The underlying suggestion was that Mary Kay women, working for God and family, would never do anything or sell anything that might undercut the economic or sexual "stability" of the heterosexual family.

The egalitarian nature of Ash's "miracles" for women was an important facet of her business model and in keeping with other direct-sales companies. Presumably any woman could follow her biblically mandated formula for climbing the corporate ladder. (Mary Kay's sellers and customers were primarily white but not exclusively so.) Another evangelical direct-sales executive, Richard DeVos of the Michigan-based Amway corporation, also traded in Pealian mind change, feminine (and masculine) uplift, personal inspiration, and revivalistic fervor. Like Ash, DeVos was fully invested in what one scholar called "charismatic capitalism." "If I expect good things to happen, they usually do!" he wrote in *Believe!*, DeVos's foremost summary of his own philosophy of economics. "This is an exciting world," he continued. "It is cram-packed with opportunity. Great moments wait around every corner. It is a world that deserves an upward look." Unlike Baptists like Ziglar and Ash, DeVos was a member of the Christian Reformed Church, which sided more with hardline Calvinism but nevertheless retained a positive approach toward missions and conversions. DeVos also followed Norman Vincent Peale's approach to positive thinking and was optimistic about the potential for personal and professional change. "Life, like it or not," he wrote in Calvinistic fashion, "is a harsh regimen." But, he clarified, "rewards are contingent on behavior. It is a rule of life: one reaps what he sows. One accepts the consequences of his behavior. That is not an artifact of capitalism; it is a rule of nature itself." Delayed gratification, however, was not necessarily another rule of nature. Like Ash, DeVos thought direct selling was the best means to personal autonomy and spiritual nourishment. Amway's sellers immediately watched a part of their sales land in their bank accounts. Self-starting, highly motivated entrepreneurialism was the key to immediate reward. (Regulators and disgruntled sellers, of course, questioned such assurances in the late 1970s and early 1980s, routinely pulling Amway into the courts as a pyramid scheme.) Given his company's emphasis on individualism and the narrative of financial salvation through work, DeVos cast the state as anathema to God-blessed free-market capitalism. Personal responsibility and free choice was sacrosanct since everyone was "answerable at the level at which he finds himself." All were equal in the labor market, and only hard work and the right mind—mixed with devotion to God, who would likewise direct where charity should or should not go—stood between DeVos's devotees and the blessings of business.[14]

Ash's and DeVos's friend, Zig Ziglar, preached a similar message of uplift, touring the country and running seminars for executives, middle managers, and salaried and hourly employees alike. After his conversion in 1972, his company became another evangelical business. "All of my staff [members] are strong, born-again Christians. Every action they take," he told a reporter, "is of a loving, caring, concerned Christian."[15] But his business was not merely in public speaking. Between the 1970s and 1990s, Ziglar authored or coauthored more than two dozen books. The titles illustrated Ziglar's interests: *Steps to the Top, Selling 101, Secrets of Closing the Sale, Top Performance, Better Than Good, Over the Top, Breaking Through to the Next Level,* and *Staying Up, Up, Up in a Down, Down World.* By the 1980s, Ziglar was regularly publishing with evangelical press Thomas Nelson. Each of his books aimed to "inspire" and "uplift" the struggling or directionless business professional, but Ziglar did not copy other positive thinking or self-help authors. He branded himself as a different type of motivational leader, one whose southern experiences legitimized his pitch and whose version of southern history "proved" his views about the mind's revival—and the mind's relationship to personal wealth and satisfaction. Ziglar's gospel linked the individual to the corporation and a transcendent and effectual God to both. His was a new corporate revival.

Get Motivated

The most popular of Ziglar's books was his first, and it served as the most concise summary of his views about religion, race, gender, business, state, and society. First published in 1974, *See You at the Top* was a longer version of a speech he gave more than 3,000 times in the late 1960s and early 1970s. Initially titled *Biscuits, Fleas, and Pump Handles* and published by a vanity press, the book was retitled for broader appeal by Pelican Publishing (a New Orleans–based press run by a Baptist layman) and published with additional commentary as *See You at the Top.* Ziglar's thesis was straightforward: "You can have everything in life you want if you just help enough other people get what they want."[16] Ziglar offered yet another version of the evangelical service ethic, not a coincidence since many in his revival and reading audience were involved in retail, sales, technology, and other service sectors. He spiritualized service and likened it to Paul's quips about serving two masters (meaning Christ or Satan) and, of course, the servant-leader model of a previous generation of evangelical businessmen. As he later told an admiring reporter, "I would never go back to serving Satan. In short, I'm committed to serving Christ." Serving the latter made him a more effective leader in business. "As a speaker, before I became a Christian I covered things I believed in, but didn't give instruction as to how you implement them."

Now, he was "a 'how-to' teacher . . . and not just a motivational teacher," teaching a foolproof method of mutual service and positive thinking that ensured what Philippians 4:13 seemed to promise, that anyone could become a business leader. No matter the circumstances, one could "do all things through Christ who strengtheneth me."[17]

But in presenting his case, Ziglar also followed Peale's philosophy, arguing that one needed to have a strong self-image and the right habits of mind before one could help others get what they want and, feasibly, attain financial security or the executive's office. To be sure, Ziglar wrote, "Positive thinking won't let you do <u>anything</u>. . . . I don't care how positive I got, I couldn't play quarterback for an NFL football team. . . . but it will let you do <u>everything</u> better than negative thinking will." To clear out "garbage dump thinking" and develop an entrepreneurial self, Ziglar offered a wide variety of analogies and suggestions, many similar to what Peale and other positive thinkers promoted: practice self-esteem exercises, visualize goals, "actualize" goals, and have faith in God's economic promise and provision. Like Peale, Ziglar's exegesis of passages and parables from the Bible also supported the notion that God approved of self-esteem and the pursuit of financial success. As Ziglar put it, "I love the Bible, and believe it should be made available as a course in every school, because God so clearly demonstrates the difference between positive and negative thinking." In particular, he admired the Bible "because of its beautiful simplicity and clarity" and chastised anyone who made excuses about its more esoteric passages or lessons: "Personally, I feel God speaks quite clearly." For Ziglar, the Bible's approachability made it a professional shortcut. One did not need any formal schooling or an MBA degree to climb the corporate ladder. One merely needed to acknowledge that the Bible was right, read it, believe it, and put its lessons into practice. Still, there was room for interpretation. Ziglar might privately assert a certain interpretive fundamentalism regarding the Bible—by his judgment, only the King James Version, New King James Version, or New International Version made the grade as translations—and fall in with those fighting in defense of the concept of biblical "inerrancy" in evangelical seminaries and denominations like the SBC in the 1970s. (*Christianity Today*'s editor Harold Lindsell, for instance, was an inerrantist, as was Ziglar's mentor, W. A. Criswell.) But Ziglar demonstrated evangelical flexibility and pragmatism for the sake of maximum appeal when reading the Bible as a book of business ethics. Ziglar himself admitted as much on one occasion, noting that his retelling of David's defeat of Goliath as "proof" of God's affirmation of strivers was "slightly Ziglarized."[18]

Like other southern evangelical business leaders, Ziglar "proved" his points by using a redacted version of southern history. Ziglar never addressed the history of his home region in terms that any archive-diving historian would recognize. No serious acknowledgement of African American struggles, the civil rights movement, or the federally subsidized regional defense economy appeared in *See You at the Top* or any of his subsequent books on business. Neither Jim Crow and its lingering effects, especially in terms of the desegregation or resegregation of American cities, nor the continuing obstacles facing minorities in the workforce, were treated as germane. The Mississippi of his youth and the region at large, in Ziglar's recasting, had not merely escaped the burdens of its past. The burdens of southern history had apparently never really been there and certainly left no long-term legacy. Thus, as in the biographies told by other evangelical businessmen, Ziglar's transformation from small-town country boy to big-time businessman was solely due to his entrepreneurial drive and commitment to—as he put it—"God's promise for my life."

His personal transformation was also aided by a number of good decisions, each best illustrated by a didactic, pithy story he claimed to have drawn from the rural culture of his native South. Ziglar spoke of biscuits cooking. "Don't get cooked in the squat," he told his readers and audiences, borrowing the idea from an off-hand comment he had overheard at a wealthy neighbor's house in Yazoo City. The cook—most likely a black woman, although Ziglar only referred to her as Maude—referred to burned biscuits as "squatting to rise, but they just got cooked in the squat." For Ziglar, people were biscuits. They ought to rise and not "squat," or wait around for the right conditions. The yeast of "positive thinking" would allow them to rise. Also, taught Ziglar, do not become like a flea. As he supposedly learned as a bored kid in Mississippi, fleas routinely tried to jump out of a jar if one put a lid on it. But then they gave up and, defeated, they stayed in the jar even after the lid was removed. Unlike the flea, one needed to recognize when the lid was lifted and, of course, keep jumping and trying. But if a defeated attitude was debilitating, then mediocrity was particularly insidious, like water boiling a frog in a pot. It crept up on the frog, eventually cooking it to death due to its unwillingness or inability to work its way off the stovetop. (Ziglar nationalized the frog; Americans in the 1970s were suffering from an epidemic of complacency brought on by "Communism," which "started under another banner back in the 30's." Secular culture and "liberal legislation" was subsequently "boiling" around the frog, which was in "hot water" that was only "getting hotter.") Frogs appeared in other books and speeches. "An ol' boy said it best," he noted. "Friend, if you've got to swallow a frog, you just don't want to look at that sucker too long. He ain't gonna get no pertier! As a matter of fact, the longer you look, the uglier he gets.' That's the way unpleasant tasks are."[19]

Ziglar's southern colloquialisms ("roun' tuit," "ain't," "half-a-minder," "gonna doer") and his thick Mississippi accent played up his identity as a revivalist with gravitas granted by a rural upbringing outside urban, corporate America. Ziglar worked in a time when "the South" remained as it had in H. L. Mencken's day and throughout postwar history, as a vital image of "difference" in American culture.

From the 1960s through the 1980s, television shows from *Beverly Hillbillies* to *Hee Haw* to *Dallas* routinely featured class-based southern stereotypes. After its first issue in 1966, *Southern Living* magazine popularized regional difference via middle-class consumerism. In the 1970s, southern civic elites posited their cities as "beyond" the region's racial past and having "good business climates." But Ziglar put a different spin on regionalist imagery and stereotype, tapping into an invented southern past as a plain-folk resource for folksy wisdom about the power of positive thinking and hard work. And, during public seminars, he delivered messages of uplift in a style borrowed from the sawdust evangelical past but updated for inspiring a different kind of "born again" experience, a reframing of the mind and body toward working diligently and mindfully in the corporate economy of the 1970s and 1980s.

Ziglar was the Billy Graham of corporate salvation. Whether delivering his message at a public seminar or in one of his books, Ziglar wanted to instill in his audience the same beliefs that his story of uplift instilled in him. "I mention these things not to impress you with what God has permitted me to do, but to encourage you as to what you do with what *you* have," he preached. Ziglar's personal history—which only mentioned Mississippi poverty as a resource for his corporate folk tales or as a foil for his later success—reaffirmed the need for his readers to impart this message to others. To sustain this message's universal applicability, cherry-picking through much of modern southern history was not an option. It was *necessary* for Ziglar's myth of individual and national redemption through work. To make a future secure through effort, any limitations to that future, especially those framed by the past, had to fade from memory—or had to appear like they never existed. Ziglar's faith, like that of Taylor, Pew, Wade, and the previous generation of Christian executives, assumed a level playing field. But his faith was also like other narratives of southern economic transformation through business. It posited the possibility of another "New South," redeemed through economic incorporation in a new regional and national economy. But in his faith there were no Old South ghosts to bury or segregationist burdens left to throw off. Ziglar acknowledged no remaining racial or economic sins in need of redemption, other than those caused by present-day negative thinking or by unconverted critics of his evangelical redemption narrative—and of course, the sins committed by the enemies of Ziglar's vision for a more Christian and free-market America.[20]

Like evangelical conservatives before him, Ziglar regularly used his books as a platform to praise the "free market enterprise system." For Ziglar, the free market was the primary solution to liberal politics and moral "decline," which he collapsed into one another. Ziglar was unequivocal about the solution. Positive thinking and hard work—along with a reduction in business regulations by the state—would fight communism, liberalism, and other ungodly "-isms."

To underscore his point, he held up African American achievements as exemplary of what was possible in a positive-thinking, free-market society. "The Negro," Ziglar wrote in *See You at the Top*, "has made more progress in this generation than any people in recorded history. His progress has been in direct proportion to the change in his self-image." He admitted that "prejudice still exists, but progress is being made daily" and "the complete solution will come with education, love, and understanding by both black and white, that skin color and ability have no correlation."[21] In this color-blind present and unlike liberal state policy in the past, whether during the 1930s and especially since the Great Society of the 1960s, the "free enterprise system" presumably placed no limits on personal success through personal responsibility. The nation's racial past, only mentioned in passing by Ziglar, was hardly relevant to the present. Rather, like conservatives who believed in the sanctity of their "color blindness" when calling for the creation of an "opportunity society" or for cuts to state services, Ziglar asserted that the free market insured that success "has nothing to do with age or education. Nothing to do with whether you are black or white, male or female, overweight or underweight, extrovert or introvert or whether you are Catholic, Jew, or Protestant." Rather, "it has everything to do with your God-given rights as a free person to work as long as you wish, as hard as you wish and as enthusiastically as you wish to get everything in life you really want."[22]

Ziglar's books and opinions joined a growing cottage industry in evangelical business writing. Since the burdens of the past were particularly acute in the South, a region long defined by economic underdevelopment and hard-to-miss forms of legal and institutional racism, the books produced by southern business leaders were most forthright in advocating the redemptive power of work blessed by God. Many biographies and autobiographies noted this fact, beginning their stories in the poverty-stricken—but routinely un-racist—southern past of the early twentieth century. For instance, Chick-fil-A's S. Truett Cathy wrote of the hardships of growing up on a failing farm in Georgia during the Great Depression. "Rural life," Cathy remembered, "left many scars," including memories of a depressed and abusive father and a sister stricken with polio. William B. Walton of Holiday Inn had a similar experience. He was forced into the adult responsibilities of work, budgeting, and fatherhood at the age of twelve, after his own father abandoned his family in the midst of the Depression. David Green, founder of Hobby Lobby, grew up in rural Oklahoma just a few miles from the Texas state line. Green found retail stores to be fascinating and enchanting places. "Not that our family came to shop very often," he wrote in his autobiography. "We simply didn't have the money."[23]

To be sure, not every evangelical business writer came from humble beginnings in the rural South. Cecil B. Day, Alvah Chapman (chairman of Knight-Ridder), and Jack Eckerd (founder of Eckerd Drug Stores) all came from families of relative means. Still, tales of hard times and hard luck featured in the popular literature produced by evangelical businessmen. In the 1970s, evangelicals made the "how to" rags-to-riches success story, a story as old as Benjamin Franklin and Horatio Alger, their own.[24]

Other evangelical writers offered a different interpretation of southern poverty, writing guides for how individuals might overcome personal troubles through a combination of faith and careful planning. Beginning in the mid-1970s, personal and business debt captured evangelical imaginations and the worries of middle-class and working-class Americans. The struggling economy, as well as shifts in male wages, rising health-care and educational costs, and rising consumer prices meant that more Americans were taking on personal debt. In other words, they were becoming poorer and, therefore, drawing a step closer to the poverty that Ziglar and other evangelical businessmen cast themselves as having left behind. In this context, the stage was set for a new kind of evangelical business and businessman: the Christian financial counselor. And one of this new market's first shapers was a Floridian, evangelical businessman, and friend of Ziglar's named Larry Burkett.

Burkett was at the forefront of an emerging evangelical financial advice industry in the 1980s. He was born in 1939 to a Depression-stressed family that was, as he put it, "somewhere between poor and very poor." Like many southerners hoping to escape poverty, he joined the military. After a medical discharge, Burkett enrolled in Orlando Junior College, graduated, and then worked for the space program before moving up to become vice president of an electronics manufacturing firm. As with other white southerners and evangelicals, the federal government helped Burkett move up in the business world, granting him a leg up through the military, student provisions, and a career in the Sunbelt's aerospace and technology sector. But he took a religious lesson from his story of personal uplift and perseverance, especially after "God reached down and touched me" in 1971. "Once that happened," he later wrote, "I knew I was not going to stay in the electronics field."

Burkett left the private sector for the parachurch sector. He joined Campus Crusade for Christ after his conversion and began developing a Christian personal finances guide. Burkett left in 1976 to found Christian Financial Concepts. The year before, his first book—*Your Finances in Changing Times*—had come out with Moody Press, a major evangelical publisher. Dr. James Dobson picked up the book and invited Burkett to appear on his syndicated radio show, *Focus on the Family*. Sales of the book increased, making a solid showing in Christian bookstores and resulting in Burkett starting his own 30-minute call-in show, eventually known as "Your Money Matters." By 1984, Burkett's career was in full stride.[25]

Like his company, Burkett and his books focused on maintaining Christian commitments in an unsteady economy. In 1975, when his first book came out, the economy was still reeling from the recent oil shocks and inflationary spikes. Like Ziglar and Ash, Burkett spiritualized such crises, arguing that the "way a Christian uses money is the clearest outside indicator of what the inside commitment is really like." True Christians treated money with respect, avoided debt, and tithed generously. They were not supposed to become paupers for Christ, but neither should they embrace a lavish lifestyle. "Somewhere between the careful ant and the foolish hoarder" lay the right attitude toward earned wages, since "God wants us to have some surplus but not an attitude of selfishness or greed." Self-styled "Christian" business owners could and should have five priorities, in the following order: evangelism, discipleship, funding "God's work," providing for needs, and, finally, earning profits. Burkett also argued for the same service-oriented managerial strategies that other evangelical corporate leaders advocated. "If you find that you can't give the same honor and regard to the lowest-ranked employee in your business," wrote Burkett, "you need to stop right here and resolve it with the Lord."

Burkett's books and radio shows made him one of the most prominent evangelical counselors in the country. By the late 1990s, over 1.3 million copies of *Your Finances in Changing Times* had been sold, and Burkett's radio show was airing on hundreds of stations. Cancer slowed his career by the turn of the century, and it took his life in 2003. Yet, Burkett left a legacy. His company—renamed Crown Financial Concepts in 2000—continued operations after his death. His teachings also continued to both inspire and compete against other evangelical personal finance counselors, such as Atlanta's Dave Ramsey, whose radio show reached millions each week and whose Financial Peace University series sold millions of copies to individual purchasers and churches alike.[26]

Burkett's books were a part of a burgeoning new market. Dozens of books appeared in the 1970s and 1980s detailing how conservative evangelicals—yet again casting themselves as merely "Christians"—might address myriad questions about work, ranging from personal debt to professional advancement to bookkeeping at a small business. This was an uncoordinated phenomenon, but it demonstrated the willingness and ability of evangelicals to shape public discourse regarding the personal, social, or familial costs and benefits of working in a corporate economy defined by flatlining professional wages and instability. Backed by the growing "Christian" book industry and corporate modes of marketing and distribution, evangelical writers crowded out other reflections on the "proper" relationship between work, faith, the state, the company, and society. Indeed, whereas progressive Protestants might have driven public debates and book purchases a generation before, evangelical writers had taken the lead. In the process, the notion of a *liberal* "Christian businessperson" became something of an oxymoron, especially in the books, tapes, and videos stocking the shelves of Christian bookstores and mass-market retailers. If the "Christian" businessperson could no longer be a liberal, then the "Christian" business writer—at least in terms of books sold and mass distribution networks—was more often than not an evangelical preaching an evangelical business ethic: work hard, be pragmatic, be open-minded, serve well, expect to change the world. Most of all, have faith in free enterprise.

Writers came from various backgrounds. Some were theologians or seminary professors, finding the Bible's support for "faith at work" through exegesis. Most were businessmen or former pastors. Given the legal environment after Title VII, writers encouraged other born-again businessmen or businesswomen to make a nonoffensive and noncoercive "faith" a component of the workplace. Still, an emphasis on "leadership" through "character" was notable. "Leadership" was a catch-all term, but taking cues from Peter Drucker or the service ethic, it generally implied that the best entrepreneurs or executives were not the authoritarian bosses of the past but sensitive "leaders" who led their employees through their "character," another catch-all term that generally meant a combination of tolerance, sensitivity, patience, wisdom, and forgiveness. John C. Maxwell, a former pastor trained at Fuller Seminary and tutored by megachurch pastor of feel-good prosperity Robert Schuller, sold millions of books on how to organize and oversee churches and businesses via "leadership principles" derived from his reading of the Bible. Maxwell toured the country, touting the need to recognize "leaders" in business as role models for subordinates, albeit best showing their managerial authority through relational care, personal inspiration, and "servant leadership." Maxwell's contemporary and competitor, Fred Smith, taught similar lessons. Smith was a former watch company executive from Texas who also preached leadership as a new managerial gospel. Smith had served on the board of Youth for Christ and Graham's crusades in Ohio before writing articles for *Leadership*, a sister magazine of *Christianity Today* (he also served on its board). Smith's version of "leadership" joined together the servant-leader ethos, the responsible management teachings of his hero Peter Drucker, and the personal discipline strategies of Oswald Chambers, an early-twentieth-century Baptist writer who authored miniature devotionals. Like Maxwell, Smith's client list was quite lengthy. Not only did he keep up a busy schedule speaking to pastors and congregational groups, he also provided exclusive mentoring services to businesses. By the time of his death in 2007, he had been contracted with Genesco, Mobil Oil, Caterpillar, Campbell-Taggart, Jefferson Standard Life Insurance Company, and the Taft law firm.[27]

Evangelical executives like Wal-Mart's Don Soderquist, Herman Miller's Max De Pree, and ServiceMaster's C. William Pollard also promoted the leadership ethic with books of their own. To be sure, as historian Bethany Moreton has shown, the infatuation with leadership addressed the concerns of businessmen managing increasingly female workforces and engaging in "nonmanly" service work.[28] But the leadership ethic was only one business philosophy of many, and it usually did not stand apart from other managerial concepts preached by evangelicals. Evangelical business authors also reaffirmed habits of mind and "positive thinking." Others pulled in anecdotes and references that had little to do with new spins on "servant leadership" but harkened back to the Rotarian social service ethic of the early twentieth century, Drucker's community-focused model, or biblical injunctions regarding "Christ-like stewardship" and corporate "discipleship." Other books were indistinguishable from the latest treatise on "corporate social responsibility" or rereading of common sense "business ethics," albeit with a splash of biblical citation. Others wrote "business-conscious" versions of the Bible itself, reissued by mass-market Bible publishers. On this score, another synergy between the new flock of evangelical business writers and the Christian book industry was readily apparent. The Bible most often cited by writers as the rock solid foundation for Christian business ethics was the New International Version, itself a recent product of not just conservative theologians and scholars but pointed, top-down planning and marketing campaigns.

Free Market Revivals

Ziglar did not promote a specific managerial theory. Instead, he promoted a free-market faith, proclaiming that anyone could become an entrepreneur and, if they optimistically expected forthcoming blessings, rise through the ranks of corporate America to join the elite. He promised, as a businessman grounded in such a faith, he would "see you at the top."

Ziglar was an itinerant revivalist for the free market, touring the nation and leading seminars on positive thinking, salesmanship, self-development, and business performance. At times, a seminar was a standalone affair, with Ziglar as the only speaker. At other times, Ziglar was joined by other inspirational speakers or business executives. Regardless of where or to whom he was pitching his materials and message, Ziglar intended his seminars to be more than just another run-of-the-mill business meeting. They were meant to be exciting, inviting revivals. Ziglar's revivalism revealed that his free-market faith was not a rationalist discourse, espoused by someone with an MBA or PhD citing charts, graphs, and data about microeconomic or macroeconomic "growth" and "incentivized self-interest." Ziglar was not a professor. He did not appeal to the head. Rather, Ziglar attempted to manufacture consent to the free market by emphasizing its emotional, experiential, and transcendent characteristics. For Ziglar, one did not merely prove, defend, or promote the free market. The free market was something that someone "believed" in, with all of one's heart, mind, and soul. It was a faith integrated into one's faith in Christ, country, and one's own work.

For Ziglar, the free-market faith needed revivalists to barnstorm for it, whooping it up for corporate leaders, mid-level managers, salaried professionals, hourly and part-time workers, and would-be entrepreneurs alike. Indeed, working in the modern economy, as Ziglar freely admitted, could be tiresome, boring, or mundane. More specifically, service work was rarely blissful and—especially amid the economic turmoil of the 1970s—all work seemed a chancy affair. Once again, Ziglar drew from his Mississippi upbringing to build a metaphor for what it meant to believe wholeheartedly in the free market. In *See You at the Top*, Ziglar wrote about a prop he had used since his early days as a motivational speaker: a chrome-plated replica of an old-fashioned, hand-driven water pump. The pump was a symbol for "the story of America, the story of the free enterprise system and the story of life." The pump's lesson was simple. First, start with full effort, pumping away with determination and dedication. Then, prime the pump by putting "*you* in whatever you do." Next, "work at it with the right attitude and the right habits . . . [and] keep at it with bulldog tenacity and persistence." Finally, when the blessings of effort flowed like water gushing out of the pump, "keep it flowing with a little steady effort."[29]

Though the full meaning of the pump analogy might have been lost on his readers, Ziglar's illustration served as a form of antistatist, free-market rhetoric. In the place of liberal Keynesian economic theory, which emphasized pump-priming the economy via state expenditures in times of stagnation, Ziglar emphasized pump-priming via individual effort. The lessons taught by the water pump were also entirely democratic, available to anyone. To Ziglar, all had equal opportunity in the democracy of the free market, regardless of their present or past circumstances. The choice to prime the pump, and keep pumping, was the only thing that differentiated the winners from the losers, the blessed from the rest.

Reporters covering Ziglar often came away impressed by his public-speaking skills and persona, both of which took cues from the Mencken-era, regionalized trope of the Bible Belt revivalist (See Fig. 6.1). "When Ziglar talks, people listen," asserted one reporter in 1990. "He kneels, he gesticulates, he mimes a robber sticking up a bank," wrote another reporter about a seminar in Washington, D.C. in 1995, "He speaks in the rolling cadences of a good Southern Baptist preacher." Similarly, a year later, an Atlanta reporter noted that "he had the movements and rhythms . . . of a Southern preacher." These stylistic cues mattered, since he was in the business of convincing others of, as another reporter put it, "the gospel of good old American gung-ho individualism." Preaching like a Baptist minister was one part entertainment, one part invigoration. The audience had to be inspired to work. Ziglar, by his estimation, had to touch their souls to motivate their minds and bodies. It was one of his longest-lasting methods for free-market revivalism. Even in 2006, at the age of eighty, Ziglar impressed one San Antonio reporter with a "style similar to an evangelical preacher."[30]

Figure 6.1 Zig Ziglar routinely incorporated stories and sayings derived from his southern upbringing to promote his free-market faith during a career that spanned over four decades. Courtesy of Randy Miramontez/Shutterstock.com.

For women, African Americans, and others underrepresented in the post–Title VII corporate applicant pool or boardroom, Ziglar's meritocratic parables often held a certain appeal. Ziglar's past, however mythical, signaled that, if he could make it up from Mississippi, perhaps they could as well. The limits of race, class, and gender no longer mattered. Only the revival of the mind and heart, inspired by a faith in the free market, stood between the rapt listener and rapturous enjoyment of the American Dream. Elizabeth Sage, a single mother and secretary at an electric company, appreciated the suggestions presented at a seminar that featured a double billing of Ziglar and Peale, primarily because it showed her how to work as a woman in the workplace. "The field [for sales] is opening up for women," she said. "I know I can do it, but I need confidence." Raised in a home that emphasized "that a woman should only stay home and take care of the children and not work," Sage found having a "positive mental attitude" empowering, even though she had not fully translated that optimism into professional success. "I get these angry feelings," she said, "and find if I just say to myself the words in the book [on positive mental attitude] . . . it helps. It makes me feel better." Karen Beckwith's career was likewise stuck in a rut when she attended a Ziglar seminar in the early 1990s. Ziglar offered Beckwith encouragement that, even though her business was floundering, its best days were ahead as long as she kept her chin up and eyes open for business opportunities. "I've had a hell of a life," she explained. "But what are you going to do, go around being [angry] all the time?" She preferred Ziglar's route: "It's all in your attitude." Marcus Tappan, a black businessman who had experienced relative success as a dentist, agreed. Ziglar's books and tapes had "contributed a lot to my success," particularly Ziglar's advice about goal-setting. As a result, Tappan believed that Ziglar's suggestions were applicable beyond the business world. A mentor to inner-city youth, Tappan was sure that Ziglar's tapes and philosophy could grant troubled kids the direction they needed to pursue a viable career and attain lasting security and happiness.[31]

Despite these accolades, Ziglar's gospel could be off-putting. May Lou Doyle, who ran a Philadelphia public relations firm, wanted her money back after hearing Ziglar for the first time. "He didn't do a thing for me," she said. "I came specifically for him. I'd heard him for years. I came here wanting to feel that feeling, the it, whatever that it was. And I didn't get it." Still, she gave Ziglar the benefit of the doubt. "Maybe it doesn't happen overnight," she reflected. "Maybe I should give him another chance. I'm still going to buy his book." David Hamilton, an Atlanta jewelry retailer, likewise found that Ziglar's message was some sometimes lost on his employees. "Some of them . . . take the concepts and run with it," he said. "Some of them, you know, it just kind of goes in one ear and out the other."[32]

Reporters could be as pensive about Ziglar's appeal as his audience. Economic uncertainty seemed to contribute to Ziglar's popularity among Americans struggling to make ends meet in the recession of the 1970s and uneven recovery of the 1980s. "For Zig Ziglar and other preachers of this new success gospel," wrote Robert Friedman in 1979, "the fear of falling behind—the modern-day equivalent of the fear of eternal damnation—has created an ideal selling climate for their self-improvement wares." Friedman concluded that "to sales managers, independent entrepreneurs, and junior executives squeezed by the realities of corporate and governmental power, the myth of limitless individual power is as shining as a new set of stainless steel cookware." But generalized prosperity also seemed to fuel Ziglar's popularity as well, especially in states with robust or growing local economies. Writing for the *Texas Monthly*, Mimi Swartz believed that Ziglar's application of "Christian principles to getting ahead" were attractive because of Texas's booming oil and petrochemical sectors. Why not believe in Ziglar's message? As she noted, "By 1979 everybody seemed to be making it very big, or at least they were about to." Ziglar offered a clear-cut explanation for this economic boom and, indeed, all economic booms. It was "the payoff for Ziglar's cowboy Christian values—hard work, faith in God, honesty in all deeds." The free market was not a grand puzzle to figure out. With just a touch of belief and a will to work, it was a perpetual revival to experience.[33]

But like any revival, it was always in danger of unraveling. Like many before him, Ziglar thought his Christian America was in danger. Ziglar's culture war, however, was one that began with the entrepreneurial self and extended into corporate and political life. Truly believing in the free market meant defending that faith with fervency, confidence, and aplomb, the very same characteristics that seemed to promise success in the private sector.

Of Corporate Revivals and Culture Wars

Ziglar rarely expressed his social or political views during his business seminars. Like any business executive, he was concerned about alienating an audience that might not fully agree with his beliefs. This concern did not stop Ziglar from inviting his audiences to convert, á la Billy Graham, through a "decision for Christ" moment at the end of seminars. It also did not stop Ziglar from putting his happy-go-lucky business tips alongside fiery social jeremiads in each of his books, nearly all of which connected the economic vitality of the person and nation to the relative influence of political elites, the media, rebellious college students, feminists, homosexuals, and communists—all presumably parading under the banner of "liberalism."[34]

Like other conservative evangelical businessmen, Ziglar posited that cultural change started with the individual and with conversion to his brand of faith-based economics. As a businessman-revivalist fully committed to preaching the verity and sublimity of free enterprise, Ziglar privileged emotional appeals and the promise of self-made, tangible, near-immediate, "worldly" results. "The extra power the Lord has given me as I live through Him," wrote Ziglar, "the effectiveness in my profession, and the love of my fellow human beings all add up to a substantial number of reasons for serving the Lord *now*. Eternity is my bonus. . . . But, the *now* benefits of serving Christ are also immense." These "now benefits" came in two forms. First, material rewards followed conversion. "Faith," he wrote, "added effectiveness to my busyness and success to my business." "If you want financial strength and security," he continued, "it is available if you will follow God's teachings." Ziglar urged his readers to read the Bible, specifically the Book of Proverbs. The former was "the greatest book on business ever written" and the latter offered "the greatest lessons on business success ever written." More important, financial success could create "wealth to glorify Him and spread His Gospel." Second, conversion automatically offered a new outlook on social and cultural affairs. There were God's dictates and Satan's lures. Conversion helped one recognize the difference because it put one squarely within the story that God was telling about the nation, the nation's economy, the nation's sexual and social sins, and the ties that bound each to one another. For Ziglar, the Devil's influence on contemporary America was obvious. "I believe—no, I *know*—that Satan and hell exist in a very real sense." Thus Ziglar wanted to recruit his readers in fighting Satan every step of the way. Engaging in this fight as angry, condescending people was self-defeating. Instead, devoted evangelicals needed to exude optimism, confidence, and surety—the very qualities that would grant them "success" in corporate life. In other words, by bringing the principles of Ziglar's free-market faith and corporate gospel to bear on the culture wars of the 1970s and 1980s, evangelical conservatives could emerge victorious over their economic, sexual, educational, and political enemies.[35]

For Ziglar, those foes were legion. In general, he laid the blame for America's decline at the feet of nameless, faceless liberals who had been overly tolerant of changing moral and sexual standards. In *See You at the Top*, Ziglar only half-jokingly traced the beginnings of America's moral "decline" to Rhett Butler's profanity at the end of the 1939 film *Gone With the Wind*. "The liberals scoffed and said it was ridiculous for us to worry. What harm could one little word do?" Ziglar wrote. "The next year saw another word added to the acceptable list for the family theatre [*sic*] and we were on our way—down." Ziglar then expressed his dismay about the proliferation of pornography "to the magazine racks of the family bookstore" before resigning that "you can view movies like *Last Tango in Paris* and *Deep Throat* in 'family' theaters [and] you can tune in on talk shows and listen to the open endorsements of free love, trial marriage, homosexuality, etc." Much like Jerry Falwell, Pat Robertson, James Dobson, and a host of other conservative activists, Ziglar thought the situation had become dire by the mid-1970s. Liberals had brainwashed American youth into no longer thinking of extramarital sex as "dirty." Liberals had allowed television to normalize instant gratification and moral laxity. Liberals had encouraged population and poverty controls via the loosening of restrictions on abortion.[36]

Ziglar's books on culture and family, *Confessions of a Happy Christian* (1978) and *Dear Family* (1984), expounded on these views. Using an allegory that detailed "Satan's sales meetings," Ziglar described how Satan wanted to woo Americans into a bum contract, namely the false benefits of drinking, gambling, pornography, and extramarital or premarital sex. Satan reserved a special affinity for the homosexual man. Satan had already encouraged his minions to "start beating the drums for homosexuality" since "you will recall at Sodom and Gomorrah we really had it going good" and "in Rome and Greece and all of the other eighty-eight civilizations that fell, homosexuality was the final straw." Following the conservative view of homosexual men as activists invested only in sexual conversion, Ziglar's Satan also advocated "getting a few of the churches saying that homosexuality is a 'lifestyle'" and assuring that Americans would "believe *anything* as long as we can get a celebrity to endorse it." Ziglar called for his readers to support Anita Bryant. "I agree with Anita Bryant," wrote Ziglar. "I don't want a homosexual—either known or unknown—teaching our children in public schools, because you cannot logically suppress the emotional feeling of the individual who teaches our children." Opposing Bryant's politics was tantamount to supporting the educational accreditation of robbers, prostitutes, drug addicts, wife-beaters, child molesters, egomaniacs, "or any other person who espouses his sin as being all right." Even in the mid-1980s, after conservative Christians had moved to the forefront of American party politics, homosexuality remained a point of particular grievance for Ziglar. In a book published in the midst of Ronald Reagan's reelection campaign, Ziglar wrote a mock question about whether homosexuals are "born that way." He answered affirmatively that they were not.[37]

The first line of defense against cultural liberalism was what Ziglar saw as the ultimate contractual organization: the family. Ziglar mirrored other conservatives in lauding the family, imagined as a male-led, heterosexual, and heteronormative household, as the wellspring of "family values," a catch-all term that to Ziglar meant sexual restraint, parental respect, educational achievement, religious devotion, national pride, *and* private-sector achievement. Like other evangelicals from Billy Graham and L. Nelson Bell in the 1960s to S. Truett Cathy in the 1980s, Ziglar added a professional twist and focused on the economic logic of family values. The biblical ordering of authority in the male-led family was essential for cultivating a sense of right and wrong and readying children, men, and women for the workplace. "The family needs a leader," Ziglar wrote in *Raising Positive Kids in a Negative World*, another parental advice book, "because while it is far *more* than a business, it *is* a business." Money had to be handled and partitioned. As the family's "employees," children needed to be trained and to affirm the biblical injunction to "honor thy father and mother." Ziglar argued, "The individual who should be the chairman of the board of the family is the man, the husband, the father." Since "our society is organized that way," he continued, the woman should be "second in command," although Ziglar was quick to argue that she was not "second in importance." Men were not released from their familial responsibilities. They too were under a contract. Husbands had to help with housework, mediate communication among family members, and, especially, illustrate their own subordination to God's will and commandments. Such religious devotion further signaled to children—whether girls or boys— the importance of all forms of authority, whether religious, familial, legal, or professional. It instructed them in how to avoid costly errors in judgment, such as having sex before marriage or having an abortion, both of which Ziglar viewed as deleterious to the "positive thinking" needed for business success. The result of this form of familial management would be happy, productive, and obedient citizens and employees.[38]

Ziglar routinely held up his own marriage as an example. Jean and Zig Ziglar married in 1946, and he dedicated *See You at the Top* to her, referring to her as "Sugar Baby" and "the Redhead." Ziglar most often used "the Redhead" as a nickname for his wife in his books and seminars, conveying that her identity was primarily marked by physical appearance and in relation to him and his career. She was the perfect "helpmate," advancing his career and the family business—and her family *as* a business—by caring for their children and household while routinely encouraging him in mentally, spiritually, and physically healthful routines. In gratitude, Ziglar was a "Romeo at Home," which he encouraged other men to become, listening to their wives with sincerity and serving them through heartfelt romance. In turn, women should follow the female ideal set by Jean Ziglar, keeping the home in order, staying positive, and treating service-oriented, domestic work as a primary and fitting career for a woman. In Marion Wade's parlance, women could and should be "service masters" in the household. Or, if in a career, women should remember to be as service-minded at home as on the job. Regardless of what women did Monday through Saturday, Ziglar taught that men were crucial for leading their families in a godly and professional manner, thereby empowering their wives to fight the good fight for the sexual, professional, and religious sanctity of the home and, by proxy, the nation itself.[39]

If a family failed to affirm Ziglar's religious and moral imperatives and violated God's familial contract, then all manner of troubles would surface. In particular, Ziglar worried that sexual "dysfunctions" would threaten to limit the potential of children for professional and personal development. Like other evangelical conservatives, Ziglar expressed dismay about how sex education had been left to teachers and public schools. He argued that "sex education *must* be taught from an early age by the parents." Otherwise, children were in danger of losing their virginity, becoming sexually attracted to their parents, or developing a professionally debilitating sexual addiction. Familial authority was likewise linked to homosexuality. In keeping with the evangelical preference for attributing homosexuality to nurture over nature, Ziglar added, "Many homosexual men have reported that their homes and childhood were mother dominated." In other words, men had abdicated their familial duties to raise boys to be "men." As such, preventing homosexuality lay with *both* the father and mother, with the former showing proper forms of authority and affection and the latter joining the father in encouraging "masculine activities or attitudes in the son." Ziglar suggested two books published by Thomas Nelson and Moody Press, respectively—Frank M. duMas's *Gay Is Not Good* and George Rekers's *Growing Up Straight*—to help parents "who want to make certain their kids are never trapped in homosexuality." By encouraging open discussions between parents and children, coupled with a proper sense of authority and mutual respect, Ziglar was certain that his readers could "raise positive, moral kids who [were] sexually straight" and ready for a fulfilling and financially viable career.[40]

Like other conservatives and a number of their past backers in big business, Ziglar saw the souls of youth as key fronts in the culture wars. As a businessman, he thought privately produced goods were the best way to teach students the lessons they needed; hence, he advocated for the insertion of privately developed curricula in public schools. To that end, Ziglar developed the I CAN program, a for-profit curriculum on entrepreneurialism, patriotism, and character development for use in elementary and secondary schools. Commercial self-help materials, of course, had been available for purchase in America throughout most of the twentieth century, although most were sold for private use, to supplement in-office seminars, or to provide at-home training for sales staff. But Ziglar aimed the I CAN program at school-age children and intended to translate the lessons and suggestions of his books and seminars to the classroom environment.

Ziglar first released the I CAN program in 1977. I CAN's purpose was straightforward: "PREPAR[E] TODAY'S YOUTH FOR AMERICA'S TOMORROW." By the early 1980s, it was in use in public school districts nationwide. One estimate calculated that nearly 3 million students learned from I CAN in the 1980s and early 1990s. Materials came in a packet for each class and consisted of twelve cassette recordings, daily motivational tapes, speech training tapes for teachers, a teacher's guide, and various other guides and workbooks for both student and teacher. Copies of *See You at the Top* were included so students could receive first-hand tips on entrepreneurialism and internalize Ziglar's views of positive thinking, work, sex, family values, the state, and Christian patriotism. Teachers worked from designed lesson plans that used workbook exercises, group work, and role-playing to help students sell themselves, work in groups, and increase both their self-esteem and their appeal to potential employers and customers.

Despite Ziglar's high expectations, I CAN had mixed results. For instance, a comprehensive study of I CAN's use in Georgia's school districts in the early 1980s revealed that it fell short of its intended goals. In general, I CAN improved the work attitude of students enrolled in marketing and distributive education, but it failed to enhance their self-esteem or their "human relations skills." Later, Ziglar admitted the shortcomings of the program, writing, "my biggest disappointment has been our I CAN character-building course for schools." But Ziglar expressed dismay only about the course's disappointing profit margins, arguing that, "we have confirming data that where the course has been taught, drug usage goes down; violence is reduced; attendance increases; grades go up; relationships among parents, teachers, and students improve; and the overall school attitude is definitely better."[41]

Of Fundamentalist Friends and
Conservative Associates

Along with winning him profit and popularity, Ziglar's books, seminars, and extracurricular activities were an effective networking strategy, embedding him squarely within a broader conservative movement that, by the 1970s, was increasingly aligning with evangelicals. This aspect of Ziglar's seminars was often missed by his audience or by reporters. For as much as Ziglar publicly presented himself and his message as apolitical or nonpartisan, he sought out the patronage of other leaders in the motivational movement, as well as conservative advocates and ideologues. One of Ziglar's closest friends, business writer and speaker W. Clement Stone, toured with him for nearly a decade after the publication of *See You at the Top*. Stone was the author of the 1960 book *Success Through a Positive Mental Attitude* and the founder of *Success Unlimited*, a monthly digest for the motivational industry. He was also the primary organizer of Success Unlimited Rallies, a series of inspirational seminars similar to Ziglar's in tone and message. A donor to Richard Nixon's presidential campaigns, Stone's political leanings also fit well with Ziglar's. Thus Ziglar often spoke at Stone's seminars. Once Ziglar did so in front of a 23-by-30-foot American flag, reminding his listeners that there was no contradiction between patriotic nationalism, religious piety, and accumulationist ambition. Ziglar taught, "The best way to help the poor is not to be one of them," adding that, "I think God made diamonds for his crowd, not for Satan's . . . Moses was a millionaire." Stone's seminars, Ziglar remembered, "represented a huge boost to my career." Not only was Ziglar able to hold down steady work, but he was also "privileged to share the platform with . . . other outstanding speakers," including Norman Vincent Peale, Cavett Robert, Ira Hayes, Heartsell Wilson, Don Hutson, Bill Gove, and Paul Harvey.[42]

Many of Ziglar's friends and associates were A-list or B-list celebrities on the inspirational circuit or in the broader conservative movement. A white southerner like Ziglar, Cavett Robert founded the National Speakers Association in 1972. Ira Hayes and Bill Gove both served as the presidents of the organization and, in that capacity, advanced Robert's mix of entrepreneurial lessons, business presentation skills, patriotic appeals, and free-market philosophy. Born poor in Oklahoma, Paul Harvey was, like Ziglar, raised in a conservative, evangelical environment. Harvey also affirmed Ziglar's politics. In an era before Rush Limbaugh and Sean Hannity, Harvey regularly publicized his disdain for liberals to approximately 22 million radio listeners per week. Harvey rarely minced words. On race, he stood strongly against quotas and forced busing ("America's schools are going downhill—by bus!"), environmental policing (the liberal media was responsible for "incit[ing] hysteria"), and liberal economics (the economy after

Reagan was "sunny-side up *without* inflation!"). Although Harvey's isolationist conservatism kept him from favoring Reagan's Cold War foreign policy, and his support for the Equal Rights Amendment infuriated some of his socially conservative listeners, he remained decidedly within the conservative camp. Harvey even coined the term "Reaganomics" as an endorsement of Reagan's supply-side and deregulatory philosophy. He also lauded the "Americanism" held by "grassroots Americans" who might, for instance, join the Farm Bureau and therefore uphold the "traditional values" of "freedom with . . . responsibility based on moral and religious concepts . . . family, national security, law enforcement, property rights [and] . . . allegiance to our flag."[43]

Of all his associations in conservative America, Ziglar's friendship with Dallas pastor W. A. Criswell was the closest and longest. Ziglar began attending Criswell's First Baptist Church in Dallas (FBCD) shortly after his conversion experience in 1972. Over the next decade, he developed an acute attachment to Criswell's theological and political point of view.

As pastor of the SBC's largest church, Criswell had been a major player in the denomination's power structure since the mid-1950s. Initially a staunch defender of racial segregation, Criswell had publicly repudiated this position in 1968. As Curtis A. Freeman has shown, however, Criswell was a fitting example of strategic accommodation to the civil rights movement. Like many other conservative evangelicals, Criswell still saw individual effort as the key to social mobility while generally ignoring or dismissing "structural explanations of racism as either irrelevant or wrongheaded."[44]

Criswell's church was a nexus of big-business influence and evangelical activity. Writing in 1973, Neal Peirce observed that Dallas exhibited a Sunbelt "new money syndrome" combined to a "Protestant complexion . . . [of] Deep South roots" to create in an urban religious culture "where sermon titles like 'God's Business Is Big Business' are not considered offensive." FBCD fit into— and helped advance—this probusiness ethos. FBCD boasted the membership of some of the most important businessmen in the city, state, and nation. The majority of FBCD's middle- to upper-middle-class members drove into town from the affluent suburbs of Dallas to attend Sunday morning services and partake in a wide range of recreational and ministerial activities. High-profile members of the Dallas business community collaborated with Criswell as members of the deaconate, managing the transformation of FBCD from notable downtown congregation to megachurch.[45]

FBCD's members were also its financial backbone. By 1960, Criswell's 12,000-member church boasted a budget approaching $1.5 million ($11.5 million, inflation adjusted). Businessmen like Charlie Roberts (vice president of Sears Roebuck), A. B. Tanco (a Dallas oil executive), and Frank Ryburn Jr.

(a prominent corporate lawyer) oversaw the church's operations and budget. Each served on the church's board of deacons in the 1940s and 1950s and
strongly supported Criswell's intent to counter the suburban out-migration of
members with "a *total* church ministry," one that included extensive recreational
and educational facilities, Christian entertainment offerings, and weekday family-centered activities. In Criswell's estimation, church management was a job
best left to white men with business experience. In 1952, Dean Willis, a former
city manager from Black Mountain, North Carolina, who had worked in business administration, accepted Ryburn's invitation to become the church's business manager. In that capacity, Willis turned FBCD into an evangelical operation
strongly informed by corporate models. Organizational boards were specialized
and streamlined. "Stewardship" campaigns pushed hard to break fundraising
records. IBM accounting machinery kept track of 6,600 individual financial
accounts and $22,000 in weekly income. Under Willis's direction, the church
appraised downtown properties, filled collection plates for their purchase, and
negotiated prompt sales.[46]

By the late 1950s and early 1960s, FBCD was the largest property owner in
downtown Dallas. It was also the largest and most well-funded Baptist congregation in the world and the most powerful church in the South. Hundreds of other
new-money and old-money Texas elites, as well as thousands more members of
the Dallas middle class, called FBCD home. The controversial, right-wing oilman H. L. Hunt—though a nominal believer and off-and-on attendee—joined
FBCD in 1960 in a highly publicized baptism of himself and his entire family.
Prominent evangelicals, such as Billy Graham and Paul Harvey, were members.
Despite suburban out-migration in the 1960s, FBCD remained a downtown
fixture and was well connected to the city's power brokers. After 1974, "the
[church's] membership roll included dozens of millionaires and literally hundreds of nationally prominent businessmen," wrote a biographer of Dr. Jimmy
Draper, FBCD's associate pastor. "As a whole, the membership at Dallas cut
across economic and social lines from one extreme to the other," he remembered, "but the decision-makers were decidedly affluent."[47]

The model that Criswell developed at FBCD certainly made an impression
on a young Southern Baptist pastor from California named Rick Warren. Warren
founded a small church in 1980, joining Criswell's approach to the managerial
ideas of Peter Drucker. Warren also credited Donald McGavran, the founder of
the Church Growth Movement, a market-and-stats obsessed church-planting
school, for his pastoral style: "Just as God used W. A. Criswell to sharpen the focus
of my life mission from ministry in general to being a pastor, God used the writ-
ings of Donald McGavran to sharpen my focus from pastoring an already established church to planting the church I would pastor." McGavran came to Fuller
Seminary in 1965 after years as a missionary in India and an underappreciated

pastoral trainer, enticed by C. Davis Weyerhaeuser, a timber executive and long-time backer of Fuller and other evangelical ventures. McGavran would teach and train "church planters" at Fuller, and his philosophy of well-planned, stats-driven pastoring and "church worker typologies" translated into the highly influential tome *Understanding Church Growth*, first published in 1970, and a number of follow-up books with practical tips for pastors and congregational planning boards. Warren certainly put this blend of corporate managerialism and church planting to good use. By 1995, his suburban Saddleback Church was one of the largest churches in America and a model—among others, such as Bill Hybels's Willow Creek Community Church and, of course, precursors earlier in the century—for the modern megachurch. To Warren, Criswell was "an organizational genius," setting up the model for future megachurches and innovating strategies for church growth that "only became known as traditional after everyone copied him!"[48]

Ziglar also credited Criswell with granting him personal and spiritual direction. "He taught me the importance of daily Bible study," Ziglar recalled. Criswell gave Ziglar the impetus for "teaching—not preaching—biblical principles in my public and corporate seminars." Criswell also led Ziglar to accept "that the Bible is the inerrant Word of God." Agreeing with Criswell on this matter did more than fuel Ziglar's belief that his business-friendly exegesis of the Bible was warranted. It encouraged Ziglar to draw a stark line between himself and anyone who doubted the Bible's inerrant lessons—however Ziglarized at a seminar—for the social and cultural upheavals of the 1960s and 1970s.[49]

In the SBC, Ziglar approved of Criswell's coalition of right-wing pastors and their fight for what they called "fundamental" interpretations of the Bible. Many of their claims and qualms harkened back to the first years of American fundamentalism. Fundamentalists at the SBC asserted the scientific and historical accuracy of the Old and New Testament, along with literalist interpretations of the virgin birth and the atoning death of Christ on the cross. Yet, when compared to the fundamentalism that split northern churches a half-century before, the fundamentalism of the 1970s and early 1980s was quite new, at least for Southern Baptists. Though a conservative denomination and a relatively safe haven for fundamentalists ever so slightly to the left of radicals like J. Frank Norris, progressive strains had long run through the SBC. Since the 1920s and especially since World War II, denominational universities expanded far beyond religious training, teaching the liberal arts and sciences, albeit in accord with Baptist theology, which rejected evolution or materialist perspectives on cosmic or human origins. Progressive elements also undergirded numerous humanitarian organizations and missions groups in the SBC, even during the segregationist era, providing arenas for biracial interaction if not quite notions of racial equality. Baptist views on race and race relations were no less complicated, ranging from theological segregationism to gradual integrationism to "goodwill" moderation to open opposition to Jim Crow to a preference for privacy and avoidance of the moral or theological implications of white supremacy. To be sure, the SBC had moved behind the broader push for family values in the 1970s, but that was in the midst of intense discussion and debate about female ordination and a woman's right to a legal abortion, the latter of which even a staunch conservative like W. A. Criswell did not initially see as either a problem or non-negotiable. (In 1973, he was not overly alarmed by the *Roe v. Wade* decision, stating "I have always felt that it was only after a child was born and had life separate from its mother, that it became an individual person, and it has always, therefore, seemed to me that what is best for the mother and for the future should be allowed." The next year, the SBC voted for a resolution that endorsed a middle-of-the-road, case-by-case approach.)

The fundamentalist push within the denomination was, in large part, an effort to marginalize any remaining progressivism or moderation in the denomination, ideally to put higher walls around a fundamentalist bastion that, like fundamentalism itself, had certain porous boundaries. Theological and social issues certainly drove what journalists called the "conservative resurgence" in the SBC, but its infrastructure was provided by well-heeled churches with pastors operating in the corporate mode, exuding a top-down influence in their churches that they wanted to transfer to the denomination at large.

In the 1980s, along with other fundamentalists—like Paige Patterson, of Criswell's own college; Texas Appeals Court Judge Paul Pressler; Adrian Rodgers of Belleview Baptist Church in Memphis; and Dr. Charles Stanley of Atlanta's First Baptist Church, the city's largest and wealthiest Baptist congregation—Criswell worked to reframe the denomination's bylaws, purge the SBC of more moderate pastors, and jettison from denominational seminaries any professor who balked at fundamentalism. On the last matter, in particular, Criswell was blunt: "There are plenty of other places the infidels can teach."[50] Criswell's views on women's status in the denomination and throughout American society were equally conservative and in line with male authoritarianism in business. Although women had been ordained by local SBC churches by 1988, Criswell wanted prohibitions on female authority and supported resolutions that "preserve[d] a submission (of women) that God requires." By that time, he also fervently opposed *Roe v. Wade* and the Equal Rights Amendment while calling for an end to church–state separation, a winner-take-all battle against communism, and a vigorous campaign against homosexuality. So too did most "self-identified fundamentalists" in the denomination, a full 63 percent of whom also believed "people on welfare don't want to work."[51]

Ziglar was another activist in this fundamentalist fight. Though he might "Ziglarize" biblical parables for the sake of conveying his points about work and business, Ziglar used the doctrine of "inerrancy" to challenge moderates and posit literalist arguments against homosexuality or for male familial authority. For his efforts, he earned a spot in the denomination's new order, elected by his fellow fundamentalists to the SBC's vice-presidency in 1984. An editor at the *Indiana Baptist* believed that Ziglar's election reflected "the desire for conservative leadership [in the convention]" and proved that fundamentalist interests were "well entrenched."[52] Conservatives in the convention wrote Ziglar to congratulate him. "I know that serving as Vice President of the Convention is going to cost you a bundle financially," wrote an Oklahoma Baptist fundamentalist. "However, I know that the Kingdom value is going to be multiplied many times." More moderate Baptists were hardly as excited. "I was delighted to be a part of your election," wrote a South Carolina congregant. "I am disturbed, however, about the possibility of you being involved in the attempt to move Southern Baptists from being a positive, gospel-preaching denomination, to be a rigid, doctrinaire self-righteous group of Christians." "Your leadership," the writer hoped, "is needed for all of us, and not just for part of us," especially since "I'm being told by people in my denomination that I no longer qualify as a Southern Baptist" even though "[m]y differences with fundamentalists are minimal." Letters conveying a mix of hope and trepidation also came in from prominent Baptist educators, state convention presidents, and business leaders.[53]

One Baptist business leader, however, was very happy for Ziglar. Dan Cathy, the son of S. Truett Cathy and an executive at Chick-fil-A, wrote to Ziglar, "How surprising it was to learn of your election." His father was more moderate and remained mum during the Baptist fights, but the younger Cathy sided with Ziglar. Dan Cathy was "confident that your leadership will be very refreshing to many who have not had the opportunity to work with you before. As a Baptist, it certainly makes me proud to know that we have an individual such as yourself in such a vital, leadership role." As a gift to Ziglar, Cathy included two "Be Our Guest" cards in his letter, which Ziglar and his wife could redeem at any participating Chick-fil-A for a free chicken sandwich. Ziglar was appreciative. "I really covet your prayers as well as the prayers of the outstanding people you have at Chick-fil-A," he wrote in response. Ziglar was very happy to hear that sales were "up approximately 17 percent" at Chick-fil-A. "This doesn't surprise me in the least," he wrote. "Not only are you folks in God's will, but you—as businesspeople—are thoroughly professional and well-versed in sound business principles. God bless you in everything. Have a good forever—SEE YOU AT THE TOP!" Reading between the lines, it is apparent that Cathy saw Ziglar as a role model and agent for a similar sort of social and religious perspective that Chick-fil-A's business model—though created by a more moderate Baptist than Ziglar—nevertheless invigorated every time sales went up.[54]

As the SBC's vice president, Ziglar chose to focus specifically on educational policy at denominational universities, once more conveying his interest in youth as the "point of sale" for religious and social values. Concerning Philip Johnson, a Mormon professor of Spanish at the denomination's flagship Baylor University, Ziglar thought his teaching appointment should be downgraded to "a caretaker position" away from students. Bob Patterson, a religion professor at Baylor, earned Ziglar's opprobrium for teaching that evolution was compatible with creation accounts in Genesis. Ziglar also attacked James M. Dunn, an SBC lobbyist working in Washington, for his former association with People for the American Way, a citizens' organization committed to preserving the establishment clause and fighting "against the religious right." In private correspondences, Ziglar openly wondered "as to why more of the pastors do not speak out concerning abortion and homosexuality, as well as pornography and some of the other issues of the day." Pastors, thought Ziglar, should be more political. "I teach a large Sunday school class," he wrote, "and I frequently deal with all these issues. [Hence,] I personally believe our pastors have a responsibility to stay abreast of these issues and to periodically inform their congregations of them." In the face of intense criticism from moderate Baptists, Ziglar stayed firm in his opposition to Mormon appointments at SBC-affiliated schools. Still, he lost face with his Mormon fans. "Come on ZIG! Give Us a Break," wrote one angry devotee. "I['ve] lost a lot of respect for you" and "that you made such a 'Stinkin'-Thinking,' 'Garbage-In, Garbage-Out' statement." "I read one of your books and was very impressed with your positive attitude," wrote another. "Now I find that your Christian treatment only applies to those who are Baptists." This was an accurate characterization. While on the seminar circuit Ziglar was open-minded, preaching an inclusive, meritocratic, positive-thinking gospel for businesses. At the SBC, he was a fundamentalist. But Ziglar's approach was not terribly different from that of other evangelical businessmen. Strategic engagement with culture, mainstream appeal, and "open-mindedness" had its advantages, providing the financial capital to build the social capital that, in turn, built political capital in the institutions, organizations, and social spheres that mattered most to their crusades for conservative evangelicalism.[55]

Ziglar's work as the SBC's vice president lasted only one term. In 1985, Ziglar stepped down and a conservative pastor from Texas named Winfred Moore won the post by a two-to-one margin.[56] All in all, Ziglar's brief time in power at the SBC did not bring any groundbreaking change or new direction in the denomination's slow-rolling transformation into a bastion of right-wing evangelicalism. It did, however, signal his personal connections in the conservative movement and his full-fledged commitment to defending Baptist fundamentalism. Ziglar's associations with the leaders of some of the SBC's wealthiest and most powerful congregations also revealed a relatively short distance between his evangelical business and social ethic and their own. Indeed, the conservative conversion of the SBC, which indisputably had wide-ranging political implications in the 1970s and 1980s, was not a radical departure from the theological and gendered conservatism of other evangelical business leaders. Mary Kay Ash's vision of a properly ordered home fit with the visions of Ziglar, Criswell, Stanley, and Pressler—and, to a degree, with the vision of S. Truett Cathy and W. Maxey Jarman and other Baptists on the conservative end of evangelicalism's political spectrum. The social model of business service masters, once the province of Rotary Clubs, was now the theology of the ideal Baptist home and properly run "Christian" business.[57]

Ziglar's revival was an important complement to other forms of business-backed and business-framed evangelicalism. By 1988, one might laud "servant leadership" at Chick-fil-A or the more universalist "soul of the firm" at ServiceMaster. Or, one could affirm Cathy's marketplace mission by applying for a franchise, getting a job, buying a chicken sandwich, or sending one's kids to work part-time at Chick-fil-A. One could buy any number of consumer goods from a set of evangelical culture industries that, by their very corporate nature, embodied the evangelical ideal of racial, cultural, and familial identity via the almighty dollar. Even for someone on the bottom rung of the new, postindustrial or suburban-centric economy, Ziglar's southern-born but supposedly universalist faith in personal redemption via a God-blessed meritocratic "free market" was worth considering, primarily because—like classic evangelicalism—it seemed to give a shortcut to the top; that is, if only one cleared out the "garbage-dump" thinking and bought another of Ziglar's many tomes on achieving one's best life now.

Ziglar's efforts, as well as the efforts of his friends and contemporaries across the evangelical business spectrum, demonstrated that conservative evangelicals could navigate the transition to a more "open" workplace and marketplace by defining the terms of what it meant to be "conservative," "Christian," "successful" and "for families." In this way, Ziglar was part of a broader movement that aligned the interests and aspirations of business with the interests and aspirations of evangelicals holding a certain faith in politics. In the same years as Ziglar's marketplace missions and corporate revivals, Baptist businessmen from the moderate Jimmy Carter to the conservative Jerry Falwell shaped the nation's political economy while evangelical businessmen-turned-politicians and lobbyists attempted to move from the private sector to the public. Blessed by business once again, evangelicals endeavored to embed themselves in the nation's political structure.

Conclusion

In 1980, conservative Republican Ronald Reagan won the presidential election with the help of millions of conservative evangelicals. Many liberals and members of the press were baffled but generally chalked it up to a concern with "social" issues such as abortion or gay rights. But Reagan's routine paeans to "free enterprise" were not contraventions of evangelicals' social and political aspirations. They were an articulation of them. And, in the 1980s, as in the 1950s or 1930s or 1910s, conservative evangelicals once again tapped into sympathizers in the nation's business elite to advance their vision of a business-friendly, Christian America.

Baptist pastor Jerry Falwell led the way, coordinating donations, corporate strategies, and grassroots fundraising with particular skill and fervor. His political rise was as much a story of circumstance—the economic anxieties of the 1970s, the particular foibles of the Carter administration, the courting of conservative politicians like Reagan, and the specific concerns of evangelicals over matters of desegregation, privatization, sex, and religious rights—as anything else. But most of all, and most often missed in accounts of Falwell's rise to public prominence, was the fact that he spoke to a new generation of small-time and executive-class donors willing to back his brand of "us versus them" rhetoric. His style of evangelicalism matched the evangelicalism of the business world. It was a faith grounded in social engagement and in the protection of privacy and promotion of private enterprise. It was oriented around results, technology, pragmatism, individualism, and corporatism.

In the early 1970s, Falwell moved beyond the segregationist views of his early pastoral career, encouraging new forms of "post-racial" political engagement by evangelicals in collaboration with other conservatives, regardless of whether they were evangelicals or not. Liberty University, the private college he founded in 1971, might push fundamentalist doctrines in its curriculum, but it also served as a hub for conservative evangelicals of various denominational and political persuasions, much like Harding College or Pepperdine College had for two decades. His megachurch, Thomas Road Baptist Church in Lynchburg,

Virginia, was also following in the path of other Southern Baptist churches like W. A. Criswell's in Dallas, linking economic prosperity, middle-class status, and sexual conservatism. Falwell disliked Jim Bakker's Heritage USA and many facets of the new evangelical culture industries, criticizing the collusion of counterculture and evangelicalism in Christian rock bands. But he was also instrumental in promoting televangelism and championing alliances among Jews, Mormons, and Catholics through the Moral Majority, an umbrella organization he established in 1979 to unify participants in what journalists alternatively called "the Religious Right" or "the Christian Right."

Through the Moral Majority, Falwell stumped for the election of Ronald Reagan and other conservatives to state offices and Congress. "It is now time to take a stand on certain moral issues," Falwell wrote in 1980, "and we can only stand if we have leaders. We must stand against the Equal Rights Amendment, the feminist revolution, and the homosexual revolution. We must have a revival in this country." Looking for common ground, Falwell linked religious, economic, and social concerns much as other evangelical businessmen did. Individualism, meritocratic work, free enterprise, and opposition to the welfare state were just as important (and informed by race and white privilege) as any forthcoming revival in public morality and Christian influence in politics. "God is in favor of freedom, property, ownership, competition, diligence, work, and acquisition," he claimed. "All of this is taught in the Word of God, in both the Old and New Testaments." For Falwell, the Book of Proverbs had "a clearly outlined" ethic, namely in favor of "the free-enterprise system," which Jesus also endorsed. Therefore, "Ownership of property is biblical. Competition in business is biblical." Falwell made work, material reward, personal affirmation, and free enterprise a component of his political package, writing economic issues into his 1980 jeremiad, *Listen America!* Sounding like plenty of evangelical businessmen over the course of the previous century, Falwell wrote, "I believe that America was built on integrity, on faith in God, and on hard work. I do not believe that anyone has ever been successful in life without being willing to add that last ingredient—diligence or hard work." He continued, "We now have second- and third-generation welfare recipients. Welfare is not always wrong. There are those who do need welfare, but we have reared a generation that understands neither the dignity nor the importance of work."[1]

Fired up by concerns about private Christian education, private property, and taxation—which intersected with concerns about racial integration, homosexuality, feminism, and abortion—conservative evangelicals were open to political mobilization. Funding such a mobilization, however, was arduous work. To coordinate the effort, Falwell turned to corporate modes of organizing sentiments, manufacturing consent, and pulling in donations. Falwell welcomed the advice and support of Epsilon Data Management, a Massachusetts-based marketing outfit founded in 1968 by four junior faculty members at Harvard Business School. An innovator in computerized database marketing, Epsilon helped Falwell streamline his pitch to potential donors and automate contribution records. Other conservatives used similarly high-tech methods. By the early 1980s, seven of the top ten televangelists in the nation were Epsilon clients while another conservative activist, Richard Viguerie, had the names and addresses of 15 million conservatives stored on 3,000 rolls of magnetic tape and available for use. Falwell's methods, under the guidance of Epsilon, were particularly effective. Falwell used a wide variety of standard marketing techniques to catch the attention of his readers. Direct mailings created the illusion of intimacy and like-mindedness, delivered ultimatums, played up the clash of "Christians" versus "government," confirmed the fears and desires of the reader, and gave off a tone of measured excitement about joining a worthwhile cause. In addition to Epsilon's staff, Jerry Huntsinger, a pastor and religious marketer, wrote attractive copy for mailings and fine-tuned aesthetics, while Janice Gleason, the only woman on Falwell's marketing staff, wrote copy that working women and mothers—a vital target audience for Falwell—might find appealing. Empowered by the latest business techniques and strategies, Falwell built his so-called moral majority.[2]

The result was a windfall for Epsilon. "The rest of the company was barely making money," remembered John Groman, an Epsilon executive, "[but] the earnings on these accounts were fantastic." The revenues brought in from evangelical televangelists in the late 1970s and early 1980s were 30 percent of Epsilon's total revenue, allowing the company to go public in 1984. Epsilon's contributions to Falwell's emerging political movement were likewise important, bringing in much-needed dollars for Falwell's direct-mail campaigns, for his ministry at Thomas Road, and for his work at Liberty University. In addition, the high-profile status of mass marketing campaigns helped Falwell to attract so-called "superdonors." Corporate executives contributed regularly to Falwell's operations and Liberty University during the 1980s. They included Arthur Williams (of A. L Williams and Associates life insurance company), Art DeMoss (the head of Liberty Life insurance group and big-time donor to Chuck Colson's Prison Fellowship), Bo Adams (an Arkansas cotton gin owner), Don Hershey (the director of Hershey Equipment Company, a poultry and grain equipment manufacturer), and Nelson Bunker Hunt.[3]

Hunt was an especially worthwhile grab for Falwell, and he helped to take Falwell's brand of evangelical conservatism deeper into Washington D.C.'s political culture. His father, H. L. Hunt, had long underwritten right-wing causes, especially radical ones. In the 1950s and 1960s, H. L. Hunt set up a conservative nonprofit organization, Facts Forum, Inc., and funded various conservative radio programs. No fan of Dwight D. Eisenhower, Hunt cottoned to radical anti-communists Carl McIntire, Billy James Hargis, and Robert W. Welch Jr. of the

John Birch Society. Other right-wing endeavors showed Hunt's unique blend of personal eccentricity and political outlook. *Life Line*, a right-wing radio program, regularly advertised Hunt's line of "HLH"-branded food products, which included "Gastro-Majic" health tablets. In 1960, Hunt also published *Alpaca*, a paperback political novel that romanticized a plutocratic America where the Constitution allowed the rich more votes. Hunt supported Lyndon B. Johnson in the 1960 election but not out of party loyalty and certainly not out of a liberal kinship. Hunt, in some ways like the very Southern Baptists around him in Texas, feared a Catholic takeover of the country if John F. Kennedy were elected. Though he had extramarital affairs and a healthy gambling habit, H. L. Hunt was a member at W. A. Criswell's megachurch and backed George Benson's anti-communist activities at Harding College. Along with several other Texas business leaders—including H. E. "Eddie" Chiles, chairman of the Western Company of North America and later owner of the Texas Rangers baseball club, and Mike Richards, chairman of two prominent Houston banks—H. L. Hunt lauded and endorsed the early career of James Robison, a Houston-born evangelist and one of the most prominent voices for strident protest against what Robison called the "demonism and liberalism" behind evolutionists, homosexuals, the ERA, anti–free marketers, and the welfare state. Like Ziglar, Graham, Taylor, and other evangelical conservatives before him, Robison also aligned "man's attitude toward God" and "his quality of production." "Preachers like myself," he argued, "can have an important impact on economic matters," increasing the nation's gross national product "by steering employers and employees to Christian morality." With the help of a new generation of big businessmen, voices like Falwell's and Robison's—though certainly more strident than Taylor's or at times Ziglar's and Graham's—kept up the long mission of making matters of national import inseparable from matters of God and Mammon.[4]

When H. L. Hunt died in 1974, Nelson Bunker Hunt inherited his share of the family fortune and picked up where his father left off, continuing to donate money and lend his personal endorsement to right-wing and conservative evangelical causes. Bunker Hunt was worth nearly $2 billion and his interests were in more than oil. For years before his father's death, the younger Hunt had been involved in American political activism. Somewhere between $250,000 and $300,000 of Hunt's money went to segregationist George Wallace's 1968 presidential bid. In addition to oil and real estate holdings, the younger Hunt's stake in the emerging Libyan oil fields underwrote his conservative endeavors, although his failed and borderline criminal attempt to corner the world silver market in 1979 showed the limits of his economic and political influence. Despite such setbacks, by the early 1980s Hunt had broadened and strengthened his financial and personal connections to a wide range of conservative initiatives. In 1980, Hunt sponsored a rally for televangelist Pat Robertson, then thinking about a presidential run. In 1981, Hunt gave $1 million to the Moral Majority. In 1982, he raised money for the National Conservative Political Action Committee, all for the sake of backing conservative candidates in Texas Congressional elections. The race-baiting Jesse Helms also took Hunt's money for an Institute of American Relations, "one of several non-profit foundations" that one observer claimed "undertook research on a host of social, economic, and foreign policy problems."[5]

Along with his brother William H. Hunt and Texas oil heir T. Cullen Davis, infamous from 1976 to 1979 for his trial and acquittal on murder charges, Nelson Bunker Hunt was foundational to the creation of the Council for National Policy (CNP) in 1981. The CNP was a secretive, nonprofit organization that linked conservative business leaders to evangelical activists for the sake of developing political strategies to restore free enterprise and "moral values" in America. It was majority white (99 percent), male (96 percent), and Christian (99 percent). It was also a regional organization, as the vast majority of members (84 percent) hailed from the South or west of the Mississippi River. Nearly every major evangelical activist joined the CNP in the early 1980s, as its membership ballooned by 1985. Among its members were Jerry Falwell, James Dobson, Pat Robertson, Bill Bright, James Robison, the Religious Roundtable's Ed McAteer, Christian Voice's Gary Jarmin, libertarian Gary North and reconstructionist Rousas Rushdoony, creationist Henry Morris, televangelist D. James Kennedy, writers Tim and Beverly LaHaye, and Amway's Richard DeVos.[6]

The 1980 presidential election gave the CNP room to maneuver in D.C. Reagan's win was years in the making. He built his political career in California among southern migrants and suburbanites, many white middle-class evangelicals just a few years removed from the farms of the South and Midwest. As such, Reagan knew how to speak the evangelical language of economic, spiritual, and political revival. His political genealogy also overlapped with that of many plain-folk and elite evangelicals, whether in their common attraction to the racial and economic overtures of Barry Goldwater or George Wallace or in terms of institutional affiliations, namely the church communities and evangelical front groups and institutions that had also depended on corporate largesse throughout the postwar period. Hardly an evangelical himself, Reagan had clarified his position on matters of evangelical concern by the time he was putting together a primary challenge to Gerald Ford in 1976. In the ensuing four years, he built another run at the White House (in part) on the votes, voices, and dollars of conservatives and moderate rightists from evangelical America.

Willing to speak more openly about the value of religious faith and backing off from his earlier support for abortion bills, Reagan courted evangelical voters who had become more willing to overlook personal "flaws" in Republican candidates and unify around school choice, anti-abortion, "family values," and their derision of or disappointment with Jimmy Carter. The shift was apparent eleven weeks before the 1980 presidential election, when Hunt-backed evangelist James Robison invited Reagan to speak in front of a similarly Hunt-backed organization, the Religious Roundtable. Meeting in Dallas, Texas, the audience was a sampling of politically inclined evangelical and conservative Christian organizations: the Christian Voice, the Pro-Family Forum, the National Prayer Campaign, the Eagle Forum, the Right to Life Committee, the Fund to Restore an Educated Electorate, and the Institute for Christian Economics. Robison and Falwell both spoke, with Robison offering a call to action that made Reagan's handlers squeamish but pleased Reagan. "I'm sick and tired," Robison told attendees, "of hearing about all the radicals and the perverts and the liberals and the leftists and the Communists coming out of the closet. It's time for God's people to come out of the closet." Reagan, who followed Robison onstage, agreed, albeit with more measured language. Aware it was a nominally nonpartisan gathering, Reagan intimated, "You can't endorse me, but . . . I want you to know that I endorse you and what you are doing." Reagan was clear. He strove to be the "born again" candidate. If elected, he implied, the age of Reagan would cater to the preferences of those gathered in Dallas. Sixty-seven percent of white evangelicals supported Reagan over the Southern Baptist, Sunday school–teaching incumbent, Jimmy Carter. Four years later, during his reelection campaign, a whopping 76 percent voted for Reagan.[7]

In one sense, Reagan turned out not to be the hard-charging culture warrior that his most fervent evangelical supporters thought they were sending to the White House. As a pragmatist working with a Congress controlled by Democrats, Reagan ran into substantial resistance on social policy. There was little he could realistically do to limit abortion. Reagan also appointed a pro-choice judge, Sandra Day O'Connor, to the Supreme Court while failing to get another conservative, Robert Bork, to join Antonin Scalia on the bench. Similarly bound and influenced by Congress and grassroots activists, Reagan's administration waffled on federal funding of AIDS research, angering conservative evangelicals who saw such subsidies as promoting homosexuality. In terms of pushing the state in the direction of "family values" or sexual conservatism, little from Reagan's two terms in office seemed worth praising.

But in another sense, Reagan *was* the culture warrior that evangelicals wanted him to be. Their so-called "social positions" were inseparable from their economic aspirations, and Reaganomics was broadly in line with evangelical desires. The long crusades by evangelical businessmen or evangelicals and their corporate backers were routinely aimed at creating a society oriented around businessmen's authority. Shifts had certainly occurred among such evangelical businessmen over the years. Until his death in 1978, Herbert Taylor, for instance, continued supporting various evangelical activities, from Young Life to Billy

Graham, and stayed on the board at Fuller Seminary as it became coed and adopted a more moderate, if still conservative, orientation. Taylor's pragmatic moderate streak also animated other evangelical organizations and institutions, from Howard E. Butt Jr.'s Laity Lodge to Billy Graham's evangelistic activities, *Christianity Today*, and the Billy Graham Evangelistic Association, all of which tempered the conservatism of their early Cold War crusades. Business organizations like the Christian Business Men's Committee, International and Full Gospel Business Men's Fellowship, International stayed evangelistic in orientation and largely white and male. But they also opened their doors to women around the same time that women entered the workforce in greater numbers during the 1960s and 1970s. Both groups continued sponsoring missionary endeavors but also became more like social clubs for like-minded businessmen and women who, like other evangelical business people, sought perpetually fresh lessons regarding what it meant to be a "Christian" in a competitive corporate marketplace. The contingency of capitalism, however, also left a few major shapers of conservative evangelicalism behind. For instance, after a failed run at the Tennessee governor's office in 1970, W. Maxey Jarman had returned to Genesco in 1972 as the company's executive officer. His son, Franklin Jarman, wanted the post and engineered a hostile takeover of the company in 1973, kicking his father out. Their internal power struggle merely added to the company's problems. Competition from upstart Nike had undercut Genesco's appeal, both because Jarman was wary of moving their company into the sport shoe market and because of Nike's use of outsourcing and cheaper, foreign labor. A dependence on downtown stores like Kress, now under serious stress from suburban and small town retailers like K-Mart and Wal-Mart, put further pressure on Genesco. From 1974 to 1976, Genesco remained profitable, but it was losing market share and dividends were dropping. In 1977, the board of directors fired the younger Jarman. The elder Jarman watched from afar in his later years as the company fired thousands of workers and went into deeper and deeper debt. In 1980, when Jarman died, Genesco owed shareholders approximately $40 million in unpaid dividends. Jarman's company survived, but as a near-victim of the very "free market"—as global as ever—that he and other evangelical businessmen had endorsed.[8]

Even so, if he had lived long enough to see it, Jarman likely would have remained in favor of Reagan's political economy. Except for deficit spending, which exploded during Reagan's first and second terms due to defense build-ups, Reagan's domestic policies were generally endorsed by conservative evangelicals (many of whom also held few qualms about the late Cold War build-up in the very military-industrial complex that had nurtured Jarman and LeTourneau). Across-the-board tax cuts passed Congress, slashing rates on top earners and dropping capital gains tax rates while deepening yearly deficits. Reagan's standoff and dissolution of PATCO, a union that had supported his candidacy, proved his anti-union streak. On deregulation, Reagan continued a path pioneered by his predecessor. Jimmy Carter had been a savvy businessman during his prepolitical days in Georgia. A military veteran and talented engineer who benefitted like LeTourneau from the military-industrial complex, Carter had used state provisions to turn himself into an up-and-coming agribusinessman after inheriting a portion of his father's farm holdings in 1953. As mechanization, fertilization, and federal subsidization pushed smaller farmers into town to escape debt and declining competitiveness in a rapidly changing southern agricultural market, Carter bought up land and set up a large warehouse, farming peanuts alongside other marketable crops. By the time he considered a run for the state Senate in the early 1960s, Carter's warehouse was, according to Randall Balmer, "the third-largest business in its tax district, and the farms and warehouse combined into a multi-million-dollar-a-year operation." Simply put, Carter was one of the wealthiest men in rural Georgia.[9]

Though more of a moderate like Taylor than an ideologue like Jarman, Carter spoke intermittently during his 1976 campaign and subsequent presidency about his identity as a "Christian businessman" and the importance of the "free-market system." As president, Carter was a mixed bag on matters of political economy. His administration both expanded corporate regulations and approved a series of market liberalization bills. Carter's evangelicalism had little if anything to do with his economic policies. The intractability of inflation and public angst over the decade's continuing economic "malaise" were more salient. Still, he and Congress kept to a certain free-market faith with the Revenue Act of 1978. It did not radically alter the tax code but did cut individual and business taxes across the board and slashed capital gains rates, thereby signaling the administration's willingness to accept investment-class prescriptions for the nation's economic ailment. Regarding transportation, especially, Carter followed a precedent set by Gerald Ford's signing of the deregulatory 4R acts in 1976. Before Reagan ousted him from the Oval Office, Carter also signed a streak of free-market bills that withdrew federal regulations on rails and airlines. Carter's deregulatory gestures turned into gospel truth during Reagan's administration, as did big tax cuts, which were premised on sheer faith in supply-side growth and free-market, corporate prosperity. Congressional deal-making and rising deficits forced Reagan to sign tax increases in 1982 and 1983 before earning bipartisan agreement for another round of cuts in 1986. Overall, however, the trend was toward a corporate-friendly political economy, although the social pros and cons were mixed. Economic data showed a notable uptick in standard measures of "growth" and "prosperity." From 1983 to 1988, GDP increased, consumer spending went up, and unemployment went down. Other measures, however, were less encouraging. Income inequality, personal and public debt, and the percentage of children in poverty rose year after year from 1981 to 1989.

It was an economic bifurcation into haves and have nots not seen in America since the early days of Herbert Taylor's business career in the 1920s.[10]

Evangelical leaders like Falwell viewed the election of 1980 and Reagan's landslide reelection in 1984 with a sense of self-satisfaction. They were now clearly political insiders, even though Falwell's own Moral Majority faced financial problems after a rush of fundraising in 1980 and 1981. The organization's total debt rose to approximately half a million dollars by 1982. Three years later, by the beginning of Reagan's second term, the Moral Majority's financial health was in question and membership in steep decline. Falwell left the organization in 1987, and it collapsed soon after. He later claimed that the organization's dissolution was acceptable since "our goal has been achieved," namely of having the "religious right . . . solidly in place." Outsiders viewed this as an excuse.[11] But, in a way, Falwell was right. Though legislative output was mixed, conservative evangelicals' political power was undeniable, especially in a Republican Party whose fate was intimately connected to a base of white evangelical voters who—to varying degrees and in varying ways—saw the GOP as the only outlet for their socioeconomic views. Moreover, the state had now cemented business's centrality as a determiner of human value and citizenship. Religious rights, political rights, and human rights were bound up in the rights conferred by work and the rights conferred to corporations.

Evangelicals' insider status in Washington, D.C. was not only measured by what Reagan or the Republican Party did or did not do for them. It was also measured by how evangelical activists learned the rules of the inside-the-beltway game, creating lobbying groups and think tanks that made their economic or political views a fixture of the D.C. scene. During Reagan's first term, an investigation by leftist writers Deborah Huntington and Ruth Kaplan discovered "an astonishing degree of interconnection among certain individual evangelical organizations, and between the evangelical organizations and the ultra-conservative, business-funded lobbying and educational organizations." Huntington and Kaplan were impressed by "how few of these [conservative] groups stand alone . . . there is at least one individual in almost every group who links it to another. . . . In many cases, these relationships form a complex web." Money tied everyone together: $20.5 million in donations between eighteen different organizations from 1975 to 1981, including Campus Crusade for Christ, the Fellowship of Christian Athletes, the Oral Roberts Evangelical Association, the Billy Graham Evangelical Association, Young Life, and Intervarsity Christian Fellowship. Several groups received funding from long-time backers, such as the Pew family and Hearst estate, and new ones, like Nelson Bunker Hunt, the rabidly anti-union Joseph Coors of Colorado, and Mormon hotel executive Willard Marriott, a friend and supporter of Billy Graham and his crusades. Probusiness organizations also interlocked with a number of evangelical organizations, often in ways not easily measured or untangled. Activist Gary Jarmin, to take just one example, was a treasurer for the Christian Voice Moral Government Fund and legislative director for Christian Voice, a Christian think tank and lobbying group, as well as a staffer for the Stop OSHA Campaign and former legislative director for the American Conservative Union, one of the nation's oldest right-wing lobbyists.[12]

Other inside-the-beltway lobbying groups appeared to represent evangelical conservatives. For instance, the Family Research Council (FRC) was the well-funded political wing of James Dobson's nonprofit Focus on the Family organization. Edgar Prince, whose son Erik would later found the mercenary-for-contract company Blackwater, gave money to the FRC, as did the DeVos family. The Moral Majority might be kaput, but by 1989 the FRC was joined by other groups with connections to business or with long mailing lists of donors, such as Pat Robertson's Christian Coalition, which formed after Robertson's failed 1988 campaign for president. Another advocacy group, Students for America, drew on support from businessmen sympathetic to Jesse Helms and was led by upstart evangelical politico Ralph Reed, who perhaps more than any other political leader—Falwell included—extended evangelical influence in the states during the late 1980s and 1990s.

Still, evangelical political power had its limits. As lobbying organizations, each node on the network was best "understood only as individual organizations within the spectrum of religious activity" rather than "representative of any social force as a whole." In addition, financial data was often scarce for specific donors, as was specific information about what donations bought. Some donors undoubtedly saw their support for evangelical organizations as best measured by legislative wins and losses, but others might have been inclined to support such organizations for other reasons. By Huntington and Kaplan's estimation, it was "difficult to separate promotion of the Christian gospel from an effort to preserve the political and economic status quo."[13]

But that was the point. Individual conversions might remain an important measure of relative social influence to evangelicals, but to be a conservative Christian by the time Reagan left office in 1989 was to consider economic policy and legislative or electoral politics—and, if wealthy and evangelical, political lobbying, think tanks, or tax-free philanthropies—as similarly worthwhile investments. The substance of evangelical politics was also in fuller alignment with a half-century's worth of efforts by businessmen to channel evangelical energies through strategic, rational, results-oriented, collaborative methods, as well as through the market exchanges upon which evangelical businesses rested. Indeed, outside of Washington, D.C., the alignment of conservative evangelicals with corporations and state politics was hard to miss. The prevalence of evangelicals in myriad businesses, in large-scale media empires, and on the cutting edge of cultural production showed that the achievements of the 1970s and 1980s had been built on years' worth of crafting ways to be "religious" in corporate environs and on business-based terms. Millions of conservative evangelicals placed their faith in the paramount notion that what was good for business was good for America. In the 1990s and 2000s, an evangelical businessman from Texas named George W. Bush built his gubernatorial career and presidential campaign on such a "base" of faith, winning huge majorities of support from conservative evangelicals and backing from businessmen who, whether evangelical or not, supported his attempt to continue a nearly century-long crusade to align the purposes of a state with the bottom-line pursuits of a "faith-based" corporation.

Bush's victories confounded liberals. As with any election, multiple factors first put Bush in the Oval Office (the controversial Supreme Court decision in *Bush v. Gore* the most notable) and returned him there four years later. But more broadly, his political life and career signified exactly how conservative evangelicalism had survived and thrived for decades. Bush's convictions, on matters of faith and business, survived not in spite of the private sector, or the corporation, or progressivism, or the federal state but in dialogue with each—or often, because of each.[14]

Businessmen and business institutions had encouraged such a strategic interchange and use of secular spheres and corporate or government provision since the days of Henry P. Crowell and Herbert J. Taylor. So too had the mass evangelism of Billy Graham, the global missions of R. G. LeTourneau, and the corporate evangelicalism and marketplace missions of Marion Wade, Maxey Jarman, Howard E. Butt Jr., S. Truett Cathy, and Zig Ziglar. With the blessing of like-minded or interested business leaders, evangelicals carved out their place in the corporate economy and intertwined their social and political interests with local, national, and international markets. They directed thousands of small businesses and not a few Fortune 500 companies; they established a profitable set of culture industries; and they played a role in promoting and proliferating both moderate and more right-wing forms of conservative evangelicalism in American corporate culture and high-level politics. Evangelicals also strategically engaged with certain individuals and factions in corporate America—especially conservative businessmen, their money, their methods, and their organizations—for the sake of advancing evangelical ambitions in public life. In doing so, evangelicals successfully embedded born-again Christianity in the very institutions, businesses, organizations, and political networks that make up present-day corporate capitalism.

At the same time, conservative evangelicalism became grounded in private-sector modes of thought and action. Evangelicals used business methods, businesses, and business executives not merely to defend specific religious claims about the nature of God or the inerrancy of the Bible but to enshrine private preferences regarding property, wealth, work, race, and gender that progressives or state policies had long ago decided were secondary or irrelevant to the social good. At the same time, conservative evangelicalism also became ever more private thanks to its big-business romance. It became secluded in private spheres that, though diverse and diffuse in the American corporate landscape, remained niche or notably dependent on seeking ever-new ways to revive or defend a "religion" that often had more corporate, progressive, or secular characteristics than conservative evangelicals either realized or were willing to admit. Defending "religious freedom"—a secular notion—in corporate spaces, particularly through appeals to the law, as in recent court cases involving "Christian" businesses like Hobby Lobby, merely exemplifies the latest (or perhaps last) stand of a religion inextricably wedded to business terms and a businessman's authoritative definition of "religion," to appeals to family values or free enterprise, and to the defense of personal "rights" to "religious freedom" in the very arena that first and routinely nurtured conservative brands of evangelicalism, namely the corporation.

Conservative evangelicalism's future, however, hinges on more than any one court decision. It remains to be seen what sorts of new corporate revivals are forthcoming among conservative evangelicals—or whether the long push to align corporate money, institutions, and interests with the evangelical faith is past its heyday. Yet, it is instructive to remember that, as in the past, conservative evangelicalism's place in American society exists because of an infrastructure of money and power that, for the better part of a century, undergirded evangelical activities and activism. Thus, regardless of proclamations of an "end to the culture wars" from liberal or conservative observers, regardless of the promise to expand the moral ambitions of evangelicalism to include environmental concern or poor relief, whatever happens next will be informed by a long business history of financial, social, and corporate relations that shaped the rise and reach of conservative evangelicalism.[15]

In political seasons bare and fruitful, in markets bear and bull, in perennial debates over individual rights and the social good, the pursuit of a more evangelical, more conservative, more "Christian" America will likely continue. And conservative evangelicals will likely do as they have done over the course of the twentieth century. They will, as R. G. LeTourneau put it, keep striving to do "a missionary job in a businesslike way," one customer, one contract, one donation, and one dollar at a time.

NOTES

Introduction

1. "Corporations: Partnership with God," *Time*, July 28, 1952, 65–67; "Ship Dedicated," *NOW*, August 1, 1952, Box B3V, LET; R. G. LeTourneau, *Mover of Men and Mountains: The Autobiography of R. G. LeTourneau* (Chicago: Moody Press, 1960, 1967), 251.
2. Clipping, "Evangelist's Early Beginning Recalled," *Longview News-Journal*, October 24, 1968, n.p., Folder, "R.G. LeTourneau," Box L0S, LET; Darren Dochuk, "Moving Mountains: The Business of Evangelicalism and Extraction in a Liberal Age," Kim Phillips-Fein and Julian E. Zelizer, eds., *What's Good for Business: Business and American Politics Since World War II* (New York: Oxford University Press, 2012), 72–90.
3. Social and political historians have recently begun to explore how business interests and agency shaped public life and social movements in the modern American past. Adding conceptual nuance and historical contingency is the next step in this developing literature, as are business histories of specific social organizations and movements generally considered as "grassroots" in origin and articulation. I would argue that the concept of social, religious, or political "movement" should be wholly revisited and revised, as historians uncover how activist interests have "moved" in a society and political context filled with varying business interests, agents, obstacles, and benefactors. For an introduction to this business turn in modern American social and political history, see Phillips-Fein and Zelizer, *What's Good for Business*, 3–15. Also, for an older, groundbreaking study of how the corporate elite shaped various aspects of postwar religion, society, and politics, see Elizabeth Fones-Wolf, *Selling Free Enterprise: The Business Assault on Labor and Liberalism, 1945–1960* (Urbana: University of Illinois Press, 1995).
4. On the leaders of the Christian Right, see William Martin, *With God on Our Side: The Rise of the Religious Right* (New York: Broadway Books, 1997), David John Marley, *Pat Robertson: An American Life* (Lanham, MD: Rowman & Littlefield, 2007), John G. Turner, *Bill Bright and Campus Crusade for Christ: The Renewal of Evangelicalism in Postwar America* (Chapel Hill: University of North Carolina Press, 2008), Daniel K. Williams, *God's Own Party: The Making of the Christian Right* (New York: Oxford University Press, 2010), David Edwin Harrell, Jr., *Pat Robertson: A Life and Legacy* (Grand Rapids, MI: Wm B. Eerdmans, 2010), and Michael Sean Winters, *God's Right Hand: How Jerry Falwell Made God a Republican and Baptized the American Right* (New York: HarperOne, 2012). On the grassroots history of conservative evangelical politics before the 1970s, see Darren Dochuk, *From Bible Belt to Sunbelt: Plain-Folk Religion, Grassroots Politics, and the Rise of Evangelical Conservatism* (New York: W. W. Norton, 2011). Other studies of the modern conservative movement that focus on grassroots religious activists, especially evangelicals, include Lisa McGirr, *Suburban Warriors: The Origins of the New American Right* (Princeton, NJ: Princeton University Press, 2001) and Joseph Crespino, *In Search of Another Country: Mississippi and the Conservative Counterrevolution* (Princeton, NJ: Princeton University Press, 2007).

5. A number of scholars have considered corporate executives as religious practitioners, specifically conservative evangelical ones. But they have focused on more contemporary examples and not delved deeply into historical precedents. More problematically, they have presented evangelical executives as having few enemies and in conflict with almost no one over matters of cultural or political import. D. Michael Lindsay, *Faith in the Halls of Power: How Evangelicals Joined the American Elite* (New York: Oxford University Press, 2007); David Miller, *God at Work: The History and Promise of the Faith at Work Movement* (New York: Oxford University Press, 2007); Lake Lambert III, *Spirituality, Inc.: Religion in the American Workplace* (New York: New York University Press, 2009); Lewis D. Solomon, *Evangelical Christian Executives: A New Model for Business Corporations* (New Brunswick, NJ: Transaction, 2011).

6. Kim Phillips-Fein, *Invisible Hands: The Businessmen's Crusade Against the New Deal* (New York: W. W. Norton, 2009) mentions evangelical leaders with business backing in the 1950s. But the formal start of big business's interest in conservative Christian activists, and the receptivity of conservative evangelicals to corporate sponsorship and support, only begins in her book in the 1970s.

7. Joe Creech, *Righteous Indignation: Religion and the Populist Revolution* (Urbana: University of Illinois Press, 2006); Michael Kazin, *A Godly Hero: The Life of William Jennings Bryan* (New York: Knopf, 2006); Jarod Roll, *Spirit of Rebellion: Labor and Religion in the New Cotton South* (Urbana: University of Illinois Press, 2010); William A. Mirola, *Redeeming Time: Protestantism and Chicago's Eight-Hour Movement, 1866–1912* (Urbana: University of Illinois Press, 2015); Elizabeth Fones-Wolf and Ken Fones-Wolf, *Struggle for the Soul of the Postwar South: White Evangelical Protestants and Operation Dixie* (Urbana-Champaign: University of Illinois Press, 2015); Heath Carter, *Union Made: Working People and the Rise of Social Christianity in Chicago* (New York: Oxford University Press, 2015).

8. William Bond, "Minutes of the Christian Laymen's Crusade Meeting Held at the Benjamin Franklin Hotel," Nov. 1, 1941, Box J4J, Folder F19, LET, quoted in Sarah Ruth Hammond, "'God's Business Men': Entrepreneurial Evangelicals in Depression and War" (PhD dissertation, Yale University, 2010), 80. Portions of this book are dedicated to the memory of Sarah. I had the privilege of meeting her and wish that she was still here to read it. Parts of the opening chapters depend on her dissertation on the CBMCI, LeTourneau, and other businessmen's organizations in the 1930s and 1940s. As happens in academic work, we were two scholars coincidentally working on a similar research project, usually laboring independently with similar sources. Those sources collected and interpreted by Sarah in her dissertation and published work are faithfully noted, both for the sake of honest scholarship and to honor her life and work.

9. Like Dochuk, Bethany Moreton's *To Serve God and Wal-Mart: The Making of Christian Free Enterprise* (Cambridge, MA: Harvard University Press, 2009) locates the origins of conservative evangelicalism's business history in the Ozarks and small-town western South during the early twentieth century. But evangelicals had tapped into business institutions and the social and cultural power afforded by corporations before Wal-Mart's founding in 1962 and rapid growth from the 1970s onward, the primary decades of Moreton's study. Also, evangelical sensibilities and aspirations found articulation in corporate institutions located in cities and diverse, urban spaces outside the Ozarks, or "Wal-Mart Country," which was a relatively homogenous environment in terms of race and demography. For instance, on Chicago's importance in the shaping of modern evangelicalism, see Timothy E. W. Gloege, *Guaranteed Pure: Moody Bible Institute, Business, and the Making of Modern Evangelicalism* (Chapel Hill: University of North Carolina Press, 2015). Large, economically and racially diverse cities and "white flight" suburban zones were also formative in the business history of modern conservative religion, culture, and politics. See McGirr, *Suburban Warriors*, Dochuk, *From Bible Belt to Sunbelt*, Eileen Luhr, *Witnessing Suburbia: Conservatives and Christian Youth Culture* (Berkeley: University of California Press, 2009), Darren E. Grem, "The Marketplace Missions of S. Truett Cathy and Chick-fil-A," and Darren Dochuk and Michelle Nickerson, eds., *Sunbelt Rising: The Politics of Place, Space, and Region* (Philadelphia: University of Pennsylvania Press, 2011), 293–315.

10. Scholars have long documented the use of businesses and business techniques to "sell" religion as a consumer experience in America. See R. Laurence Moore, *Selling God: American Religion in the Marketplace of Culture* (New York: Oxford University Press, 1994), Colleen McDannell,

Material Christianity: Religion and Popular Culture in America (New Haven, CT: Yale University Press, 1998), Douglas Carl Adams, *Selling the Old Time Religion: American Fundamentalists and Mass Culture, 1920–1940* (Athens: University of Georgia Press, 2001), Heather Hendershot, *Shaking the World for Jesus: Media and Conservative Evangelical Culture* (Chicago: University of Chicago Press, 2004), Jay R. Howard and Jon M. Streck, *Apostles of Rock: The Splintered World of Contemporary Christian Music* (Lexington: University of Kentucky Press, 1999), Eileen Luhr, *Witnessing Suburbia*, and David W. Stowe, *No Sympathy for the Devil: Christian Pop Music and the Transformation of American Evangelicalism* (Chapel Hill: University of North Carolina Press, 2012). Rather than viewing the marketplace for such consumer goods as the product of large-scale corporate enterprise—or as a type of scaled and integrated big business unto itself—scholars have typically cast it as simply a modern iteration of early market capitalism, quasi-democratic in nature and with origins in the colonial period or early American shopkeepers' republic. Hence, the corporate interests that shaped the consumption of such "religious" goods and services have not received much attention.

11. Gaines M. Foster, *Moral Reconstruction: Christian Lobbyists and the Federal Legislation of Morality, 1865–1920* (Chapel Hill: University of North Carolina Press, 2002); Tisa Wenger, *We Have a Religion: The 1920s Pueblo Indian Dance Controversy and American Religious Freedom* (Chapel Hill: University of North Carolina Press, 2009); Stephen K. Green, *The Second Disestablishment: Church and State in Nineteenth-Century America* (New York: Oxford University Press, 2010); Sarah Barringer Gordon, *The Spirit of the Law: Religious Voices and the Constitution in Modern America* (Cambridge, MA: Harvard University Press, 2010); David Sehat, *The Myth of American Religious Freedom* (New York: Oxford University Press, 2011).

12. Wendy L. Wall, *Inventing the "American Way": The Politics of Consensus from the New Deal to the Civil Rights Movement* (New York: Oxford University Press, 2008); Kevin M. Schultz, *Tri-Faith America: How Catholics and Jews Held Postwar America to Its Protestant Promise* (New York: Oxford University Press, 2011); Jonathan P. Herzog, *The Spiritual-Industrial Complex: America's Religious Battle Against Communism in the Early Cold War* (New York: Oxford University Press, 2011); Kevin M. Kruse, *One Nation Under God: How Corporate America Invented Christian America* (New York: Basic Books, 2015).

13. Kim Phillips-Fein, "Conservatism: A State of the Field," *The Journal of American History* 98.3 (December 2011): 723–743, quoted on 739.

14. Richard Howard LeTourneau, "A Study of the Basic Requirements for Success in an International Business-Christian Missionary Venture" (PhD dissertation, Oklahoma State University, 1970), 69, 82–83, 111, Box L1I, LET.

15. Numerous books offer such a conspiratorial take, casting conservative evangelicals as engaged in a quest to overtake American public life, one that—if successful—would turn the nation into a theocracy. For two examples, see Chris Hedges, *American Fascists: The Christian Right and the War on America* (New York: Simon & Schuster, 2006) and Kevin Phillips, *American Theocracy: The Peril and Politics of Radical Religion, Oil, and Borrowed Money in the 21st Century* (New York: Viking Press, 2006). Though less conspiratorial in tone but still inattentive to the limits of evangelical political influence, see Jeff Sharlet, *The Family: The Secret Fundamentalism at the Heart of American Power* (New York: Harper, 2008).

16. On the power of the "embattlement" narrative in modern evangelicalism, see Christian Smith, *American Evangelicalism: Embattled and Thriving* (Chicago: University of Chicago Press, 1998) and, when taken to certain flamboyant extremes, Jason C. Bivins, *Religion of Fear: The Politics of Terror in Conservative Evangelicalism* (New York: Oxford University Press, 2008).

17. On the evangelical left's fate in modern America, see David R. Swartz, *Moral Minority: The Evangelical Left in an Age of Conservatism* (Philadelphia: University of Pennsylvania Press, 2012) and Brantley W. Gasaway, *Progressive Evangelicals and the Pursuit of Social Justice* (Chapel Hill: University of North Carolina Press, 2014).

Chapter 1

1. Herbert J. Taylor, *The Herbert J. Taylor Story* (Downers Grove, IL: Intervarsity Press, 1968), 25–32. This truncated biography of Taylor aligns with Hammond, " 'God's Business Men,' " 148–164.

2. "Dedicate Organ in Park Ridge April 20," *Chicago Tribune*, April 6, 1941, 3–1; Orvis F. Jordan, *A History of Park Ridge* (Park Ridge, IL: George L. Scharringhausen Jr., 1961), 164.

3. US Census Data, 1930, 1960, cited in "Park Ridge, IL," *The Encyclopedia of Chicago*, http://www.encyclopedia.chicagohistory.org/pages/2203.html; Jordan, *A History of Park Ridge*, 64, 163–165. First Methodist is likely the historic, "virile church" Jordan refers to when describing "Methodist service to the community." First Methodist of Park Ridge was the only Methodist church in the community until a Second Methodist was founded around 1960 while another at the time of his book's publication—Good Shepherd Methodist Church—was "operating in a schoolhouse, pending the erection of a new building." Ibid., 170.

4. On the *Dartmouth* case, see Gordon Wood, *Empire of Liberty: A History of the Early Republic, 1789–1815* (New York: Oxford University Press, 2009), 465–466. On the postbellum manifestations and power of "the corporation," see Martin J. Sklar, *The Corporate Reconstruction of American Capitalism, 1890–1916: The Market, The Law, and Politics* (Cambridge, UK: Cambridge University Press, 1988). On the rise of managerialism, see Alfred P. Chandler, *The Visible Hand: The Managerial Revolution in American Business* (Cambridge, MA: Harvard University Press, 1993). On welfare capitalism and paternalism, especially in the southern context, see Jacquelyn Dowd Hall et al., *Like a Family: The Making of the Southern Cotton Mill World* (Chapel Hill: University of North Carolina Press, 1987). On advertising, philanthropy, and public relations, see Roland Marchand, *Advertising the American Dream: Making Way for Modernity, 1920–1940* (Berkeley: University of California Press, 1986) and *Creating the Corporate Soul: The Rise of Public Relations and Corporate Imagery in American Big Business* (Berkeley: University of California Press, 1998).

5. Charles Lippy, *Do Real Men Pray? Images of the Christian Man and Male Spirituality in White Protestant America* (Knoxville: University of Tennessee Press, 2005), 113–142; Leo Ribuffo, "Jesus Christ as Business Statesman: Bruce Barton and the Selling of Corporate Capitalism," *American Quarterly* 33.2 (Summer 1981): 217–221; Wayne Elzey, "Jesus the Salesman: A Reassessment of *The Man Nobody Knows*," *Journal of the American Academy of Religion* 46 (1978): 151–177.

6. Jeffrey A. Charles, *Service Clubs in America: Rotary, Kiwanis, and Lions* (Urbana: University of Illinois Press, 1993), 34, 24–25.

7. On early interactions between evangelical revivalism and business culture, see Kathryn Teresa Long, *The Revival of 1857–58: Interpreting an American Religious Awakening* (New York: Oxford University Press, 1998), and Lippy, *Do Real Men Pray?*, 113–142; Thekla Ellen Joiner, *Sin in the City: Chicago and Revivalism, 1880–1920* (Columbia: University of Missouri Press, 2007), 21–62; George M. Marsden, *Understanding Fundamentalism and Evangelicalism* (Grand Rapids, MI: Wm. B. Eerdmans, 1991), 1–6, 11–85. On the whiteness of Christ and turn-of-the-century America, see Edward J. Blum and Paul Harvey, *The Color of Christ: The Saga of Race and the Son of God in America* (Chapel Hill: University of North Carolina Press, 2012), 141–172.

8. Richard Ellsworth Day, *Breakfast Table Autocrat: The Life Story of Henry Parsons Crowell* (Chicago: Moody Press, 1946), 161, quoted in Timothy E. W. Gloege, "Consumed: Reuben A. Torrey and the Construction of Corporate Fundamentalism" (PhD dissertation, Notre Dame University, 2007), 264.

9. Kathleen Minnix, *Laughter in the Amen Corner: The Life of Evangelist Sam Jones* (Athens: University of Georgia Press, 1993), 112; Gloege, "Consumed," 142–163; Moody quote from ibid., 148; Gloege, *Guaranteed Pure*, 3.

10. Gloege, "Consumed," 148–150, 250–402, and *Guaranteed Pure*, 59–65, 122–130, 138–161.

11. Charles R. Erdman, "The Church and Socialism," in *The Fundamentals: A Testimony to the Truth*, Vol. 12.

12. Stewart quoted in Ernest Sandeen, "Toward a Historical Interpretation of the Origins of Fundamentalism," *Church History* 36.1 (March 1967): 77–80; Gloege, *Guaranteed Pure*, 162–189.

13. George M. Marsden, *Fundamentalism and American Culture: The Shaping of Twentieth Century Evangelicalism* (New York: Oxford University Press, 1980), 109–117, 141–198; Matthew Avery Sutton, *American Apocalypse: A History of American Evangelicalism* (Cambridge, MA: Harvard University Press, 2014), 148–157.

14. Edward J. Larson, *Summer for the Gods: The Scopes Trial and America's Continuing Debate Over Science and Religion* (New York: Basic Books, 1997); Mary Beth Swetnam Mathews, *Rethinking Zion: How the Print Media Placed Fundamentalism in the South* (Knoxville: University of Tennessee Press, 2006); Mencken quoted in S. T. Joshi, ed., *H. L. Mencken on Religion* (Amherst, MA: Prometheus Books, 2002), 120; On the class composition and politics of the Klan, see Nancy MacLean, *Behind the Mask of Chivalry: The Making of the Second Ku Klux Klan* (New York: Oxford University Press, 1994), 52–97. On the Klan's form of Protestantism, see Kelly J. Baker, *Gospel According to the Klan: The KKK's Appeal to Protestant America, 1915–1930* (Lawrence: University of Kansas Press, 2010), 34–69; Lyle W. Dorsett, *Billy Sunday and the Redemption of Urban America* (Grand Rapids, MI: Wm. B. Eerdmans, 1991).

15. Sutton, *American Apocalypse*, 157; George M. Marsden, *Reforming Fundamentalism: Fuller Seminary and the New Evangelicalism* (Grand Rapids, MI: Wm. B. Eerdmans, 1987), 28.

16. Darryl G. Hart, *Defending the Faith: J. Gresham Machen and the Crisis of Conservative Protestantism in Modern America* (New York: Boker, 1994); Heather Hendershot, *What's Fair on the Air? Cold War Right-Wing Broadcasting and the Public Interest* (Chicago: University of Chicago Press, 2011), 105.

17. Grant Wacker, *Heaven Below: Early Pentecostals and American Culture* (Cambridge, MA: Harvard University Press, 2001), 1–8; Edith Blumhofer, *Aimee Semple McPherson: Everybody's Sister* (Grand Rapids, MI: Wm. B. Eerdmans, 1993); Matthew Avery Sutton, *Aimee Semple McPherson and the Resurrection of Christian America* (Cambridge, MA: Harvard University Press, 2007), 1–6, 56–62, 66–89, 125–127, 188–195; Kevin Starr, *Material Dreams: Southern California Through the 1920s* (Oxford: Oxford University Press, 1990), 136–139; James N. Gregory, *The Southern Diaspora: How the Great Migrations of Black and White Southerners Transformed America* (Chapel Hill: University of North Carolina Press, 2005), 225–226.

18. Matthew Avery Sutton, "Was FDR the Antichrist? The Birth of Fundamentalist Antiliberalism in a Global Age," *The Journal of American History* 98.4 (March 2012): 1052–1074.

19. Leo P. Ribuffo, *The Old Christian Right: The Protestant Far Right from the Great Depression to the Cold War* (Philadelphia: Temple University Press, 1983), 154–155.

20. "Black on Blacks," *Time*, April 27, 1936, 10–11; Elna C. Green, "From Antisuffragism to Anti-Communism: The Conservative Career of Ida M. Darden," *The Journal of Southern History* 65.2 (May 1999): 287–316; Walter Davenport, "Savior from Texas," *Collier's*, August 18, 1945, 13, 79–81; Glenn Feldman, *The Irony of the Solid South: Democrats, Republicans, and Race, 1865–1944* (Tuscaloosa: University of Alabama Press, 2013), 129; Marc Dizon, "Limiting Labor: Business Political Mobilization and Union Setback in the States," *The Journal of Policy History* 19.3 (2007): 313–344; Victor Riesel, "Let's Look at Labor IV: How to Choke Unions," *The Nation*, July 31, 1943, 124–126.

21. Gary K. Clabaugh, *Thunder on the Right: The Protestant Fundamentalists* (Chicago: Nelson Hall, 1974), 111; Allan J. Lichtman, *White Protestant Nation: The Rise of the American Conservative Movement* (New York: Grove-Atlantic Monthly Press, 2009), 96–97; George W. Robnett to Herbert J. Taylor, September 27, 1940, Box 11, Folder 9, HJT; Clipping, Rev. John Evans, "Church League Warns Pastors of Polls Crisis," *Chicago Daily Tribune*, September 2, 1940, n.p., Box 11, Folder 9, HJT; "An Urgent Appeal . . . To Every Churchman In America," n.d., Box 11, Folder 9, HJT.

22. James D. Davidson, Ralph E. Pyle, and David V. Reyes, "Persistence and Change in the Protestant Establishment, 1930–1992," *Social Forces* 74.1 (September 1995): 164–166; Fones-Wolf, *Selling Free Enterprise*, 219.

23. Hammond, "'God's Business Men,'" 169; Gregory Eow, "Fighting a New Deal: Intellectual Origins of the Reagan Revolution" (PhD dissertation, Rice University, 2007); Phillips-Fein, *Invisible Hands*, 3–25.

24. "Personalia," *The Rotarian*, March 1954, 46.

25. Ibid.; Taylor correspondences, 1940, 1949, cited in Heidebrecht, "Pragmatic Evangelical," 110.

26. Hammond, "'God's Business Men,'" 162–172, 180; Don Cusic, *The Sound of Light: A History of Gospel and Christian Music* (Milwaukee, WI: Hal Leonard, 2002), 183–184; "Rotary's Mid-Century," *Newsweek*, February 28, 1955, 31–32.

27. Hammond, "'God's Business Men,'" 169–174; "Herbert Taylor," American National Business Hall of Fame, http://anbhf.org/laureates/herbert-taylor; William F. McDermott, "Broke

in 1933; On Top in 1941," *The Rotarian*, March 1942, 34–36. Also quoted in Hammond, "'God's Business Men,'" 174.

28. Judson A. Rudd to H. J. Taylor, May 6, 1950, Box 16, Folder 55, HJT. For examples of many invitations to speak regarding the Four-Way Test, see Joseph Stevans to H. J. Taylor, February 9, 1958, and H. J. Taylor to Joseph Stevans, April 4, 1958, Box 72, Folder 6, HJT; "Rotary President Taylor: 50 Years to the Good," *Newsweek*, February 28, 1955.

29. Pamphlet, "14 Prominent Business Men Look at Life," Box 11, Folder 7, HJT.

30. David R. Enlow, *Men Aflame: The Story of Christian Business Men's Committee International* (Grand Rapids, MI: Zondervan, 1962), 13–20; Miller, *God at Work*, 34; Hammond, "'God's Business Men,'" 84–87.

31. Arnold Grunigen Jr., "Around the King's Table," *The King's Business* (April 1936), 122, quoted in Hammond, "'God's Business Men,'" 90–91.

32. Gloege, "Consumed," 12, 250–402, and *Guaranteed Pure*, 194, 166–168.

33. For clarity I refer to this as the CBMCI throughout the rest of the book.

34. Enlow, *Men Aflame*, 13–14, 19, 87–109; Miller, *God at Work*, 33–34; Joel Carpenter, *Revive Us Again*, 122.

35. Tom Olson, "The CBMCI of Capernaum" (1942), Box 3, Folder 10, VWP.

36. Pamphlet, 15th Annual CBMCI Convention, Atlantic City, NJ, October 15–19, 1952, Box 3, Folder 10, VWP.

37. Carpenter, *Revive Us Again*, 116–119.

38. On this point, I follow and build on the insights provided in Hammond, "'God's Business Men,'" and Gloege, *Guaranteed Pure*.

39. Paul Arnsberger, Melissa Ludlum, Margaret Riley, and Mark Stanton, "A History of the Tax-Exempt Sector: A SOI Perspective," *Statistics of Income Bulletin*, Winter 2008, 105–135; Nina J. Crimm and Laurence H. Winer, *Politics, Taxes, and the Pulpit: Provocative First Amendment Conflicts* (New York: Oxford University Press, 2011), 110. The dizzying number of laws regulating tax exemption and deductions that followed out of the tax codes of the 1910s and 1930s cannot be adequately covered within the confines of this book. Nevertheless, the general rule of thumb held for evangelical businessmen as they followed the law. State provisions and allowances encouraged them—like any other business executive or philanthropist—to donate portions of their income (however defined) from their businesses and personal wealth as a means to kill two birds with one stone: support various evangelical enterprises as a proxy for their religious or political sensibilities and potentially receive a tax break for their generosity.

40. Robert Walker to Mr. Smiley (?), n.d., Box 12, Folder 13, HJT. This letter was most likely written in 1940 or 1941.

41. The CWF's wide range of recipients is detailed in Report of Activities of the Christian Workers Foundation, July 1, 1940–June 30, 1941 and Annual Report of the Christian Workers Foundation, July 1, 1941–June 30, 1942, Box 11, Folder 1, HJT; Bruce Shelley, "The Rise of Evangelical Youth Movements," *Fides et Historia* 18.1 (1986): 47–63; "These Rotarians!!!" *The Rotarian*, October 1968, 48; Marsden, *Reforming Evangelicalism*, 24–25, 51; "Taylor, Herbert J(ohn)," in Randall Herbert Balmer, ed., *Encyclopedia of Evangelicalism* (Louisville, KY: Westminster John Knox, 2002), 674–675.

42. Herbert J. Taylor to Clyde H. Dennis, April 17, 1940, Box 11, Folder 21, HJT.

43. Herbert J. Taylor, *God Has a Plan for You* (Carol Stream, IL: Creation House, 1972), 50, quoted in Shelley, "The Rise of Evangelical Youth Movements," 47. On the 1960s and youth conservatism, see John A. Andrew III, *The Other Side of the Sixties: Young Americans for Freedom and the Rise of Conservative Politics* (New Brunswick, NJ: Rutgers University Press, 1997). On the role of teenagers and college-age students in the "new Right" and "new Left," see Rebecca E. Klatch, *A Generation Divided: The New Left, the New Right, and the 1960s* (Berkeley: University of California Press, 1999).

44. Jordan, *A History of Park Ridge*, 144; Flyer, Victory Youth Rally, Chicago Stadium, Saturday, October 21 [1944], Box 72, Folder 1, HJT; Pamphlet, "Twin-City Youth Rally," June 23, 1945, Box 72, Folder 2, HJT; Cover, *Youth for Christ Magazine*, April 1945, Box 72, Folder 1, HJT.

45. Torrey Johnson to Herbert J. Taylor, November 25, 1946, Box 72, Folder 3, HJT; Pamphlet, "Twin-City Youth Rally," Box 72, Folder 2, HJT; Charles R. White, "Report of Business

Manager," *Minutes of the Second Annual Convention, Youth for Christ International, Inc.,* July 22–29, 1946, 59–65, Box 72, Folder 3, HJT; Harold E. Fey, "What About 'Youth for Christ'?" June 20, 1945, *The Christian Century,* n.p., Box 72, Folder 2, HJT.

46. "Meet Billy Graham," *Youth for Christ Magazine* (March 1945), 10–11, Box 72, Folder 1, HJT.

Chapter 2

1. L. Nelson Bell to J. Howard Pew, November 2, 1965, Box 231, Folder C, JHP; J. Howard Pew to L. Nelson Bell, November 8, 1965, Box 231, Folder C, JHP.

2. Bell quotation from Sutton, "Was FDR the Antichrist?"1068.

3. Lichtman, *White Protestant Nation,* 123–125.

4. Harold Ockenga, "The New Evangelicalism," in Matthew Avery Sutton, ed., *Jerry Falwell and the Rise of the Religious Right: A Brief History with Documents* (Boston: Bedford/ St. Martin's, 2012), 31–34; Harold Ockenga, "Can Fundamentalism Win America?" *Christian Life,* June 1947, 13–14. The context for this article is detailed in Sutton, *American Apocalypse,* 314–315.

5. Ockenga, "The New Evangelicalism," 31–34.

6. Harold Ockenga, "Resurgent Evangelical Leadership," *Christianity Today,* October 10, 1960, 11–15.

7. Harold Ockenga, "Christ for America," in *United We Stand: A Report of the Constitutional Convention of the National Association of Evangelicals, May 3–6, 1943,* quoted in Williams, *God's Own Party,* 17; "Session II—Communism and Our Christian Heritage," 1–2, Box 40, Folder "Communism," NAE. Thanks to Ken and Elizabeth Fones-Wolf for this document; Lichtman, *White Protestant Nation,* 124–125; for additional context, see Williams, *God's Own Party,* 16–18.

8. Hammond, " 'God's Business Men,' " 224–265; Ken and Elizabeth Fones-Wolf, "What Was Different About Southern Textile Workers?" Paper presented at the 2013 Southern Labor Studies Conference, in author's possession; Carpenter, *Revive Us Again,* 158–159.

9. Billy Graham, *Revival in Our Time: The Story of the Billy Graham Evangelistic Crusades* (Wheaton, IL: Van Kampen Press, 1950), 13; William McLoughlin, *Billy Graham, Revivalist in a Secular Age* (New York: Ronald Press, 1960), 45–48, 51; Miller, *Billy Graham and the Rise of the Republican South,* 15; Marshall Frady, *Billy Graham: A Parable of American Righteousness* (New York: Simon & Schuster, 2006), 204.

10. McLoughlin, *Billy Graham,* 51; Grant Wacker, *America's Pastor: Billy Graham and the Shaping of a Nation* (Cambridge, MA: Harvard University Press, 2014), 263–266.

11. Wacker, *America's Pastor,* 337, n24; William Martin, *A Prophet With Honor: The Billy Graham Story* (New York: W. Morrow, 1991), 94–95, 117–118.

12. McLoughlin, *Billy Graham,* 97–102, 109; Heidebrecht, "Pragmatic Evangelical," 109.

13. Michael G. Long, *Billy Graham and the Beloved Community* (New York: Palgrave Macmillan, 2006), 143–148, 151–156; Billy Graham, "God Before Gold," *Nation's Business,* September 1954, 34–35, 55–56; McLoughlin, *Billy Graham,* 109.

14. Graham, "The Answer to Corruption," *Nation's Business,* September 1969, 49.

15. On the 1964–1965 World's Fair and its social and cultural context, see Joseph Tirella, *Tomorrow-Land: The 1964–1965 World's Fair and the Transformation of America* (Guilford, CT: Globe Pequot Press, 2014); Lawrence R. Samuel, *The End of Innocence: The 1964–1965 World's Fair* (Syracuse, NY: Syracuse University Press, 2007), 21–23; "The Hall of Free Enterprise at the New York World's Fair, 1964–1965," 3, Folder 1, Box 215, JHP; Clipping, "Free Enterprise Hall Rises at World's Fair," *New York World-Telegram and Sun,* June 1, 1963, n.p., Folder 1, Box 215, JHP.

16. "Plan of Fair," *Official Preview: New York World's Fair, 1964–65* (New York: Time-Life Publications, 1964), n.p., Folder "American Economic Foundation, Hall of Free Enterprise, 1964," Box 215, JHP; Samuel, *The End of Innocence,* 22; Bill Cotter and Bill Young, *The 1964–1965 World's Fair* (Charleston, SC: Arcadia, 2013), 37–38.

17. "Graham Defines America's Plight: It's Lack of God," n.p., May 27, 1951, Box 1, Folder 12, NAV.

18. This is according to an "early biographer" of Graham, quoted in Stephen J. Whitfield, *The Culture of the Cold War* (Baltimore, MD: Johns Hopkins University Press, 1996), 79–80. The biographer was William McLoughlin.

19. Clipping, Louis Cook, "God's Super Salesman," *Detroit Free Press* (1953), n.d., Box 2, Folder 45, NAV; Martin, *A Prophet With Honor*, 115; Billy Graham, "Satan's Religion," *The American Mercury*, August 1954, 41, 45–46.

20. Miller, *Billy Graham and the Rise of the Republican South*, 26–33.

21. "Graham Says Youth 'Obsessed With Sex,'" *The Free Press*, July 29, 1957, Box 4, Folder 29, NAV; "Billy Tells Women to Roost, Not Rule," n.p. (1953), Box 2, Folder 45, NAV.

22. Herbert Weiner, "Billy Graham: Respectable Evangelism," *Commentary*, September 1957, 262; Frady, *Billy Graham*, 248–249; "Heaven, Hell & Judgment Day," *Time*, March 20, 1950, 72–73; Cook, "God's Super Salesman"; "The New Evangelist," *Time*, October 25, 1954, 55.

23. Martin, *A Prophet With Honor*, 135–136; Frady, *Billy Graham*, 221–222; Graham, *Just As I Am*, 178–184; Price Waterhouse & Co. to the Executive Committee of Billy Graham New York Crusade, Inc., December 16, 1957, Box 4, Folder 25, NAV; Cook, "God's Super Salesman."

24. J. Howard Pew to Graham, June 22, 1956, Box 48, Folder "Billy Graham," JHP; "Follow-Up in the Seattle Campaign," Box 1, Folder 36, NAV; "Personal Workers Meeting," *Greater Seattle Gospel Crusade, Instructions for Personal Workers*, Box 1, Folder 36, NAV; "To All Counselors," Box 1, Folder 39, NAV; "Notes on Personal Work Meeting, 9-10-51, To All Counselors," Box 1, Folder 39, NAV. For convert databases from 1951, see Box 1, Folders 4, 7, 28, NAV.

25. Frady, *Billy Graham*, 292.

26. Roger Hull, "A Report to the Public," December 16, 1957, Box 4, Folder 25, NAV; "Standard Operating Procedure and Outline for Counselor Training" and assorted flow charts, Box 4, Folder 31, NAV; "Organization Plan for Billy Graham New York Crusade, Inc.," Box 4, Folder 30, NAV; J. Howard Pew to Howard E. Isham, December 14, 1956, Box 48, Folder "Billy Graham," JHP; "Invocation Delivered at Billy Graham Evangelistic Association Crusade" (July 18, 1957), Martin Luther King Jr. Papers Project.

27. The "Gotham budget" of $900,000 and Beavan and Haymaker's involvement, noted in the previous paragraph, is cited here. Clipping, James E. Wallace, "Efficient Evangelist: Billy Graham Unites the Bible, Business Methods as He Starts New York Crusade," *The Wall Street Journal*, May 10, 1957, 1, Box 5, Folder 1, NAV.

28. "God's Groceryman," *Time*, April 26, 1954, 86; McLoughlin, *Billy Graham*, 160, 163–164; Charts, Box 1, Folder 1-3, Folder 14, RLP; Joe E. Barnhart, *The Billy Graham Religion* (Philadelphia: Pilgrim Press, 1972), 182.

29. Martin, *A Prophet With Honor*, 139–140.

30. Peter W. Williams, *Popular Religion in America: Symbolic Change and the Modernization Process in Historical Perspective* (Urbana: University of Illinois Press, 1989), 202; Pamphlet, "It's Great! Oil Town, U.S.A." Box 3, Folder 3, VWP; Martin, *A Prophet with Honor*, 140, 306; Frady, *Billy Graham*, 231–232.

31. Douglas A. Sweeney, "*Christianity Today*," in Mark Fackler and Charles Lippy, eds., *Popular Religious Magazines of the United States* (Westport, CT: Greenwood Press, 1995), 144–151; John Pollack, *Billy Graham: Evangelist to the World* (New York: Harper & Row, 1979), 171; Harold J. Ockenga to Russell MacGuire, June 2, 1954, Box 39, Folder O, JHP.

32. L. Nelson Bell to J. Howard Pew, January 14, 1955, Box 41, Folder B, JHP.

33. T. Jeremy Gunn, *Spiritual Weapons: The Cold War and the Forging of an American National Religion* (Westport, CT: Greenwood Press, 2009), 127–128; Fones-Wolf, *Selling Free Enterprise* (Urbana: University of Illinois Press, 1994), 236–244. Pew's paternalistic views regarding race came to the forefront over a segregated shipyard in Chester, Pennsylvania. Joe Pew, a brother and executive at the facility in question, thought that hiring more black workers would show the Pew family's goodwill toward black workers, cut labor costs, and perhaps pull in a few black voters for the family's favored Republican candidates. J. Howard Pew likely agreed, although he did nothing to oversee desegregation at the facility or in the surrounding town. Economic and political interest, rather than a curtailing of white privilege or lauding of black civil rights, animated Pew's approach toward race. The Pew family's strategic engagement with race also did not go uncontested by black activists and workers, as detailed in John

M. McLarnon, "Pie in the Sky vs. Meat and Potatoes: The Case of Sun Ship's Yard No. 4," *Journal of American Studies* 34 (2000): 67–88.

34. J. Howard Pew to Harold Ockenga, October 21, 1954, Box 39, Folder O, JHP; J. Howard Pew to L. Nelson Bell, January 17, 1955, Box 41, Folder B, JHP; Lichtman, *White Protestant Nation*, 216–217.

35. Billy Graham to J. Howard Pew, March 25, 1955, Box 42, Folder "Christianity Today, Folder #2," JHP; Lichtman, *White Protestant Nation*, 215–216; J. Howard Pew to Jasper Crane, June 6, 1956, Box 47, Folder "Re: Christianity Today; Solicitation Letter," JHP; J. Howard Pew to L. Nelson Bell, May 24, 1956, Box 47, Folder "Re: Christianity Today; Solicitation Letter," JHP.

36. J. Howard Pew to W. E. Winn, May 17, 1957, L. Nelson Bell to the Members of the Finance Committee, May 25, 1957, Harold Ockenga to J. Howard Pew, February 1, 1957, Harold Ockenga to J. Howard Pew, March 26, 1957, and Untitled budget, February 15, 1957, all in Box 53, Folder "Christianity Today, 1957," JHP.

37. "Memorandum in Support of the Application of Christianity Today, Inc. to Qualify for an Exemption Under Section 301(c) [*sic*] of the Internal Revenue Code of 1954," 5-6, 10, Box 5, Folder 12, CTR.

38. Loose paper, "Board of Trustees," "Outline for Christianity Today Readers," Box 42, Folder "Christianity Today, Folder #2," JHP; "Memorandum in Support of the Application of Christianity Today, Inc." 7, Box 5, Folder 12, CTR.

39. On the encounter between Barth and Henry, see Molly Worthen, *Apostles of Reason: The Crisis of Authority in American Evangelicalism* (New York: Oxford University Press, 2013), 15–16.

40. Estimates on exact circulation in the late 1950s and 1960s vary, although most fall somewhere around these numbers. See Frank W. Price, "*Christianity Today*: An Appraisal," *Christianity and Crisis*, October 27, 1958, 148–151; Phyllis Alsdurf, "Evangelicalism and the Presidential Election of 1960: The 'Catholic Question' in *Christianity Today* Magazine," in Lynn S. Clark, ed., *Religion, Media, and the Marketplace* (New Brunswick, NJ: Rutgers University Press, 2007), 171–197 (esp. 194, n5); George, "Henry, Carl Ferdinand Howard (1913–)," in Timothy Larsen et al., eds., *Biographical Dictionary of Evangelicals* (Downers Grove, IL: Intervarsity Press, 2003), 198.

41. Howard Butt Jr. to Bell, April 15, 1957, Box 1, Folder 48, CTR; Bell to Howard J. Butt Jr., April 16, 1959, Box 1, Folder 48, CTR; Butt Jr. to Bell, April 21, 1959, Box 1, Folder 48, CTR; Bell to Butt Jr., April 27, 1959, Box 1, Folder 48, CTR.

42. Memorandum in Support of the Application of Christianity Today, Inc., 10, Box 5, Folder 12, CTR.

43. Bell to Butt Jr., May 25, 1960, Box 1, Folder 48, CTR; Bell to Pew, October 4, 1962, Box 1, Folder 59, CTR.

44. Martin, *A Prophet With Honor*, 139–140; Bell to Charles A. Pitts, March 29, 1957, Box 1, Folder 60, CTR; Charles A. Pitts to Walter F. Bennett et al., July 27, 1959, Box 1, Folder 60, CTR.

45. Donald T. Critchlow, *The Conservative Ascendancy: How the GOP Right Made Political History* (Cambridge, MA: Harvard University Press, 2007), 22; Kenneth W. Shipps, "*Christianity Today* (1956–)," in Ronald Lora and William Henry Longton, eds., *The Conservative Press in Twentieth-Century America* (Westport, CT: Greenwood Press, 1999), 174–176.

46. Bell, "A Layman and His Faith: The Fifth Freedom," *Christianity Today*, June 22, 1959, 19; "Ten Books on Ethics and Economics," *Christianity Today*, June 22, 1959, 12–14, 38.

47. Sweeney, "*Christianity Today*," 146; Hoover once wrote at the editors' request a three-part contribution on communism and religion. See J. Edgar Hoover, "Red Goals and Christian Ideals," *Christianity Today*, October 10, 1960, 3–5, "Communist Propaganda and the Christian Pulpit," October 24, 1960, 53–55, "Soviet Rule or Christian Renewal," *Christianity Today*, November 7, 1960, 96–99; Clipping, "Christianity and Communism," *Christianity Today*, January 19, 1959, 19, Box 1, Folder 1, CTR; L. Nelson Bell, "Triplet of Evils," *Christianity Today*, September 29, 1958, 19.

48. Bell, "Triplet of Evils," 19; "Evangelicals and Public Affairs," *Christianity Today*, January 27, 1964, 26.

49. Alsdurf, "Evangelicalism and the Presidential Election of 1960"; "The Assassination of the President," *Christianity Today*, December 6, 1963, 24–25; Harold J. Ockenga, "The Death of

a President," *Christianity Today*, December 20, 1963, 39; "Race Tensions and Social Change," *Christianity Today*, January 19, 1959, 23.

50. "Civil Rights and Christian Concern," *Christianity Today*, May 8, 1964, 28–29.

51. J. Howard Pew, "The Mission of the Church," *Christianity Today*, July 3, 1964, 11–14.

52. The Board of Directors, "The Mission of the Church," *Christianity Today*, July 17, 1964, 3.

53. "Bible Battles," *Time*, May 10, 1976, 57; Shipps, "*Christianity Today* (1956–)"; Mary Sennholz, *Faith and Freedom: A Biographical Sketch of a Great American, John Howard Pew* (Grove City, PA: Grove City College, 1975), 154–156; Dan D. Nimmo and Chevelle Newsome, eds., *Political Commentators in the United States in the 20th Century: A Bio-Critical Sourcebook* (Westport, CT: Greenwood Press, 1997), 23; Doris Jean Waller, "A Historical Analysis of *Christianity Today* Magazine" (PhD dissertation, University of Mississippi, 2007), 54–55; "Of Prophetic Robes and Weather Vanes: An Interview with Kenneth Kantzer," *Christianity Today*, April 7, 1978, 23, 25; Martin, *A Prophet with Honor*, 211, quoted in Sweeney, "*Christianity Today*," 147–148.

Chapter 3

1. On speaking engagements, see Boxes J4A through J4E, LET; Rachel K. McDowell, "Churches to Mark Bible Sunday Here," *The New York Times*, December 6, 1947, 16; "R. C. LaTourneau [*sic*] To Speak Here," *Atlanta Journal*, December 12, 1939, n.p., Vertical File, UGA; "'God's Businessman' Coming," *The Lethbridge Herald*, April 11, 1959, 13; Ken Durham, "LeTourneau, Robert Gilmour," in *The Handbook of Texas*, https://tshaonline.org/handbook/online/articles/fle36; Clipping, "Tech Graduation," *NOW*, June 15, 1953, n.p. in Folder "Loose Files Folder #2," Box B4S, LET; LeTourneau, *Mover of Men and Mountains*, 212.

2. Hammond, "'God's Business Men,'" 22–25; LeTourneau, *Mover of Men and Mountains*, 106–133.

3. LeTourneau, *Mover of Men and Mountains*, 161–168, 174–189; Hammond, "'God's Business Men,'" 33–35, 250–251; Lamar Q. Ball, "New Industry in Georgia Born of a Chance Meeting," *Atlanta Constitution*, April 9, 1939, 1-A, 18-A; "LeTourneau Equipment is Big Feature with Yancey," *Atlanta Constitution*, July 17, 1939, 12; Clipping, "The LeTourneau Plant Passes Its 5th Milestone in It's [*sic*] Fantastic Growth," *Royston Record*, December 2, 1943, n.p.; LeTourneau, *Mover of Men and Mountains*, 210–211; Pamphlet, "Industrial Chaplain" (R. G. LeTourneau, Inc.: n.d), 1, in Folder 15-17-4, Box J2Z, LET; "LeTourneau's One Stop Community," *NOW*, December 6, 1946, 4–7; "Plant Chapel," *NOW*, March 1, 1946, 1–5.

4. Robert Haralson Selby, "Earthmovers in World War II: R. G. LeTourneau and His Machines" (PhD dissertation, Case Western Reserve University, 1970), iii–v, 30–32, 392, 416; "Milestones," *Time*, June 13, 1969, 90; *Summary of War Contract Terminations Relative to World War II* (June 10, 1946), n.p., in Box F2X, LET.

5. Charles Reagan Wilson, "Bulldozer Revolution," in Charles Reagan Wilson et al., eds., *The Encyclopedia of Southern Culture* (Chapel Hill: University of North Carolina Press, 1989), 736; "Corporations: Partnership with God," 65. Dozens of military-related contracts are available in Box FOD, LET; "R. G. LeTourneau is Building Missile Carriers for Britain," *The Wall Street Journal*, June 6, 1957, 17; "New $24 Million Order," *Longview Morning Journal*, August 29, 1968, 1-A.

6. "LeTourneau, Robert G(ilmour)" in Balmer, *The Encyclopedia of Evangelicalism*, 402–403; LeTourneau, *Mover of Men and Mountains*, 205; "Corporations," *Time*, May 23, 1953, 92.

7. "Free Enterprise," *NOW*, June 15, 1956, 1, 3.

8. Walter J. Brooking, "A Work-Study Plan," *The Journal of Higher Education* 18.6 (June 1947): 307–311; Kenneth R. Durham, *LeTourneau University's First Fifty Years* (Longview, TX: LeTourneau University, 1995), 114; "LeTourneau College Is Now Coeducational," *NOW*, July 15, 1961, 2; "Tech Students Come from Far and Near," *NOW*, October 16, 1959, 2; William R. Glass, *Strangers in Zion: Fundamentalists in the South, 1900–1950* (Macon, GA: Mercer University Press, 2001), 101–105; "Operation No. 6 East Texas Factory and School" and "LeTourneau Tech Will Demonstrate Educational Plan," *NOW*, February 25, 1946, 2–5.

9. Selby, "Earthmovers in World War II," 399–401; "Texas Army Hospital to be LeTourneau Technical School," *NOW*, February 8, 1946, 2; "LeTourneau Tech Will Demonstrate Educational Plan," 4–5; Dochuk, *From Bible Belt to Sunbelt*, 54–55.

10. Marion E. Wade, *The Lord is My Counsel: A Businessman's Personal Experiences with the Bible* (Englewood Cliffs, NJ: Prentice-Hall, 1966), 77–82, 96–100; Lewis D. Solomon, *Evangelical Christian Executives: A New Model for Business Corporations* (New Brunswick, NJ: Transaction, 2004), 59–60, 65–68.

11. Quoted in Lambert, *Spirituality, Inc.*, 63.

12. Howard Bowen, *The Social Responsibilities of the Businessman* (New York: Harper, 1953); Thomas F. McMahon, "The Contributions of Religious Traditions to Business Ethics," *Journal of Business Ethics* 4 (1985): 341–342, 344–345.

13. Timo Meynhardt, "The Practical Wisdom of Peter Drucker: Roots in the Christian Tradition," *Journal of Management Development* 29.7–8 (2010): 616–625.

14. Nancy MacLean, *Freedom Is Not Enough: The Opening of the American Workplace* (Cambridge, MA: Harvard University Press, 2008), 30–34; Paul Finkelman, "Civil Rights, State Actions, and," in P. Finkelman, ed., *Encyclopedia of African American History, 1896 to the Present: From the Age of Segregation to the Twenty-First Century* (New York: Oxford University Press, 2009), 397; Anthony S. Chen, *The Fifth Freedom: Jobs, Politics, and Civil Rights in the United States* (Princeton, NJ: Princeton University Press, 2009), 115–169; William P. Jones, *The March on Washington: Jobs, Freedom, and the Forgotten History of Civil Rights* (New York: W.W. Norton, 2013), ix–40.

15. Wade, *The Lord is My Counsel*, 45.

16. *ServiceMaster Industries, Inc., 1968 Annual Report*, Box 24, Folder 41, HJT; *ServiceMaster Industries, Inc., 1969 Annual Report*, Box 24, Folder 41, HJT.

17. Jarman quoted in David Swartz, "Left Behind: The Evangelical Left and the Limits of Evangelical Politics" (PhD dissertation, University of Notre Dame, 2008), 52, n86.

18. Bill Carey, *Fortunes, Fiddles and Fried Chicken: A Nashville Business History* (Franklin, TN: Hillsboro Press, 2000), 172–176.

19. Ibid.; Orville Prescott, "Books of the Times," *The New York Times*, July 23, 1956, 27.

20. "Personality: A Prayerful Enterpriser," *The New York Times*, August 5, 1956, F-3; "Last Summer's Joy," *Faith and Freedom* (April 1957), 19; Carey, *Fortunes, Fiddles and Fried Chicken*, 176–182.

21. W. Maxey Jarman, *A Businessman Looks at the Bible* (Westwood, NJ: Fleming H. Revell Company, 1965), 6, 15–17, 153–159.

22. Michael Bowlin, "HEB Started in Kerrville," *Kerrville Daily Times*, September 17, 1989, 10-E; "Charles C. Butt New H.E.B. President," *San Antonio Express*, July 20, 1971, 3-A; "Hard Work and Golden Rule Built H.E.B., Says Founder," *The Brownsville Herald*, April 16, 1953, 30.

23. "Oral History Memoir," Howard E. Butt Jr., May 13, 1982, BOH; "Texas Grocery Man Devotes Long Hours Evangelizing as 'Gospel Bootlegger,'" *The Daily Chronicle*, March 7, 1955, 9; "Busy Texan is 'Gospel Bootlegger,'" *Council Bluffs Nonpareil*, March 27, 1955, D-1.

24. "Local Men to Be With 900 at Laymen's Meet," *Corpus Christi Times*, January 13, 1961, 8-B; "Spectator Religion," *The Morning Herald*, May 8, 1961, 14.

25. Howard Hovde, *A Dream That Came to Life: The History of the Laity Lodge Retreat Center* (Macon, GA: Smith and Helwys, 2007), 17–21; Al McCulloch, "Christian Renewal Goal of Mountainside Center," *The Corpus Christi Call-Times*, August 10, 1969, 1-B; "Laity Lodge Attracts Over 18,000 Annually," *Kerrville Mountain Sun*, April 4, 1984, 9; "Oral History Memoir," Howard E. Butt Jr., May 13, 1982, BOH.

26. "Enterprise: The Monster-Maker," *Newsweek*, November 16, 1959, 89, 90, 92; Lorimer, *God Runs My Business*, 186–191; "Wings for Missionaries," *Time*, September 17, 1945, 77–78.

27. Bob Hall, "Case Study: Coca-Cola and Methodism," in Samuel S. Hill Jr., ed., *On Jordan's Stormy Banks: Religion in the South* (Macon, GA: Mercer University Press, 1983), 147–150; Kathryn W. Kemp, *God's Capitalist: Asa Candler of Coca-Cola* (Macon, GA: Mercer University Press, 2002), 7–14; Greg Grandin, *Fordlandia: The Rise and Fall of Henry Ford's Forgotten Jungle City* (New York: Metropolitan Books, 2009). Ford never visited Fordlandia and, after a series of labor revolts and declining productivity, it folded.

28. "The Navigator," *Time*, July 2, 1956, 58–59; Nancy Calvert, "Dawson Trotman" in James Dixon Douglas, ed., *Twentieth-Century Dictionary of Christian Biography* (Carlisle, UK: Paternoster Press, 1995), 394; Martin I. Klauber and Scott M. Manetsch, *The Great Commission: Evangelicals and the History of World Missions* (Nashville: B&H Publishing

Group, 2008), 123; Robert H. Krapohl and Charles H. Lippy, *The Evangelicals: A Historical, Thematic, and Biographical Guide* (Westport, CT: Greenwood Press, 1999), 308–309.

29. Dan L. Thrapp, "Faith Navigators Founded by Sailor," *Los Angeles Times*, May 30, 1954, 1–13; Notebook, *National and International Scope of The Navigators Ministry* (1953), Box 2, Folder 42, NAV.

30. "Glen Eyrie Finance Campaign: Suggestions for Workers," n.d., 1–2, Box 2, Folder 42, NAV.

31. Marshall Sprague, *Newport in the Rockies: The Life and Good Times of Colorado Springs* (Athens: Ohio University Press, 1980), 339; *The Glen Eyrie Story* (Colorado Springs: Navigators Press, 1961), 3, 5–16; Thrapp, "Faith Navigators Founded by Sailor"; Michael Leccese, "Navigating Change," *Landscape Architecture* 89 (April 1999): 52.

32. Todd Hartch, *Missionaries of the State: The Summer Institute for Linguistics, State Formation, and Indigenous Mexico, 1935–1985* (Tuscaloosa: University of Alabama Press, 2006), xv; William Lawrence Svelmoe, *A New Vision for Missions: William Cameron Townsend, the Wycliffe Bible Translators, and the Culture of Early Evangelical Faith Missions, 1896–1945* (Tuscaloosa: University of Alabama Press, 2008), 213.

33. Lawrence Routh to Cameron Townsend, June 3, 1954, Document 10594, WBT; Interview of Vernon William Patterson by Paul Ericksen, March 5, 1985, Tape 6, VWP; Cal Hibbard, "'Founding Fathers' of SIL and WBT" (2003), unpublished, WBT; George M. Cowan to Henderson Belk, November 23, 1960, Document 19155, WBT.

34. Dawson Trotman to Cameron Townsend, August 19, 1942, Document 03215, WBT; Trotman to Townsend and Kennedy Nyman, November 18, 1948, Document 05600, WBT; Trotman to Townsend, June 12, 1945, Document 407201, WBT.

35. Flora M. Rhind (?) to Cameron Townsend, September 23, 1952, Document 07901, WBT; Maxey Jarman to Lawrence Routh, October 12, 1963, Document 21602, WBT; Maxey Jarman to Lawrence Routh, November 23, 1964, Document 22149, WBT; Jarman to Townsend, July 22, 1970, Document 27750, WBT; John G. Pew to Cameron Townsend, April 13, 1961, Document 20264, WBT; Pew to Elaine and Cameron Townsend, December 13, 1967, Document 25247, WBT; Townsend to W. C. Welchel, December 16, 1966, Document 23864, WBT; Samuel R. Milbank to William Nyman, September 26, 1957, Document 13780, WBT; Invoice, December 3, 1964, Document 22115, WBT; Norman J. Hollenbeck to Willis, December 6, 1965, Document 23046, WBT; Frank Sherrill to Dale Keitzman, April 16, 1963, Document 21577, WBT; Frank Sherrill to Lawrence Routh, November 5, 1964, Document 22144, WBT. On how businessmen could recommend one another for WBT's board, see Lawrence Routh to Board of Directors, July 1, 1954, Document 10126, WBT.

36. W. Cameron Townsend to Crowell Trust, May 2, 1960, Document 23679, WBT; Henry C. Crowell to Townsend, May 5, 1949, Document 06045, WBT; Henry C. Crowell to Townsend, January 9, 1951, Document 07179, WBT.

37. Crowell to Townsend, November 20, 1948, Document 05384, WBT.

38. Crowell to Townsend, January 9, 1951, 1–3, Document 07179, WBT; The Henry Parsons Crowell and Susan Coleman Crowell Trust to Townsend, June 22, 1966, Document 24064, WBT; Townsend to Crowell Trust, April 11, 1967, Document 24960, WBT; Crowell Trust to Townsend, June 1, 1968, Document 26319, WBT; Crowell Trust to Townsend, July 7, 1970, Document 27286, WBT; Crowell Trust to Townsend, June 10, 1970, Document 27788, WBT.

39. "Why Liberia?" in Dick, *R. G. Talks About*, 173–174, Box J2L, LET.

40. "Basic Philosophy," Document #701 (1960?), Folder, "Loose Files, Folder #1," Box B5S, LET; "Bulldozers and Bibles," *NOW*, May 1, 1953, n.p., in Folder, "Loose Files, Folder #2," both in Box B4S, LET.

41. LeTourneau, "A Study of the Basic Requirements for Success," 45–46; "It's a Small World," *NOW*, February 15, 1952, 3–4.

42. LeTourneau, *Mover of Men and Mountains*, 257–258; "Peru," Document #702 and "National Needs," Document #703 (1960?) in Folder, "Loose Files, Folder #2," Box B4S, LET.

43. On the nature and intent of these letters, see Robert J. Burket to R. G. LeTourneau, October 1, 1956; Homer Lee Marrow to R. G. LeTourneau, n.d., Frank Sowers to Editor, September 10, 1956; Rev. Harry Ketchem to R. G. LeTourneau, October 5, 1956, all in Folder, "Colonizer

Inquiries, 500–600," Box B5G, LET. Also, see Richard V. Stafford to R. G. LeTourneau, November 30, 1953, Obiora Agusiobo to R. G. LeTourneau, January 7, 1954 and May 6, 1954, all in Folder "Specialists (Lumbering—Forestry)," Box L0S, LET.

44. LeTourneau, "A Study of the Basic Requirements for Success," 49–50; "Christian Initiative," *NOW*, May 15, 1954, 2, Box B3W, LET.

45. Roy G. LeTourneau to R. G. LeTourneau, December 11, 1959 and Roy G. LeTourneau to Richard L. LeTourneau, November 30, 1959, in Folder "Letters from Roy LeTourneau," Box B5G, LET; Roy G. LeTourneau to R. W. Blakeley, March 21, 1960, Roy G. LeTourneau to R. G. LeTourneau, March 22, 1960, Draft of Contract, LeTourneau del Peru, Inc. and Gulf Oil, April 14, 1960, R. G. LeTourneau to Roy G. LeTourneau, April 22, 1960, all in Folder "Peru Corres. 1-1-60-61," Box FOV, LET.

46. Pamphlet, "They Took Two!" (LeTourneau Incorporated, 1957?) and Clipping, Lee Kelly, "Bush, LeTourneau Share Ties" *Longview News-Journal*, January 22, 1989, 1-E, 2-E, Box J8U, LET; "Oil Platform is En Route to Iran," *The New York Times*, November 24, 1958, 45.

47. Oden and Olivia Meeker, "Letter from Liberia," *The New Yorker*, November 29, 1952, 106, 109; "Liberia Report," *NOW*, April 6, 1961, 3; "Peru," *NOW*, February 1, 1962, 3; LeTourneau, "A Study in the Basic Requirements," 124–125.

48. Raymond Stadelman, "Resume of Annual Costs and Production of Crude Rubber," (n.d.), 1–2, Box L0A, LET; "Giant Tires," *NOW*, March 8, 1946, 3–5; "Liberia," in Dick, *R. G. Talks About*, 206–207; For salary records related to the Liberian project, see bank books and bank receipts stored in Box L0A, LET.

49. "Development vs. Exploitation," *NOW*, November 15, 1951, 3–4.

50. "An Act Approving the Statement of Understanding Made and Entered Into on the 18th Day of January A.D. 1952 by and Between the Republic of Liberia Represented by the Secretary of State and R. G. LeTourneau" (Monrovia: Authority Government Printing Office, 1953), 2–8; "An Act to Create and Establish LeTourneau of Liberia, Ltd., and to Define Its Powers, Approved May 13, 1953" (Monrovia: Authority Government Printing Office, 1953), 14–15, in Folder "Loose Files #2," Box B4S, LET.

51. Views about the particular successes and failures of Point Four vary. Several scholars have cast it as an ineffective program and a side story in American foreign policy during the Truman Administration. For this view, see *Robert A. Pollard, Economic Security and the Origins of the Cold War, 1945–1950* (New York: Columbia University Press, 1985), 207; Robert A. Packenham, *Liberal America and the Third World: Political Development Ideas in Foreign Aid and Social Science* (Princeton, NJ: Princeton University Press, 1973), 48–49. Others see it as having more significance, despite its shortcomings. For Point Four's attempts at reorganizing the world economy, see Gabriel Kolko, *Confronting the Third World: United States Foreign Policy, 1945–1980* (New York: Pantheon, 1988), 145. For its involvement in the "green revolution," see John Perkins, *Geopolitics and the Green Revolution: Wheat, Genes, and the Cold War* (New York: Oxford University Press, 1997), 43–44. For a review of these various takes on Point Four, as well as a political history of the program and its ambiguous legacy, see Sergei Y. Shenin, *The United States and the Third World: The Origins of Postwar Relations and the Point Four Program* (Huntington, NY: Nova Science Publishers, 2000), x–xi, 171–181.

52. R. Fansmeier, "The Churches and Point IV," *Inter-American Economic Affairs*, 7 (Summer 1953): 82–83, quoted in Shenin, *The United States and the Third World*, 165.

53. Guild Walker, "Peru Will Exploit Great Resources," *The New York Times*, January 5, 1955, 45; LeTourneau, "A Study in the Basic Requirements," 82–83, 69, 111, 85–89, 129–132.

54. Sam Pope Brewer, "Catholics Protest Texan's Peru Plan," *The New York Times*, October 1, 1953, 11.

55. Memo, Richard H. LeTourneau, "Administrative Changes," June 24, 1966, document #999, Folder, "Loose Files Folder #2," Box B4S, LET; Walter Knowles to Richard LeTourneau, September 21, 1970, and Clipping, "LeTourneau Jungle Lands Return to the Authority of the State," n.d. in Folder "Peru (1970)," Box B5G, LET.

56. T.E. McCully to B.H. Romine, April 20, 1959, Box 3, Folder 13, VWP.

57. Pamphlet, "15th Annual C.B.M.C.I., 1952, Box 3, Folder 10, VWP; February News-Flash, 1955, Bookmark, Pray and Plan Now, 1958, Box 3, Folder 12, VWP; T. E. McCully to B. H. Romine, April 20, 1959, Flyer, Crusade for Christ Closing Rally and 1958 Devotional

Calendar, Box 3, Folder 13, VWP; David Enlow to Vernon Patterson, October 16, 1959, Box 3, Folder 13, VWP.

58. T. E. McCully to Gordon Hallmark, April 17, 1959, Box 3, Folder 13, VWP; Pamphlet, 26th Annual Christian Business Men's Committee International Convention, 1963, and Flyer, "Enjoy This European Fellowship," 1963, Box 3, Folder 18, VWP. The CBMCI used the terminology of the day, referring to Sri Lanka as Ceylon and Taiwan as Formosa. T. E. McCully to Former Directors, May 6, 1959, Box 3, Folder 13, VWP.

59. "Downey Dairy Owner Isaac Shakarian Dies," *Los Angeles Times*, November 8, 1964, A-2; Ed Ainsworth, "A Lot of Faith: A Lot of Cows," *Los Angeles Times*, May 8, 1960, I-19; "Old-Fashioned Revival Tent Series to Begin," *Los Angeles Times*, September 3, 1949, A-3.

60. "Revivalist Oral Roberts Due Here in September," *Los Angeles Times*, July 21, 1951, A-3; David Edwin Harrell Jr., *All Things Are Possible: The Healing and Charismatic Revivals in Modern America* (Bloomington: Indiana University Press, 1975), 146–149; J. R. Zeigler, "Full Gospel Business Men's Fellowship International," in Stanley M. Burgess and Eduard M. Van der Maas, eds., *The New International Dictionary of Pentecostal and Charismatic Movements*, rev ed. (Grand Rapids, MI: Zondervan, 2002), 653–654; Demos Shakarian with John and Elizabeth Sherrill, *The Happiest People on Earth* (Old Tappan, NJ: Fleming H. Revell, 1975), 118–119, FPC.

61. Several key figures in the "prosperity gospel" movement within Pentecostalism certainly knew about the FGBMFI. An early member in the FGBMFI, prosperity preacher Kenneth Hagin met John Osteen—the father of later prosperity preacher Joel Osteen—at a meeting in the 1960s, exchanging ideas and developing a friendship that lasted for three decades. Thanks to Phil Sinitiere for this tip. *Full Gospel Men's Voice*, February, 1953, 1–13, FPC.

62. Ibid.

63. Harrell, *All Things Are Possible*, 147.

64. R. Marie Griffith, "A 'Network of Praying Women': Women's Aglow Fellowship and Mainline American Protestantism," in Edith L. Blumhofer, Russell P. Spittler, and Grant A. Wacker, eds., *Pentecostal Currents in American Protestantism* (Urbana: University of Illinois Press, 1999), 135–136; Walter J. Hollenweger, *The Pentecostals* (Minneapolis: Augsburg, 1972), 6–7, quoted in Harrell, *All Things Are Possible*, 146–148; Shakarian et al., *The Happiest People on Earth*, 9; Dochuk, *From Bible Belt to Sunbelt*, 343.

65. *A Manual for Young Life Staff* (n.d.), A-4, A-5, Box 493, Folder "Young Life," FFR; Evon Hedley to Herbert J. Taylor, September 24, 1958, Box 72, Folder 6, HJT.

66. "Special July 4th Features! A Day Filled with Inspiration and Blessing," Box 72, Folder 6, HJT; "Some Basic Program-Points for a United Evangelical Front," (n.d., but probably 1948), 1–2, Box 72, Folder 4, HJT; "A Good Business Investment: Youth for Christ 'World' Program, 1962 Budget, $227,469.00," Box 72, Folder 19, HJT.

67. Turner, *Bill Bright and Campus Crusade for Christ*, 107–112; Kenneth L. Woodward, with John Barnes and Laurie Lisle, "Born Again!" *Newsweek*, October 25, 1976, 76, 78.

68. Turner, *Bill Bright and Campus Crusade for Christ*, 107–112, 176.

69. L. Edward Hicks, "*Sometimes in the Wrong, but Never in Doubt*": *George S. Benson and the Education of the New Religious Right* (Knoxville: University of Tennessee Press, 1994), 21–22, 30, 45–46, 57, 65–68, 72, 77; Harold V. Knight, "Whooping It Up for Adam Smith," *The Nation*, August 2, 1952, 87–89; Mark Sherwin, *The Extremists* (New York: St. Martin's Press, 1963), 96–99; Also see Lori Lyn Bogle, *The Pentagon's Battle for the American Mind: The Early Cold War* (College Station: Texas A&M University Press, 2004), 151–152; George Thayer, *The Farther Shores of Politics: The American Political Fringe Today* (New York: Simon & Schuster, 1967), 274.

70. Elected officials educated at Bob Jones University include Alan Cropsey, a Michigan state senator; Glenn Hamilton, a member of the South Carolina House of Representatives; Daniel Verdin, a South Carolina state senator; Terry Haskins, former Speaker Pro Tempore of the South Carolina House of Representatives; Tim Hutchinson, a former US Senator from Arkansas; and Asa Hutchinson, a former US Representative and member of the Department of Homeland Security. A complete list would be much too lengthy, but some of the more important pastors include Ed Dobson, former pastor of Calvary Church, Grand Rapids, Michigan; David Hocking, former pastor of Calvary Church of Santa Ana, California and

director of Hope for Today Ministries; Billy Kim, past president of Baptist World Alliance; David Stertzbach, pastor of Trinity Baptist Church in Williston, Vermont, and founder of Vermont Defense of Marriage Committee; Ken Hay, founder of The Wilds Christian Camps.

71. Mark Taylor Dalhouse, *An Island in a Lake of Fire: Bob Jones University, Fundamentalism, and the Separatist Movement* (Athens: University of Georgia Press, 1996), 131; Archie Vernon Huff, *Greenville: The History of the City and County in the South Carolina Piedmont* (Columbia: University of South Carolina Press, 1995), 398.

72. "George Pepperdine, Founder of College," *The New York Times*, August 1, 1962, 31; Audrey Gardner, "A Brief History of Pepperdine College," (MA thesis, Pepperdine College, 1968), 34–45; Candace Denise Jones, "White Flight?: George Pepperdine College's Move to Malibu, 1965–1972" (MA thesis, Pepperdine University, 2003); Dochuk, *From Bible Belt to Sunbelt*, 51–54, 66–74, 218, 322; "College Dedicated at Pepperdine U," *Los Angeles Times*, April 21, 1975, I–21; ; "Petrogrants," *Newsweek*, July 4, 1977, 75–76; James R. Wilborn, "The Importance of Corporate Support," *Pepperdine People Magazine*, Winter 1981; Jerry Rushford, ed., *Crest of a Golden Wave: Pepperdine University, 1937–1987* (Los Angeles: Pepperdine University Press, 1987), 213. Thanks to Darren Dochuk for providing copies of materials or notes summarizing the archival materials at Pepperdine.

Chapter 4

1. "Chick-fil-A Inc.," in *Telephone Directory, Greater Atlanta, GA, White Pages* (Atlanta: Southern Bell Telephone and Telegraph Company, 1976, 1986), n.p.; Report, Borden D. Dent, "Trade Area Analysis of Atlanta's Regional Shopping Centers" (Atlanta: Department of Geography, Georgia State University, 1978), 18–19, 31–32, 34–50, UGA; Report, "Shopping Centers" (Atlanta: *Atlanta Journal-Constitution*, 1978) 46–47, 51, 53, UGA; S. Truett Cathy, *Eat Mor Chikin: Inspire More People* (Decatur, GA: Looking Glass Books, 2002), 118; Teri Peitso, "King of the Malls," *Business Atlanta*, February 1986, 28, 38.

2. S. Truett Cathy, *It's Easier to Succeed Than to Fail* (Nashville: Thomas Nelson, 1989), 69–70, 78.

3. "The Law," Equal Employment Opportunity Commission, http://www.eeoc.gov/eeoc/history/35th/thelaw/civil_rights_act.html. On the 1972 amendments, see http://www.eeoc.gov/eeoc/history/35th/thelaw/eeo_1972.html.

4. MacLean, *Freedom Is Not Enough*, 35–113.

5. For total claims of racial discrimination to the EEOC, see ibid., 76. By 1984, religious discrimination had bumped up to 2.4 percent of total claims. Jews and Seventh-Day Adventists brought nearly half of all claims. Gloria T. Beckley and Paul Burstein, "Religious Pluralism, Equal Opportunity, and the State," *The Western Political Quarterly* 44.1 (March 1991): 188–190.

6. Susannah P. Mroz, "True Believers? Problems of Definition in Title VII Religious Discrimination Jurisprudence," *Indiana Law Review* 39 (2005–2006): 146–147.

7. Ibid., 147–148; Robert J. Friedman, "Religious Discrimination in the Workplace: The Persistent Polarized Struggle," *Transactions: The Tennessee Journal of Business Law* 11.2 (2010): 148–149.

8. Raymond F. Gregory, *Encountering Religion in the Workplace: The Legal Rights and Responsibilities of Workers and Employers* (Ithaca, NY: Cornell University Press, 2011), 64–65; David L. Gregory, "Religion in the Workplace," in Paul Finkelman, ed., *The Encyclopedia of American Civil Liberties* (New York: Routledge, 2006), 1299–1303; Friedman, "Religious Discrimination in the Workplace," 155–157; Beckley and Burstein, "Religious Pluralism, Opportunity, and the State," 198–200.

9. Sehat, *The Myth of American Religious Freedom*, 249–250; Kruse, *One Nation Under God*, 165–201; Williams, *God's Own Party*, 111–120; Andrew Hartman, *A War for the Soul of America: A History of the Culture Wars* (Chicago: University of Chicago Press, 2015), 1–8, 78–79, 87–92, 203–208.

10. Cathy, *It's Easier to Succeed*, 52–67; Cathy, *Eat Mor Chikin*, 75–79; "Chick-fil-A Growing Strong," *Athens Banner-Herald*, February 15, 1981, 8-C; Pamphlet, "Creating the Original Chick-fil-A Sandwich," in author's possession.

11. On economic losses and gains in the Atlanta metropolitan area from the 1970s to the 1990s, see Larry Keating, *Atlanta: Race, Class, and Urban Expansion* (Philadelphia: Temple

University, 2001), 7–40; Robert D. Bullard, Glenn S. Johnson, and Angel O. Torres, "Dismantling Transportation Apartheid: The Quest for Equity" and Charles Jaret, Elizabeth P. Ruddiman, and Kurt Phillips, "The Legacy of Residential Segregation," in Robert D. Bullard, Glenn S. Johnson, and Angel O. Torres, eds., *Sprawl City: Race, Politics, and Planning in Atlanta* (Washington, DC: Island Press, 2000), esp. 52–53, 128–131; Kevin M. Kruse, *White Flight: Atlanta and the Making of Modern Conservatism* (Princeton, NJ: Princeton University Press, 2005), 234–235, 243–245.

12. Peitso, "King of the Malls," 28; *Fulton County Review*, August 2, 1940, 4. Hapeville was actually closer to 99 percent white in the 1940s and 1950s. *Sixteenth Census of the United States: 1940*, vol. II, no. 2 (Florida–Iowa), Table 30, 359; *Seventeenth Census of the United States: 1950*, vol. II, pt. 11 (Georgia), Table 39, 11–84; *Eighteenth Census of the United States: 1960*, vol. 1, pt. 12 (Georgia), Table 21, 12–62.

13. Jason Sokol, *There Goes My Everything: White Southerners in the Age of Civil Rights, 1945–1975* (New York: Knopf, 2006), 182–187, 231–237. On intracity fractures created during the civil rights era and the multiple political and rhetorical conceptions of "white flight," see Kruse, *White Flight*.

14. "A Study of Greenbriar Mall in Metropolitan Atlanta" (Atlanta: The Atlanta Journal and Constitution Research and Marketing Department, 1973), 5, 8–10, 16, UGA; Cathy, *Eat Mor Chikin*, 84–86.

15. Roger Ricklefs, "Christian-Based Firms Find Following Christian Principles Pays," *The Wall Street Journal*, December 8, 1989, B-2; Cathy, *It's Easier to Succeed*, 153–159; John W. White, *The Great Yellow Fleet* (San Marino: Golden West Books, 1986); Wayne King, "A Taste for Profits," *The New York Times*, June 16, 1974, 149; "What Makes Rossi Run?" *Forbes*, November 15, 1971, 50–51; "Beatrice Foods: Adding Tropicana for a Broader Nationwide Network," *Business Week*, May 15, 1978, 114–116; Dale White, "Juice King Revolutionized Industry," *Sarasota Herald-Tribune*, February 22, 1999, 1-B. For a hagiographic treatment of Rossi, see Sanna Barlow Rossi, *Anthony T. Rossi, Christian and Entrepreneur: The Story of the Founder of Tropicana* (Downers Grove, IL: Intervarsity Press, 1986).

16. William Kaszynski, *The American Highway: The History and Culture of Roads in the United States* (Jefferson, NC: McFarland, 2000), 156–159; Kenneth Jackson, *Crabgrass Frontier: The Suburbanization of the United States* (New York: Oxford University Press, 1985), 253–255.

17. Walton was not related to Sam Walton, the founder of Wal-Mart. William B. Walton and Mel Lorentzen, *Innkeeper* (Wheaton, IL: Tyndale House, 1987), 122. Lorentzen was a professor at Wheaton and associate director of the Billy Graham Center at the college at the time of publication. Walton, like many evangelical businessmen before him, counted Graham as a friend, spiritual mentor, and professional inspiration. On the back of the first edition, Graham commended Walton's "courageous moral stands . . . in secular business, even though it was very costly to [Walton] personally."

18. Ibid., 149–171.

19. M. Howard Gelfand, "Growing ServiceMaster Industries Inc. Thrives by Calling on God and Hospitals," *The Wall Street Journal*, January 23, 1973, 14; Solomon, *Evangelical Christian Executives*, 61, 63–65; Ted Gregory, "Kenneth T. Wessner, 71, Ex-Chief of ServiceMaster," *Chicago Tribune*, April 1, 1994, http://articles.chicagotribune.com/1994-04-01/news/9404010105_1_wheaton-college-professional-boards-chief.

20. Solomon, *Evangelical Christian Executives*, 68–72; C. William Pollard, *The Soul of the Firm* (Grand Rapids, MI: Zondervan, 1996), 20–21.

21. William J. Ventura II, "The Personal Values Communicated by Truett Cathy and Their Effect on the Culture of Chick-fil-A: A Quantitative Case Study" (PhD dissertation, Regent University, 2006), 99.

22. Cathy, *It's Easier to Succeed*, 135–143.

23. For earlier iterations of the "family" motif in corporate management, see Julie Kimmel, *The Corporation as Family: The Gendering of Corporate Welfare, 1880–1920* (Chapel Hill: University of North Carolina Press, 2002).

24. Cathy, *Eat Mor Chikin*, 111; Cathy, *It's Easier to Succeed*, 161, 133; Lewis Grizzard, "Chicken Man," *Atlanta Journal/Atlanta Constitution, Atlanta Weekly*, November 28, 1982, 62–66; Marc Rice, "Chick-fil-A Founder Uses Spiritual Principles in Business, Personal Life," *Athens Daily*

News, September 23, 1991, 4-A; Diana West, "Profile: Pioneer Restauranteur Services Big Helpings of Scholarships, Too," *The Rotarian*, July, 1997, 50.

25. Cecil Burke Day Jr. and John McCollister, *Day by Day: The Story of Cecil B. Day and His Simple Formula for Success* (New York: Jonathan David, 1990), 23–29, 73–86, back cover.

26. Deen Day Sanders, interview transcript, May 27, 2008, in author's possession; Day and McCollister, *Day by Day*, 74–76; Edward J. White, Jr., interview, July 9, 2008, in author's possession. Day also engaged in a variety of humanitarian efforts, including "prison ministries or senior citizens or children or youth or . . . youth detention, halfway houses, [and] inner city things." Flexibility existed among certain evangelical businessmen and women about the application of evangelical tenets to corporate life, resulting in genuinely beneficial—and admirable—forms of philanthropy. These socially conscious "exceptions" (if they can be termed that) often proved the rule, namely these entrepreneurs' disdain for state-based solutions to pervasive social or familial problems.

27. Solomon, *Evangelical Christian Executives*, 90–91, 93, 102–103; Kathryn Lofton, "The Spirit in the Cubicle: A Religious History of the American Office," in Sally Promey, ed., *Sensational Religion: Sense and Contention in Material Practice* (New Haven, CT: Yale University Press, 2014), 135–158.

28. Solomon, *Evangelical Christian Executives*, 25–27, 98; Moreton, *To Serve God and Wal-Mart*, 107–111.

29. West, "Profile," 50.

30. Solomon, *Evangelical Christian Executives*, 102–103, 109–111, 97; Laura L. Nash, *Believers in Business* (Nashville: Thomas Nelson, 1994), 262.

31. "Reell Precision Manufacturing, Inc: A Matter of Direction," in Kenneth E. Goodpaster and Laura L. Nash, eds., *Policies and Persons: A Casebook in Business Ethics*, 3rd ed. (New York: McGraw Hill, 1998), 135–150.

32. Clipping, John P. Moody, "Religion Plays Role in Labor Relations at Glassport Firm," *Post-Gazette Daily Magazine*, May 30, 1973, n.p., Box 585, Folder 4, FFR; Clipping, "Glassport Exec Gives Prayer Plan to Ford," *Pittsburgh Post-Gazette*, October 10, 1974, 12, Box 586, Folder 2, FFR; Clipping, Edward Verlich, "Bible Produces at Pittron, Ford Told," *The Pittsburgh Press*, October 20, 1974, 1-C, Box 586, Folder 2, FFR; Wayne T. Alderson to Gerald R. Ford, October 4, 1974, Box C4, Folder "Presidential Handwriting, 10/4/1974," http://www.fordlibrarymuseum.gov/library/document/0047/phw19741004-04.pdf.

33. Keith Haddock, *Bucyrus: Making the Earth Move for 125 Years* (St. Paul, MN: MBI, 2005), 47–52; Alex Zimmerman, "Obituary: Wayne Alderson, Made Career Helping People See the Value in One Another," *Pittsburgh Post-Gazette*, February 24, 2013, http://www.post-gazette.com/news/obituaries/2013/02/24/Obituary-Wayne-Alderson-Made-career-helping-people-see-the-value-in-one-another/stories/201302240351; R. C. Sproul, *Stronger Than Steel: The Wayne Alderson Story* (New York: Harper & Row, 1980); John Stott, *Our Social and Sexual Revolution: Major Issues for the Next Century* (New York: Baker, 1999), 40; Tony Campolo, *Wake Up, America!: Answering God's Radical Call While Living in the Real World* (New York: HarperCollins, 1991), 69–72; Charles Colson and Jack Eckerd, *Why America Doesn't Work* (Dallas: Word, 1991), 136; Zig Ziglar, *God's Way Is Still the Best Way* (Nashville: Thomas Nelson, 2007), 34–38.

34. Solomon, *Evangelical Christian Executives*, 11–12, 124–135; Norm Miller, *Beyond the Norm* (Nashville: Thomas Nelson, 1996); Dan McGraw, "The Christian Capitalists," *US News & World Report*, March 13, 1995, 53.

35. James Robison, "Jews Assail 'Christian Yellow Pages,'" *Chicago Tribune*, March 13, 1977, 4; *Christian Yellow Pages—Dallas Area* (December 1976), 4–9, 17, 22, 25, DPL; *Christian Yellow Pages—Dallas Area* (December, 1977–1978), 4–7, 10–13, 20–25, DPL.

36. Pam Belluck, "Drivers Find New Service at Truck Stops: Old-Time Religion," *New York Times*, February 1, 1998, 1-1; Erika Duckworth, "A Deep Faith Drives Family and Its Trucking Company," *St. Petersburg Times*, April 3, 1994, 1-H.

37. *Christian Yellow Pages—Dallas Area* (December, 1977–1978), 3, 26, DPL.

38. Aubrey B. Haines, "Buying 'Christian,'" *The Christian Century*, September 21, 1977, 804–805; "The CYP Concept," *Christian Yellow Pages—Dallas Area* (December, 1976), 3, DPL; Janis Johnson, "'Christian Yellow Pages' Under Fire," *The Washington Post*, February 25, 1977, D-14.

39. "Christian Directory Is Sued," *Merced Sun-Star*, August 24, 1977, 12; "'Christian-Only' Ads Charged With Bias," *The New York Times*, September 7, 1977, 36; Russell Chandler, "Business Directory Drops Religious Ban," *Los Angeles Times*, November 22, 1977, D-1, D-8; David M. Ludington, "A Study of the Christian Yellow Pages as an Advertising Tool for Small Businesses" (Mt. Berry, GA: Berry College, 1990), n.p., in author's possession; "Christian Yellow Pages Loses a Round Over Ads," *The Wall Street Journal*, October 1, 1984, 1; Steve Maynard, "All in the Family," *Houston Chronicle*, January 18, 1986, 3; Tammerlin Drummond, "In God We Advertise," *Los Angeles Times*, July 29, 1992, 2.

40. Ricklefs, "Christian-Based Firms Find Following Christian Principles Pays," B-1, B-2.

41. Nabil A. Ibrahim, Leslie W. Rue, Patricia P. McDougall, and G. Robert Greene, "Characteristics and Practices of 'Christian-Based' Companies," *Journal of Business Ethics* 10.2 (February 1991): 123–132; quote on 128; Lambert III, *Spirituality, Inc.*, 55–56; Ricklefs, "Christian-Based Firms Find Following Christian Principles Pays," B-2.

42. Ricklefs, "Christian-Based Firms Find Following Christian Principles Pays," B-2.

43. Ibid., B-1, B-2; McGraw, "The Christian Capitalists," 54, cited in Shirley J. Roels, "The Business Ethics of Evangelicals," *Business Ethics Quarterly* 7.2 (March 1997): 111–112; Ibrahim et al., "Characteristics and Practices of 'Christian-Based' Companies," 125.

44. Arthur Asa Berger, *Shop 'til You Drop: Consumer Behavior and American Culture* (Lanham, MD: Rowman & Littlefield, 2005), 100–101; Jim Osterman, "Chick-fil-A Hops into Easter with 'Taste' Promotion," *Adweek*, Southeast Edition, March 30, 1987, 6; "Chick-fil-A Cranks Up Expansion," *Atlanta Constitution*, February 13, 1993, C-2.

45. On urban space as "queer" or "deviant," see George Chauncey, *Gay New York: Gender, Urban Culture, and the Making of the Gay Male World, 1890–1940* (New York: Basic Books, 1995). In a later period, on suburban environs as "heterosexual" or "normative," see Clayton Howard, "The Closet and the Cul du Sac: Sex, Politics and Suburbanization in Postwar California" (PhD dissertation, University of Michigan, 2010) and, to a lesser extent, Karen Tongson, *Relocations: Queer Suburban Imaginaries* (New York: New York University Press, 2011).

46. Cathy, *Eat Mor Chikin*, 134–139; Ventura, "The Personal Values Communicated by Truett Cathy," 94–95; "Move Over, Colonel Sanders: The Chick-fil-A Fast Food Empire Espouses Christian Principles," *Canadian Business and Current Affairs, Western Report*, October 10, 1994, n.p.; Ouida Dickey and Doyle Mathis, *Berry College: A History* (Athens: University of Georgia Press, 2005). By the late 1990s, the WinShape campus at Berry had added the WinShape Wilderness program to create "adventure experiences that encourage spiritual transformation."

47. Cathy, *It's Easier to Succeed*, 81–82, 93; WinShape affirmed the work of Life Innovations, Inc., which published regular research reports on the benefits of companies supporting "marriage and family wellness." See, for instance, Report, Matthew D. Turvey and David H. Olson, "Marriage & Family Wellness: Corporate America's Business?" (Minneapolis: Life Innovations, Inc., 2006).

48. Sharon Jayson, "Chick-fil-A Offers Marital Advice on the Side," *USA Today*, June 22, 2006, 1-D; On WinShape Marriage's programs, see http://www.winshape.org/marriage/.

49. "Be Your Own Boss," *The Wall Street Journal*, November 19, 1987, 39; Cathy, *It's Easier to Succeed*, 135–143, 126–131, 160; Cathy, *Eat Mor Chikin*, 97–100; Renee Gibson, "Chick-fil-A Chief at Home in Rome," *Rome News-Tribune*, April 17, 1989, 4; Nancy J. White, "Truett Cathy Helps the Lord Run Chick-fil-A," *Atlanta Constitution*, May 30, 1985, 1-C, 7-C.

50. Cathy, *It's Easier to Succeed*, 127; "Chick-fil-A: Not Just Chicken Feed," *Incentive*, January 1989, 24.

51. "Chicken Chain Won't Hire Men with Earrings," *The Associated Press State and Local Wire*, February 2, 2000, n.p.

52. Robert J. Grossman, "Home Is Where the School Is," *HR Magazine*, November 2001, 58–65; Nahal Toosi, "Atlanta-Based Chick-fil-A Chain Seeks Home-School Students as Employees," *Knight-Ridder/Tribune Business News*, August 8, 1998, http://www.accessmylibrary.com/coms2/summary_0286-5591332_ITM.

53. "Chick-fil-A: Not Just Chicken Feed," 24; Frederick F. Reichheld, *Loyalty Rules: How Today's Business Leaders Build Lasting Relationships* (Cambridge, MA: Harvard Business Press, 2001), 78.

54. Jan Jarboe, "What Does H.E.B. Stand For, Anyway?" *Texas Monthly*, April 1988, 158–159; Dana Scarton, "Schools Display Mixed Reaction to ServiceMaster," *The Pittsburg Press*, September 1, 1984, W10; Ted Goldman, "School Issue Focuses on Public vs. Private," *St. Petersburg Times—Hernando Times*, March 25, 1991, 1; Collins Conner, "Union Takes On School Privatization," *Hernando Times*, May 6, 1991, 1; Michael Powell and Vernon Loeb, "School Contractor Demands More Pay," *The Washington Post*, November 19, 1996, B-06.

55. Robert Bryce, "Not Clucking Around," *The Austin Chronicle*, November 3, 2000, http://www.austinchronicle.com/news/2000-11-03/79226/.

56. Ibid.; Harris Collingwood, "These Campaign Gifts Ain't Chicken Feed," *Business Week*, July 24, 1989, 27; "Texas Businessman Hands Out $10,000 Checks in State Senate," *The New York Times*, July 9, 1989, 23; Roberto Suro, "Lobbying Becomes Bolder in Texas," *The New York Times*, July 23, 1989, 18.

57. In 1999, Pilgrim dumped over 3 million gallons of wastewater each day into a creek near one of his factories in east Texas, drawing pause from the Texas Natural Resources Conservation Commission, which was considering a permit request from Pilgrim to double his processing capacity and, presumably, his environmental impact. Still, Danny Crooks, a judge who lived in a county transformed by a Pilgrim plant, thought such environmental drawbacks did not outweigh the economic benefits the company brought to his community. "When you smell that [smell]," he claimed, "it smells like money." Bryce, "Not Clucking Around"; Carol Countryman, "Shame of Pilgrim's Pride," *The Progressive*, August 1994, 11; Christopher Helman, "Fowl Play," *Forbes*, February 11, 2008, 42, 44.

58. Steve Striffler, *Chicken: The Dangerous Transformation of America's Favorite Food* (New Haven, CT: Yale University Press, 2005), 15–71; Ling Li, *Supply Chain Management: Concepts, Techniques, and Practices* (Singapore: World Scientific, 2007), 296–297.

59. Perdue Farms and Wayne Farms, of course, were not the only companies to do this. For a fuller account on the connections between industrial food and immigration, see Leon Fink, *The Maya of Morganton: Work and Community in the Nuevo New South* (Chapel Hill: University of North Carolina Press, 2003).

60. Julie Ardery, "Mayberry Shake-Up: Economic and Ethnic Change Comes to Surry County, North Carolina," *Reports on Rural America* 1.1 (2006): 18; Shelly Howell, "News Shorts," *Meat Processing*, September 28, 2004, http://www.meatnews.com/index.cfm?fuseaction=article&artNum=8262; "OSHA Cites Alabama Poultry Processor Following Fatal Accident, Agency Proposes $59,500 in Penalties" OSHA Region 4 News Release Number: 04-1853-ATL 206 (2004), http://www.osha.gov/pls/oshaweb/owadisp.show_document?p_table=NEWS_RELEASES&p_id=11036; Ahmed El Amin, "Top Poultry Processors Faulted for High Salmonella Rates," *Food Production Daily*, July 6, 2006, http://www.foodproduction-daily.com/Quality-Safety/Top-poultry-processors-faulted-for-high-Salmonella-rates; Ann Bagel, "All Things Unequal," *Poultry*, October/November 2005, 36.

61. Client list and quote from http://en.wikipedia.org/wiki/Wayne_Farms and http://www.foodprocessing-technology.com/projects/wayne/; "Chick-fil-A Tops Its Own Sales Record, Despite Economic Crisis," *QSR Magazine*, January 29, 2009, http://www.qsrmagazine.com/articles/news/story.phtml?id=7982; Giannina Smith, "Chicken Fight: McDonald's Looks to Challenge Chick-fil-A," *St. Louis Business Journal*, May 13, 2008, http://www.bizjournals.com/stlouis/stories/2008/05/12/daily33.html; "Not All Businesses Suffering: Christian-Owned Chick-fil-A Profits Up in 2008," *Black Christian News*, February 7, 2009, http://www.blackchristiannews.com/news/2009/02/not-all-businesses-suffering-chick-fil-a-profits-up-in-2008.html.

62. The evangelical executives for each of the listed companies were, respectively, Elmer Johnson, Jim Beré, Dick Crowell, Thomas Phillips, Jerry Dempsey, Charles Olcott, Dave Thomas, Jack Eckerd, Alvah Chapman, Jack Willome, Bob Buford, Rich Snyder, Allen Morris, John C. Snyder, Jack Turpin, Ed Yates, William H. Rentschler, Jim Carreker, Ed Williamson, Steven Reinmund, Joe Martin, W. Robert Stover, David V. Cavan, Dick Capen, Christopher A. Crane, Neal Clark Warren, Bob Reese, David Green, James Leininger, John F. Baugh, Do Won Chang, and David Steward. Of these evangelical executives, all are white males, except Do Won Chang and David Steward. For interviews with several of these business executives, see Laura L. Nash, *Believers in Business* (Nashville: Thomas Nelson, 1994) and Kenneth E. Goodpaster and Laura

L. Nash, eds., *Policies and Persons: A Casebook in Business Ethics*, 3rd ed. (New York: McGraw-Hill, 1998), 135–150; Merrill J. Oster and Mike Hamel, *The Entrepreneur's Creed: The Principles and Passions of 20 Successful Entrepreneurs* (Nashville: Broadman and Holman, 2001); "The Ins and Outs of In-N-Out," March 6, 2006, http://www.gilroydispatch.com/printer/article.asp?c=180266; R. G. Ratcliffe, "Conservative Liberal With His Offerings," *Houston Chronicle*, September 21, 1997, 1-A, 21-A; McGraw, "The Christian Capitalists," 53–62; Matthew Myers, "CEO Profile of David Green," *Revenue Generators*, September 2004, 4–5; David Steward and Robert L. Shook, *Doing Business by the Good Book* (New York: Hyperion, 2004); Lindsay, *Faith in the Halls of Power.*

Chapter 5

1. Heritage Village Church, *Jim and Tammy Bakker Present the Ministries of Heritage Village Church* (Toronto: Boulton, 1986), FPC; Thomas C. O'Guinn and Russell K. Belk, "Heaven on Earth: Consumption at Heritage Village, USA," *The Journal of Consumer Research* 16 (September 1989): 227, 235; William E. Schmidt, "TV Minister Calls His Resort 'Bait' for Christianity," *The New York Times*, December 25, 1985, A-8; William Cran and Stephanie Tepper, *Praise the Lord*, Frontline, video recording (New York: Network Features, 1987), UGA; Kenneth L. Woodward, "A Disneyland for the Devout," *Newsweek*, August 11, 1986, 46–47; Charles E. Shepard, *Forgiven: The Rise and Fall of Jim Bakker and the PTL Ministry* (New York: Atlantic Monthly Press, 1989), 254–256, 291–292.
2. P.J. O'Rourke, *Holidays in Hell* (New York: Atlantic Monthly Press, 1988), 93; Hunter James, *Smile Pretty and Say Jesus: The Last Great Days of PTL* (Athens: University of Georgia Press, 1993), 14.
3. Such a switch to consumption as political expression was hardly particular to evangelical conservatives. See Lizabeth Cohen, *A Consumers' Republic: The Politics of Mass Consumption in Postwar America* (New York: Knopf, 2003).
4. Jeffrey K. Hadden and Charles E. Swann, *Prime Time Preachers: The Rising Power of Televangelism* (Reading, MA: Addison-Wesley, 1981), 77–78; Jeffrey Shandler, *Jews, God, and Videotape: Religion and Media in America* (New York: New York University Press, 2009), 63.
5. Dochuk, "Moving Mountains," 79; Hadden and Swann, *Prime Time Preachers*, 78–81.
6. Hadden and Swann, *Prime Time Preachers*, 82–83, 17–27, 29–32; McGirr, *Suburban Warriors*, 105–107, 249–254.
7. Williams, *God's Own Party*, 17; Sara Diamond, *Roads to Dominion: Right-wing Movements and Political Power in the United States* (New York: The Guilford Press, 1995), 97–98; "FCC Enforcing 'Fairness Doctrine,'" *Christianity Today*, February 28, 1964, 43; "Should the Critics Be Stifled?" *Christianity Today*, December 8, 1967, 29–30; Hendershot, *What's Fair on the Air*, 137–169.
8. Peter Horsfield, *Religious Television: An American Experience* (New York: Longman, 1984), 8– 10, 22; Jeffrey K. Hadden, "The Rise and Fall of American Televangelism," *Annals of the American Academy of Political and Social Science*, May 1993, 118; Louis Gorfain, "Pray TV," *New York*, October 6, 1980, 48; Hadden and Swann, *Prime Time Preachers*, 81; Broadcast Institute of North America, "Religious Programming on Television: An Analysis of a Sample Week" (1973).
9. Horsfield, *Religious Television*, 10; Hadden, "The Rise and Fall of American Televangelism," 123.
10. Ralph Clark Chandler, "The Fundamentalist Heritage of the New Christian Right," in David G. Bronson and Anson Shupe, eds., *New Christian Politics* (Macon, GA: Mercer University Press, 1984), 56–57; Razelle Frankl and J. K. Hadden, "A Critical Review of the Religion and Television Research Report," *Review of Religious Research* 28 (1987): 111–124.
11. Larry Martz and Ginny Carroll, *Ministry of Greed: The Inside Story of the Televangelists and Their Holy Wars* (New York: Newsweek, 1988).
12. Hadden and Swann, *Prime Time Preachers*, 123–124.
13. Mary Mitchell, "Biggest Bargain Family Vacation in Dixieland," *Saturday Evening Post*, May–June 1982, 78; Andrew Kopkind, "Jim Bakker's Lost America," *Esquire*, December 1987,

175–183; Woodward, "A Disneyland for the Devout," 46–47; Kathy English, "At Heritage USA It's Pray and Play," *Toronto Star*, April 5, 1987, 8-A; James A. Albert, *Jim Bakker: Miscarriage of Justice?* (Chicago: Open Court, 1998), 30.

14. Harry Genet, "PTL: Please Toss a Lifesaver," *Christianity Today*, December 15, 1978, 41.

15. Megan Rosenfeld, "Heritage USA and the Heavenly Vacation; South Carolina Theme Park Caters to Born-Again Christians," *Washington Post*, June 15, 1986, H1; Albert, *Jim Bakker*, 35–36.

16. Albert, *Jim Bakker*, 390; Shepard, *Forgiven*, 240; Schmidt, "TV Minister Calls His Resort 'Bait' for Christianity," A8.

17. Mitchell, "Biggest Bargain Family Vacation in Dixieland," 78–81; Martha Fay, "God's Country," *Life*, August 1987, 87; Woodward, "A Disneyland for the Devout," 47; "Fun and Games for Bible-Thumpers," *The Economist*, October 19, 1985, 29.

18. Rosenfeld, "Heritage USA and the Heavenly Vacation," H1, H8.

19. Anne L. Borden, "Making Money, Saving Souls: Christian Bookstores and the Commodification of Christianity," in Lynn Schofield Clark, ed., *Religion, Media, and the Marketplace* (New Brunswick, NJ: Rutgers University Press, 2007), 68, 71–72; Jan Blodgett, *Protestant Evangelical Literary Culture and Contemporary Society* (Westport, CT: Greenwood Press, 1997), 52; Howard E. Butt Jr., "Business, Books, and Christians," paper presented at the CBA Annual Convention, July 16, 1973, 2–3, 9–11, Box 18, Folder 38, CTR.

20. On African American Christian bookstores and their connections to gospel music, see Birgetta Joelisa Johnson, "'O, For a Thousand Tongues to Sing': Music and Worship in African American Megachurches of Los Angeles, California" (PhD dissertation, University of California, Los Angeles, 2008), 244–245. Although it is difficult to determine how much racial matters shaped its foundation, the African American Christian Booksellers Association incorporated in 1994 as an entity separate—but at times overlapping—with the historically and majority white CBA.

21. McDannell, *Material Christianity*, 246–247, 259; Carol Flake, *Redemptorama: Culture, Politics, and the New Evangelicalism* (New York: Penguin Books, 1984), 152–166; Paul Boyer, "Back to the Future: Contemporary American Evangelicalism in Cultural and Historical Perspective" in Alex A. Schäfer, ed., *American Evangelicals in the 1960s* (Madison: University of Wisconsin Press, 2013), 17–36.

22. Daniel Wojcik, *The End of the World as We Know It: Faith, Fatalism, and Apocalypse in America* (New York: New York University Press, 1997), 46; Glenn W. Shuck, *Marks of the Beast: The Left Behind Novels and the Struggle for Evangelical Identity* (New York: New York University Press, 2005), 5, 37–41; Boyer, *When Time Shall Be No More*, 5, 126–140.

23. "Don v. Devil," *Time*, September 8, 1947, 65–74; David Van Biema, "Beyond the Wardrobe," *Time*, November 7, 2005, 111; "C. S. Lewis Goes Marching On," *Time*, December 5, 1977, 92; Bob Smietana, "C. S. Lewis Superstar," *Christianity Today*, December 2005, 28–32; Philip Graham Ryken, "Lewis as the Patron Saint of American Evangelicalism," in Judith Wolfe and Brendan N. Wolfe, eds., *C. S. Lewis and the Church: Essays in Honour of Walter Hooper* (London: T&T Clark, 2011), 174–185; "History of the Marion E. Wade Center," http://www.wheaton.edu/wadecenter/Welcome/History.

24. Randall Balmer, *Mine Eyes Have Seen the Glory: A Journey into the Evangelical Subculture in America*, 2nd ed. (New York: Oxford University Press, 1993), 196–199; Diego Ribadeneira, "From Dads to Students, There's a Bible for You," *The Boston Globe*, April 10, 1999, A-1; Murdoch made another move in 2011, buying evangelical publishing giant Thomas Nelson. See "HarperCollins to Acquire Thomas Nelson," *Publishers Weekly*, October 31, 2011, http://www.publishersweekly.com/pw/by-topic/industry-news/industry-deals/article/49334-harpercollins-to-acquire-thomas-nelson.html.

25. W. Maxey Jarman to Harold Lindsell, December 16, 1975, Box 26, Folder 10, CTR; W. Maxey Jarman to Harold Lindsell, October 17, 1975, Box 26, Folder 10, CTR; "Overview Committee Meeting Participants," November 17, 1975, Chicago, Illinois, Box 26, Folder 10, CTR; W. Maxey Jarman to Harold Lindsell, March 25, 1976, Box 26, Folder 10, CTR; Ribadeneira, "From Dads to Students, There's a Bible for You," A-1.

26. Mark Kellner, "Faith Sales Shift," *The Washington Times*, July 24, 2002, A-2.

27. David W. Stowe, *No Sympathy for the Devil: Christian Pop Music and the Transformation of American Evangelicalism* (Chapel Hill: University of North Carolina Press, 2011), 11–33; McGirr, *Suburban Warriors*, 243–244; Flake, *Redemptorama*, 172; Julian Wagner, "The New Rebel Cry: Jesus is Coming!" *Time*, June 21, 1971, 56–63.

28. Thomas Frank, *The Conquest of Cool: Business Culture, Counterculture, and the Rise of Hip Consumerism* (Chicago: University of Chicago Press, 1998); Joseph Heath and Andrew Potter, *Nation of Rebels: Why Counterculture Became Consumer Culture* (New York: HarperCollins, 2004); Grace Elizabeth Hale, *A Nation of Outsiders: How the White Middle Class Fell in Love with Rebellion in Postwar America* (New York: Oxford University Press, 2011).

29. Howard and Streck, *Apostles of Rock*, 30–31.

30. Stowe, *No Sympathy for the Devil*, 31, 34–57, 81–123, 137–149.

31. Ibid., 58–80, 142; Turner, *Bill Bright and Campus Crusade for Christ*, 138–144.

32. Stowe, *No Sympathy for the Devil*, 155; Andrew Beaujon, *Body Piercing Saved My Life: Inside the Phenomenon of Christian Rock* (Cambridge, MA: Da Capo Press, 2006), 24–26. Though a journalistic instead of scholarly account, Beaujon nevertheless conducted valuable interviews with a slew of industry insiders and originators.

33. This "separational" element in contemporary Christian music ran alongside other impulses, however, what Jay R. Howard and Jon M. Streck have aptly termed "integrational" and "transformational." In the former arrangement, Christian musicians attempted to penetrate the secular music market by blending secular musical stylings with Christian lyrics. In the latter arrangement, they attempted to use their music to change the broader culture, trying to bring it into alignment with evangelical moral and political tenets. See Howard and Streck, *Apostles of Rock*.

34. William D. Romanowski, "Evangelicals and Popular Music: The Contemporary Christian Music Industry," in Bruce David Forbes and Jeffrey H. Mahan, eds., *Religion and Popular Culture in America*, rev. ed. (Berkeley: University of California Press, 2005), 103–122; quote on 114.

35. Beaujon, *Body Piercing Saved My Life*, 26–28; Paul Baker, *Contemporary Christian Music: Where It Came From, What It Is, Where It's Going* (Westchester, IL: Crossway Books, 1985), 153–154; "Acquisitions, New HQ Noted at NRB Show," *Billboard*, February 20, 1999, 67–68.

36. Stowe, *No Sympathy for the Devil*, 247; Steven Holden, "Evangelical Pop a Hit of the Record Business," *The New York Times*, February 20, 1985, C-17; Baker, *Contemporary Christian Music*, 154–155.

37. Moira McCormick, "The A&M/Word Impact," *Billboard*, October 19, 1985, G-33; Howard and Streck, *Apostles of Rock*, 62; Beaujon, *Body Piercing Saved My Life*, 33, 37–43.

38. Joanne Brokaw, "3 Things You Need to Know About Christian Music and the Economy," Belief Blog, http://blog.beliefnet.com/gospelsoundcheck/2008/10/3-things-you-need-to-know-abou.html; "My Interview with Paul Baloches Busts the Myth of the Millionaire Musician," Belief Blog, http://www.beliefnet.com/columnists/gospelsoundcheck/2008/08/my-interview-with-paul-baloche.html.

39. Bob Lochte, *Christian Radio: The Growth of a Mainstream Broadcasting Force* (Jefferson, NC: McFarland, 2006), 10–12. Like Arbitron and other radio industry sources, Lochte counts "Christian, Contemporary Christian, Christian Hit Radio, Christian News/Talk, Gospel, Southern Gospel, Inspirational, and Religious" as "Christian Radio," although the subgenre with the greatest growth was non-gospel "Christian music."

40. Williams, *God's Own Party*, 235–236.

41. Lochte, *Christian Radio*, 9, 80–81.

42. Charles E. Shepard, "PTL's Bakker Rebuts News Reports of FCC Allegations," *Charlotte Observer*, February 1, 1986, 1-A, 6-A; Gary L. Wright, "Bakker, 3 Others Indicted," *Charlotte Observer*, December 6, 1988, 10A, 12-A–13-A; Richard N. Ostling, "Of God and Greed," *Time*, June 8, 1987, 70.

43. Beaujon, *Body Piercing Saved My Life*, 37; Carey, *Fortunes, Fiddles, and Fried Chicken*, 436.

44. Hendershot, *Shaking the World for Jesus*, 56; Howard and Streck, *Apostles of Rock*, 153. Global music sales are estimated annually by IFPI, a London-based market research group. In 2001 total sales in the United States equaled $13.4 billion, or almost 40 percent of world sales. See *The Recording Industry World Sales, 2001* (London: IFPI, 2002), 3, http://www.ifpi.org/content/library/worldsales2001.pdf.

Chapter 6

1. Michael Vitez, "He Delivers Hope," *The Philadelphia Inquirer*, November 17, 1995, A-1; Joe L. Kincheloe, "Zig Ziglar: Motivation, Education, and the New Right," *Vitae Scholasticae* 4 (1985): 203; Tom Van Riper, "At 80, Zig Ziglar Decides to Slow Down," *Forbes*, March 27, 2007, http://www.forbes.com/2007/03/27/zig-ziglar-retires-face-cx_tr_0327autofacescan01. html.
2. Zig Ziglar, *Confessions of a Happy Christian* (Gretna, LA: Pelican Publishing, 1980), 55.
3. Ibid., 55–57, 70–71; Kincheloe, "Zig Ziglar," 203.
4. Donald Meyer, *The Positive Thinkers: Popular Religious Psychology from Mary Baker Eddy to Norman Vincent Peale and Ronald Reagan*, 2nd ed. (Middletown, CT: Wesleyan University Press, 1988), 177–194; Carol V. R. George, *God's Salesman: Norman Vincent Peale and the Power of Positive Thinking* (New York: Oxford University Press, 1993), 104–106, 109–119, 181–183; Robert S. Ellwood, *The Fifties Spiritual Marketplace: American Religion in a Decade of Conflict* (New Brunswick, NJ: Rutgers University Press, 1997), 83–84.
5. Zig Ziglar, *Zig: The Autobiography of Zig Ziglar* (New York: Doubleday, 2002), 118–120, 134–161; Kincheloe, "Zig Ziglar," 204.
6. Sue Young, *The Heart of a Leader: My Friendship with Mary Kay* (Bloomington, IN: iUniverse Books, 2009), 36; Ziglar, *God's Way Is Still the Best Way*, 78; Ziglar, *Zig*, 161–162.
7. Robert Friedman, "Inspiration, Inc." *Esquire*, September 1979, 24–33; Kincheloe, "Zig Ziglar," 204; Ziglar, *Confessions of a Happy Christian*, 69–71; Ziglar, *Zig*, 162–164.
8. Tammi Ledbetter, "Zig Ziglar Identifies Requirements for Success of Bold-Mission Thrust," undated manuscript (1986?), 1–2, Box 1, Folder 20, ZIG. Throughout his career, Ziglar believed that conversion—especially in the dramatic, life-changing mode of evangelicalism—was the key to personal peace and professional purpose. For an example of Ziglar's late-career advocacy of evangelical tenets, see Ziglar, *God's Way Is Still the Best Way*, 147–160.
9. "Doors to Executive Suite Were Closed, So She Started Her Own Company," *Chemical Week*, August 6, 1975, 40; Chris Hutchins, "How Mary Kay Became a Makeup Powerhouse," *Cox News Service*, December 4, 2001, n.p. Also see biography of Mary Kay Ash, "About Mary Kay," http://www.marykay.com/en-US/About-Mary-Kay/CompanyFounder/Pages/About-Mary-Kay-Ash.aspx.
10. May Kay Ash's company was similar to Amway, Shaklee, United Science of America, and Tupperware, all of which had a strict division of labor between men in authority and married women in sales or personnel positions. Mary Kay's market also overlapped with Home Interiors & Gifts, another woman-run, Texas-based, direct-sales company run by Ash's friend and contemporary Mary Crowley. Nicole Woolsey Biggart, *Charismatic Capitalism: Direct Selling Organizations in America* (Chicago: University of Chicago Press, 1989), 93–95.
11. Kathy Peiss, *Hope in a Jar: The Making of America's Beauty Culture* (New York: Metropolitan Books, 1998), 262; Virginia Payett, "Two Female 'Giants,'" *Abilene Reporter-News*, June 19, 1970, 8-B.
12. Bess Winakor, "Mary Kay: She's Queen of Cosmetics," *Corpus Christi Times*, March 4, 1976, C-1; Biggart, *Charismatic Capitalism*, 95.
13. John Crudele, "Mary Kay to Go Private Again," *The New York Times*, May 31, 1985, http://www.nytimes.com/1985/05/31/business/mary-kay-to-go-private-again.html; Mary Kay Ash, *Miracles Happen: Expect Great Things and Great Things Will Happen*, 3rd ed. (New York: HarperCollins, 1994; orig. 1981), 61, 65; Winakor, "She's Queen of Cosmetics," C-1.
14. Richard DeVos and Charles Paul Conn, *Believe!* (New York: F.H. Revell, 1975), 59, 54, 47–48, 71, quoted in Michael Lienesch, *Redeeming America: Piety and Politics in the New Christian Right* (Chapel Hill: University of North Carolina Press, 1993), 98–99, 101. Charles Paul Conn, an evangelical writer who also wrote a book with Jack Eckerd, another evangelical businessman, ghost-wrote the book for DeVos.
15. Ledbetter, "Zig Ziglar Identifies," 3, Box 1, Folder 20, ZIG.
16. Zig Ziglar, *Biscuits, Fleas, and Pump Handles: Zig Ziglar's Key to "More"* (Dallas: Update, 1974), ix–x; Ziglar thought the lesson important enough to repeat it several times. Zig Ziglar, *See You at the Top*, 43rd printing (Gretna, LA: Penguin, 1987; orig. 1974), 117, 144, 382. On race, see

ibid., 57. Later editions, including the twenty-fifth anniversary edition, cut out these reflections and the use of the term "Negro." The rest of the chapter refers to this edition, primarily because by the late 1980s Ziglar's thoughts on matters of economy, religion, and politics had matured to the point that editions from the late 1980s arguably represented their fullest presentation. Later editions cut out certain secondary opinions, moved sections around, or otherwise edited material that not only showed Ziglar's editing of his own ideas but also slightly modified the book's pagination.

17. Ledbetter, "Zig Ziglar Identifies," 2, Box 1, Folder 20, ZIG.
18. Ibid.; Ziglar, *See You at the Top*, 215.
19. Ziglar, *See You at the Top*, 37–38, 187–188, 353–355; Zig Ziglar, *Over the Top* (Nashville: Thomas Nelson, 1994), 39. Of course, fleas do jump out of jars when the lids are removed, and frogs actually clamber out of pots of water when the temperature reaches a certain point. But as with other facets of Ziglar's storytelling, myth held more meaning than fact.
20. Ziglar, *See You at the Top*, 94–101; On the formulations of "the South," "the Old South," "the New South," and "Sunbelt South" in the American imagination, see James C. Cobb, *Away Down South: A History of Southern Identity* (New York: Oxford University Press, 2005).
21. Ziglar, *See You at the Top*, 351–380, 57.
22. Ibid., 325–326.
23. Cathy, *Eat Mor Chikin*, 12–15; Cathy, *It's Easier to Succeed Than to Fail*, 34–39; Walton, *Innkeeper*, 15–23; David Green, *More Than a Hobby* (Nashville: Thomas Nelson, 2005), 1–2.
24. "Alvah Chapman, Miami Newspaper Titan, Dies at 87," http://www.huffingtonpost.com/ 2008/12/29/alvah-chapman-miami-newsp_n_153914.html; "Jack Eckerd, 91, Founder of a Chain of Drugstores," *The New York Times*, May 20, 2004, A-25.
25. Larry Eskridge, "Money Matters: The Phenomenon of Financial Counselor Larry Burkett and Christian Financial Concepts," in Larry Eskridge and Mark A. Noll, eds., *More Money, More Ministry: Money and Evangelicals in Recent North American History* (Grand Rapids, MI: Wm. B. Eerdmans, 2000), 311–350; Balmer, "Burkett, Larry (1939–)," *Encyclopedia of Evangelicalism*, 111–112.
26. Eskridge, "Money Matters," 329–330, 337–339; Larry Burkett, *Using Your Money Wisely: Biblical Principles Under Scrutiny* (Chicago: Moody, 1990), 59; Burkett also experimented with apocalyptic themes in books like *The Coming Economic Earthquake* and *Whatever Happened to the American Dream?* as well as his popular novels, *The Illuminati* and *The Thor Conspiracy*. Politically, Burkett cheered on the rise of a new "Christian Right," helping to found the Alliance Defense Fund in 1994 and working on behalf of socially conservative Republican candidates. Balmer, "Larry Burkett (1939–)," 111–112; Ginia Bellafante, "The Anti-Debt Crusader," *The New York Times*, October 30, 2005, http://www. nytimes.com/2005/10/30/magazine/the-antidebt-crusader.html?_r=0; Paul Harvey, "Fix the Economy God'$ Way: Dave Ramsey's Great Christian Recovery," *Religion Dispatches*, July 25, 2011, http://www.religiondispatches.org/archive/atheologies/ 4905/fix_the_ economy_god%E2%80%99$_way%3A_dave_ramsey%E2%80%99s_great_christian_ recovery_/.
27. John C. Maxwell, *Developing the Leader Within You* (Nashville: Thomas Nelson, 1993), *Developing Leaders Around You* (Nashville: Thomas Nelson, 1995), and *Failing Forward— Turning Mistakes into Stepping Stones for Success* (Nashville: Thomas Nelson, 2000); "Leadership Guru Dies," *Christianity Today*, October 1, 2007, 20; Pamphlet, "Fred Smith, Sr." (n.d.); Smith, "Leadership is an Art" (n.d.). Also see "About Fred Smith, Sr.," http://www. breakfastwithfred.com/about/.
28. Moreton, *To Serve God and Wal-Mart*, 67–85, 100–124.
29. Ziglar, *See You at the Top*, 322–326.
30. Paul Christopher Sancya, "Guru of Inspiration Captures Crowd," *Post-Tribune*, April 25, 1990, n.p.; Vitez, "Let a Thousand Gurus Bloom," *The Washington Post*, February 12, 1995, W-17; Colin Campbell, "Pumps and Pitches in a Den of Success," *Atlanta Journal-Constitution*, April 21, 1996, C-1; Meena Thiruvengadam, "Part Revival, Part Pep Rally," *San Antonio Express-News*, http://www.redorbit.com/news/education/506900/part_revival_part_pep_rally/ index.html.

31. Megan Rosenfeld and Robert Wilson, "Success Unlimited," *The Washington Post*, June 17, 1978, B-1; Megan Rosenfeld, "The Secrets of a Confidence Man," *The Washington Post*, November 1, 1992, F-1.

32. Vitez, "He Delivers Hope," A-1; David Hamilton, interview transcript, September 14, 2008, in author's possession.

33. Friedman, "Inspiration, Inc.," 25–26; Mimi Swartz, "Myth-o-Maniacs," *Texas Monthly*, February 1993, 140–145.

34. On visions of masculinity, femininity, the family, and "breadwinner conservatism" that precluded queer, homosexual, transgender, and other "sexual others" as viable "family" members in the American body politic, see Robert O. Self, *All in the Family: The Realignment of American Democracy Since the 1960s* (New York: Hill and Wang, 2012), esp. 276–307.

35. Ziglar, *Confessions of a Happy Christian*, 9, 27–29, 45, 86.

36. Ziglar, *See You at the Top*, 276–277.

37. Ziglar, *Confessions of a Happy Christian*, 61–64, 108–110; Ziglar, *Dear Family* (Gretna, LA: Pelican, 1984), 129–136; Mark D. Jordan, *Recruiting Young Love: How Christians Talk About Homosexuality* (Chicago: University of Chicago Press, 2011).

38. Ziglar, *Raising Positive Kids in a Negative World* (Nashville: Thomas Nelson, 1985), 23–40, 87–102, 129–130.

39. On the emotional appeal of the heterosexual home and home defense, see Linda Kintz, *Between Jesus and the Market: The Emotions That Matter in Right-Wing America* (Durham, NC: Duke University Press, 1997), esp. 17–53, 111–139, 187–204, 237–272. On sexuality and the "gender dangers" of the 1970s and 1980s, see Moreton, *To Serve God and Wal-Mart*, esp. 116–124; Ziglar, *See You at the Top*, 133–144.

40. Ziglar, *Raising Positive Kids in a Negative World*, 167–180; for the multitude of ways that Ziglar linked sexual values, family, child-rearing, and business "success," see Ziglar, *Dear Family*, 85–153.

41. *The I CAN Course Teacher's Guide* (Dallas: Zig Ziglar Corporation, 1977); Pamphlet, "Preparing Today's Youth for America's Tomorrow" (1980), in author's possession; Earl C. Meyer, "The Effects of the Ziglar 'I CAN' Program on the Self-Concept, Human Relations Skills, and Work Attitude of Cooperative Marketing and Distributive Education Students in Selected Secondary Schools in Georgia" (PhD dissertation, Georgia State University, 1982), 93–94, 136–137, Appendixes H, I, UGA; Ziglar, *Zig*, 215–216.

42. Rosenfeld and Wilson, "Success Unlimited," B-1; Ziglar, *Zig*, 166–167.

43. Cavett Robert, *Cavett Robert: Leaving a Lasting Legacy* (Minneapolis: Creative Training Techniques International, 1998); Joseph DiSanto, "A Lover's Quarrel With Reagan," *National Review*, February 24, 1984, 48–49; William E. Schmidt, "Paul Harvey's Soapbox of the Air," *The New York Times*, September 24, 1988, 1–54; Brant Short, "'Hello Americans': Paul Harvey and the Rhetorical Construction of Modern Agrarianism," *Journal of Radio and Audio Media*, 1.1 (1992): 43–54.

44. Barry Hankins, *Uneasy in Babylon: Southern Baptist Conservatives and American Culture* (Tuscaloosa: University of Alabama Press, 2002), 242; Curtis W. Freeman, "'Never Had I Been So Blind': W. A. Criswell's 'Change' on Racial Segregation," *The Journal of Southern Religion*, 10 (2007): 1–12, http://jsr.fsu.edu/Volume10/Freeman.pdf. On the persistence of "color-blind" perspectives in evangelicalism, see Michael Emerson and Christian Smith, *Divided by Faith: Evangelical Religion and the Problem of Race in America* (Oxford: Oxford University Press, 2001), 69–114.

45. Neal R. Pierce, *The Great Plains States of America: People, Politics, and Power in the Nine Great Plains States* (New York: W. W. Norton, 1973), 343.

46. Mark G. Toulouse, "W. A. Criswell" in Charles H. Lippy, ed., *Twentieth-Century Shapers of American Popular Religion* (Westport, CT: Greenwood Press, 1989), 98; Leon McBeth, *The First Baptist Church of Dallas, Centennial History, 1868–1968* (Grand Rapids, MI: Zondervan, 1968), 234, 247–270, 276–288, 353.

47. Swanee Hunt, *Half-Life of a Zealot* (Durham, NC: Duke University Press, 2006), 48–50; James McEnteer, *Deep in the Heart: The Texas Tendency in American Politics* (Westport, CT: Greenwood, 2004), 107; John Perry, *Walking God's Path: The Life and Ministry of Jimmy Draper* (Nashville: Broadman & Holman, 2005), 117.

48. Shayne Lee and Phillip Sinitiere, *Holy Mavericks: Evangelical Innovators in the Spiritual Marketplace* (New York: New York University Press, 2009), 129–148; Donald McGavran and George G. Hunter III, *Church Growth: Strategies That Work* (Nashville: Abington Press, 1980), 16–18; Donald A. McGavran, *Effective Evangelism: A Theological Mandate* (Phillipsburg, NJ: Presbyterian and Reformed Publishing, 1988), 79–91; Donald A. McGavran and Win Arn, *How to Grow a Church: Conversations About Church Growth* (Glendale, CA: Regal Books, 1973), 174–177; McGavran, *Understanding Church Growth* (Grand Rapids, MI: Wm. B. Eerdmans, 1970), 44–51. McGavran's "evangelistic typology" was not his own but borrowed in part from Ralph D. Winter's 1974 address to the plenary session of the International Congress on World Evangelization in Lausanne, Switzerland. See Donald A. McGavran and Winfield C. Arn, *Ten Steps for Church Growth* (New York: Harper & Row, 1977), 111–113. For Warren's debt to McGavran and Criswell, see Rick Warren, *The Purpose Driven Church: Growth Without Compromising Your Message and Mission* (Grand Rapids, MI: Zondervan, 1995), 25–29.

49. Ziglar, *Zig,* 167.

50. Criswell quotation from Williams, *God's Own Party,* 117; Joe E. Barnhart, *The Southern Baptist Holy War* (Austin: Texas Monthly Press, 1986), 123; Nancy Ammerman, *Baptist Battles: Social Change and Religious Conflict in the Southern Baptist Convention* (New Brunswick, NJ: Rutgers University Press, 1995), 80–89. On the various strains in Texas Baptist culture and politics, see Blake A. Ellis, "An Alternative Politics: Texas Baptist Leaders and the Rise of the Christian Right, 1960–1985" (PhD dissertation, Rice University, 2011); Gayle White, "The Baptist Pope," *Atlanta Journal-Constitution,* June 2, 1991, M-1, M-4.

51. Russell Chandler, "Southern Baptist Ultraconservatives Turn Tide at Convention, Go on Roll," *Los Angeles Times,* June 16, 1984, 11; Ammerman, *Baptist Battles,* 99–106.

52. David T. Morgan, *The New Crusades, the New Holy Land: Conflict in the Southern Baptist Convention* (Tuscaloosa: University of Alabama Press, 1996), 64–67.

53. Jerry Don Abernathy to Zig Ziglar, June 20, 1984, Box 1, Folder 1, ZIG; Marion D. Aldridge to Zig Ziglar, November 30, 1984, Box 1, Folder 1, ZIG.

54. Dan T. Cathy to Zig Ziglar, June 19, 1984 and Zig Ziglar to Dan T. Cathy, July 3, 1984, Box 1, Folder 3, ZIG.

55. "Mormon Professor Faces Furor at Baptist University," *The New York Times,* July 8, 1984, 1–30; Zig Ziglar to Billie Good, November 6, 1984, Box 1, Folder 7, Zig Ziglar to Thomas A. Dannelley Jr., July 11, 1984, Box 1, Folder 2, ZIG; Raymond J. Barton to Zig Ziglar, August 19, 1984, Box 1, Folder 2; Lucy Bodily to Zig Ziglar, July 10, 1984, Box 1, Folder 2, ZIG.

56. Jesse C. Fletcher, *The Southern Baptist Convention: A Sesquicentennial History* (Nashville: Broadman and Holman, 1994), 283.

57. Such a vision endures today. Andy Stanley, Charles Stanley's son, heads a megachurch in suburban Atlanta that has preached "complementarian" roles for men and women. His church's stance largely accords with SBC doctrine. Article XVIII of the SBC's "Baptist Faith and Message," adopted in 1998 and revised in 2000, proclaims that "a wife is to submit herself graciously to the servant leadership of her husband." http://www.sbc.net/bfm2000/bfm2000.asp.

Conclusion

1. Jerry Falwell, *Listen America!* (New York: Doubleday, 1980), 3–23.

2. Dirk Smillie, *Falwell, Inc.: Inside a Religious, Political, Educational, and Business Empire* (New York: St. Martin's Press, 2008), 87–95; Phillips-Fein, *Invisible Hands,* 213–214.

3. Smillie, *Falwell, Inc.,* 93, 105; Winters, *God's Right Hand,* 301.

4. Robert G. Sherrill, "H. L. Hunt: Portrait of a Super-Patriot," *The Nation,* February 24, 1964, 182–195; "People," *Time,* February 29, 1960, 43; David R. Jones, "H. L. Hunt: Magnate with Mission," *The New York Times,* August 17, 1964, 1; William Martin, "God's Angry Man," *Texas Monthly,* April 1981, 152–157, 223–235; "James Robison (1943–)," in Glenn H. Utter and John W. Storey, eds., *The Religious Right: A Reference Handbook,* 2nd ed. (Santa Barbara: ABC-CLIO, Inc., 2001), 110–111; Flake, *Redemptorama,* 128–130.

5. Dan T. Carter, *The Politics of Rage: George Wallace, the Origins of the New Conservatism, and the Transformation of American Politics*, 2nd ed. (New York: Simon & Schuster, 2000), 336–337. On the silver market and Hunt family, see Charles R. Geisst, *Wheels of Fortune: The History of Speculation from Scandal to Respectability* (Hoboken, NJ: Wiley, 2002), 231–240. At one point or another, Nelson Bunker Hunt had been on the John Birch Society's governing board and was affiliated with the arch-conservative Manion Forum and anti-union Southern States Industrial Council and the borderline neo-Nazi organization, the International Council for the Defense of Christian Culture. Chandler Davidson, *Race and Class in Texas Politics* (Princeton, NJ: Princeton University Press, 1992), 76–77.

6. Davis's trial and acquittal is detailed in Gary Cartwright, *Blood Will Tell: The Murder Trials of T. Cullen Davis* (New York: Harcourt, 1979); Lichtman, *White Protestant Nation*, 357–360.

7. J. Brooks Flippen, *Jimmy Carter, the Politics of Family, and the Rise of the Religious Right* (Athens: University of Georgia Press, 2011), 284–286, 11; Williams, *God's Own Party*, 187; Daniel K. Williams, "Reagan's Religious Right: The Unlikely Alliance Between Southern Evangelicals and a California Conservative," in Cheryl Hudson and Gareth Davies, eds., *Ronald Reagan and the 1980s* (New York: Palgrave Macmillan, 2008), 135–150.

8. Carey, *Fortunes, Fiddles and Fried Chicken*, 186–192.

9. Randall Balmer, *Redeemer: The Life of Jimmy Carter* (New York: Basic Books, 2014), 1–13.

10. Steven F. Hayward, *The Age of Reagan: The Fall of the Old Liberal Order, 1964–1980* (New York: Three Rivers Press, 2001), 523–529; Laura Kalman, *Right Star Rising: A New Politics, 1974–1980* (New York: W. W. Norton, 2010), 240–249; Dennis S. Ippolito, *Deficits, Debt, and the New Politics of Tax Policy* (Cambridge: Cambridge University Press, 2012), 105–106; "4R" was the abbreviation for the Railroad Revitalization and Regulatory Reform Act of 1976. Carter signed the Airline Deregulation Act of 1978, Staggers Rail Act of 1980, and Motor Carrier Act of 1980. Mark H. Rose, Bruce E. Seely, and Paul F. Barrett, eds., *The Best Transportation System in the World: Railroads, Trucks, Airlines, and American Public Policy in the Twentieth Century* (Columbus: Ohio State University, 2006), 185–211; Phillips-Fein, *Invisible Hands*, 236–262.

11. Ribuffo, *The Old Christian Right*, 266; Falwell quoted in Patrick Allitt, *Religion in America Since 1945: A History* (New York: Columbia University Press, 2003), 198.

12. Deborah Huntington and Ruth Kaplan, "Whose Gold is Behind the Altar? Corporate Ties to Evangelicals," *Contemporary Marxism* 4 (Winter 1981–1982): 62–94.

13. Ibid. Helms, who had organized businessmen in his native North Carolina to resist the desegregation of public and private spaces, was a natural fit as a point-man on matters evangelical and business related. During the 1960s and 1970s, he had couched his arguments against civil rights activism in terms of "private rights" and had long used religious rhetoric against the "socialism" of racial protest. Moreover, Helms was backed by powerful business interests ranging from Piedmont mill owners like Roger Milliken to conservative players like Henry Salvatori, Richard Mellon Scaife, and Joseph Coors. See Phillips-Fein, *Invisible Hands*, 221–225.

14. On the renewed scholarly interest in religious liberalism, see Matthew S. Hedstrom, *The Rise of Liberal Religion: Book Culture and American Spirituality in the Twentieth Century* (New York: Oxford University Press, 2012); David A. Hollinger, *After Cloven Tongues of Fire: Protestant Liberalism in Modern American History* (Princeton, NJ: Princeton University Press, 2013); Elesha Coffman, *The Christian Century and the Rise of Mainline Protestantism* (New York: Oxford University Press, 2013).

15. Omri Elisha, *Moral Ambition: Mobilization and Social Outreach in Evangelical Megachurches* (Berkeley: University of California Press, 2011), 1–35; Brian Steensland and Philip Goff, eds., *The New Evangelical Social Engagement* (New York: Oxford University Press, 2013); David Platt, *Radical: Taking Back Your Faith from the American Dream* (Colorado Springs, CO: Multnoma Press, 2010).

INDEX

Note: Page numbers followed by n indicate notes. Page numbers in italics indicate photographs.